HEINEMANN GNVQ

INTERMEDIATE

Business

Carol Carysforth • Mike Neild

Heinemann Educational Publishers,
Halley Court, Jordan Hill, Oxford OX2 8EJ
A division of Reed Educational & Professional Publishing Ltd.

Heinemann is a registered trademark of Reed Educational & Professional Publishing

OXFORD MELBOURNE AUCKLAND
JOHANNESBURG BLANTYRE GABORONE
IBADAN PORTSMOUTH (NH) USA CHICAGO

First published 1993

Third edition published 2000

05 04 03 02
10 9 8 7

A catalogue record for this book is available from the British Library on request

ISBN 0435 456024

Cover designed by Sarah Garbett

Typeset by 🅰 Tek-Art, Croydon, Surrey

Printed and bound in Great Britain by The Bath Press Ltd., Bath

Tel: 01865 888058 www.heinemann.co.uk

Contents

Dedication

With love to Sam, the newest member of the family. May good health, happiness, kind friends and an enquiring and open mind be yours forever.

Acknowledgements

The authors would like to record their thanks and gratitude to all those who so freely gave of their time and expertise to help in the writing and production of this book.

Particular thanks are due to Catherine Crowe, LLB; Joanna McGowan, BA(Hons), GIPD; and Susan Holden, LLB, for their specialist assistance with many of the legal aspects of this book and to Peter Nangle, MEd, for his invaluable help and advice on retailing. Our gratitude is also due to Sheila Goodman and her colleagues – particularly Jane Lunnon and Pam Mayoh – who helped with many of the research statistics illustrated in Unit 2.

Thanks are also owed to our colleagues at Heinemann – particularly Alex Gray for his hard work and patience, which was much appreciated. As ever, no book of ours would be complete without reference to our friend and development editor Margaret Berriman, who yet again had faith in our abilities, who kept us on track throughout the writing of this book and who always seemed to ring or email at the right time to keep us motivated!

The authors and publishers would also like to thank the following individuals and organisations for permission to reproduce photographs and other copyright material:

p.5 The Savoy, pp.31, 32, 34, 42 Unipart; p.63 Alton Towers; p.66 Kwik-Fit; p.71 Argos; p.73 Robert Harding; p.77 Virgin Group; p.118 Unipart; p.128 Virgin Group; p.131 Littlewoods; p.133 J Allan Cash; p.135 Virgin Group; p.135 The Body Shop; p.138 Co-operative Bank; p.139 Delta-T; p.143 J Allan Cash; p.156 Empics; p.166 Birdwells; p.170 Trafford Park Shopping Centre; p.173 J Allan Cash; p. 177 Unipart; p.182 Robert Harding; p.186 J Allan Cash; p.190 J Allan Cash; p.227 The Prince's Trust; p.288 Unipart; p.304 Debenhams; p. 315 Toys 'Я' Us; p. 349 Office of Fair Trading; p.354 Consumers' Association; p. 357 Oftel.

Carol Carysforth and Mike Neild
June 2000

Investigating how businesses work

Many of the people you see every day are going to work in a business organisation – offices, shops, banks or factories. A business can be a firm of solicitors, an estate agent, a garage, a football club, a farm, a mining company, a local council. Even your local charity shop is part of a larger organisation run in a similar way to a commercial business. Your school or college can also be described as a business organisation.

You may be curious about what these different organisations actually do. What type of work is carried out in them? What are they trying to achieve? How are they organised so that people work together productively, rather than get in each other's way?

This unit answers all these questions. By the time you have completed it you will know that:

- many types of organisations are known as businesses – and they are all involved in trying to achieve certain aims.

- all businesses set objectives or targets, and measure their success by how well they meet these.

- to operate, a business has to perform certain functions which help it to achieve its aims and objectives.

- businesses have to organise or structure their functions to meet their aims and objectives.

- the people who are employed in businesses need to understand the aims of their organisation and work together to achieve these. This is one of the reasons that people who work on the same type of activities are grouped together. They must also be able to communicate easily so that everyone is kept informed of new developments.

This unit will be assessed through your portfolio work. Your tutor will give you further details about the work you must do as you progress through the unit.

1.1   THE AIMS AND OBJECTIVES OF BUSINESSES

At the end of this section you should be able to:

- find out what a business actually does and describe its activity
- identify the main aims of a business
- suggest appropriate objectives for a business
- explain how businesses evaluate their success at meeting their aims and objectives
- apply what you have learned about business activities, aims and objectives to a medium-sized or large business of your choice.

Overview of aims and objectives

The main purpose of a business is sometimes stated in a **mission statement**. By reading this you can usually determine what the business actually does. For instance, Bill Gates has said that Microsoft's mission is 'taking the Internet, combining it with great software and turning that into the most powerful tool of all time'. You can tell from this that Bill Gates is involved with computers and software development. The mission statement for British Airways is 'to be the undisputed leader in world travel'. From this you know that British Airways operates in the travel market.

However, it is one thing to state a mission or purpose, and another to achieve it. You may decide your purpose is to become 'healthy, wealthy and wise' – but how do you do this? An obvious way is to decide the **aims**, or goals, you will need to achieve this. In this case your aims may relate to losing weight, saving money and obtaining your GNVQ Intermediate Business award. In business, the main aims are usually concerned with one or more of the following:

1 making a profit
2 providing goods and services to the local or wider community
3 surviving as a business or expanding
4 maximising sales or improving the quality of a product or service
5 providing a highly competitive service
6 providing a charitable or voluntary service
7 being environmentally friendly.

At this point the business needs to identify specific practical targets it needs to accomplish to achieve its aims. These are called **objectives**. It is usual for objectives to be quantified (i.e. expressed as a number) so that success can be easily measured. For instance, British Airways has the aim of 'being the airline of first choice in key markets'. An objective linked to this could be 'to increase sales of air tickets to business passengers by 5 per cent a year in Europe'.

The link between the mission statement and the aims and objectives is shown in Figure 1.1 below.

Term	Business	Personal
Mission	The purpose of the business	To be healthy, wealthy and wise
Aims	The goals the business wants to achieve	To be physically fit To save more money To pass my current course
Objectives	Practical steps to achieve the goals – usually quantified	To lose 10 lbs in weight in 3 months To visit the gym twice a week To get a part-time job by November To complete Units 1 and 2 by Christmas

Figure 1.1 The link between the mission, aims and objectives in business and in personal life

Understanding business aims

Making a profit

Broadly speaking, profit is the difference between what a business has earned and what it has spent over a given period. If you owned your own business, then the profit is the amount you would be able to keep, or re-invest in the business, each year. You may therefore think that the aim of making a profit is so obvious, there is no need to discuss it. However, you would be surprised at some of the organisations which *don't* make a profit! For instance, the calculations for the costs of producing the original Mini car were so inaccurate that, although it was a bestseller, it actually lost money for several years because it was sold too cheaply! More recent examples of organisations which have seen a fall in their profits include Marks & Spencer, British Airways, Levi and EMI. This can happen in a bad year when a company has poor sales, yet the costs of running the business stay the same or increase. In this case, the aim for the next year may be just to survive as a business and work hard to keep costs down and improve sales.

Profit is extremely important for all businesses as no business can survive for very long if it is not profitable. You will learn about profit in more detail when you study Unit 3.

Providing goods or services to the local or wider community

All business organisations make goods, provide goods or provide services. A manufacturing organisation makes goods. For instance, Heinz makes food products and Nike makes sports clothing and equipment. A retailing organisation, such as Tesco, sells a variety of goods made by other organisations. Banks, such as NatWest, provide financial services to both businesses and private individuals.

Some organisations provide a mixture of goods and services. Marks & Spencer sells goods in its stores and also sells financial services. British Aerospace makes and sells planes and provides a variety of technical services to its customers. In fact, many organisations that manufacture or sell goods offer some type of after-sales service for their customers. An obvious example is a car dealership where customers buy a car and then take it back regularly for servicing or for repairs if anything goes wrong.

Some organisations provide goods or services locally, such as a newsagent or dentist. Others provide goods and services nationally (such as Dixons or Kwik-Fit) or internationally (such as Coca-Cola or IBM).

Figure 1.2 Car dealerships often have an after-sales service

Surviving as a business or expanding

In a bad year, when profits are low, a business may concentrate on simply surviving. If sales cannot be improved, the only way profit can be increased is by reducing costs. In some cases this may mean reducing staff. Because of the fall in its profits Marks & Spencer's cut some of its management jobs to save money.

Sometimes people running small local businesses are content just to survive. They are happy to earn enough to pay their bills, enjoy themselves and save some money. Not everyone wants to be Sir Richard Branson or Bill Gates!

However, many businesses aim to expand. If they are local they may want to grow to spread over a region or the country. An example of a company that started locally but has since expanded is Pizza Express, which plans to open 40 new outlets a year.

The decision whether to operate locally or nationally is often largely determined by the type of goods or services offered. If you were offering a mobile phone service, manufacturing carpets or publishing books, it would not be profitable to sell only to your local community. National organisations are often household names – Vodafone, Penguin, Dixons and Boots operate nationally and are known to most people.

Organisations which operate worldwide may be even more well-known. Coca-Cola, Tommy Hilfiger, Levi, Microsoft and IBM are world famous American organisations. British ones include Cadbury's, BP, Virgin and ICI.

Some organisations grow larger by buying other businesses or by joining with another business. This is the most rapid method of expansion. If one business buys another, this is usually known as a **takeover**. The world's biggest retailer, Wall-Mart, paid £7 billion to take over Asda, the British supermarket chain, in 1999. The American company bought Asda because of its aim to expand internationally. Buying Asda will double its international sales. Wall-Mart also has a target of $200 billion sales by 2002, another aim the takeover will help it to achieve. Not all takeovers are successful, however. In 1999 BSkyB tried to buy Manchester United Football Club, but was thwarted by the government, which can rule against a takeover or merger if it thinks this would not be in the best interests of consumers.

A **merger** is when two companies, often in the same line of business, join together, such as the banks Lloyds and TSB. This is usually done to reduce operating costs and increase profits as premises can be combined, staff can be reduced, and the overall customer base increased.

SNAPSHOT

A cut above the rest?

Toni and Guy is a hair-salon chain probably better known for doing the hair of personalities such as David Beckham rather than for its business aims. However, when you look at the history of Toni and Guy it is relatively easy to identify what those aims have been.

Toni and Guy started life in Clapham, south London, 35 years ago with one salon. Today there are 227 salons worldwide. The overseas network includes 45 salons in America, 15 in Germany, 9 in Australia, 3 in Canada and 14 in Japan. At home there are 108 franchised outlets (see page 135) and 12 salons which are operated by the company. Its annual sales in 1998 were £140 million with worldwide profits of £9 million.

In addition to the hair-salon chain, the same organisation – Mascolo Brothers – also owns a haircare products company called TIGI, a salon-furniture business known as Innovia, and a new salon concept which it has named Essenuals. It has started a chain of British cash-and-carry businesses to provide hairdressing supplies and a shopfitting company called Straight Impact.

Maximising sales or improving quality

There are two major aspects of providing goods and services that businesses must consider:

1 the **quality** of their goods and services
2 the **price** they charge for them.

Quality relates to the performance of a product, how long it lasts, how well it is made, what additional features are included. High-quality service is offered by many service providers. In a top restaurant you would expect excellent food, attentiveness by the staff and attractive, comfortable surroundings. If you paid to fly first class you would expect the same thing. If you stayed in a five-star hotel you would want this too, plus a range of additional facilities, such as 24-hour room service.

Quality goods and services cost more – both to make and to buy. You wouldn't expect to buy an Armani suit for the same price as a suit in Next, or stay at the Savoy hotel for the same price as a Comfort Inn. Armani and the

Figure 1.3 The Savoy is all about luxury

Savoy have both deliberately decided to offer high quality for those who can afford it. This is therefore one of their aims. Next and Comfort Inns, on the other hand, want to sell their goods or service in quantity and therefore price them for the mass market. This is one of their aims. Quality is still important, because customers will always want value for money. However, keeping the costs of running the business within forecast levels is more important to businesses aiming for the mass market. This is because if costs rise they would have to put up their prices, and they would lose customers.

If a business aims to **maximise** sales, this simply means it wants to sell as many goods as possible. It can do this in several ways, such as by reducing the price, spending more on advertising and promotion or offering additional services to customers. All these strategies help to improve sales. Tesco is an example of a supermarket which has reduced prices with its value campaign, spent money advertising its stores and has introduced incentives, such as its loyalty card, to maximise sales. It has become the leading supermarket in the country.

However, businesses which are renowned for quality would not want to maximise sales, as they wish to keep their exclusive appeal. Several years ago Porsche withdrew its cheapest model car because it said that too many people were buying it, and it was concerned that it would lose its appeal for the super-rich! Knowing who your customers are, and how to please them, is a very important part of business strategy – as you will see when you learn about marketing, sales and customer service later in this unit.

Providing a highly competitive service

Some organisations aim to sell large volumes of goods at a low price all the time and provide a highly competitive service. The supermarkets Netto and Aldi, for instance, sell goods at lower prices than Tesco, Sainsbury or Safeway. They are not interested in features such as loyalty cards and spacious stores. They focus all their attention on keeping prices as low as possible.

In the airline industry, Easyjet and Ryanair offer cut-price flights, without any 'frills', such as free drinks or meals on board. Their prices are much lower than standard airlines, such as British Midland or British Airways.

Usually, the more competitors there are in a particular industry, the cheaper the goods or services offered. For many years, Kelloggs was almost the only supplier of breakfast cereals and its prices were high. Now many supermarkets sell their 'own brand' cereals and Kelloggs is having to drop its prices in order to compete.

Another example is Internet provision. When the Internet first became available, there was a limited number of service providers, all of them charging between £10 and £20 a month for access to the service. Then organisations such as Dixons and Tesco started offering a free Internet service, putting pressure on the other providers to drop their prices to stay in business.

Providing charitable or voluntary services

Not all organisations offer a commercial service. Charitable organisations, such as Save the Children or Shelter, provide a service but in a rather different way. In this case the money they raise goes to support a special cause and provide a service for those in need. Voluntary organisations, such as the Samaritans, recruit unpaid helpers to provide a service as well as asking for donations.

We don't talk about charitable or voluntary organisations 'making a profit'. They obtain

money through running events, operating charity shops and appealing for donations. From this money they have to deduct the cost of running the charity or voluntary service. The eventual figure is the **surplus** they have made at the end of the year, which can be used to support their particular aims.

Oxfam is currently the UK's richest charity. In 1998 its income amounted to £98 million and it is expected to pass the £100 million figure very shortly. Oxfam employs 50 staff in its fundraising department and operates 873 charity shops with a turnover (sales value) of £60.4 million. The surplus from its shops alone amounts to over £16 million a year.

The largest charities are run like a business with expert, salaried staff in charge of fund-raising and the accounts and administration. There are 135,000 active charities in the UK with a gross income of £13.1 billion and nearly half a million employees, together with an army of volunteers. Good organisation and management is vital if a charity is to achieve its aims and objectives.

Being environmentally friendly

Today many business organisations are serious about environmental concerns, such as pollution, waste disposal, recycling and energy use. They are aware that the public cares about 'green issues' and that no business can afford bad publicity for being environmentally unfriendly. The government also has environmental aims and has asked all industries to show how they will reduce energy use, water use and pollution. If industry fails to do this, it is likely the government will introduce specific targets that all business organisations will have to meet.

Some organisations are prepared to go further than what the government is asking. Some electricity suppliers, for instance, are offering electricity from renewable sources which they

Figure 1.4 Real estate developments take account of the environment

call 'green electricity'. Tarmac, the construction company, has its own environment panel which advises managers on environmental aims and BP's chief executive, Sir John Brown, has publicly committed his company to action on climate change. Ford has advertised that its Focus car contains 20 recycled parts and many supermarkets have collection banks for recycling bottles, newspapers and drink cans adjacent to their car parks.

Key areas important to companies with environmental aims include:

- using 'environmentally-friendly' materials, and reducing use (by reducing wastage) as much as possible

- designing products for re-use and using recycled and recyclable packaging

- disposing of all waste properly. Even offices need to be aware of how to dispose of fluorescent lights and solvent materials. Waste disposal is important. The person who collects and disposes of waste must be registered to carry it and must dispose of it at a site licensed to deal with that particular type of waste.

- reducing the energy and water that is used – by switching off lights, closing doors and windows, investing in draught-proofing and insulation. According to environmentalists, a large office, using fluorescent lights for two hours less each day can save up to £700 each year.

- storing rubbish in suitable sacks, containers or skips and separating different kinds of waste for easy disposal. An office which stores waste paper separately for recycling saves on its waste disposal costs as well as being environmentally friendly.

Businesses can check how environmentally friendly they are by carrying out an environmental audit. This is a check of all the areas above. Successful companies which can show they operate an environmental management system can apply for a quality standard, such as ISO 14001. It is predicted that in the future very large companies will only use suppliers who operate to such standards, so that many businesses will come to focus much more on environmental concerns.

Here is a summary of the main aims of businesses. Use this to help you when you answer the Activity questions below.

Business aims	
1 Make a profit	2 Provide goods or services to the local community
3 Provide goods or services to the wider community	4 Survive as a business
5 Expand	6 Maximise sales
7 Improve quality	8 Provide a highly competitive service
9 Provide a charitable or voluntary service	10 Be environmentally friendly.

ACTIVITY

1   The aims of a business relate to the product or service which it provides. What type of aims would you therefore expect each of the following businesses to have?
a   a hospital
b   a football club
c   a computer manufacturer
d   a bank
e   a supermarket.

2   The specific aims of organisations may vary depending upon their priorities, e.g. high quality versus low price. In groups of three or four, discuss which aims you think are important to each of the following business organisations. Remember, most businesses have more than one aim!

a   McDonald's   b   Tesco
c   NSPCC   d   Ford
e   Microsoft   f   Coca-Cola
g   Porsche   h   Marks & Spencer
i   Body Shop   j   Royal Mail
k   Kwik-Fit   l   Toys 'Я' Us

CASE STUDY 1.1

Mercedes has developed the world's most expensive production car, CLK-GTRs, a two-seater which costs £1 million! Only 25 will be produced and a deposit of £250,000 is required. The car will do 8 miles to the gallon but is so powerful that it needs a new clutch every 3,000 miles. The boot will only fit two specially-fitted briefcases and inside the car is so small that the steering wheel has to be dismantled before the driver can get in! It is thought that the several people who have bought one have no intention of driving them, but just want to keep them in their garage in pristine condition.

Activities

1   What do you think Mercedes' aims were in developing this car?
2   What do you think is the aim of people who 'keep them in their garage in pristine condition'?
3   Do you think more of these cars will be produced in the future? Give a reason for your answer.
4   How do you think Mercedes' aims compare with those of a car company such as Fiat or Ford?
5   What do you think is the aim of most people when they buy a car?

Figure 1.5 The Mercedes symbol stands for quality

Setting objectives

An objective is a target which contributes towards a main aim or goal. If one of your aims is to achieve your GNVQ Business Intermediate award, one of your objectives might be 'to achieve at least 95 per cent attendance over the year'. Another could be 'to complete your portfolio work on this unit by a certain time'. Each objective is challenging, otherwise there is little point in setting it. The objective of staying in bed every Saturday until lunchtime would not be challenging, and wouldn't help you to achieve much!

Objectives are far more manageable than 'aims' because they are more specific. In fact, good objectives are said to be **SMART**.

S	specific
M	measurable
A	agreed
R	realistic
T	time constrained

Pizza Express set a target of opening 40 new outlets a year. This is an example of a SMART objective. If Pizza Express had set a target of 'growing so large in the future it will operate all over the world', this would not have been a 'SMART' objective. There is no time-scale against which it can be measured. It is also unrealistic, given Pizza Express's current size.

Objectives provide a focus for the managers and the employees of a business, and ideally they should be involved in setting, or agreeing their own objectives.

Sometimes the main responsibility for achieving an objective falls on a particular group, in other cases everyone is involved in helping achieve it. For instance, in the search for a cure for Aids, the pharmaceutical companies' research teams were mainly

Figure 1.6 How staff treat customers helps the company achieve its objectives

responsible for achieving this objective. When supermarkets compete to sell more products than their competitors, or aim to maximise sales, their sales and marketing people have to devise promotional ideas to help achieve this. Companies that need to reduce costs to survive may place much of the responsibility for how to achieved this on their accounting and finance teams.

However, without the cooperation and commitment of all staff, objectives are more difficult to achieve. Supermarkets need friendly and efficient checkout operators to encourage customers to return again and again. Manufacturing companies desperate to reduce costs will have little success if there is high wastage through carelessness or if office staff fail to turn off their lights every night.

It can be difficult to achieve objectives consistently, so staff may be offered incentives, such as profit-related pay or sales commission, as an encouragement to maintain the level of performance needed to go on achieving the objectives set.

SNAPSHOT

Carried away with objectives!

There are dangers in setting objectives without thinking about the consequences. If a hospital has the objective of treating twice as many patients a year, there is a danger that patients may be sent home too soon, perhaps with disastrous results. So, those who set objectives must consider whether undesirable side-effects are likely to occur.

The New York Police Department learned this lesson the hard way. They set an objective for every police officer to increase his or her arrest rate. They even linked this to bonus payments. The idea was successful and the arrest rate soared. The only problem was that many of the people arrested had done nothing wrong! Zealous officers, keen to meet their targets, were locking up as many people as they could whether they were guilty or not!

ACTIVITY

1 The specific objectives set by a business organisation will depend upon its overall aims. Examine the list of objectives below and identify to which of the aims on page 7 each one relates.
   - To sell more of a product than a competitor.
   - To open more stores or outlets over a wider area.
   - To provide more goods or services than in the previous year.
   - To produce a new product.
   - To provide a new service.
   - To improve an existing product or service.
   - To use only recycled paper.
   - To increase sales in all charity shops.

2 All the above objectives are very useful but not SMART. Convert each one so it includes a measurable target and a time-scale. Make it more realistic by including a business you have heard of. To help, the first two are done for you.
   - Airtours has the objective of selling 10 per cent more holidays than Thomsons over the next twelve months.
   - McDonald's intends to open a further 100 outlets in Britain during the year 2001.

3 You work for a motor car manufacturer which wants to improve quality in its cars. It also wants to improve performance and include additional features for customers. However, during the last two months there have been very negative press reports that your company's cars are 'gas-guzzlers' and environmentally unfriendly.

In groups of three or four,

   a identify three main aims you think the company should have
   b write two SMART objectives under each aim.

Evaluating performance

All businesses operate in a changing and uncertain world. So, although they may set aims and objectives, they may not always achieve these. Furthermore, aims and objectives go out of date and need to be reviewed at regular intervals.

Businesses therefore need to check regularly whether they are on target to achieve their objectives. If not, they will need to find out what has gone wrong and what can be done about it. They will also need to check that their aims and objectives are still achievable or whether they need to be revised.

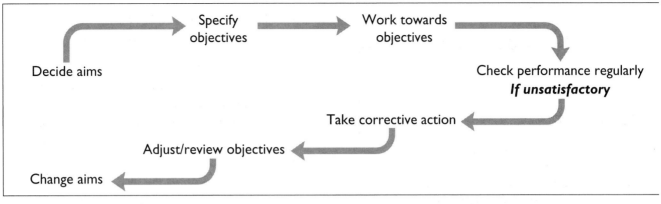

Figure 1.7 How to check aims and objectives

The process for checking aims and objectives is shown in Figure 1.7. Remember that if objectives are SMART they are measurable, so it is relatively easy to check if they are being met. It also helps if they have a time-scale, as you know then the period over which you are checking your achievements. However, it is wise to check regularly to make sure that you are on track to succeed. If you want 200 new customers to visit your shop in a year, then you should be aiming for about 50 every three months. You shouldn't wait for a year before you start to add them up.

When businesses set objectives they normally work out the targets they will use to measure success and how frequently. A car manufacturer designing a car which uses 10 per cent less petrol can measure its success on a test track. A superstore aiming to reduce customer complaints by 15 per cent a year can count the complaints one year and then count them (each month) during the following year.

If every objective is regularly checked then corrective action can be taken if things are going wrong. A company which wants to increase sales by 10 per cent may decide to run an advertising campaign if sales are not improving, or cut costs in a 'value' campaign. An airline trying to reduce delays may consider buying an additional plane if maintenance problems are causing too many hold-ups.

Only if the objectives are met will the business aims be met. However, sometimes external circumstances can mean that both the objectives and the aims must be changed. A charitable organisation aiming to increase aid in Britain may, for instance, change that aim and the objective if there is a sudden crisis elsewhere that deserves priority, as occurred in the case of the Kosovo refugees.

 ACTIVITY

1   Write out your own aims for the next 12 months.

2   Under each aim, write at least three SMART objectives for yourself.

3   Now decide how you are going to measure your progress in each case and how often.

4   Draw a flow chart to show the action you would take if your performance was unsatisfactory (see Figure 1.7 for how to do this).

5   Suggest two external circumstances that could arise which would mean you had to change your aims.

Check your answers with your tutor.

CASE STUDY 1.2

Sir Neville Sims, chief executive of Tarmac, the construction company, has publicly stated his commitment to environmental concerns and has said that in the future businesses are unlikely to survive if they do not take environmental issues seriously.

Tarmac set up an environmental panel in 1995 to set targets and report annually on the environmental performance of the company. In 1997 the company achieved 60 per cent of the 82 targets set for the year. This was a distinct improvement on 1996, when only 30 per cent of the targets were achieved. Forty-eight targets were fully met in 1997, which included establishing environmental policies across the company. Limited progress was made on 13 targets and there were problems in other areas. Tarmac was fined for pollution in two cases and was in trouble for destroying hedgerows and trees while working on the Manchester airport development.

Figure 1.8 Some companies take environment issues seriously

Sir Neville says that he is aware the group must continue to improve its performance but he also knows that many of the projects the company undertakes will always be controversial. He considers the role of Tarmac in the future will be to influence how these projects are carried out so that environmental damage is minimised. However, not everyone is convinced. Friends of the Earth is sceptical about Tarmac's claims. It argues that Tarmac is still more interested in profits than the environment and simply issues glossy brochures and gives fine speeches to mask the problem.

Activities

1   What do you think is one of the main aims of the Tarmac company?
2   Give an alternative word for 'targets'.
3   What do you understand by the words 'annually', 'distinct', 'controversial', 'influence', 'minimised' and 'sceptical'?
4   How many targets were set in 1997?
5   a   What percentage of targets were met in 1997?
    b   What percentage of targets were met in 1996?
    c   Can you calculate the percentage increase in success between these two years?
6   Was the company successful in meeting its targets in 1997? Give a reason for your answer.
7   a   What is Friends of the Earth and what does it do?
    b   Do you think companies like Tarmac simply try to mislead the public? Or do you think they should be encouraged in their efforts? Discuss your views as a group.

Section review

Refresh your memory of the section by writing short answers to each of the following questions and activities.

1   *In two or three sentences, explain what is meant by the phrase **business aims**.*

2   *Why is it sensible for a business to have aims?*

3   *Describe three aims that a business might have.*

4   *Briefly explain why targets or objectives are important in helping a business to achieve its aims.*

5   *Suggest two objectives for a company which identify expansion as its main aim.*

6   *In relation to your own school or college.*

   a   *As a group, identify what you consider is the main purpose of the institution – and compare this with the official mission statement. Can you explain any differences you find?*

   b   *Explain what you consider to be the main activity carried out by your institution.*

   c   *Identify three aims of your school or college. How do these relate to the service which is provided?*

   d   *How environmentally friendly is your institution? Find out whether it has any environmental quality standard and what measures are taken to adopt environmentally friendly policies.*

1.2 FUNCTIONAL AREAS WITHIN BUSINESS

At the end of this section you should be able to:

- describe the different functional areas of business
- explain how each contributes to the overall business activity
- give examples of job roles associated with each area
- explain how different functional areas interact to achieve the aims and objectives of the business.

Overview of functional areas

In the same way that businesses have a purpose, so do the individuals who work there. You know this yourself if you have a part-time job. You have a specific set of duties to carry out and you may have a job title that indicates what you do, in other words, it states your **function**. If you work in a supermarket you may be employed as a check-out operator or a shelf-filler or a customer services assistant. All these are different functions which must be undertaken for the supermarket to operate efficiently.

In a large organisation, people with the same type of jobs work together in **functional areas**. These are areas which relate to the main functions which must be carried out within the business, and all have a specific purpose. The functions you need to know about are:

- human resources

- finance

- administration

- production

- marketing and sales

- customer service.

In many businesses you will find that the functions match the title of the departments, e.g. the human resources department, finance department and so on. In other cases a function may take place in several different departments, as you will see when you read about administration.

These are not the only functions that take place in businesses. You will also need to learn about other functions, such as quality control and research and development. Sometimes these are a separate department and sometimes they are part of another, larger one.

Each functional area operates to support the business's aims and objectives and a range of activities goes on in each one. How the functional areas interact with one another is important. For a business to be efficient and effective, there must be close links between the people who work in different functional areas, especially when their activities overlap. How the overall business is structured to include all these functional areas is discussed in Section 1.3. For now, we will concentrate on the purpose of different functional areas and the activities that are carried out.

Human resources

The purpose of the human resources function

Human resources is concerned with the **employees** who work for the organisation. Wise organisations regard staff as the most important resource. Other resources include money (called **capital**), equipment, buildings, land and materials. However, if the employees are not motivated and only do the minimum work that is required, then all the money or equipment in the world won't make the business successful. On the other hand, if the employees are keen to do their best, are well trained and committed to the aims of the business, then most organisations will be successful. This is why the employees – or human resources – are so important.

If you worked for a business, what would help to make you keener to work hard? In other words, what would motivate you? Obviously you would want a respectable salary, but this isn't everything. You would also want:

• to do work you found interesting and challenging (but not so challenging it was overwhelming)

• good working conditions

• to be treated fairly by your boss

• to know that you were working in a safe environment

Figure 1.9 Hospital staff

• to have opportunities to take further training

• to be able to develop yourself and have the opportunity to gain promotion

• to have protection against victimisation, harassment, discrimination and unfair dismissal

• to be treated equally, no matter what your gender or race or whether you were disabled in some way.

These are areas with which the human resources staff are involved. The overall purpose of the human resources function can therefore be identified as:

• to attract and retain good, high-quality staff

• to train and develop all staff to enable them to reach their maximum potential

• to ensure that the organisation avoids unlawful or unfair discrimination

• to ensure that the organisation operates within the law in relation to employment and health and safety.

The activities of the human resources function

To fulfil its purpose, human resources staff are involved in specific activities. These include:

• the recruitment, retention and dismissal of staff

• the training, development and promotion of staff

• the monitoring and maintenance of good working conditions

• health and safety

• liaison with employee organisations and trade unions.

All of these areas are considered separately, and in detail, on pages 23–44.

Job roles in human resources

Exact job roles and job titles vary considerably from one organisation to another. The larger the organisation, the more likely it is there will be several staff working in the human resources department. There may be a **human resources director** who is a senior manager in the organisation. This is likely to be the case in a large manufacturing organisation which employs thousands of workers. A medium-sized company with fewer employees may have a **human resources manager** who oversees a much smaller number of staff. In a small organisation you may find each manager is responsible for the 'human resource' aspects relating to his or her own department. You may even find that a company you are investigating doesn't use the term 'human resources department' but refers to its 'personnel department'. Both terms describe a similar type of function.

An example of some of the job roles you may find in an organisation is given in Figure 1.10 below.

Typical job title	Function and responsibilities
Human resources director	Deciding the overall staffing policies of the organisation. Advising senior management. Setting the HR budget. In charge of all the HR functions in the organisation.
Human resources manager	Managing the HR department and staff, involved with industrial relations and trade union negotiations, implementing the organisation's HR policies.
Recruitment officer	Responsible for the recruitment and selection of staff.
Training/staff development officer	Responsible for training and staff development.
Personnel/staffing officer	Keeping staff records, monitoring staff welfare.
Health and safety officer	Overseeing all health and safety matters, accident monitoring and prevention.
Security officer	General security, responsible for all security staff.
HR administrative assistants	Administrative work relating to the human resources function.

Figure 1.10 Job roles in human resources

The law and the human resources function

The way in which the human resources function operates is not simply left to the business itself. There is legislation covering **employment law** and **health and safety** to ensure organisations follow certain minimum standards for their employees. This means that you have certain rights as an employee. You also have certain responsibilities to your employer in return.

Some of your rights and responsibilities are stated clearly in your **contract of employment**. This is a written document you should be given within two months of starting work. Some of these rights and responsibilities are identified in the conditions under which you are employed – known as **express terms**. They include the date your employment started, the hours you will work, your salary and how often it is paid, holiday and sickness entitlement, your job title, place of work and notice entitlement, and so on. You will learn more about contracts of employment if you study the option unit 'Individuals and the Organisations'. You are obviously expected to abide by these terms and conditions – and so is your employer.

However, when you accept a job, there are also **implied conditions** relating to your employment. These are conditions both parties can reasonably expect of each other even if they are not written down. So far as the employee is concerned, these are:

- that you will be 'ready and willing to work'. This means that you will arrive for work in person – you cannot legally ask someone else to do the job for you!

- that you will use reasonable care and skill

- that you will obey reasonable orders, such as conforming to a reasonable company dress code

- that you will take care of your employer's property

- that you will act in good faith – for instance, you will not accept bribes or give confidential information to a competitor.

In return your employer has two implied conditions:

- to treat you reasonably

- to give you the opportunity to be consulted on certain company matters, particularly those that will affect you.

In addition, your employer must not ask you to do anything which is illegal or which is dangerous and may cause you physical harm.

Any employee who does not abide by the terms and conditions in their contract of employment can be disciplined through the organisation's disciplinary policy (see page 29).

It is relatively easy to see that your rights as an employee are your employer's responsibilities to you, and your responsibilities as an employee are the rights of your employer. These are summarised, to help you, in Figure 1.11.

Employment law and equal opportunities

Rights and responsibilities don't just happen, they have evolved over many years in an effort to find a fair balance between what employers and employees can both reasonably expect. A good, responsible and caring employer who appreciates the importance of well-motivated staff will always treat them

Your rights as an employee (the responsibilities of the employer)	Your responsibilities as an employee (the rights of the employer)
1 To be provided with safe working conditions.	1 To be 'ready and willing' to work.
2 To receive written particulars of employment within two months of starting work.	2 To give a personal service.
3 To be paid a fair wage or salary in return for being 'ready and willing' to work.	3 To be reasonably competent.
4 To be provided with information concerning your rights.	4 To take reasonable care of your employer's property.
5 *In some cases*, to be provided with work.	5 To carry out reasonable and lawful instructions.
6 To have any grievances properly dealt with.	6 To act in good faith, i.e. to be honest, not work for a competitor, not give away trade secrets.
7 Not to be discriminated against on grounds of race, sex disability.	7 To comply with the express terms of your contract (e.g. hours of work, duties etc.).
8 To be allowed to choose whether or not to join a trade union.	8 To comply with health and safety procedures.
9 To be consulted over matters which will significantly affect your terms and conditions of employment.	9 To work towards the objectives of the organisation.
10 To be treated reasonably.	10 To behave responsibly towards other employees.

Figure 1.11 Rights and responsibilities of employees and employers

fairly. Equally, honest and conscientious staff will always work hard to earn their money. Sadly this wouldn't be the case in all organisations or with all employees without some formal procedures. Therefore, the rights and responsibilities of employers and employees are laid down in **employment law**. In addition, employee organisations and unions also work to check that the legal requirements are being followed and try to negotiate improvements or additional safeguards for staff where possible (see page 42).

There are four main Acts you need to know about:

- The Employment Rights Act 1996

- The Sex Discrimination Act 1975

- The Race Relations Act 1976

- The Disability Discrimination Act 1995.

The first summarises the main rights which have been agreed over several years in one Act of Parliament. The other three Acts are concerned with **equal opportunities** – and support the basic principle that all potential and actual employees should be treated equally in all matters relating to their employment. The first of these is concerned with gender, the second with race and ethnicity and the third with disabilities. The main points of each of these Acts are summarised in Figure 1.12.

To confirm that they agree and will abide by the concept of equal opportunities, most organisations have an **equal opportunities policy**. This is a statement of the equal opportunities aims of the organisation. A sample statement suggested by the Department for Education and Employment is given below:

The company supports the principle of equal opportunities in employment and opposes all forms of unlawful or unfair discrimination on the grounds of colour, race, nationality, ethnic or national origin, sex, being married or disability. We believe that it is in the company's best interests, and those of all who work in it, to ensure that the human resources, talents and skills available throughout the community are considered when employment opportunities arise. To this end, within the framework of the law, we are committed, wherever practicable, to achieving and maintaining a workforce which broadly reflects the local community in which we operate.

Every possible step will be taken to ensure that individuals are treated equally and fairly and that decisions on recruitment, selection, training, promotion and career management are based solely on objective and job related criteria.

As you already know, the next step to achieving an aim is to set objectives. The company should therefore prepare an action plan which states the main objectives to be achieved. One objective may be equal opportunities training for all the staff in a given period. Another may be to improve the percentage of certain people employed in jobs or at levels where they are under-represented, e.g. more ethnic minority employees, more women managers, a higher number of disabled workers employed, and so on.

As with any objective, progress needs to be monitored to identify how well the targets are being met. Various initiatives may be introduced to improve success, such as reviewing the recruitment procedures in the organisation, training interviewers, developing links with the local community, or introducing more flexible working schemes. Always remember, setting an aim – or equal opportunities statement – is no guarantee of achieving it! Only if specific actions are taken to help to accomplish the objectives is it likely to be successful.

The Employment Rights Act 1996

This Act covers virtually all of the main rights of employees, i.e.:

- All employees must receive written details of their employment terms within two months of starting work, normally in a contract of employment. The Act specifies the details which must be given. If an employer makes significant changes which the employee disagrees with, then the employee may be able to claim constructive dismissal and complain to an employment tribunal.
- All employees are entitled to an itemised pay-slip which shows gross and net pay and details of any deductions.
- An employee asked to work on a Sunday can 'opt-out' by serving notice.
- All female employees are eligible for maternity leave and can return to work afterwards on the same terms and conditions as before.
- An employee cannot be dismissed for acting as a trade union official or health and safety representative.
- Employees must be allowed time off work for jury service or ante-natal care.
- Any employee suspended from work on medical grounds is entitled to receive payment for up to 26 weeks.
- Employees have a right to a minimum period of notice (between 1 and 12 weeks), depending upon the length of time they have been continuously employed. An employer not giving this notice would be guilty of wrongful dismissal.
- Employees have the right not to be unfairly dismissed by their employer, and, if this occurs, can present their complaint to an employment tribunal.
- Employees dismissed through redundancy have the right to receive a redundancy payment if they have more than two years' service. In certain cases this includes employees who are laid off or kept on short time. If an employee is redundant and the employer is insolvent or bankrupt, then the employee can apply to the Secretary of State for payment.

The Sex Discrimination Act 1975

This Act makes it illegal for anyone to be discriminated against on grounds of gender (or gender reassignment) – either directly or indirectly. In employment this applies to recruitment and selection for jobs and promotion, training, the way you are treated in a job, dismissal and redundancy. **Direct discrimination** is where one gender is excluded, e.g. 'only men need apply'. **Indirect discrimination** is where a *condition* would make it more difficult for one sex to comply, e.g. 'only those over 6' 6" need apply'. Even if this is done unintentionally, the organisation is still guilty. There are some special exceptions, such as in acting or live-in jobs, if the employer can show a Genuine Occupational Qualification (GOQ) applies. Note, too, that the **Equal Pay Act 1970** means that jobs where the work is of 'equal value' must be paid at the same rate for men and women.

The Race Relations Act 1976

This Act makes it unlawful for anyone to be discriminated against on grounds of colour, race, nationality or ethnic origin. Again both direct and indirect discrimination apply, e.g. 'only white people need apply' or 'only those who speak English as their first language need apply'. Again there are certain special circumstances under which it can be justified, e.g. restaurants for authenticity, but these are relatively rare.

The Disability Discrimination Act 1995 (applies to businesses with over 15 employees)

This Act is concerned with discrimination against people with disabilities in employment, when obtaining goods and services or buying/renting land or property. The disability may be physical, sensory or mental but must be relatively long-term (i.e. last more than 12 months). Employers must *not* treat a disabled person less favourably than able-bodied persons whether in recruitment, training, promotion or dismissal unless it can be justified. Employers must also be prepared to make reasonable adjustments to the workplace to enable a disabled person to do the job. Disabled persons who suffer discrimination can complain to an employment tribunal. Discrimination in this case is not divided into 'direct' and 'indirect' but is 'less favourable treatment that cannot be justified'.

Figure 1.12 Main points of employment law

SNAPSHOT

Fair words don't always equal fair play!

In 1999 much press coverage was given to 'institutional racism' in the police force, particularly following the Macpherson enquiry into the Metrolopitan police following the murder of Stephen Lawrence. What is institutional racism and how is this linked to equal opportunities?

Today virtually all companies claim to have equal opportunities policies. They may state this on their job advertisements. They say they do not differentiate between applicants on grounds of sex, race, religion, ethnicity, colour or disability. This, actually, is a requirement of law – as you can see from Figure 1.12. Some employers go even further in saying they do not discriminate on grounds of age or sexual orientation – although neither of these are covered by law at the present time.

*Any organisation can **say** it has an equal opportunities policy. But does it really? Some women have complained they were miserable in the army or the fire service because they were not made to feel welcome by the predominantly male workforce. Some ethnic minority ex-police officers have made similar complaints about the police force. They believed the internal operations and procedures of the police force and its culture were against them and in favour of the white officers who implemented them.*

*These sort of problems defeat any attempt to implement a **real** equal opportunities policy. The police force however is now making an effort to change its internal culture and to attract more ethnic minority applicants. Perhaps the renewed interest in equal opportunities will help to make it a reality and not mere words.*

CASE STUDY 1.3

Employees who feel they have been treated unfairly can take their case to an employment tribunal. These are independent bodies set up to provide an inexpensive and speedy method of determining disputes between employers and employees. They are usually made up of a legally qualified chairperson and two lay members who are appointed by the Secretary of State for Trade and Industry. The employee making the complaint is often supported by their union, but this isn't a legal requirement. The tribunal can order a company to reinstate the employee or award compensation.

The first person to be compensated for unfair treatment under the Disability Discrimination Act was Mrs Barbara Tarling, who was sacked after 17 years with the same company. Mrs Tarling was born with a club foot and by 1996 the pain in her leg had become much worse. Her job involved standing at a machine all day and her productivity had deteriorated because of the pain. Her employer started disciplinary procedures against her and then dismissed her.

Mrs Tarling's union, the Transport and General, took the case to a tribunal, which

CASE STUDY (continued)

awarded her £1,200 for injury to her feelings and ordered the company, Wisdom Toothbrushes in Haverhill, to reinstate her. They found her a job that she could do sitting down.

The Equal Opportunities Commission (EOC) and the Commission for Racial Equality (CRE) help to bring cases for employees who suffer sex or racial discrimination, and from April 2000 the Disability Rights Commission has undertaken this role for people with a disability. In addition, under the Employment Rights (Disputes) Act 1998, disputes relating to unfair dismissal can be settled by the Advisory, Conciliation and Arbitration Service (ACAS), rather than a tribunal.

The success of the EOC and CRE is worth noting. According to the EOC, the average settlement for sex discrimination cases was £16,445 in 1998. A few others have received much higher awards, such as personnel director Christine Esplin, who was sacked when she claimed the same pay as the merchandise director. She received £140,000 in compensation. In addition her employers agreed to amend their equal opportunities policy.

In a case concerning racial discrimination, a quantity surveyor was awarded more than £41,000 compensation after being passed over for promotion by Bridgend Council because he was black. In another case, two chartered surveyors found out at a seminar that they were paid less than their colleagues and believed they had a case on the grounds of racial discrimination. The difference? They were Welsh, whereas their colleagues were English.

Activities

1 Under what Act did Mrs Barbara Tarling bring her case to an employment tribunal?
2 Did she win or lose her case? Explain your answer.
3 a What is an employment tribunal?
  b What powers does it have?
4 a You are not a member of a union but you are unfairly dismissed. Can you still go to an employment tribunal?
  b Where else could you take your complaint?
5 Under what Acts were the following cases brought?
  a Christine Esplin
  b The surveyor employed by Bridgend Council.

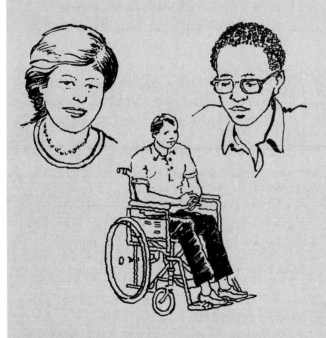

Figure 1.13 Some employers may discriminate against certain people

CASE STUDY (continued)

6   If an Irish worker in a Scottish company found he was paid less than his male colleagues, could this be classed as discrimination? Explain your answer and state under what Act he might have a case.

7   If you have Internet access, find out more about the work of the EOC, CRE and ACAS by accessing their web pages.

Then write a paragraph on each, explaining what they do.
Contact them on the following sites: www.eoc.org.uk, www.cre.gov.uk, www.acas.org.uk.

8   Look back at the article on institutional racism. Discuss with your tutor what is meant by the 'culture' of an organisation.

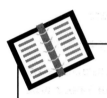

SNAPSHOT

Keeping up to date with the law

Employment rights change quite frequently and it is important that all employers and employees keep up to date with any changes. Since the Employment Rights Act was passed, other significant legislation has improved workers' rights still further. Under the Employment Relations Act 1999, female employees gained improved maternity leave, parents were granted up to three months' unpaid leave to look after young children and all workers gained the right to take leave in the case of a family emergency. Workers had already benefited from the National Minimum Wage Act in 1998, which stipulated a minimum wage rate per hour for all adults and specified amounts for young workers. Working hours were regulated in the Working Time Regulations 1998 which came in force in the autumn of 1999. For most employees the working week cannot be any longer than 48 hours, unless an 'opt-out' relevant agreement is in place, with specified rest breaks and a four weeks' annual holiday entitlement. Part-time employees will have the right to equal pay, treatment and benefits by April 2000 when the European Directive on Part-time Work is implemented.

ACTIVITY

Find out your rights under each of the above Acts by answering the following questions. You can find out the information you need from the Internet or from your library. Web sites to try include: www.tuc.org.uk, www.open.gov.uk, www.emplaw.co.uk.

1   Under the Employment Relations Act:
   a   for how long must you have worked for an employer to be able to claim unfair dismissal?
   b   a female worker joins a company and two months later finds out she is pregnant. How many weeks maternity leave can she take?
   c   can the parents of a 10-year-old take parental leave?

2   Under the National Minimum Wage Act 1998, what is the minimum amount per hour that can be paid to a 19-year-old employee?

3   Under the Working Time Regulations 1998:
   a   what is your weekly rest period entitlement?
   b   what three occupations are exempt from the regulations?
   c   can your employer force you to sign a paper 'opting out' of the regulations?

4 What is 'whistleblowing'? What Act has been passed to protect 'whistleblowers'?

Discuss as a group why the government has decided this Act is important.

Investigating human resource activities

On page 16 you read that there were several activities carried out in human resources by a variety of people. Now that you are familiar with some of the legal constraints on this function, it is time to examine these in more detail.

Recruitment, retention and dismissal

The human resources department is responsible for recruiting new staff to the organisation. The cost of recruitment is high, but mistakes are even more expensive. Appointing someone who cannot do a job or who does not get on with other people is disastrous. Companies try to keep their staff turnover as low as possible – in other words, they want to **retain** the staff they recruit. This not only saves money on recruitment and training, but helps staff to feel they are working in a stable environment. It encourages good teamwork, which is disrupted if there is a high turnover of staff.

Recruiting employees

Most organisations have a specific recruitment policy which everyone must follow. Everyone involved in interviewing and selecting staff should be trained so that they follow the law relating to equal opportunities policies and know how to interview applicants to get the best results. The recruitment policy is likely to specify:

- that all jobs must be detailed on a job description and advertised vacancies linked to an appropriate person specification (see page 25)
- the sources of recruitment to be used for particular jobs
- how jobs must be advertised
- the method by which candidates must apply for a job
- the procedure for shortlisting candidates
- a set procedure for interviewers
- a set procedure for consulting referees.

This type of policy reduces the possibility of anyone being treated unfairly – or being able to claim that they were discriminated against when they applied for a job. It also tries to ensure that the best possible candidate for each job vacancy is offered the position.

Sources of recruitment and advertising
There are a number of sources of recruitment available to employers. They may:

- contact the careers service or a local college
- contact the job centre
- contact a recruitment agency
- contact an employment consultant
- advertise in the local or national press
- advertise in professional and trade journals
- advertise internally.

The careers service is usually the first point of contact if an organisation wants to employ a young worker or a trainee under the Modern Apprenticeship scheme. The careers service will advertise the vacancy and inform the organisation of interested applicants. Some careers services also have job vacancy boards in the local college. Some organisations may contact a college direct if they have a vacancy for a young, skilled worker in a particular area.

The local job centre is more appropriate for adult vacancies, particularly for manual work. If a driver, mechanic, foreman, cook or cleaner is required then the human resources staff would notify the job centre, who will advertise the vacancy and notify the firm about interested applicants.

Recruitment agencies are common, particularly in large cities. They also handle vacancies for temporary staff. This is useful for an organisation that needs seasonal workers, or holiday or maternity cover. The temporary worker is usually employed by the agency itself, which pays the worker's wage and charges the company at a higher rate – the difference being the agency's profit. Most agencies also handle permanent vacancies. They do not charge for advertising these, nor for interviewing their clients, but they do charge the company if someone they recommend gets the job. Recruitment

agencies are often used for administration, clerical, secretarial, IT and accounts staff.

If the vacancy is at managerial level, then an employment consultancy may be asked to find suitable applicants. They often know which senior managers in other organisations are interested in changing companies and may even 'head-hunt' one of these. This means contacting the person to see if they would be interested in a vacancy about to arise in another company. A consultancy places job advertisements, usually in prestigious newspapers or professional journals, and does the preliminary selection process. This saves the company a lot of work, but obviously there is a charge at the end of it.

Despite all these sources of recruitment, the most popular one is advertising in a local or national newspaper or a trade journal. National newspapers are used for relatively high salaried prestigious jobs, that people would be willing to move location for. They are also used where there is local skills shortage. In these cases the company may pay relocation expenses for the person they choose. Most local papers have a 'jobs night' when you can scan all the current vacancies in the area. This saves you buying the paper every night to see what is available.

Last – but by no means least – many companies advertise vacancies internally. This is sensible if the job provides a promotional opportunity for current staff. Indeed, some companies have a policy of only advertising the lowest level jobs externally. Above this level, they prefer promoting their own staff. This has the benefit of motivating employees, but has the disadvantage of limiting the number of new staff who enter the organisation. New staff can bring in new ideas and new methods of working that can be valuable and save the organisation from becoming too insular (look up this word!). Probably a balance of new staff and promoted staff is the ideal in most companies.

Figure 1.14 Job centres are one source of jobs

Advertising a vacancy

Display advertisements are expensive and can cost hundreds of pounds – even in a local paper. So they have to be effective enough to attract the right calibre of applicants. If they make the job sound easier than it is, people who do not have the necessary skills or qualifications will apply. If they make the job sound too hard, good candidates will be put off and may not apply.

Writing an advertisement to attract the right candidates is not easy and there are guidelines for human resources staff who do this. They usually start from a **job description** which states the duties and responsibilities of the job. This is drawn up by the manager who will be responsible for the employee. The manager then writes a **person specification**. This lists the **essential** and **desirable** characteristics of any candidates. These characteristics, and the conditions of employment that apply, usually form the main part of the advertisement. Applicants must also be told how to apply or find out further information. A closing date is often specified, by which time all applications must be received. You will learn more about job descriptions and person specifications if you study the option unit 'Individuals and the Organisation'.

Most organisations also include a statement about their equal opportunities policy (see page 18).

Methods of applying for a job

Candidates may be asked to apply for a job in various ways.

- They can be asked to telephone the company. This is rare but is increasingly used by organisations employing telephone sales or customer services staff – and who want to check how candidates will sound over the telephone.

- They can be asked to call in to the human resources department. This may be used for job centre vacancies, where skilled or unskilled manual workers are required, or for temporary seasonal staff who are required urgently.

- They can be asked to write a letter and attach their CV (curriculum vitae). You may have already prepared a CV for yourself. This lists your personal details, education, qualifications, working experience (full and part-time), hobbies and interests and gives the name of two referees. Letters and CVs must be well constructed and clearly set out, particularly if you are applying for a job where your written English skills will be important.

- They can be asked to complete an official application form. However, application forms vary. Those for basic jobs may be short and straightforward. Those for more senior positions may be longer and

DATAPLAN CORPORATION

Finance Trainee

required for busy data communications company.

The successful applicant must have excellent numeracy skills and a flair for, and interest in, financial matters. A minimum of GNVQ Advanced Level Business (with financial options) or AAT level 3 is required. The ability to work as a member of a team is essential, together with a good knowledge of spreadsheets and a related IT qualification.

Although college leavers will be considered, preferably applicants will have gained one or two years' experience in a commercial environment or have a good track record of work experience. Ideally, applicants will also possess good communication skills and be able to demonstrate their ability to deal effectively with a wide range of people at all levels.

The successful candidate will be required to work towards higher level financial qualifications and career prospects are excellent.

Hours 9 – 5.30. Salary negotiable, depending upon age and experience.

For full details including a job description and application form contact Nikki King, Human Resources Assistant, on 02837-809010. Completed application forms should be returned to the Human Resources Department, Dataplan Corporation, 14 Riverside Square, Hightown, HG1 8EG, quoting reference 839.28.

Dataplan Corporation is an Equal Opportunities employer and welcomes applications from all sections of the community.

Figure 1.15 You need the right advertisement to get the right person

contain blank spaces where applicants have to explain why they want that particular job. Again, neatness, spelling and accuracy will all be taken into account, particularly where this is a vital prerequisite for the job.

Shortlisting candidates

A good advertisement for an attractive job will probably attract far more candidates than a company could possibly interview. So, before anyone is selected for interview, someone has to go through the applications and decide which candidates are the most suitable. This is not an easy task, particularly if you have 20 good applicants and can only interview 6 of them!

The first starting point is the essential characteristics listed in the person specification. Unless candidates have *all* the essential requirements they are not usually shortlisted. This is obvious, if you think about it, given that the company has specified that these are all essential!

The second stage is to look at the list of desirable characteristics to see which candidates have the 'best mix' of these. Some people may have all of them, which puts them at the top of the list. Others may just have a few of them. If there are still too many applications then the neatness and style of the application itself is one of the things likely to be taken into account.

The shortlisted candidates then receive a letter, asking them to attend an interview. You may think it would be courteous for the company to send letters to everyone who has not been shortlisted, but the high cost of producing and mailing these letters means that most organisations don't do it. Some companies in their advertisements or applications do tell candidates that they will have been unsuccessful if they are not contacted within a certain time.

Interviewing candidates

These are some of the formats for interviews:

- one-stage interviews, carried out by human resources staff

- two-stage interviews, the first carried out by human resources staff, the second carried out by the manager of the new employee

- panel interviews.

The human resources staff will usually be involved in interviews for manual staff, unskilled staff, junior staff and first stage interviews for many other vacancies. The candidates chosen for further interview or an important job will have a final interview with the manager they will work for, as he or she will approve the final decision.

Senior staff are often appointed by a panel of interviewers, which usually includes a senior member of the human resources department. The panel may comprise various managers or directors of the organisation.

Interviewers should be trained so that they know *how* to question applicants and *what*

Figure 1.16 A candidate being interviewed for a senior post

type of questions to ask. Good interviewers are skilful at encouraging candidates to talk about themselves. They are also aware that certain types of questions cannot be asked because they would be discriminatory, and disadvantage certain applicants. You cannot, for instance, ask all female applicants whether they can cope with a job if they have a family and assume that all male applicants will have no difficulty!

Some interviews contain a psychometric assessment or skills test to check the abilities of applicants. For some senior positions, candidates may have to attend an assessment centre for a day – or even a weekend – and undergo a variety of tests and activities.

Towards the end of an interview the candidate should be given the opportunity to ask questions – for instance, about training opportunities or to clarify any queries. Candidates should be thanked for attending and told how, and when, they will be notified of the result. It is considerate to make a rapid decision and, once the chosen candidate has accepted, to notify all other interviewees promptly.

Consulting referees

It is normal to ask candidates to list the names and addresses of two people who can provide a reference. If you are ever asked to give the names of referees, do make sure you obtain their permission first, so they are forewarned. Referees should not be members of your own family, as it is assumed they will always say good things about you!

Applicants currently employed may not wish to give the name of their current employer as a referee, as they may not want their employer to know they are 'looking around'. They are within their rights to ask that their current employer is not contacted, unless they are offered the job.

References are usually requested before the interview, but for shortlisted candidates only.

Copies are passed on to the interviewers. If the interviewer wishes to offer a person the job, but has no reference from the current employer, the job may be offered 'subject to satisfactory references' and confirmed at a later date.

ACTIVITY

1   You are employed in the human resources department of a large organisation as a trainee recruitment officer. Read the previous section again and list all the tasks:
    a   which are routine, and which you would be expected to do as part of your job
    b   for which you would need training or advice and would only carry out under the guidance of your own boss.

2   Form into groups of two or three and list all the factors which would be important to you in relation to staying with an organisation. Then score each item on your list out of 10, to see which would be the most important factors to you and which would be the least important. If you are studying the option unit 'Individuals and the Organisation', then you will find this list useful later.

Retaining employees

All companies are keen to retain good staff. This saves them the cost of hiring and retraining someone else. So what can organisations do to make sure they keep their staff?

First, organisations must ensure that new staff settle in quickly and understand their job and their contribution to the organisation's objectives. This is usually done through an **induction programme**. The new employee will spend a short time learning about the company, touring the premises, finding out about health and safety requirements and their rights and responsibilities as an employee. They will be introduced to their immediate colleagues and receive training and support for the first few weeks. This is beneficial for everyone as the employee settles in quicker and also becomes productive faster and makes fewer mistakes.

In the last activity you were asked to list the factors you would consider most important in retaining employees. Several studies have been done to see what helps employees to stay interested in their job and keen to work hard. These studies are about **motivation**.

One famous study was by Frederick Herzberg who investigated what factors contribute to job satisfaction. This is what he concluded.

- Some factors actively help to *increase* job satisfaction or motivation. Herzberg called these **motivators**. They include:

  - interesting work
  - having responsibility
  - being praised for doing a good job
  - being able to achieve
  - personal growth
  - opportunities for advancement.

Interestingly, all these are concerned with the content of the job and opportunities for undertaking more challenging work.

- Some factors cause dissatisfaction if they are not present but, on their own, will not create job satisfaction. Herzberg called these **hygiene factors**. The most important of these are:

  - company policies and administration
  - your relationship with your boss or supervisor
  - working conditions
  - salary
  - your relationships with your colleagues
  - your own personal life.

So, if you work in a modern office with a group of lively colleagues and an excellent canteen, this will help to prevent you becoming dissatisfied – even if the job is rather boring. But if you want to really enjoy your work, job content is far more important.

You will learn more about induction programmes and motivation if you study the option unit 'Individuals and the Organisation'.

Today most organisations have a clear procedure that employees can use if they wish to complain about being treated unfairly. This is known as the **grievance procedure**. Most grievance procedures cover three main areas:

- money – such as a mistake in your pay packet

- work issues – such as a change in your job content, the amount of time off you are allowed or the amount of overtime you must work

- discriminatory or unfair treatment.

It is always hoped that any problems can be sorted out informally and quickly, but this is

Figure 1.17 A good canteen can make a difference

not always possible. In this case the employee may use the official grievance procedure. There are usually three stages.

1   The employee has an interview with his/her line manager at which all the facts are checked. (Your line manager is your immediate boss.) At this stage the problem may be solved. The employee can be accompanied at this interview by someone else of his/her own choosing, such as a colleague, solicitor or union representative.

2   If the problem is not resolved, an interview is held with a more senior manager, usually outside the department. This may be the human resources manager. Sometimes a joint committee of union and management representatives is called.

3   An interview with an outside third party who will make a recommendation. The Advisory, Conciliation and Arbitration Service (ACAS), which you first encountered on page 21, is an official body which is often involved at this stage.

Using the formal grievance procedure is relatively rare. In most organisations, where there is good management, committed employees and good communication, any problems are usually solved informally and amicably at an early stage. Through early resolution of problems, the grievance procedure helps staff retention.

Dismissing employees

There are very few managers who like to dismiss an employee, though this may be necessary. There are several reasons why an employee may be dismissed.

1   Because he or she has breached the terms of their contract of employment (see below). In other words, they have committed an offence which is not permitted by the organisation. An obvious example is theft.

2   Because he or she is redundant. In this case, there is no longer any work for that person to do.

3   Because an employee has misled an employer at interview about his or her ability to undertake a critical aspect of the job (such as a word operator not being able to type!) and so is incapable of doing the work.

4   Through involvement in unlawful activities, such as a 'wildcat' strike where there hasn't been a proper ballot (see page 44).

5   For some other substantial reason, e.g. continually refusing to comply with reasonable requests.

Dismissal for breach of contract

Any employee who breaches their contract is usually dealt with through the organisation's **disciplinary procedures**. These are, in effect, the opposite of grievance procedures, as in this case it is the organisation which has the complaint about an employee, rather than the other way round.

The company's disciplinary procedures are in writing and will state clearly what type of disciplinary action may be taken and by which managers. It will also inform employees of their right of appeal if they feel the complaint against them is unfair.

There are usually three stages to a disciplinary procedure.

1   A verbal warning for a minor offence.
2   A written (or final) warning for a serious offence or a repeated minor offence.
3   Suspension, demotion, transfer or dismissal for a very serious offence. This is often called **gross misconduct**.

If a serious offence is committed the company may terminate the employee's contract without notice. This is called **summary dismissal** or instant dismissal. Offences which would prompt this include stealing, drunkenness, attacking another employee or gross breach of organisational rules (e.g. clocking in another employee who is late or absent).

Normally, however, dismissal is the last resort and only occurs when all other options have been exhausted. If an employee is disciplined, the first stage is usually a disciplinary interview where the claim is fully investigated and the employee can put forward his or her own case in defence.

Redundancy

An employee is made redundant when he or she is dismissed because there is no longer any work for them to do. Other possibilities will usually be looked at before taking such action. It may be possible to offer the person appropriate alternative work or to ask for voluntary redundancies. Some organisations stop recruiting staff if work is becoming scarce and don't replace staff who leave. Not replacing staff is known as **natural wastage**.

Sometimes compulsory redundancy is the only option. To do this the organisation must have an agreed procedure which involves the relevant trade unions to make sure the process is as fair as possible. The employees must be told the reason for the redundancies and the method of selection must be fair – a manager cannot legally use redundancy as a method of getting rid of unpopular staff! Sometimes companies use the 'last in, first out' criterion which means the most recent employees leave first. In other cases a whole section of staff may be selected for redundancy, such as staff in a particular regional office which is being closed.

Staff being made redundant must be told about the payments they will receive and their legal rights, as well as the time scale over which dismissals will occur. Sometimes free counselling or retraining is offered to help redundant employees find other work.

SNAPSHOT

Know your rights on dismissal

If you are dismissed fairly there is little you can do. You may have been dismissed because you are incapable of doing a job, misled your employer during the interview about your abilities, breached the terms of your contract of employment, behaved badly or have genuinely been made redundant.

However, employees may be dismissed unlawfully. So, what can they do? The first step is to understand the different types of dismissal that can take place.

Wrongful dismissal *occurs if your employer ignores the notice period in your contract of employment or as set down in the Employment Rights Act of 1996, even though you hadn't committed gross misconduct.*

Unfair dismissal *is when you are dismissed for no good reason after you have been employed for 12 months or longer.*

Constructive dismissal *is when your employer or boss makes your life so difficult for you that you are forced to leave.*

As you have already seen, if an employment tribunal agrees that you should not have been dismissed it can insist that your employer reinstates or re-employs you. Or it can order the employer to pay you compensation. Usually this is the best option, as few people want to return to work for an employer who has treated them badly.

Training, development and promotion

Staff training

It is normal to specify minimum qualification levels in job advertisements. Why, then, should companies want to continue to train their employees after they have started work?

There are several important reasons for providing staff with training opportunities.

- New staff need to be made familiar with organisational methods of working that may be different from their previous workplace and with health and safety requirements (see induction programmes, page 27). They may also need extra training for their specific job – even if they have been promoted from somewhere else within the company.

- Jobs change – and so do the skills people need. For instance, the company may introduce new methods of working or new equipment or software. All staff will have to be trained to maintain organisational efficiency. Training helps people to keep up to date.

- People are more motivated if they continue to learn and develop. They are also eligible for promotion within the company if they have gained experience and additional qualifications.

- Staff may be interested in improving and extending their knowledge and skills so that they can undertake more varied work.

- Newly promoted staff may need training to be able to cope with their new responsibilities.

Training opportunities can be provided **on-the-job** or **off-the-job**. If you receive training 'on-the-job' you remain in the workplace, in your normal working situation. This is appropriate when you are learning to operate equipment, e.g. a photocopier or telephone system. 'Off-the-job' training occurs when you leave your normal working environment to receive special instruction. This can still be within the company, as when you attend an induction programme or fire training in

Figure 1.18 On-the-job training

another part of the building. Sometimes you may go to an outside organisation, such as doing a course at an FE college or specialist centre to gain a specific qualification. Your employer may allow you some time off for this but, more likely, you will be expected to do some of this in your spare time.

Staff development

Most organisations now expect their employees to take an active role in their own training and self-development. This is usually a key part of an **appraisal scheme**. Under this scheme, each employee has a confidential interview with his or her manager, usually once a year. This covers the work the employee has done well during the year, areas where the employee feels less confident and identifies where future training may be useful. It is the employee's chance to make a positive contribution to his or her own self-development and future prospects. A good manager will listen carefully to the employee's concerns and help to address them. He or she will also want to link the employee's future ambitions with the overall aims and objectives of the organisation.

In this way the organisation benefits from highly trained staff and the employee benefits by being able to do a wider range of jobs and apply for better paid jobs. So, employees should be even more interested in their own self-development than their employers!

Self-development is more than being 'expected' to be trained. It puts the onus on the employee to *want* to continually improve by being involved in new experiences and improving and extending his/her own skills. These are often called 'CV enhancing activities'. They are likely to include challenges such as:

- keeping up to date with IT developments and learning new software packages

- developing team work skills and learning

Figure 1.19 Learning more will help your career

how to be a productive member of a team and, later, how to manage a team and motivate other people

- continually improving presentation and communication skills

- learning a new language

- developing numeracy and analytical skills so that a report containing a few statistics does not seem like a foreign language!

This type of commitment often means giving up your spare time and *volunteering* to become involved in activities which will improve your overall abilities and worth as an employee, either to your existing employer or to a future employer if you wish to change jobs and move 'onwards and upwards' somewhere else.

Promotion opportunities

Many people thinking of joining a company will be interested in career development and promotion opportunities. It is likely that there will be greater opportunities in larger organisations than small ones. This is because a larger organisation is more likely to have different grades of jobs – from junior to more senior. Hard-working staff will then have the opportunity of progressing to higher paid and more responsible jobs – in other words, being promoted.

Some people, however, prefer to move around and gain their experience with different employers. They feel it broadens their skills to work in different environments before they reach their career goal. In this case a person may be quite happy to work for a small organisation with limited promotion prospects, provided the experience is relevant to their future aims.

There are several factors which influence someone's potential to be promoted, such as:

- their interest in the work and the organisation itself

Figure 1.20 Promotion feels good

- their ability to manage their current job and responsibilities extremely well

- their commitment, enthusiasm and willingness to help out when necessary

- their ability to get on well with other people

- the additional training and qualifications they have achieved since starting with the company

- the amount of interest and commitment they have shown in their own personal development

- their potential to take on a more responsible position (e.g. if they show they can cope when someone senior is off sick).

This may seem a tall order, but remember that internal applicants for a job are likely to be competing with external applicants. It is now very rare for anyone to be promoted without being interviewed – and the higher the job, the tougher the competition and the more difficult the interview. There is no reason to promote a person who is not particularly keen to get on, or has never shown any interest in achieving higher-level qualifications, when there are dozens of good external applicants to choose from!

However, companies are very keen to retain hard-working employees. They would therefore generally prefer to reward such a person with a promotion than to disappoint and upset them. An employee's aims and ambitions are therefore often discussed as part of the appraisal process, and an employee would be dissuaded from applying for a promotion which was inappropriate. Equally, a good manager will help to guide his or her staff to undertake suitable training and staff development that will help them to succeed.

Working conditions

At an interview you should be told about your conditions of employment and you should be informed of your working conditions, which are slightly different.

Your terms and conditions of employment are contained in your contract of employment (see page 16) and include:

- the address at which you will work

- your hours of work plus the degree of flexibility which is required

- any arrangements or requirements relating to overtime or unsocial working hours

- your pay and any additional payments, such as overtime rates, bonuses or commission

- your holiday entitlement per year – both personal leave and statutory days

- whether you will receive sick pay and on what basis

- your pension rights

- any fringe benefits, such as staff discounts or luncheon vouchers

- notice periods.

However, working conditions also includes aspects such as:

- the physical environment, such as good lighting and ventilation, modern furnishings and equipment, adjustable heating, lack of noise, restful colour scheme

- the job content, e.g. varied, interesting and challenging work

- promotion prospects within the organisation

- training opportunities (see page 30)

- welfare policies, such as loans to employees, compassionate leave for family emergencies, stress counselling, medical checks etc.

Figure 1.21 Some companies care for their staff

Human resources staff are often involved in assessing the working conditions of staff and recommending improvements to managers. They will also help to organise events which contribute to the well-being of employees. Some organisations offer free medical screening or visits by Relate counsellors to talk to any staff experiencing personal relationship problems.

SNAPSHOT

To have and to hold . . .

It has long been recognised that employers who have a reputation for taking care of their staff attract the best applicants and keep them. This is cost-effective because it saves on having to recruit and train new staff. Unipart is a leader in this area. Its 2,000 staff at its head office near Oxford enjoy a wide range of facilities in a high-tech, purpose-built complex, which includes an information centre and a well-being centre. On Tuesday lunchtime you can learn holiday Spanish and on Wednesday enjoy an aromatherapy session.

Other businesses are concentrating on more family-friendly policies to attract and retain staff. Family-friendly policies range from extended maternity leave, financial help with nursery care, workplace nurseries, flexible working, job sharing and paid leave if a child is sick or if a couple plan to adopt. Midland Bank provides more than 800 nursery places for its staff, together with a wide range of family-friendly policies, which attracts 85 per cent of its female staff back to work after maternity leave. The retail store Littlewoods also offers paternity leave, and has done so since the 1970s. They say that this helps them to keep good staff and to motivate staff to work harder. The staff see it as a company that cares about them. All companies are now required to give paternity leave as outlined in the Employment Rights Act.

Health and safety

Employees want to work in a safe environment. The law requires both employers and employees to conform with health and safety legislation. What does this mean in practice, and how does it affect the human resources function?

Most organisations will have a health and safety officer who has overall responsibility for all health and safety policies and training. He or she will advise managers about their responsibilities for health and safety and make sure all employees are kept informed, too. This is because health and safety laws place a responsibility on *both* employers and employees, so if you do not cooperate with your employer in this then you are guilty of an offence.

The most important Act of Parliament relating to health and safety is the **Health and Safety at Work Act 1974 (HASWA)**. The Act sets out the general duties and responsibilities that employers have to their employees and to members of the public, and those that employees have to themselves and each other. The Health and Safety at Work Act is an 'umbrella' Act which includes various Regulations that can be revised to ensure the law is kept up to date. The **Workplace (Health, Safety and Welfare) Regulations 1992**, for instance, gives more specific details of the responsibilities of employers under HASWA.

All organisations must display details of the Act in a prominent place, and this includes your school or college. A person who is negligent under the Act can face criminal prosecution for breaching a health and safety requirement.

The agency which enforces the Act is the **Health and Safety Executive (HSE)**, which has its own inspectorate and advisory service. An inspector can visit any industrial premises without warning to investigate an accident or complaint or to inspect the premises. Offices and shops are visited by an environmental health officer employed by the local authority. If the inspection shows that there are unsatisfactory working practices then the employer is issued with an Improvement Notice, which gives a specific time for any problems to be rectified. If working practices are so poor that the safety of the workers or the public is at risk, then a Prohibition Notice can be issued. In this case the employer must stop operations immediately. The employer however can appeal if they feel the decision is unfair. However, if the employer loses the appeal and still fails to put matters right, the company can be fined or the owner imprisoned.

ACTIVITY

1   Extracts from the Health and Safety at Work Act 1974 are shown in Figure 1.22. Read this carefully and decide which part of the Act the following actions would contravene.

   a   An office worker overloads a high shelf above a desk with some heavy files.

   b   A caretaker leaves a stack of boxes behind the front door.

   c   The same caretaker leaves a graffiti removing solvent on top of the reception counter.

   d   An employee refuses to leave the building when the fire alarm sounds. He assumes it is a drill and says he has too much work to finish.

   e   An office worker breaks a glass and throws it, unwrapped, into the waste paper bin.

   f   A young hairdressing trainee has never been told to wear gloves when colouring a client's hair.

   g   The same trainee sets off the fire extinguisher as a joke.

h When the heating breaks down the office supervisor finds an old fan heater. Although the plug is loose and the heater rattles alarmingly when carried, she still switches it on.

2 The Health and Safety at Work Act requires all employers 'as far as is reasonably practicable' to ensure the health, safety and welfare of their employees.

   a What do you think is meant by the phrase 'as far as is reasonably practicable'?

   b Give an example of an action which *would* be reasonably practicable, and one which

would not, to safeguard people walking up and down a steep stone staircase with a drop at one side.

3 Check through the Workplace (Health, Safety and Welfare) Regulations shown in Figure 1.23 and identify one example, in your own school or college buildings, where each requirement has been fulfilled.

The Health and Safety at Work Act 1974

1 Applies to all work premises. Anyone on the premises is covered by and has responsibilities under the Act, whether employees, supervisors, directors or visitors.

2 Requires all employers to:
- 'as far as is reasonably practicable' ensure the health, safety and welfare at work of their employees. This particularly relates to aspects such as:
  - safe entry and exit routes
  - safe working environment
  - well-maintained, safe equipment
  - safe storage of articles and substances
  - provision of protective clothing
  - information on safety
  - appropriate training and supervision.
- prepare and continually update a written statement on the health and safety policy of the company and circulate this to all employees (where there are five or more of them)
- allow for the appointment of safety representatives selected by a recognised trade union. Safety representatives must be allowed to investigate accidents or potential hazards, follow up employee complaints and have paid time off to carry out their duties.

3 Requires all employees to:
- take reasonable care of their own health and safety and that of others who may be affected by their activities
- cooperate with their employer and anyone acting on his or her behalf to meet health and safety requirements.

Figure 1.22 The Health and Safety at Work Act 1974

Workplace (Health, Safety and Welfare) Regulations 1992

Most of the Regulations cover specific areas of health, safety and welfare to supplement general duties on employers who have to ensure the workplace is safe and without risks to health under the HASWA 1974.

Employers and others in control of workplaces are required to comply with a set of requirements covering:

1 **Work environment**, i.e.:
- effective ventilation
- reasonable temperature
- adequate and emergency lighting
- enough space
- suitable workstations
- protection from adverse weather conditions for workstations outside a building.

2 **Safety**, i.e.:
- traffic routes for pedestrians and vehicles to circulate in a safe manner
- properly constructed and maintained floors
- safe windows and skylights
- safely constructed doors, gates and escalators
- safeguards to prevent people or objects falling from a height.

3 **Facilities**, i.e.:
- sufficient toilets and washing facilities
- adequate supply of wholesome water
- adequate seating
- suitable accommodation for clothing
- rest areas, including provision for pregnant women or nursing mothers
- provision for non-smokers in rest areas
- adequate facilities for people who eat at work.

4 **Housekeeping**, i.e.:
- proper maintenance of all workplaces, equipment and facilities
- cleanliness of workplaces.

Figure 1.23 Workplace (Health, Safety and Welfare) Regulations 1992

Health and safety regulations

Since the introduction of the HASWA, several other Regulations have been introduced. You do not have to learn these by heart, but it is important that you know they exist. The main ones are listed below.

- **The Reporting of Injuries, Diseases and Dangerous Occurrences Regulations 1992 (RIDDOR).** Organisations must notify the HSE of any serious or fatal injuries and keep records of certain specific injuries, dangerous occurrences and diseases.

- **The Control of Substances Hazardous to Health 1999 (COSHH).** Hazardous substances must be stored in a special environment and users provided with protective clothing.

- **The Electricity at Work Regulations 1989.** These relate to the design, construction, use and maintenance of electrical systems.

- **The Noise at Work Regulations 1989.** Employers must check noise hazards and reduce these where possible and provide ear protectors to employees where necessary.

- **The Management of Health and Safety at Work Regulations 1999.** Employers must carry out risk assessments, eliminate unnecessary risks, control significant risks and provide information on risks to all employees.

- **Display Screen Equipment Regulations 1992.** Employers must assess the risks of using VDUs and workstations, pay for eye tests and spectacles or lenses if prescribed for VDU work, and plan work activities to incorporate rest breaks.

- **Provision and Use of Work Equipment Regulations 1998.** Employers must make sure all equipment is well-maintained and provide appropriate training and instructions for users.

- **Personal Protective Equipment at Work Regulations 1992.** Protective clothing and equipment must be provided when risks cannot be eliminated. This must be free of charge, fit properly and be maintained in good condition.

- **Manual Handling Operations Regulations 1992.** These relate to lifting and handling items. Where possible an automated or mechanised process must be used but employees who have to move items should be trained properly to minimise injury.

- **The Fire Precautions Act 1971 – updated by the Fire Precautions (Workplace) Regulations 1997 and amended Regulations in 1999.** All designated premises require a fire certificate giving a plan of the building,

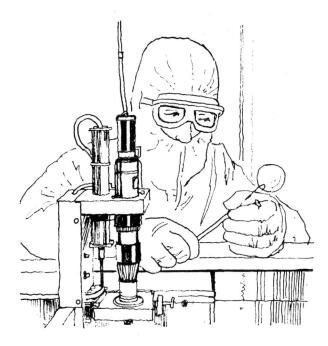

Figure 1.24 Special clothes are needed in certain conditions

Figure 1.25 Special equipment is needed for certain items

specified design and in the correct colours, i.e. red for a prohibited action, blue for a mandatory (must do) action, yellow for warning and green for a safe condition.

In addition, under the **Employers' Liability (Compulsory Insurance) Regulations 1969** all employers must take out insurance against accidents and ill health to their employees. This means that if you were injured as an employee in the course of your work, you could claim compensation and this would be met through the employer's insurers. Without this protection, some firms may say that they could not afford to pay employee's claims, even if the injury had been caused by organisational negligence.

showing the position of fire-resistant doors, fire extinguishers and break-glass alarms. There must be a proper fire alarm system and protected means of escape. Businesses which do not comply can be issued with Prohibition and Improvement Notices or prosecuted by the fire authority.

- **Health and Safety (First Aid) Regulations 1981.** The business must provide sufficient first-aiders, depending upon the risk level of the working environment. A low-risk environment should have one first-aider for each 50 employees. High-risk environments (e.g. oil rigs) have a higher ratio.

- **The Health and Safety (Safety Signs and Signals) Regulations 1996.** Specific safety signs must be displayed to identify risks and hazards. There must be written instructions on the use of fire-fighting equipment. All signs must be to a

SNAPSHOT

Could you repeat that, please?

*A health and safety risk which many people ignore is **noise**. Although the 1989 Noise at Work Regulations offer protection to people who work in noisy industries, what many people don't realise is that the risks of noise go beyond specialist workplaces. And young people are particularly vulnerable.*

If you use a mobile telephone regularly, visit nightclubs and cinemas and play music as loudly as you can, then your hearing is at risk. Some employees in 'new', expanding industries are particularly at risk. These include workers in call centres who are on the telephone constantly and motorbike couriers who encounter air turbulence and engine noise all day. Unlike workers in traditional industries, they don't wear ear protectors as they go about their jobs!

Health and safety and the human resources function

Health and safety doesn't just 'happen' in a business. It has to be carefully monitored. As you can see, there is a considerable amount of legislation with which the organisation must comply and making sure this happens is usually part of the overall human resources function. In addition to inspecting premises, the **HSE** also has an advisory role and provides guidance for employers and those responsible for implementing health and safety legislation. It also issues approved codes of practice, which give advice on how companies can comply with the law.

The first stage for a business is to draw up its **safety policy**. This is a legal requirement for organisations that employ five or more people. The policy must state, in simple terms, what the aims of the company are in relation to the health and safety of employees. It should also include the key members of staff and the arrangements for carrying out

the policy. This is likely to include arrangements covering training and instruction, company rules, emergency arrangements, the system for reporting accidents and the identification of risk areas. The policy is usually signed by a senior manager. The policy must then be revised regularly, to make sure it stays up to date.

The business will then decide its own **codes of practice**, which state the procedures all employees must follow in the event of an emergency, such as a fire, bomb scare, gas leak, or an accident, occurring. This will include how to contact a first-aider, where the medical room is situated, how to contact a doctor or send for an ambulance and when an accident report must be completed.

In many organisations a **safety committee** operates, made up of representatives from management and employees. It is this group's responsibility to check that legal requirements are being followed. They will also report to management on any working conditions which breach safety regulations or company policy. If there is no safety committee then these duties are undertaken by the **safety officer**. The committee or safety officer will also check local accident trends and recommend preventative action. They will consider reports of particular accidents and suggest actions which would prevent any recurrence. They regularly report on safety matters and make recommendations to managers.

Many businesses also have **safety representatives** who attend meetings of the safety committee. These representatives are appointed by recognised trade unions and are elected by the union members and not by the employer. They are involved in accident and hazard investigation, follow up complaints made by employees relating to health and safety, carry out inspections every three months and are involved with any consultations

Figure 1.26 Staff need to know what to do in an emergency

involving HSE inspectors. They must also be consulted by the employer as to any changes in the workplace that might affect the health and safety of the employees, or any information or training the employer plans to provide for staff.

Accidents

All organisations must record accidents and all employers with more than 10 workers must keep an accident book and accident records for at least three years. In addition to accidents, organisations usually record 'near misses' as these often indicate where improvements should be made.

If you witnessed or were involved in an accident then you would have to complete an accident report form. This includes all relevant information relating to the accident and the names of any witnesses. Serious accidents are usually investigated and, until the safety officer or representative arrives, nothing must be moved or changed. Accident monitoring involves checking that accident rates in the organisation are not above the national

average and identifies any improvements or deterioration in standards. The safety officer or safety committee can recommend improvements, where required, and then check that recommended action has been taken.

ACTIVITY

1   Obtain a copy of your school's or college's accident report form.

   a   Note the headings used and state why you think each particular piece of information is required.

   b   Assume you slipped on the main corridor this morning and sprained your ankle. Complete the form correctly stating this. The witness to the event was your best friend. Invent any other details you need to complete the form realistically.

   c   Find out how accidents are monitored in your school or college. What, for instance, would happen if several people slipped on a new floor within days of it being installed?

2   A company installs a large plate glass mirror in its reception area in an attempt to make the area look larger and more spacious. During the first week, six people walk into the mirror not realising what it is. One, a child, is quite badly injured.

   a   As an assistant to the safety officer in the company, how do you think you would be involved?

   b   The safety officer wants the mirror removed but the reception manager argues there will be no risk if a large potted plant is placed in front of it. The safety officer decides that her case will be strengthened if she refers to legal requirements. Look back at the Regulations above and find the argument she needs to use and the Regulation she should quote.

Figure 1.27 Accidents need to be investigated and the dangers removed

CASE STUDY 1.4

Any business that thinks the cost of preventing accidents is too expensive should think again. The cost of an accident can be even greater.

When organisations calculate the cost of an accident they often only take in the obvious cost and forget the hidden ones. After all, bandages and sticking plasters are cheap, but what about the time of the first-aider who was called away from work to attend to the injury? And what if the injured person then spends three days at home recovering? And then there is the time spent by safety representatives investigating the accident and making their report. Sometimes accidents can involve damage to property or equipment, which may need to be repaired or replaced.

According to the HSE, the total average accident bill will depend upon the number of employees, the type of work carried out and the value of a firm's raw materials, products or service. A large manufacturing company employing 100 people can average nearly £120,000 a year on accidents. In the transport industry the average costs are even higher. A firm employing 80 people can expect an accident bill of nearly £200,000 each year!

The cost of employee absence, often caused by health problems, is significant. According to the CBI (Confederation of British Industry), the average British employee is absent from work for almost two weeks every year and the total cost to British business was £11 billion in 1997. Another survey, by the Association of Insurance and Risk Managers, estimated that employee health problems alone cost business more than £12 billion a year. Companies are thought to lose 6 or 7 per cent of their total payroll costs to health-related issues, or 37 per cent of their profits. At this rate, a good health and safety policy appears very cheap indeed!

Activities

1 Identify five 'hidden costs' of accidents.
2 As a group suggest what type of organisation the CBI is and discuss your ideas with your tutor.
3 Suggest three types of accident which might occur which would involve damage to property, equipment or raw materials.
4 If a company has eight minor accidents a month at an average cost of £45, what would their accident bill be in a year?
5 A firm has profits of £234,000 this year, but its health-related employee costs amount to 6.5 per cent of this. What is the total loss of profits?
6 Calculate the difference between the average cost of accidents per employee

Figure 1.28 Accidents can be expensive

CASE STUDY (continued)

each year in the manufacturing industry and the average cost per employee in the transport industry.

7 Bill Evans is paid £16,120 a year. His conditions of employment state that the firm will pay him sick pay when he is ill for up to 26 weeks each year. Last year he had 'flu for two weeks in January and had an accident in May when he hurt his back. He was off for five weeks. His employer received £60 in statutory sick pay from the government for each week he was ill, excluding the first three days of each illness period. Calculate what Bill's illnesses cost his employer.

8 Suggest at least two reasons why the figures given in the CBI survey and the figures given in by the Association of Insurance and Risk Managers are different.

Employee organisations and unions

Good relations are only possible between employer and employee if both parties feel that:

- they can discuss major problems and proposed changes

- there can be discussion and consultation about key issues

- both genuinely want to work together to find a solution.

This sounds ideal. In practice, employers may have to make difficult decisions. For example, if business is poor and redundancies are likely, it may be impossible to make a decision which suits everyone. However, if there is a history of good relations and mutual trust it is possible to reach a decision which is as fair as possible under the circumstances. The fact that employees have been involved in a consultative process usually makes them more likely to accept a negotiated outcome.

It is usual for employees to rely on colleagues who have the skills, expertise and experience to negotiate on their behalf with management. In some organisations, with no recognised trade union, this may be done through a recognised staff association or through selected employee representatives or by a joint working party which represents employee interests. Sometimes this has the advantage of being more flexible. In other cases, particularly in large companies,

Figure 1.29 Staff representatives and management meet to discuss issues

employee representatives may be inexperienced and may not have any legal knowledge or access to specialist advice. In most medium and large organisations, negotiations are carried out by recognised trade union representatives. Indeed, of the 50 largest companies in the UK, 44 recognise trade unions.

Trade unions are voluntary organisations with employees free to join, or not, as they wish. There is often a subscription charge. They range from those which are very large, such as Unison with over one million members, to those at the other end of the scale, such as the Professional Cricketers Association. Trade unions offer a range of benefits and advisory services to members, represent their members

during disciplinary or grievance procedures and aim to protect and improve pay and conditions of employment. They lobby the government to introduce laws which will benefit employees. They believe that there is 'strength in numbers' and that employees together can achieve more than employees on their own.

It is the role of a senior member of the human resources team to negotiate with the trade union or staff representative on behalf of the management of the organisation. Today the buzz phrase is 'joint problem solving', that is, working together for the future of the organisation and those who work for it. Many see this as the way to forge strong working relationships in the 21st century.

SNAPSHOT

Staff associations and works councils

Employee organisations have to be independent to be able to operate freely and responsibly. They also need to be recognised and certificated to be given union status. The Blue Circle Staff Association was initially refused a certificate of independence and appealed. Several criteria were used to determine whether it could function independently, including whether or not it was funded by the company, Blue Circle Cement; the status of those running the association (managers may not act in the overall workers' interests); the 'rules' which applied and whether the company could interfere with the running of the association.

Staff associations do not automatically have the same legal rights as independent trade unions, although many do. They may just provide an informal meeting ground for employees and employer and often have a role similar to a works council, where employees are involved in

management decision making. Certainly in the case of Blue Circle Cement, co-operation between workers and management paid dividends when the company was going through a difficult time.

Works councils are now part of many large and medium-sized multinational companies as a result of the European Works Council Directive. These organisations now have a legal requirement to inform and consult employees about important issues such as finance, business trends and future proposed changes. Between 3 and 30 employees must be elected or appointed by their colleagues to a European Works Council, which must meet with management annually, although they can meet alone to discuss issues which concern the staff. They can appoint experts to help them if they wish. Many in the European Union would like to see this extended to smaller organisations – only time will tell whether they are successful.

ACTIVITY

Year	1979	1995	1997
Total union membership (million)	13.3	7.3	7.1
Union membership as a % of the workforce			
	55	32	30

Figure 1.30 The fall in trade union membership 1979–97

1   The TUC (Trades Union Congress) is the body to which all unions are affiliated. Find out about it by accessing the TUC site on the Internet on www.tuc.org.uk. There is an excellent link to the student BizEd site where you can find out the answers to almost anything you want to know about the TUC and unions, as well as more details about your own rights as an employee. Then answer the following questions.

   a   What is the TUC's mission statement?

   b   What is the TUC's equal opportunities policy?

   c   What current campaigns is the TUC involved with?

   d   Why do unions belong to the TUC?

   e   What are the five most important reasons why people join trade unions?

2   Figure 1.30 shows the decline in union membership between 1979 and 1997.

   a   State four reasons put forward by the TUC for this decline.

   b   Calculate the total percentage decrease in the number of people who are union members between 1979 and 1997.

   c   What is meant by the term 'union membership as a percentage of the workforce'? Why do you think this figure is not higher?

   d   The Employment Relations Act 1999 allowed union recognition in organisations with more than 20 employees, where that is the wish of the majority of the workforce. What difference do you think that is likely to make to union membership in the future and why?

   e   From the latest *Labour Force Survey* in your library, complete the figures for the current year and see whether union membership is still falling or rising.

3   For a strike to be lawful, trade union members must be ballotted and a majority of those who vote must be in favour. Discuss with your tutor why such controls on strike actions have been introduced.

4   Some people argue that works councils can never be successful because workers don't understand business finance and cannot contribute anything useful to future business plans.

   a   What assistance is available to EWCs to help them overcome these difficulties?

   b   Do you agree with the claim that workers normally cannot make any useful contribution to business plans? Give a reason for your answer.

   c   Assume that works councils are introduced for all companies with more than 20 employees. How would you feel about this if you were:

      i   an employee who works for a large local company

      ii the owner of a business that employs 25 people?

5   An employers' organisation is one which represents a group of employers. The main employers organisation is the CBI, which you met on page 41. Other employers' organisations include the Road Haulage Association Limited, the National Federation of Retail Newsagents and the Federation of Master Builders.

What advantages do these organisations give their members? Discuss your ideas as a group and with your tutor.

Human resources and its affect on other functional areas

The most obvious link between human resources and the other functional areas is in the recruitment of staff. In many areas, departments notify human resources when they have a vacancy and it is up to the HR staff to make sure that this is advertised or placed with the most appropriate source for recruitment and that the paperwork is completed and the interviews scheduled according to company policy. If the vacancy also creates a promotional opportunity, the HR staff will also make sure that the vacancy is advertised internally as well as externally. Once the selection has been made, the HR department will confirm the appointment and prepare the contract of employment.

There will also be links between different functional areas and HR staff over training events and staff development activities. The training manager will not only be able to

Figure 1.31 Staff training in first aid

advise on suitable opportunities for staff, he or she will also organise internal training events, often in liaison with internal specialists, such as the health and safety officer. Normally, the HR department organises regular induction programmes which all new staff attend together, regardless of which department they will work in.

In many specialist areas, the HR function operates in an advisory capacity. It advises managers about employment law and about both employer and employee rights and responsibilities. It checks and monitors that the company's equal opportunities policy is being met. It ensures that all employees are informed about company facilities and welfare policies. It is involved if there are disputes or disagreements which need resolution through the formal disciplinary or grievance procedures. It has a key role in negotiating with union or staff representatives from different departments if any changes are being proposed.

As for health and safety, there are obvious links with all areas of the organisation. Safety representatives will work in other functional areas and, particularly in more hazardous environments such as production, there will be constant liaison between departmental managers and staff and the health and safety officer. The latter has the responsibility of making certain that the company operates within the law and will therefore advise managers on any changes that must be made or any new developments that are planned.

Finance

The purpose of the finance function

If you owned a business you would probably consider the finance function the most important of all – as you will know if you have already started to study Unit 3! This is because those who work in finance keep track of all the money going in and out of the business. If they are doing their job correctly, and if the right systems are in place, one of your managers should be able to tell you every day how much you are making (or losing!) on every single item or service you provide. They should also be able to tell you how much you are paying for raw materials, your staff and other general expenses. They also check the amount of money owed to your business and chase up any 'late payers'.

To control the financial side of the business you would allocate different departments budgets and expect them to keep to their planned levels of income and expenditure. Your financial staff would check this regularly and tell you if each one was still on target or not – and why. Given the importance of all this information to the future survival of the business, it is no

wonder finance is so crucial to business owners and executives.

Finance is very important for all the staff, too, as the payment of wages and salaries is part of that function. You have already learned that you have a legal right to be paid. In addition, most people expect to be paid the correct amount, on time, every week or month. Mistakes in the amount paid are never well received!

In your business, one of your financial managers would also be responsible for preparing all the accounts. These are a legal requirement for all companies and, as you will learn in Unit 2, in some cases are published for anyone to read. Even a small business has to prepare accounts to satisfy the Inland Revenue, who will want to know how much profit the business has earned, as the owner will be taxed on this. Knowing how to compile the accounts accurately so nothing is omitted, and with all the expenses and allowances listed so that no more tax than necessary is paid, is a crucial function in any business.

Finally, the business may need to obtain more money from time to time. It may want to finance expansion, buy additional raw materials or buy expensive equipment so that it can remain competitive. Obtaining extra finance, called **capital**, at the best rates possible is the job of the finance section. Senior staff will also give advice on planning large amounts of expenditure in line with what the business can afford, and when.

The purpose of the finance function, therefore, is to:

- keep all the financial records required by the organisation, detailing all the receipts and payments that have been made

- prepare final accounts from these records as required by law

Figure 1.32 Financial control is vital to success

- monitor the income and expenditure of different departments against their budgets

- provide continuous, up-to-date financial information for managers about business performance

- pay salaries and wages to the staff

- pay amounts owing to suppliers

- control the levels of debts owed to the company

- obtain additional finance when required, from the most appropriate source

- advise senior managers on the financial implications of major decisions.

The activities of the finance function

The overall activities of the finance function can be grouped into three main areas:

- preparing accounts

- paying wages and salaries

- obtaining capital and resources.

These are described in more detail below. You will also study the operations of the finance function in more depth in Unit 3.

Job roles in finance

The type of job roles you will find in finance will vary depending upon:

- the size of the organisation

- whether the payment of wages and salaries is undertaken by company staff or by an agency.

Typical job titles and the roles you are likely to find in a large organisation are shown in Figure 1.33.

Typical job title	Function and responsibilities
Financial director	Giving advice to senior managers on the overall financial policy of the organisation. Overseeing the company budget. In charge of all the finance function in the organisation.
Financial manager	Managing the finance function and staff. Advising on financial resources.
Chief accountant	Overseeing the preparation of the final accounts of the organisation.
Management accountant	Producing continuous financial information for management.
Credit controller	Advising on credit policies. Ensuring that money owing to the company is kept within agreed levels.
Chief cashier	Responsible for the receipt, safe-keeping, banking and accounting of all cash received.
Payroll administrator	Responsible for overseeing the company payroll and salary/wage section.
Wages clerks	Assist the payroll administrator in the production of salary and wage details.
Ledger clerks	Assist the chief accountant in the recording of all financial transactions.
Credit control clerks	Assist the credit controller in checking the credit status of new customers and existing accounts. Reminding customers of overdue payments.

Figure 1.33 Job roles in finance

Investigating finance activities

Preparing accounts

Every day millions of financial transactions take place in businesses throughout Britain. Money flows in from the sale of goods and services to customers who may pay in various ways. Supermarkets, for instance, accept payments from individuals in cash, by debit or credit card, or by cheque. People paying a telephone, gas or electric bill may choose to pay by direct debit, when the money is automatically transferred from their bank account to that of the service provider at regular intervals. Most businesses settle the majority of their bills by cheque, usually at the end of the month, after they have received a statement showing how much they owe.

Allowing businesses to settle their bills some time after they have received the goods is known as allowing them **credit**. Because this relationship involves an element of trust, the supplier will check that a new customer is creditworthy by obtaining a credit reference either from an agency or from the customer's bank. It will then make a decision as to how much credit the customer is allowed.

Every business also has to pay its own bills. It will owe money for raw materials used in the manufacture of a product and also for the services it uses and for general items – from food in the canteen to stationery in the offices. Again, it will usually buy these goods on credit and will have an account with all its suppliers. After the goods have been supplied an invoice will be issued for the total amount due. At the end of the month, a statement will be received listing all the amounts owing to that organisation. At that stage it is normal for the account to be paid by cheque.

In Unit 3 (page 209) you will cover in detail financial transactions and the documents that are used. In this unit you are more concerned with the tasks undertaken by the financial staff and how these relate to the other aspects of the business as a whole.

The finance staff have to perform a range of activities related to the checking and recording of all amounts received and paid. In each case these are entered into particular accounts. Each customer will have an account and so will each supplier. There will also be accounts covering sales, purchases and expenses.

- Money received is checked carefully and recorded against each item sold and against each customer's account.

- All monies received are banked as soon as possible.

- At the end of each month all the accounts are balanced so that any outstanding amounts are highlighted.

- Statements will be sent to customers who buy on credit.

Figure 1.34 All financial transactions must be recorded

- Customers with overdue accounts will be sent reminders to pay.

In addition, a range of activities are undertaken which relate to the payment of money by the company.

- Goods received are carefully checked when they are received to ensure no goods are faulty or missing. This is normally done by the staff who actually receive the goods, not the finance staff.

- The invoice is checked to make sure the items and amounts are correct and any promised discounts are included.

- Cheques are made out, normally only by authorised individuals. There is usually more than one signature on a company cheque for security.

- The amounts paid are recorded in the correct accounts, either against purchases or expenses.

- Finally, all the banking documents are checked and any surplus money is transferred into an interest-bearing account so that it will not be lying 'idle'.

Today many of these operations are computerised. As amounts paid in or out are entered then the accounts are automatically adjusted. As money is banked the company banking records are also updated. A summary of all the important figures can be obtained quickly and easily and this gives a continuous flow of information, which is very important to managers.

Imagine you have a shop selling 50 different lines of clothing. You want to know which items are selling well and which are not. This affects your plans for buying new stock. It may also make you decide to hold a sale to periodically get rid of all 'slow' items. You could only make decisions like this if you knew exactly which lines were the most profitable. This would be possible if you had access to records on sales which were always up to date. This is possible with a computer package.

The information you obtain is known as **management information** because your managerial decisions would be based on it. In a large organisation, it is the job of the **management accountant** to ensure this type of information is constantly available for managers.

The **financial accountant**, on the other hand, is the person responsible for assembling all the accounts information into the format required for the statutory accounts which must be prepared at the end of each financial year. Statutory means required by law. Companies must provide a profit and loss account and a balance sheet. The profit and loss account shows how much profit or loss the company made in the year. The balance sheet shows all the assets (belongings) of the company and their value and all the liabilities (debts) on a specific date. Many companies also produce a cashflow statement as well. You will learn about these in Unit 3.

These accounts provide information for those who have a financial interest in the company – as well as for the Inland Revenue which can then check that the amount of tax to be paid by the company is correct. Note that individuals pay income tax on their earnings, whereas companies pay **corporation tax** on their net profit. Calculating the tax liability of the company is also the task of the financial accountant.

Small businesses are more likely to have this work carried out by a firm of registered chartered accountants. There will be dozens in your own town. They prepare the financial accounts for local businesses, which would not find it cost-effective to employ their own specialist financial accountant.

SNAPSHOT

Living within your budget!

Most people know how difficult it is to keep within a budget. How good are you? Can you accurately plan how much you will receive next year and how much you intend to spend without going into debt? Are you 'money wise' and find it quite easy to budget so that you can save as well? Or are you totally broke after the first two or three days every week?

If you find it hard to manage your own money, think how difficult it must be to manage the money of a very large organisation. No employee will be too pleased if the money runs out and they can't get paid! So, budgeting in a business is very important.

*All the different functional areas have to prepare their own budgets, forecasting the amount they will spend in the year. A sales budget will also be prepared which shows how much the company expects to receive in income during the year and a cashflow budget will be prepared to identify the flows of cash forecast for the business. The finance team then compile a **master budget** which gives the forecasts of all costs and all revenues. Any forecasted expenditure which will not be met by sales would have to come out of savings or **reserves** (money put aside in previous years).*

All budgets are flexible to allow for unexpected changes and developments, but the finance staff will keep a close check on all departments to make sure they are not exceeding their budgets. If they are, or if there are unexpected problems, then cut backs may be needed for a time. Just like you should do, if your financial planning is going awry!

Paying wages and salaries

This is usually a computerised operation and virtually all organisations pay their staff monthly, direct into their bank account, using a system known as credit transfer. The company's bank transfers the money from the company account to all the employees' accounts each month.

However, the bank has to know how much to transfer to each individual. In addition, payroll records must be kept which show how much each person earned in gross pay, how much they earned in overtime or bonus payments, how much tax and National Insurance was deducted and the net amount paid to them. Individuals may make other payments, as to a company pension scheme or for union dues. They may receive special allowances for clothing or travel or expenses to be paid. These, too, must all be recorded.

Every employee has the legal right to receive an itemised pay statement. This must show all the current payments and deductions and give a running total for that tax year, which runs from 6 April one year to 5 April the next.

Some pay records rarely change. An individual on a monthly salary with no special payments or deductions would only need to be entered once into the system, along with his or her tax code, which is determined by the Inland Revenue. The computer then makes all the necessary calculations. However, other individuals receive variable amounts of pay, through overtime, bonuses etc., and in these cases the payroll staff have to make the correct entries each month. The tax code may change for any individual and this would have to be amended. People fall sick and may receive sick pay. Women may take maternity leave and be paid maternity pay. Temporary staff may be hired and then leave. Other employees may even be paid hourly, and their hours may vary each week or month. In other cases, employees change their address or bank account details.

Figure 1.35 Figuring out a pay slip

All these differences mean that there is a considerable amount of work for the payroll staff – besides paying out the money! Before paying out the money all the entries must be checked carefully before they are sent to the bank for processing, so that each person will always receive the correct amount of money on the due date.

 ## ACTIVITY

How well do you understand a pay slip? If you don't understand the entries, then there is little chance you could identify a mistake! If you work part-time, then you will be familiar with the layout of your current payslip, but you may not understand exactly what all the headings mean.

Ask for a volunteer in the group to bring in a payslip from their part-time job and discuss the meanings of the various entries on it. Better still, arrange for several people to do this and compare the different layouts and entries. Test your ability to

be discreet by *not* mentioning anyone's rate of pay or discussing the details outside the group afterwards.

Obtaining capital and resources

Capital is the money an owner puts into their business. Most of this will be needed when the business first starts trading. The initial capital buys all the basic requirements, such as paying for a lease or buying premises, purchasing a company van, stock, shop fittings and basic items such as a cash register, telephone and fax machine (see start-up costs, Unit 3 page 216).

The business then starts to trade and, hopefully, make a profit. The profit can be used to buy additional stock to sell. Or it can be saved and retained as further capital in case the owner wants to buy new equipment or move to larger premises. In a sense, this additional capital is the 'savings' of the business. You may remember it is usually referred to as the 'reserves'.

Figure 1.36 High street banks lend money to businesses

Businesses are similar to people. You probably know that your savings don't always cover the cost of special items you want to buy, especially if these are expensive. Businesses can experience the same thing, no matter how large they are. A company may not have enough capital in reserve to buy something it needs. In this case it may have to borrow the additional money or raise it in some other way. In this unit we will concentrate on borrowing money, in Unit 2 we will look at other methods by which large companies may raise finance.

Banks are an important source of finance for business. High street banks – known as commercial banks – lend money to a range of businesses. Other banks, called investment banks, deal with much larger companies. They will lend greater sums of money. There are also specialist lending companies which will lend money to businesses. A company can also apply for special funds. For example, a company that wants to open a factory in a redevelopment area may get a grant from the local council or even from a European fund. The sources available usually depend upon:

- who wants the money

- what they want it for

- how much they need

- what security they can offer, e.g. in assets (items owned) that could be converted to money if the loan couldn't be repaid.

Large companies have a wide choice of options and will be advised by a financial manager, who will assess all the different ones. Generally a company will want 'cheap' money, that is, it will want the lowest interest rates possible and the best repayment terms it can find. The financial manager also needs to assess whether interest rates are likely to rise or fall in the future. This will influence the length of time over which the

loan will be taken out. The length of time in which the money should be paid back can be critical. If it's too long the overall interest charges will be higher. If it's too short the company will be short of money trying to meet all its commitments, in other words, its cashflow will suffer.

Other resources may be acquired in different ways. Instead of borrowing money to buy a building, for example, a company could rent it instead. Rather than buy dozens of new computers, a business could lease them. Leasing is often preferred in cases such as company cars. The lease states the amount of money which is paid at regular intervals. At the end of the leasing period the cars are replaced with new ones and a new lease is negotiated. The leasing company will also replace cars that are damaged and pay for repairs and servicing. This can be better value for money than buying cars, which depreciate (fall) in value and need money spent on them for repairs and servicing.

ACTIVITY

1   Your friend wants to borrow £20,000 from a bank to expand his business. He is 30 and has a good reputation so the bank have offered him a loan. He has two options:
    a   a fixed interest rate loan of 15 per cent over 5 years
    b   a variable interest rate loan over 6 years.
    Discuss with your tutor the advantages and disadvantages of each option.

2   Your friend eventually decides on option a. To the original sum of £20,000 the bank adds £1,000 in administrative charges for setting up the loan.
    a   Calculate the amount of interest your friend would pay in the first year.
    b   Calculate how much he would pay off the

capital sum in the first year.

c Work out how much his total repayments would be to the bank in that year.

d Extend your calculations for the remaining period of the loan.

3 Your sister bought a secondhand car for £5,600 two years ago. This year she decides to sell it and is offered £3,800. The difference between these two figures is the amount the car has **depreciated** in value.

a By how much has the car depreciated?

b What is this amount as a percentage of the price she paid for it?

c If the car has cost her £700 in tax and insurance a year and she has paid £350 each year in repairs and servicing, how much has the car cost her per year to run?

Finance and its affect on other functional areas

All functional managers are concerned with the finance of their own areas, not just at budget preparation and agreement stage, but also day-to-day checking whether they are meeting their budget forecasts. Because financial staff are responsible for controlling the money, they will advise managers when the company is over-spending. This can mean cutting back on expenditure. The effect of this could be that new equipment cannot be purchased; the sales department may have to stop a proposed advertising campaign; production may have to reduce overtime; human resources may be told that no more staff can be hired or replaced for a while; administration may have to defer the purchase of a new photocopier.

Finance is also responsible for paying the employees' wages or salaries. So any queries about those payments will be made to the finance department.

Different functions need finance to pay for goods they have bought. Authorised personnel can sign orders to buy goods up to a pre-set level of expenditure. The canteen, for example, will need finance to pay invoices for food; administration will submit invoices for telephone services, photocopiers and stationery to finance; production will submit invoices for raw materials. Remember that the items ordered should be within the limits of the agreed budget. If a department goes over budget, it may find its future orders are scrutinised, and may be refused.

Finance depends on the buyers of goods checking them on arrival and notifying them if there are any changes or if any deliveries are incorrect. In return, the functional areas are dependent on finance paying their bills relatively promptly. Production doesn't want to telephone a supplier to be told nothing else can be delivered because the last bill still hasn't been paid!

Administration

The purpose of the administration function

The main purpose of administration is to make sure that the organisation operates as effectively as possible by performing a wide range of support activities promptly and efficiently. If you think of a business as a large engine which is constantly trying to move forwards, then administration represents all the couplings that hold it together. Unless these function properly, then no amount of energy produced in making and selling goods will work, and the business will grind to a stop. If you study the option unit 'Administrative Systems', you will learn about this function in more detail.

Many large organisations traditionally **centralised** their administration function. In these cases a large administration department provided all the support services needed by the other functional areas. Today administration is often **decentralised** and each functional area has its own administrative staff to serve its own needs. This provides greater flexibility for the organisation and better job opportunities for staff, who can transfer between departments to gain more experience and improve their skills.

The following are the key areas with which administrative staff are concerned.

- Information handling – the creation, storage, retrieval and transmission of all the documents used by the organisation, the receipt, safe storage and monitoring of all the documents received by the organisation and all the records held by the organisation.

- Communications – sending and receiving messages by telephone, fax, email; sending and receiving mail; dealing with

customers, colleagues and other visitors face-to-face.

- Making arrangements – from booking parking spaces for visitors to organising a foreign trip for a senior manager, from preparing for a small meeting to organising a large conference.

- Obtaining resources – providing stationery stock and other basic office items.

In some organisations you may find that the administration function also includes activities such as cleaning and maintenance work. The administration staff themselves will not undertake these activities, which will come under the general remit of an office manager or administration manager who will be responsible for them. You may also find that security is also part of administration, though in other companies this may be part of the human resources function. No two organisations are the same!

The activities of the administration function

There are many different activities carried out by the administrative function. For ease we will examine these in three main areas:

- clerical work, which includes mail handling, record keeping, document production, organising meetings, dealing with enquiries etc.

- cleaning and maintenance

- security.

We will also include the IT function in this section, as this is often linked to the overall administration function in many organisations.

A point to note at this stage is that it is not the range of tasks which identifies an

Figure 1.37 A range of communications

effective administration function but the way the work is done. Sloppy administration means that orders get lost, customer enquiries are not answered (or answered badly or late), documents are sent out containing mistakes, papers are mislaid, deadlines are missed. Superb administration is the opposite of all these. Not only are all enquiries dealt with promptly and courteously but even the most routine jobs are done well. In addition, the administrative staff work *with* other functional staff to fulfill the company objectives. In an ineffective organisation there may be little cooperation between them, or even open conflict or competition, which is worse!

Job roles in administration

In any organisation you investigate you are likely to find considerable differences between standard job titles and roles in administration. This is because the range of job roles carried out under the administration function can vary so much. To guide you a list of the most usual titles and job roles is given in Figure 1.38.

Investigating administration activities

Clerical or administrative work

This is a very broad heading under which dozens of tasks can be listed. For a moment, think of a busy office and all the jobs that would need doing every day. The phone would need answering, mail would need opening, visitors would arrive at reception, some by appointment and others not, fax messages would need distributing, papers need filing, documents need preparing on a word-processor, database records need updating, and so on and so on! All these are

Typical job title	Job role
Company secretary	A senior executive responsible for all the legal affairs of the company, dealing with shareholders, insurance and pension matters and organising directors' meetings.
Administration manager	Managing the administration operations of the organisation.
IT manager	Managing all the IT requirements of the company, including equipment maintenance and advising on future needs.
Office manager/ Senior administrator	Responsible for overseeing the administration operations in a particular office or department.
Chief security officer	Responsible for the security staff and for advising on security requirements.
Reprographics supervisor	Responsible for running a centralised reprographics (printing/photocopying) section.
PA/secretarial staff	Responsible for providing secretarial and administrative support, usually to senior managers.
Administration assistant	Assists with administrative tasks in a particular area.
Word processing operator/Data input clerk	Responsible for document production/input of data into a computer system.
Cleaning staff	Cleaning of general office areas, facilities and equipment.
Maintenance staff	Responsible for routine maintenance work, which may include painting and decorating.
Security	Responsible for monitoring and maintaining security to the required standard.

Figure 1.38 Job roles in administration

activities carried out by clerical or administrative staff. However, a simple list of tasks doesn't tell you very much about the main priorities of administrative staff and the importance of much of their work. It is therefore important to examine in more detail some basic duties, which may seem routine on the surface, to see how important they really are.

Mail handling

Every morning dozens of items of mail are delivered to large companies. Some are routine items but others will contain important, if not critical, information. It is therefore vital that the mail is correctly sorted and delivered as soon as possible. This is why in some large mailrooms the staff start earlier than the rest of the office staff. All the mail is usually date-stamped to show it arrived and all the envelopes are checked to make sure they are empty before being discarded. The mail is then usually collected by different departments and delivered to individual staff.

Figure 1.39 Delivering the mail

At the end of the day, a large amount of mail needs despatching. Some will be to organisations in Britain, others to overseas. There will be parcels, valuable items, rapid delivery items and routine items. All these need sorting and franking (stamped with the cost) before they can be posted. Large firms normally arrange for their mail to be collected at a certain time.

Keeping records and producing documents

A vast amount of paperwork is generated by organisations. There are forms, fax messages, telephone messages, letters, memos and reports – to name but a few! Administrative staff make sure that all the documents they create are both accurate and pleasing to the eye, so the presentation of each document must be of a high standard. Outsiders who receive communications from the company will judge the company based on the quality of these documents. You wouldn't be very impressed if you were thinking of doing business with a company which sent you a scruffy letter with three typing errors and four spelling mistakes, would you?

As you will see in Section 1.4 of this unit, communications are vitally important for organisations. So, too, is the ability to find documents. Administrative staff are responsible for the storage and maintenance of huge amounts of paperwork, either in standard filing cabinets or in a computer, or both. The aim is to find (quickly) what they put away, and to retrieve it in good condition. Having the correct information at one's fingertips is often the key to giving a good service. This is not possible if the required document is torn and crumpled at the bottom of a pile of file folders.

Organising meetings

In some companies, managers spend up to 65 per cent of their time in meetings. Some meetings are held within a department and others between different departmental staff.

They are often the quickest method of exchanging information, solving a problem or agreeing a course of action. Administrative staff are responsible for organising all these meetings. This means confirming the date, time and place the meeting will be held, booking the room, organising refreshments, making sure any paperwork is prepared, taking the minutes (or notes) of the meeting to record what was said and distributing these to all who were, or should have been, present.

Responding to enquiries

Enquiries are not only received from customers and prospective customers. They will come from inside the organisation from other departments and from managers and staff in the same departments. They will also come from outside the organisation, from suppliers or the company's bank, solicitor or insurance company, from the local council or from a national organisation such as the HSE.

All these enquiries need to be answered promptly with accurate information. No administrator can ever know enough to answer everything he or she is asked immediately. The secret is knowing who *can* answer the query and either passing the call or message to them to deal with, or finding out the information and passing it on promptly. This may sound simple, but a difficult query received when an administrator is busy trying to prepare a tricky report tests his or her ability to stay calm in a stressful situation – a key requirement for all good administrative staff.

Other duties

The range of additional duties carried out by administrative staff will depend upon the nature of the business, the functional area in which they are working and the type of duties identified as 'administrative' by the organisation. They may include:

- the purchase of all routine resources required by office staff, from small items of equipment, such as staplers and calculators, to stationery requirements, such as paper and envelopes.

- making travel arrangements. Many companies have executives, technical or sales staff who travel nationally or internationally on business, and staff who travel to attend training courses and events in different parts of the country. Booking travel and accommodation is often part of an administrator's role.

ACTIVITY

Your school or college will have administrators who undertake a wide variety of duties. Try to arrange for a senior administrator to talk to you about the range of activities which are carried out in his or her section. Before the talk, divide into groups of three or four and draft four suitable questions you could ask about the administrative function. Check your questions with your tutor in case there are any overlaps between different groups. Your visiting speaker may find it helpful to see your questions before the talk, to make sure that he or she covers everything you want to know.

Cleaning and maintenance

You should remember that a clean working environment is a legal necessity under health and safety regulations – it is also a much more pleasant place to work in! Some organisations have their own cleaning staff while others 'contract out' the work to outsiders. For this they pay a company to supply them with cleaners every day to do routine cleaning duties. If a cleaner is off sick, the supplier has to replace them as part of the contract. This is often more cost-

Figure 1.40 Contract cleaning

all year round. If not, specialist firms will be contracted to provide a service as and when needed.

Security

Security is another area often contracted out to a specialist company. If you walk around any large retail store, such as Marks & Spencer, you will see security staff in uniform. These are not employed by Marks & Spencer but by a specialist security firm. Training and supply of security staff is the responsibility of the security firm.

Some organisations employ their own security officers or security guards. They are responsible for patrolling the premises, reporting security risks (such as unlocked offices or open windows at night), logging security 'incidents' and liaising with the local police if and when required. In most cases security guards also monitor and report health and safety risks. The chief security officer will advise senior managers on any

effective (cheaper) for the company than having its own cleaning staff.

There is a difference between 'light' cleaning duties and 'heavy' cleaning duties. Light cleaning involves dusting, emptying waste bins, vacuuming office areas, cleaning toilet areas. Heavy cleaning involves cleaning windows, sweeping outside areas, washing blinds. Different staff are usually employed for these duties, and they may be part of a maintenance section.

In your school or college you will find maintenance staff employed to do general repair work. This can be anything from a faulty door lock to a leaking roof. Substantial or specialist repair work would be contracted out. A large organisation may have its own electrician, but not a plumber. It would have to call one in to do plumbing repairs. Some large institutions, such as a hospital, would employ both. Very large organisations may also have their own painting and decorating staff. It's a question of having enough work

Figure 1.41 Security is essential to many organisations

extra security precautions that need to be taken, such as the installation of CCTV, and landscaping the grounds to create banks of earth or digging a ditch or erecting of concrete blocks in front of plate glass shop windows to deter ram raiding.

In many large organisations security staff are posted at a gate house at the main entrance to the site. They are responsible for checking and logging all visitors on to the premises, issuing visitor passes and checking that all visitors have left at the end of the day. High security installations will also have security staff patrolling areas which are out of bounds to visitors No matter how senior they are, staff will be expected to cooperate with security staff in the case of an alert.

The IT function

IT is now a critical part of virtually every business. In most medium or large organisations you will find there is an IT or computer services manager who is responsible for this function. You may find that IT or computer services is a completely separate function, or it might be part of the overall administration function. For that reason it is appropriate to consider it at this point.

IT is probably the most rapidly changing area in a business. Computers installed one year are out of date three years later. Software packages that are suitable one day are replaced the next. The more dependent a business is on its computer systems the more critical it is that employees who regularly need information or input data have access to a computer, and that all are fully functional, all day and every day.

Many organisations today have a network of interlinked computers and a network administrator will be appointed to 'manage' the network. This means giving new users access to the system, dealing with queries,

setting up network services and liaising with users to develop new services that would be useful. There will be computer service staff and technicians to carry out routine repairs and maintain the system. There will also often be a computer 'help desk' that users can contact in case of a sudden problem or crisis.

The IT manager checks that all this is carried out efficiently, monitors new developments and advises senior managers about changes that should be made in the future. The major upgrading of a large computer network can cost millions of pounds. As you know, this must be covered by the budget or resourced from reserves or by borrowing money. An alternative would be to lease a new system from a large computer supplier.

The worst case scenario for most businesses today is that their computer system crashes or is disabled in some other way. So computer staff have to make sure the system is secure

Figure 1.42 Experts are needed to deal with serious computer problems

from hackers (who could find out critical company information) and from viruses. Viruses can easily be downloaded by anyone using the Internet, unless there is a virus checker in place and a system for preventing employees using their own disks on company machines, unless they've have been 'swept' for a virus. Today, safety and security goes beyond doors and windows – intruders can be far more selective in their techniques!

ACTIVITY

1   You may find it useful to find out from your school or college estates manager or maintenance department how routine repairs and cleaning are organised. Your tutor may be able to arrange for someone to talk to you about this – in the same way that you obtained information from one of the office administrators.

2   If you attend a large college you will find security staff on the premises. Discuss with your tutor the duties you think they carry out, their value to the college and the importance to you of feeling safe and secure while you are on the premises.

3   Investigate the security precautions for IT equipment in your school or college. What procedures are in place to prevent hackers or to reduce the dangers of computer viruses? What type of password system is in operation? What basic precautions can you take, as an IT user, to maintain the security of your own home area on the system.

4   Discuss with your IT tutor the type of computer system you have in your school or college. Check that you understand how a networked system operates and the type of facilities you would expect to find on a network.

SNAPSHOT

Computer rage – a sign of the times?

Everyone has heard of road rage, but what about computer rage? According to Compaq, a US computer maker, computer users are now suffering from a new form of frustration – computer rage. At its worst, furious users dash keyboards onto the floor. The Compaq study, 'Rage Against the Machine', identified that IT problems severely affected workers' productivity. Twenty-three per cent of those who responded said their work was interrupted every day because of IT problems. Two people out of five claimed that IT failures and breakdowns caused them to miss important deadlines.

Compaq has set up a computer rage hot line to help stressed out workers. Hopefully this will have numerous lines and plenty of staff to cope. Nothing infuriates already stressed out IT operators more than an engaged signal!

Administration and its affect on other functional areas

Administration has a considerable impact upon all the other functional areas, given that it provides the support services which enable these to operate effectively.

ACTIVITY

Look back at the two functional areas you previously covered, human resources and finance, and in groups of two or three list as many support services that you think administration would provide for each of these areas. Use the headings on pages 55–59 to help you. You should almost run out of paper before you run out of ideas!

Production

The purpose of the production function

There are two ways you can think about production. The first is in a narrow sense, as in the manufacture of goods. If you were making T-shirts or jeans to sell, you would be in the business of production. All manufacturing businesses have a production function, whether they are making cars, tables, computers or whatever.

However, not all businesses are in the business of manufacturing goods. Others provide a service. So, in what sense do they produce anything?

If we consider production in its widest sense, then all businesses produce *something*. Your school or college aims to produce better educated students. In this case your tutors are responsible for the production function. Your local travel agent aims to produce satisfied holiday-makers. In this case your travel agency staff are responsible for the production function. You can apply this kind of thinking to most organisations if you try.

Figure 1.43 Two kinds of production

You can then describe the purpose of production as making a product or providing a service. This will be the main purpose of a business and the reason it exists. Take away cars from Ford and it ceases to exist. Take away food from Tesco and it also ceases. Take away all the students from a college and it might as well close its doors. Production, therefore, is critical to the survival of every business.

In many organisations today, the process of meeting the main aim of the company is known as **operations**. The operations manager may be known by a variety of job titles, as you will see later, but his or her core function is to obtain the resources required by the business and transform these into the finished product or service. How this is done, and the priorities involved, will depend very much on the particular business.

The activities of the production function

Production is concerned with:

- obtaining the resources required to produce goods or provide a service

- organising the resources to produce the goods or provide the service in the most appropriate way.

In order for this to be achieved satisfactorily, several criteria must be considered:

a   the aims of the business (e.g. does it want to sell cheaply to the mass market, or make exclusive items or provide a personal service?)
b   the resources which are needed to produce the goods or provide the service
c   how the resources can be organised to achieve the aims in the most cost-effective way
d   how the operation can be monitored and controlled to achieve the desired result.

All these are considered separately below.

Job roles in production

You are likely to find that job titles and job roles vary depending upon whether a company physically manufactures a product or offers a service. Figure 1.44 shows the typical job titles you might find in a manufacturing company.

In a service organisation you may find the operations functions headed by a manager with a specific title. For instance, the store manager would oversee operations in a supermarket and the captain is the operations manager on a cruise liner or aircraft. A distribution company would employ a fleet or logistics manager, a school would have a head teacher, a college has a principal and a newspaper has an editor. Similarly, the job titles and job roles of those who actually deliver the service would be specific to the type of business. For instance, your college has tutors, hospitals have doctors and nurses, travel agents have travel consultants, banks have cashiers, newspapers employ journalists and editors.

Investigating production activities

Considering the aims of the business

You have already dealt with business aims in the first section of this unit. They are important now because the whole production or operations function has to be focused on these aims. Body Shop, as you saw, is an environmentally friendly organisation. This fundamentally affects the type of resources it uses and the way it manufactures its products and packages them. Alton Towers is a theme park that aims to provide family entertainment in a safe environment and include 'cutting-edge' rides. This affects the resources it requires, the way it organises and sets out the park and the way its staff supply the service.

Typical job title	Job role
Production director	Responsible for the entire production function and its operations.
Operations or Works manager	Responsible for the production of all goods as scheduled and to the quality required.
Purchasing manager	Responsible for the acquisition of raw materials.
Chief engineer	Responsible for all maintenance staff and for scheduling equipment maintenance and recommending modifications.
Chief designer	Responsible for the design team and the design of the finished products.
Production planners	Plan all production to maximise machine use and staffing, taking account of customer requirements.
Production controllers	Check production is going to schedule.
Quality controllers	Check quality is to the required standard.
Buyers/Order clerks	Buy the raw materials required for production.
Stores staff	Store and monitor stocks of all raw materials and components and issue these as required.
Draughtsmen	Responsible for the technical design of manufactured equipment.
Foremen	Supervise the maintenance staff and factory operatives.
Despatch clerks	Responsible for despatching the finished goods.
Designers	Responsible for the actual design of the finished product.
Engineers	Responsible for carrying out equipment maintenance.
Factory operatives	Undertake the production and assembly of manufactured items by machine or by hand.

Figure 1.44 Job roles in production (for a manufacturing organisation)

Figure 1.45 One of the rides at Alton Towers

Business aims vary in a number of ways, but the most important issues to consider are:

- whether the organisation produces for the mass market or for individuals, i.e. the **volume** of production (think of McDonald's versus a cosmetic surgeon)

- whether one product or service is offered or several, i.e. the **variety** of production (consider a shoe shop versus a department store)

- whether demand is the same all the time or varies in some way, e.g. the **variability of demand** (think of bread versus Christmas trees)

- the degree to which the organisation interacts with its customers on a face-to-face basis, i.e. the degree of **customer contact** (consider a mail order company versus your dentist).

All these factors will affect the way in which the resources are organised and controlled. Before we study this, it is necessary to identify the types of resources that are required and used in business.

Types of resources

Anyone who wants to run a business needs resources. If you decide to open a sandwich

bar then you would obviously need premises; some equipment such as a refrigerator, knives and bowls; the basic materials for making sandwiches, and your own labour to produce and sell the sandwiches. From this simple example it is possible to extract the main types of resources needed by all types of businesses, no matter what they do.

- **Buildings and land**. A manufacturing organisation needs a factory; retailers need shops; service providers, such as solicitors and accountants, need offices; distributors need warehouses. A garden centre would need land, so, too, would a farmer.

- **Equipment**. A manufacturing organisation may need complex machinery, a distributor would need a fleet of vehicles, a newspaper would require a printing press, virtually all offices use a range of equipment including computers, fax machines and photocopiers.

Figure 1.46 Many organisations need offices

- **People**. Usually a variety of different individuals are employed to produce the goods or deliver the service. You have already met some of these. Key staff will include managers, who have the overall responsibility for a particular type of function, support staff who assist them (see under administration) and operators who produce the goods. In addition, most organisations employ **specialists** of one type or another. A pharmaceutical company will employ chemists, your college has tutors who are knowledgeable in a particular subject area, an accountant needs tax experts.

- **Materials**. These include stock which is bought for resale in retail stores and the raw materials which are purchased by manufacturing organisations and assembled into the finished product. However, materials can include other items as well. A travel agent needs brochures and catalogues, a hotel needs towels, bed linen and furniture, hospitals need bed linen, bandages and drugs. It all depends upon the business you are in.

 **ACTIVITY**

Copy out the chart below and, in groups of two or three, try to complete the gaps. Then compare your suggestions.

Business	Type of buildings or land	Equipment	Specialist staff	Materials
Bakery		Ovens		
Water company		Pipes, pumps, filters	Water engineers	
Knitwear company	Factory		Designers	
Airline		Aeroplanes Catering equipment Safety equipment Check-in desks		Food Drinks Toilet items Cleaning materials
Paper company	Paper mill Warehouse			Wood pulp China clay Water
Book publisher			Editors Artists	
Vet			Veterinary surgeons Veterinary nurses	
Police				Uniforms Petrol Stationery
Radio station	Studios	Broadcasting equipment Transmitters OB Vehicles		
Shipping company				Fuel Food Uniforms

Planning and organising resources

If you visit any business you expect to see some type of order so that everything functions in an organised manner. As people walk into a hotel they expect to find a reception desk where they can check in, and someone to carry heavy bags. They expect their room to be nearby and for it to have been cleaned and the bed freshly made. If you visit a cinema you expect to buy a ticket quickly, to have someone show you to your seat and refreshments close by.

If you visited a factory you would also find the 'resources' organised in a methodical way, so that the goods could be produced in a logical manner and all the required items would be close at hand for each operator. Items kept in stock would be relatively close to the production area. In a retail store you would expect something similar, with the goods 'grouped' or organised in a sensible fashion. You expect to see vegetables in one area, clothing in another. You would be surprised if they were all muddled up! You would expect to find sufficient stocks and to meet helpful staff in smart uniforms. In a

factory few customers come into contact with the staff, so that isn't as important. You would expect less variety in your local shop and might be more prepared to accept a substitute if it didn't stock an item you wanted.

All these factors affect the number of resources that are required, the type of resources that are needed, the way in which they are used and the way the operations are organised. Therefore, before any type of production can commence, certain questions need to be asked.

- **Buildings and land**. How much space is required to manufacture the items required or provide the service? How much storage space is required for stock or raw materials? Is space required to store finished goods? Will a specific location be preferable or does it not matter?

- **Equipment**. What type of specialist equipment will be required? How many will be required to satisfy the expected number of customers/make the required number of goods?

- **Raw materials**. What quantities will be required to make the goods? Will they need any packaging materials and if so

---

Flexibility/Variability High

Manufacturing – types of production process	Service industries - types of operations process
Job production – 'one-off' products (aeroplanes, submarines, designer clothes, bridges)	**Professional services** – high degree of personal contact/individual service (consultant, solicitor, architect, dentist)
Batch production – 'groups' of items made one after another (bakery, cosmetics, clothing, frozen food, books)	**Service providers** – front office deals with customers, back office provides support services (travel agent, bank, colleges, hotels, good restaurant, car dealership)
Mass production – large runs of identical products (cars, televisions, computers, CDs)	**Mass service** – offer same type of service to many customers (fast food chain, supermarket, petrol station, football club, airport, theme park)
Flow production – continuous production of one product often using a technological process (oil, gas, steel, paper)	

Flexibility/Variability Low

Figure 1.47 Flexibility and variability in manufacturing and service industries

what type? Should any components be manufactured or 'bought in'? How much stock will be needed and where will it be stored? Can it be ordered as and when needed? What specific items or materials are required for that business, how many and what quality? Must the items be stored in a particular way and will they be on view to customers?

- **People**. What type of staff will be required and how many? How much training is required? Are customer service skills necessary for all staff? Would uniforms or a dress code be desirable? Are any specialist skills needed?

These factors are considered in relation to the four variables mentioned earlier – volume, variety, variation and customer contact – and the aims of the company. A summary of the way that flexibility and variability affects the way goods are made, or services are offered, is shown in Figure 1.47.

A worked example

As an example, consider the aims of Kwik-Fit versus an ordinary garage. First, what are the differences?

Kwik-Fit aims to:

- provide a rapid service

- provide a limited service (for instance, it changes tyres and batteries but wouldn't do repairs to body work)

- operate on an 'on demand' basis (customers just arrive, they don't have to make bookings in advance).

In contrast, a large garage servicing facility would:

- have a 'core' base of customers who use it regularly

Figure 1.48 A Kwik-Fit garage

- offer a wide range of services – they will virtually sort out any car problem their customers experience

- need to schedule routine services, although they may have to respond to some emergencies

- probably offer 'courtesy cars' to good customers whilst their vehicles are off the road.

How would this affect the resources that are required and their organisation? Let's examine these in relation to the four criteria we identified: volume, variety, variation and customer contact.

The aim of Kwik-Fit is high volume, low variety, low variability and a relatively high level of customer contact (given the customer often stays with the car during the entire operation). Staff will repeat the same tasks over again and can specialise in the work they do. They don't need to be flexible. They just need to be good at one job. They need to be able to cope with the customer on site and there should be somewhere for people to wait if it is raining. The area needs to be clean and safe, the materials need to be on site and at hand in sufficient quantities, the staff need to be trained to a high level in a specific range of tasks and should be dressed to be visually appealing to customers. The location of the firm needs to be easily accessible (preferably near a busy road or town centre) and easy to find, with enough space for queues during busy periods.

In contrast, the garage is identified by much lower volume, high variety, some variation in demand and less customer contact in the service area. This affects its resources. The workshop needs to be safe but can be 'tucked away' at the back as customers will leave their keys in reception. The appearance of the mechanics is less important. However, they will need to be trained to cope with a much wider range of problems. Spares and parts may not be held on site but can be ordered as required, particularly for more unusual items. There is not the same urgency to fit them, especially if they can be delivered the same day. The location of the garage itself is less important – although it is useful for it to be near a main road, it doesn't need to be in a town centre. Because jobs can be scheduled there is less need for forecourt or parking space and no need for a waiting area for customers. The 'front office' can deal with customers and the 'back office' can schedule jobs and work out bills, although there is usually a service manager who can deal with technical enquiries. A wide range of equipment is needed to deal with different types of repairs as well as an inspection pit and specialist equipment if the garage also does MOT testing.

 ACTIVITY

1   Copy out the following resource table and complete it for both Kwik-Fit and an ordinary garage from the information given above.

	Kwik-Fit	Ordinary garage
Buildings		
Equipment		
Staff		
Materials		

2   Now prepare a resource table yourself for *each* of the following pairs of organisations. In each case consider whether they have:
   * high or low volume
   * high or low variety
   * high or low variation
   * high or low customer contact.
   Remember that each of these factors will affect the resources that are required.
   a   McDonald's versus an expensive restaurant
   b   the Royal Mail versus an express courier service
   c   an ice cream manufacturer versus Heinz
   d   a hospital versus a recording studio.

Obtaining resources

Buying resources is undertaken by the **purchasing function** of the organisation. This may be part of production or a separate function altogether. Purchasing is separate when it is **centralised**. This means that specialist staff purchase everything required by the organisation. This is often cheaper because they can bulk buy at greater discounts. This is not possible if each department looks after its own resource needs. Purchasing may also try to standardise items to make bulk purchases for the whole company, for items as different as machine oil and paper. Purchasing staff will be responsible for any contracts and making sure that the terms of these are met. All items are normally inspected on delivery and any problems are reported back to the purchasing staff.

Resource acquisition is critical for an organisation, particularly buying raw materials. Purchasing has to make sure that supplies of the correct materials of the right quality are available when needed. Production cannot be delayed because there is a problem obtaining components. The purchase must be made at the best price (which is not necessarily the cheapest!), bearing in mind the reliability of different suppliers, essential quality, storage space, possible shortages and proposed delivery dates.

Many large organisations use a system known as **Just-in-Time (JIT)**, which saves money because it reduces the number of raw materials kept in stock and therefore the storage space required. Holding stock costs money, as the materials have to be paid for. The lower the stock held, the less money is tied up. So, instead of holding large stocks of raw materials companies often try to find one preferred supplier who will deliver goods at a moment's notice. This is known as the JIT system. Large motor manufacturers are often surrounded by satellite suppliers of components who will deliver on a daily basis.

Another modern method of obtaining goods is by computer, using **Electronic Data Interchange (EDI)**. Not only are goods purchased by this system, they are also paid for through it. Orders and invoices are passed on by computer to companies in any part of the world. Because of the speed of ordering through EDI companies can afford to hold lower stocks and save on storage costs.

Payment is made through special computer terminals which can only be accessed by a smart card and a personal security code. The payment computer automatically arranges for money to be transferred from the purchaser's bank account to the supplier's bank account, and both will receive a computerised record of the transaction.

Purchasing staff in many organisations not only obtain resources from the UK but also from overseas. This means that they must be familiar with import restrictions and regulations. They also have to be aware of how currency rates can affect the cost of supplies.

Close links between the purchasing staff and production staff are essential. Any changes to a product or to a production schedule can easily mean that changes are required to the type or quantity of raw materials required or the date when they are needed.

SNAPSHOT

Thoroughly modern methods

The Japanese have been world leaders in revolutionising production processes and they invented JIT. Large car manufacturers were surrounded by dozens of suppliers who made daily deliveries (sometimes twice a day) to the plants. The relationship benefitted both. The car plants had little need to store supplies and the suppliers had guaranteed regular orders. Everyone was happy. Toyota even changed its factory manufacturing procedures so it could use the JIT system to its fullest extent.

In Britain the Rover car company uses EDI. It trades electronically with over 270 suppliers, who have between 12 hours and one week to deliver goods. In an emergency a delivery can be made in 40 minutes. Tesco claims that 95 per cent of its orders and 60 per cent of its invoices are transmitted as EDI messages. This improves the service for customers as shelves are refilled more rapidly and it reduces space for storage, giving more sales space to generate more income.

Monitoring production

If you were the manager of McDonald's, how would you 'monitor' that your production schedules were being met? You would probably check the speed at which customers were served and the length of the queues. Your takings for the day would give you a good indication of the amount of business you had done and whether this was good or poor. If you were in charge of a manufacturing plant, you would have to check that all the planned items were being produced on schedule and that your stocks of finished items were increasing as forecast. If you were running a hospital, you would check that sufficient patients were being treated each week and being discharged.

In every organisation, checks are made to ensure that plans become reality. It is no good forecasting you will make 5,000 boxes of chocolates a week, obtaining the resources to do this, but only making 22, and then shrugging your shoulders! Remember that anything that goes wrong, or holds up production, costs the company money. The role of the production control staff is to ensure that production targets are met.

Figure 1.49 Length of queues give some idea of how fast customers are being served

If not, they need to have a very good explanation!

The control system to check that targets are met involves the following.

- **Progress control** – to check that planned output is as scheduled. In a factory the controllers traditionally walked around regularly to see what was happening. Today they are more apt to be staring at an electronic control panel or VDU! Problems can occur if there is a machine breakdown (known as **downtime**), through poor quality raw materials or because of labour problems. Not only must the problem be solved quickly, but production schedules must be readjusted to try to make up the lost time.

The McDonald's manager is doing the same thing when he or she watches the queues. There will be considerable consternation if no fries can be made because the machine breaks down. Your dentist would be annoyed if appointments had to be changed because the electricity supply failed. Cinemas do not react well to their projectors breaking down. An evening football match disrupted by a floodlights failure would be a disaster. These are 'service' equivalents of 'downtime'.

- **Quality control** – to check the quality of the finished item or service. Quality is discussed in more detail on page 89.

- **Stock and materials control** – to ensure that there is a continuous supply of all the essential raw materials or items required. Service equivalents include a hotel running out of clean towels or sheets, Kwik-Fit running out of tyres, a taxi running out of petrol, a hospital having no bandages. Good stock control is essential for all businesses.

- **Machine utilisation control** – to control the use of machines to make sure none are overloaded, over-used or under-used, and to ensure that all are regularly checked and maintained. Some organisations have a maintenance plan which shows the dates on which machines are out of operation because they are being inspected and serviced. In an office, the breakdown of a photocopier or fax can be catastrophic and computer failure can cause huge problems and great stress – as you saw on page 60!

Remember that the method of production control will vary, depending on the type of organisation. In your school or college, you will find that there is some monitoring that classes (and learning) are actually taking place. There are routine observations of classes, room checks and visits by inspectors. The end of year results of students are also monitored. In a superstore the manager often 'walks the floor' to check that sufficient stocks are available, that the queues aren't excessive at the checkouts, that customer service staff are being helpful. He or she will also examine the sales figures very carefully to make sure they are high enough!

Control therefore can be done by:

- physical and visual checking

- reading computer print-outs giving results

- asking people what they think. This is covered under marketing on page 75.

ACTIVITY

Divide into five groups. Each group should select one of the following organisations and list the methods they would use to check that 'production' was taking place as scheduled.

a   a television manufacturer
b   a parcel delivery company
c   a bank
d   an airline
e   a newspaper.

CASE STUDY 1.5

Argos is an unusual type of high street shop. Instead of a large amount of selling space and elaborate displays, it issues catalogues to customers who order from the items listed. The shopper completes a form, takes it to a terminal to pay, obtains a receipt and collects the items from a collection desk. That's if the items are in stock. The benefit is cheaper prices, but for that the customer does without the frills and, in some cases, the customer service. These difficulties resulted in problems for Argos. It identified that their failures were due to giving poor service to customers, inadequate product availability and a limited product range. In early 1999 they reported their second disastrous Christmas.

Argos became the target of a hostile take-over by Great Universal Stores (GUS) who, in the summer of 1999, announced plans to introduce Internet and interactive television shopping plus a new fashion catalogue. This will be a merged GUS/Argos catalogue covering 7,300 products and will be sent to 19 million people every six months, as well as going into all 448 Argos stores. The range of products is 30 per cent greater than traditional catalogues. Argos' expansion

CASE STUDY (continued)

Figure 1.50 An Argos catalogue

plans also include a nationwide home shopping service, with products ordered by telephone delivered to any address within 48 hours. It plans to upgrade its website and interactive TV shopping service.

Activities

1   Identify the differences between Argos and an ordinary high street shop in terms of: volume, variety, variation and customer contact.

Show clearly how this would affect its resource needs under the categories of buildings, equipment, people and materials.

2   Under each of your resource headings, identify what Argos actually provided and what, according to its critics, it *should* have provided.

3   Suggest four ways in which a company which does much of its business at Christmas should *improve* its resources at that time so it will not disappoint its customers.

4   What do you think is meant by a 'hostile takeover'? Look back at page 4 for help if you need it!

5   Why might a mail order company such as Great Universal Stores be interested in Argos? What similarities can you identify in the two businesses?

6   GUS has announced its aim of expanding Argos. From the information in the case study, identify three objectives associated with this aim.

7   Critics argue that a new catalogue or additional services won't help visitors to Argos stores. If you were in charge of 'production' or operations in Argos shops:

   a   what suggestions could you make to improve the services to customer?

   b   what controls would you introduce to check if you were being successful?

Production and its affect on other functional areas

Because production or operations is often a 'back room' activity, it is often unnoticed by a customer. When you buy a CD, for instance, you rarely think about all the 'production' work that has gone into making it: the scheduling of the recording studios, the booking of session musicians and recording engineers, the making and editing of the master tape, pressing the disk, designing the cover and distributing it to the shops. You simply buy it. However, given that production or operations is normally concerned with the main activity of the business, it obviously has close links with every other function.

Figure 1.51 What you don't see when you buy a CD

It has links with human resources for its staffing needs. Additional staff may be needed to help process a large order or to meet a high seasonal demand for the goods or service. Human resources will also organise training for new staff or for staff having to learn new skills. They will give advice if there are any labour disputes and will be involved in any union negotiations.

Finance has a critical link with production because the cost of making a product or delivering the service has to be calculated very carefully. This information is required before the selling price can be calculated and this must take into account the prices charged by competitors. It is no use making a ballpoint pen for 50p and having to sell it at 70p to make a profit if your competitors are selling the same item for 35p!

The costs of production will be calculated using current figures for raw materials, standard times of working and average wage rates. If raw materials cost more, and there is excessive downtime or slow working

resulting in high overtime payments, then these will increase the cost of production. The management accountants will therefore keep a very close watch on the production budget to ensure that targets are met as much as possible.

Production will use its own administrators, or the services of an administrative function, for many of the routine tasks that are carried out, from checking orders for raw materials to producing production schedules and maintenance reports. There will be someone on hand to answer queries from other parts of the organisation, from distributors and from suppliers.

Probably the greatest link, however, is between production and marketing and sales. This relationship is not without problems, and in some organisations there is sometimes conflict between the two departments. The reason for this is simple. Production is concerned with its own targets of producing good products (or providing a good service) in a scheduled time. Sales is concerned with selling as many products as possible. This means that keen sales staff may be tempted to promise customers deliveries within deadlines that production staff consider unreasonable, or even impossible. Sales may worry that if it does not meet the customer's demands the customer will take their business elsewhere. In other cases, a customer may want a highly individual product that production argue cannot be made. There is the famous American case of an armoured people carrier designed by a committee of generals. By the time they had finished adding bits to it (ignoring the pleas of the producers) there was hardly any room for anyone to fit inside!

The problems between production (or operations) and sales will never disappear entirely, but in a good organisation there will be an excellent communication system and clear guidelines to help everyone (see also page 105).

SNAPSHOT

Marketing and sales

The purpose of the marketing and sales function

One of the most famous thinkers on business management, Peter Drucker, said 'marketing is looking at the business through the customer's eyes'. This is the basic purpose of marketing. It is concerned with identifying what the customer needs and providing it.

In many successful businesses, marketing is considered much more than just a separate function. It is the whole philosophy, or belief, of the company. This means that everyone is highly focused on fulfilling the customer needs – whether this is for an urgent appointment, a cheap calculator or a presentation of the latest products. Staff are also keen to find out *what else* they can do to keep customers happy and what additional needs customers may have that they don't even know about! After all, no-one considered criticising their vacuum cleaner until Dyson invented a different one, 20 years ago no-one wore trainers or used a mobile phone or owned a microwave cooker, because they hadn't been invented. If you think about all the needs you have, and compare these with the needs your grandparents had at the same age, you will soon see how 'needs' can be fostered and developed simply through the introduction of new products, services and ideas.

Figure 1.52 The mobile phone

A true marketing-orientated company always tries to be 'one step ahead' of the customer (and the competition) by anticipating needs and fulfilling them. It also puts the customer at the top of its priority list in every single operation it undertakes.

The activities of marketing and sales

The activities of marketing and sales include:

- **market research**, to find out what customers need and customer opinions on proposed and existing products or services

- **promotion**, to inform the customers that their particular organisation can fulfill these needs

- **sales**, to provide the goods or service the customer now thinks he or she needs.

The contribution of marketing is vital in that it directly influences the number of sales that are made and therefore the profitability of the company.

Job roles in marketing and sales

Interestingly, the job roles in marketing and sales are usually less variable between different organisations than they are in other functional areas. However, the roles *will* vary depending on the size of the organisation. A large organisation will have more specialists and may do some of its promotional work 'in-house'. A smaller organisation will have fewer people undertaking broader roles and will contract out much of its specialist marketing requirements. It would hire the services of market research specialists and advertising consultants. Large firms also do this, but often have a specialist person in the company to liaise with them.

A broad range of job titles and job roles you may find is shown in Figure 1.53.

Typical job title	Job role
Marketing director	Responsible for the overall marketing function and its aims and objectives.
Sales director	Responsible for the sales function.
Sales manager	Responsible for sales staff and the achievement of sales targets, often within the UK.
Export manager	Responsible for overseas agents and the achievement of sales targets overseas.
Advertising manager	In charge of advertising and liaising with agency staff over publicity campaigns.
Sales coordinator	The 'link' person for travelling sales representatives who require urgent information.
Sales representatives	Sales people who visit customers in the UK and overseas.
Market researchers	Find out consumer opinions on current and proposed goods and services.
Order clerks	Accept and process sales orders.
Shipping clerks	Arrange for the transportation and delivery of orders overseas and the completion of export documentation.
Telephone sales staff	Accept and process telephone orders.

Figure 1.53 Job roles in marketing and sales

Investigating marketing and sales activities

Market research

Market research is carried out to identify customer needs and views in relation to:

- potential new products or services
- existing products or services.

It can be carried out through primary research, secondary research, or both.

Primary research

Primary research means asking someone for their views or opinions. When you carry out your case study for this unit you will undertake primary research. You will have to ask appropriate questions to find out the information you need. In market research terms this is called a **survey**. A survey may be conducted face to face, by telephone or by post. Postal surveys normally have a poor response unless a prize or incentive is offered to tempt people to complete them. Telephone surveys are popular and are cheaper than having to interview someone face-to-face. This method is often used for more in-depth surveys.

The method is to ask specific questions and have a range of possible answers listed. You then tick or mark the answer you get. The survey can be optically read and the results calculated by computer.

Figure 1.54 Primary research

Other methods of carrying out primary research include 'test marketing' a new product or service in a particular area of the country, using a testing panel or setting up a consumer panel. All Boots stores have a consumer panel to give feedback on customer views. Testing panels are used in the food industry and also in the clothing trade. One hosiery manufacturer gives new brands of tights and stockings to its female employees and asks them for their opinions before putting them on general sale. Another method is to collect reports and feedback from sales representatives who meet customers on a regular basis.

For the survey to be valid, the sample surveyed must be large enough to give significant results and it must be focused on the **key** customer. It is no good surveying car owners about a local bus service they never use, or asking pensioners about Club 18-30 holidays. However, aftershave manufacturers often ask *women* for their views because so much aftershave is actually bought by women, even if it isn't used by them! The sample may be obtained on a gender basis, by age, socioeconomic grouping (how much people earn) or by ethnicity. It all depends upon the product or service being surveyed. A company usually knows the profile of its existing and potential customers and will use this to identify those who are suitable in relation to their age, gender and income.

Secondary research

This is often known as 'desk research'. It relates to looking up facts and figures in books, magazines, on computer databases, in company files. In other words, you are looking at information that already exists, rather than creating your own.

Companies store a vast amount of information on their database systems about their customers and their buying patterns.

They can also buy information from other company databases, and obtain government statistics about consumer expenditure and details of their competitors.

Questions to ask

Questions are likely to focus on:

- similar products or services the customer already uses

- the type of product or service he or she would prefer

- the price paid for the product or service

- the price the customer would be prepared to pay for a product or service with different features

- the newspapers and magazines the customer reads and the television programmes frequently watched

- the places where the customer usually shops

- the customer's views of current products and/or services.

Marketing strategies

Companies use information from market research to plan their marketing strategies. These are the tactics they will use to try to maximise sales of the products or services. These tactics will depend very much on the type of customers they have and their needs.

The marketing mix

One of the first things the organisation must do is to decide its **marketing mix** for a particular item. This comprises the four 'P's: **product**, **price**, **promotion** and **place**. The company is trying to find out the following information in each case.

- **Product** – the type or the variety of product the customer wants, the quality required, the features and styling that are preferred, whether packaging is important, whether a guarantee or after-sales service is required.

- **Price** – what basic price the customer would pay, whether discounts or credit terms would be desirable, the price of competitors' products, whether additional price-related features would be tempting (e.g. a trade-in on an old model).

- **Promotion** – where it would be best to advertise the product, what type of personal selling would be best, what type of sales promotions could help, what publicity would be most effective, how the product should be displayed in stores (known as merchandising).

- **Place** – where to find potential customers, what kind of shops they use, what magazines and newspapers they read, how best to distribute the product, what regions to cover, what type of transport to use, where to locate shops and depots.

The marketing mix is likely to vary from one product or service to another, depending on the type of customers it attracts and their habits, needs and preferences. As an example, catering packs of common items such as coffee are not packed, priced, promoted or sold in the same way as basic supermarket products. They aim to reach a different market and do so in a different way.

The marketing mix will give you information on the business's customers and is useful in understanding a particular marketing and sales department. For instance, some businesses deal only with industrial customers, others only with private individuals, and some will deal with both. One company may sell locally but another may sell nationally or internationally. All these factors influence the way the marketing and sales function operates in a business.

Promotion

All businesses have to decide how to promote their products. They usually use a variety of methods, which will depend on the type of product or service being promoted. A local plumber would not use the same methods as an international company such as Microsoft! The range of available methods includes:

- advertising
- sales promotions
- publicity campaigns
- personal selling (see page 79).

The aim of promotional methods is to inform (or remind) the public that the product or service exists, and to stress the benefits. The hidden message is nearly always, 'you have that need, we can fulfil it with this . . . .' Promotion is often identified by the acronym AIDA. Draw **attention**. Create **interest**. Develop **desire**. Invite **action**.

Advertising

Products and services are advertised daily in the press, on television and commercial radio, in cinemas and on hoardings, in train stations and on buses. Householders also receive direct mail shots through the letterbox.

Advertisements are written to **inform** or to **persuade**, though some do both. A persuasive advertisement sells an image whereas an informational advertisement gives the facts. The company will also use a variety of tactics to enable you to recognise their product or service easily. These will include distinctive packaging, brand names (e.g. Pepsi or Fairy Liquid) or trade names (e.g. Virgin or Häagen-Dazs) and advertising slogans (e.g. 'The Real Thing').

The choice of media (press, television etc.) depends upon:

Figure 1.55 Virgin's name is one of the best known trade names

- the type of product or service
- the extent of coverage required
- the geographical distribution of the product
- the cost
- the habits of the key customer.

As an example, you will find your local newspaper has details of houses for sale in your area. Exclusive properties, however, would be advertised in expensive magazines or in particular newspaper supplements (e.g. the *Financial Times* Saturday supplement). Boats and caravans are advertised in specialist magazines. None of these products would be suitable for advertising on television because they are only of interest to specific groups. Groceries, cars, toiletries and banking services, however, are of more general interest and are regularly advertised on national television.

The company can measure the effectiveness of an advertising campaign by checking the difference in its sales. If customers are asked to respond for more information they may be asked to quote the source where they saw the advertisement. Customer service staff, too, often ask new customers where they first heard of the company (see page 82).

Direct mail shots are frequently used to promote a product, service or charity appeal. Local shops may advertise special offers by distributing leaflets. Large companies exchange databases so that customers who show an interest in a particular product might find themselves deluged by mail shots from other companies.

Sales promotions

Sales promotions are campaigns which tempt potential customers to try a product. They include offering free samples, point-of-sale demonstrations, special discounts, competitions and special offers. A company will sometimes initiate a sales promotion if sales of an existing product have fallen.

Some companies offer dealers incentives to sell their products. These can include bonus payments and prizes as well as the use of special display materials.

Publicity campaigns

Some organisations try to get free publicity by passing on news stories to the media. The aim is to keep the name of the organisation and the brand name in the public eye. Sir Richard Branson and Virgin must head the list in this category! He willingly dressed as a bride to obtain free publicity for the launch of Virgin Bride and was pictured in a reclining bed with a model to launch the new first-class seating in Virgin Atlantic! Most other companies are rather more restrained but still aim to get free press coverage when they can.

Another way of getting publicity is through sponsorship, sometimes of sporting events or football teams or concerts. Other companies sponsor particular charities (e.g. Mothercare supports Great Ormond Street Children's Hospital).

A **publicity campaign** is when a range of different promotional methods are used simultaneously to focus customer attention on a particular product or service. A direct mail shot may be linked with television and press advertising, publicity stores and point-of-sale promotions, spread over a short period of time.

CASE STUDY 1.6

Häagen-Dazs is one of the success stories of the 1990s. It has used some fairly startling marketing tactics to persuade people that its luxury ice cream is different and worth the price it charges. Not content with high summer sales, the company decided to do something about our winter eating habits – and spent over £1.5 million doing it.

Häagen-Dazs' 'winter sale' was a promotional campaign which included advertisements on national radio, posters and in national newspapers – all featuring its 'Christmas Offering'. A special Christmas flavour of rum, raisin and cream was made, the tubs were dressed in a red ribbon, and the adverts focused on the story of the 'Three Wise Men'. The slogan? 'At least one offering is 100 per cent perfect this Christmas.'

Häagen-Dazs claims that its sales only drop by 10 per cent in winter, but wants to persuade the British public that despite lower temperatures, ice cream is still a desirable product to buy.

CASE STUDY (continued)

Figure 1.56 A famous ice cream

Activities

1 What is the aim of the Häagen-Dazs campaign?
2 Would you consider its advertisements to be persuasive or informational? Give a reason for your answer.

3 What media did Häagen-Dazs use to promote its winter sales?
4 As a group, discuss why you think Häagen-Dazs did *not* include television advertising in its campaign.
5 What benefits do you think Häagen-Dazs would gain by increasing its winter sales? Think beyond immediate profits to the difficulties of operating with a seasonal product. Look back to the last section on production for help.
6 Our perception of a product is often strongly influenced by its promotional methods and advertising campaigns. What are your perceptions of Häagen-Dazs as a product?
7 How successful do you think Häagen-Dazs would be at persuading the average British family to eat ice-cream at Christmas? Give a reason for your answer.

Sales

Some marketeers believe that if you offer customers what they want, at the right price, in the right place and at the right time, then the product or service sells itself. Others believe 'word of mouth' is the best advertising, i.e. a recommendation from a friend. Regardless of this, some organisations still spend large sums of money employing staff to sell their products. This is because for certain products and services buyers expect personal attention and because promotion by itself is impersonal. The advertising message is aimed at whole groups of people, not individuals. Direct selling, in contrast, involves personal contact between the buyer and seller.

You wouldn't expect personal attention if you were buying cornflakes but you would if you wanted a new car. Personal selling is appropriate when a customer may have several queries about the product, some of them technical, and where the price may be negotiable. It is used for selling expensive products and when expert advice is required. For example, you would consult a specialist if you were spending £6,000 on audio equipment, and you would probably insist that it was professionally installed and set up correctly.

Sales people are often employed to sell complex industrial equipment. In this case it is more usual for sales representatives to visit the customer, rather than the other way round.

The sales person knows the market, keeps in touch with the customer and makes suggestions that help to result in new sales opportunities. Some sales people travel abroad and have to be familiar with the customs and the needs of foreign buyers. Many sales people are monitored closely on performance and offered incentives, such as bonus payments or commission.

An effective sales person can make a considerable difference by converting a potential customer into an actual customer. This is done through a mixture of:

- good product knowledge

- a sincere interest in the customer's particular needs

- excellent communication skills

- a persuasive manner.

People are always more tempted to buy if the sales person is friendly, approachable, lively, interested in them, hard-working and

Figure 1.57 A good salesperson can make a big difference

knowledgeable. This gives them confidence in the sales person's judgement and advice. A sales person also needs self-confidence and it helps if sales staff believe in the products or services being sold. It is much easier to sell something you think is high quality and value for money, than something you think is not!

Ethics are also an issue linked to sales. This means that you only sell something you think the buyer will benefit from. It is unethical to deliberately mislead someone and persuade them to buy an overpriced item they either do not need or which will not do what you claim. This is not a practice supported by reputable companies, but unfortunately it goes on.

Another form of selling becoming more popular is telephone selling, commonly referred to as **telemarketing**. This is cheaper than paying a sales person to visit potential customers. Firms may target a local area and 'ring round' offering a product or service. This practice can be counter-productive, however, as it can irritate many householders who feel their privacy is being invaded in their own home.

Many commercial organisations spend more on personal selling than any other part of the promotional mix. It is costly to keep a large sales force, especially one that travels around the country or even around the world. A sales force however can build strong loyalty relationships with major customers, who like having someone to look after their particular needs. The benefits of this are obvious. Sometimes sales people become so well liked that their companies fear that losing them to a competitor would mean losing some of their business as well!

Specialist sales staff also gather information from customers. Sales representatives prepare reports following visits to customers summarising key issues raised. They may find out, for instance, that the customer is planning to expand over the next twelve months, which means more sales opportunities. A customer may tell the representative about the need to order goods from the firm over the Internet, and ask if something can be done to make this possible (see primary research, page 75).

Other employees have a 'sales role' in some organisations. Travel agency staff help 'sell' you a holiday, possibly a more expensive one than you first planned to take, bank staff 'sell' you a bank service, customer service staff may suggest a new service or product. It can be very cost-effective for organisations to make staff who are in contact with customers aware of new products and services, so when the chance arises they can suggest or recommend these. Staff who can turn a brief encounter with a customer into a sales opportunity, and convert this into a sale, are worth their weight in gold. IT systems can be programmed to help. Bank's computers, for instance, can be programmed to flash a message to staff if a large deposit is being made to remind them to offer financial advice services to the customer!

 ## ACTIVITY

1 Identify the products or services below where you would:
   a expect a personal sales service
   b prefer a personal sales service
   c not require a personal sales service

i	computer	**ii**	pair of jeans
iii	magazine	**iv**	answer machine
v	camcorder	**vi**	watch
vii	sports bag	**viii**	portable TV
ix	fitted bedroom suite	**x**	car insurance

2 Your friend wants to buy a mobile phone but is worried about the health risks. Certain stores in your town offer a personal sales service and others do not. Which do you think would be best to visit and why?

3 Select an item of your choice and list its key benefits to the user. Then try to persuade the person next to you to buy it. Try to counter his or her objections by making positive suggestions, rather than shouting them down! See who survives the longest!

4 Identify the 'sales opportunity' for a member of staff in each of the following situations, and recommend a suitable response :
   a an office worker telephones an office stationery and equipment supplier. During the conversation she says their fax machine is six years old.
   b a mother accompanying her son to a college open evening says she wishes she had learned more about IT when she was young.
   c a bank clerk notices that a customer has a lot of money in a non-interest paying account.
   d Two young men in a jeweller's shop at Christmas are peering at a tray of bracelets. One is saying to the other, 'It's OK for you, you know what she wants.'

Marketing and sales – its affect on other functional areas

The degree to which a company is 'market led' will determine the impact that marketing has on all the other functions. Organisations which see marketing as a key activity argue that everyone should stay focused on the customer, even if they don't deal with them directly. They argue that everyone in the organisation operates in a chain, with the person at the end dealing with the customer. This person depends on everyone else in the chain for support.

Otherwise the person who ends up disappointed is the customer.

Therefore, no marketing and sales function can survive without the support of other parts of the organisation. Indeed, marketing is often the function that needs the most administrative support of all.

A good relationship with human resources is important because of its role in the recruitment and training of staff. Good sales staff are particularly difficult to find and often training is required, to familiarise them with company products and services and to improve their sales techniques.

Marketing has links with finance as to the sales budget, given that the level of sales is the starting point for setting the budget. Marketing and sales will forecast annual sales of different products and this results in the income forecast for the organisation. Marketing also forecasts how much it needs to spend on promotion and advertising. Sales staff will also expect finance to generate the standard paperwork (invoices, statements etc.) when they make a sale on credit. They also expect finance to tell them about the credit worthiness of new customers or warn them if an existing customer is a bad payer. Marketing may need to consult with a senior member of the finance staff if they want to offer special terms or extra discounts to a particular customer to secure a sale.

Considerable administrative help is required by marketing and sales staff. This may include keeping a comprehensive customer database, analysing and recording sales representative reports, recording sales and analysing trends, liaising with advertising agency staff, answering customer enquiries, sending out literature, helping to prepare presentation materials. Sales managers and representatives who travel abroad regularly

Figure 1.58 The Internet is one way of selling goods and services

will also need accommodation and flights booked.

The relationship between production and marketing and sales has been discussed previously (page 72). Marketing will want to satisfy the customer's needs. The orders it takes and the deliveries it promises will affect the production schedules. Marketing will consult production about technical problems and issues sales representatives have identified in products or services – and consult them about whether it's possible to implement new ideas into products or services.

Customer service

The purpose of the customer service function

When customers buy goods or services they do so to satisfy a need. They also expect certain

The future for sales – e-commerce?

Most people have heard of Amazon.com. If you have not, then this is the fastest growing book seller in the world, selling all its books over the Internet. Over a million consumers used the Internet to buy products worth more than £400 million in 1998. The figure is expected to be double in 1999 and to reach £12.9 billion by the end of 2001. Yet Britain's retailers are lagging behind.

Many of Britain's top retailers don't have a web site and only 14 of the top 100 companies sell goods over the Internet. It is forecast that by 2003 40 per cent of sales of books, computer software, music and videos will take place over the Internet, in addition to over £2 million worth of clothing products. Unless Britain reacts swiftly, most of these sales will be made by American companies. Americans already buy twenty times as many goods over the Net than we do and 95 per cent of American companies have developed extensive web sites.

Companies seriously interested in grabbing a share of Internet business are advised to take their web pages seriously. A bad site is worse than none at all, and is known in the trade as a 'cyber-turkey'. It should be easy to find, easy to follow and should be up to date. It should follow the AIDA principles. It is another form of promotional and sales strategy which is too important to ignore.

things. They expect the goods to be available when they want them. They expect the items they are sold to be safe and reliable. They have the right to get good value for money. In the UK there are laws governing **consumer protection**, which you will learn about if you study the option unit on this topic.

Giving customers an *excellent* service however, involves more than simply observing their legal rights. Customers should be treated courteously and given accurate information, staff should be trained to give prompt assistance and advice if customers have problems, customers should be offered helpful payment terms for expensive items, have their goods delivered to them and be given immediate assistance if the goods break down or are faulty.

Companies which do this often get repeat business from customers over many years. Satisfied customers also tell their friends and relatives and the company gets more business. It has been shown that a *dissatisfied* customer will tell at least seven other people about poor service, each of whom will pass on the message to about five others. At the end of the cycle, one unhappy customer can spread the word to about 60 or 70 people. It is therefore pointless spending money on expensive advertising campaigns if 'word of mouth' news about the organisation is bad!

Marketing and sales concentrates on getting new business, whereas customer service usually focuses on existing customers. Its purpose is to keep customers happy by fulfilling their expectations, by making them feel needed and important and by providing a range of services which will fulfil their ongoing needs.

The activities of customer service

You may be familiar with the type of customer service offered by a retail store. In many commercial organisations, however, the range of activities is greater than you would find at Safeway or Tesco, for example. It would include:

- providing information
- giving advice

Figure 1.59 Customer service tries to keep customers happy

- providing credit facilities
- delivering goods
- after-sales service.

All these activities are explained in more detail below.

Job roles in customer service

The number of staff employed in customer service and the roles they undertake will depend very largely on the type of business. Some businesses, such as supermarkets, deal with their customers face-to-face. In these organisations you will find a customer service desk with customer service assistants. In some businesses, however, customers may never have personal contact with anyone in the company. An example is a holiday tour company. However, if a customer has a problem or query, they may write to the customer service department. Some organisations may only deal with industrial clients and their customer service facility may

be part of the overall marketing and sales function, or operate as a separate technical service department.

A typical range of job titles and job roles is shown in Figure 1.60. However, you will have to adapt this for any organisation you study, in line with the activities it undertakes for its own customers.

Typical job title	Job role
Customer services manager	Responsible for the overall customer services function and staff.
Technical services manager	Responsible for all the technical services function and staff.
Delivery or distribution manager	Responsible for scheduling and overseeing the delivery of all new items sold.
Customer services assistant	Deals with customers, face-to-face or on the telephone. Liaises with other staff over complex issues and either responds to customers personally or ensures issue is dealt with by specialist.
Technical advisers	Deal with customers who are encountering technical difficulties.
Telephone help line staff	Deal with customer enquiries over the telephone.

Figure 1.60 Job roles related to customer service

ACTIVITY

It is argued that everyone in an organisation works for customer services, given that every member of staff who ever talks to or meets a customer has the ability to please or displease. As a group, discuss occasions when you have entered a shop or called in at a reception area or spoken to someone over the telephone and been 'put off' by that person's attitude or behaviour.

Then suggest some 'golden rules' you would introduce in your own business to prevent such situations occurring.

Investigating customer service activities

Providing information

The type of information required by customers and clients can vary a lot. An astute member of staff will realise that it is impossible to know the answer to every question immediately, but it is the way the query is dealt with that is important. A friendly smile, a promise to find out quickly and keeping that promise is more important than being a walking encyclopaedia! Customers may ask:

- a technical query about a product or service
- a general query about the organisation
- about the range of products or services supplied
- about the location of another store
- about the location of somewhere else in the area
- about general facilities available.

Customer service staff should have information to hand on products and services and should be fairly conversant with the range on offer. In a retail store they should know where these are located. They should be able to check which items are in stock, which items are not and how long they take to order. Modern computer databases have helped staff enormously and many organisations have a great deal of information available for customer service staff, literally at the touch of a few keys. The customer database should record the names and addresses of existing customers as well as details of recent purchases and amounts paid. If there is a query, the customer account can be easily accessed. Stock can also be held on a database, with delivery times and availability.

Giving advice

Advice is more precise than information. It also involves more detail, greater specialist knowledge and is tailored to the needs of the person making the request. I could give you information about the services a bank offers, but I would need to know quite a lot about each one, and understand your personal circumstances, before I could advise you which one would be best for you.

Some types of advice are more critical than others. Advice about legal, safety, financial or medical issues, for instance, *must* be correct. So, unless you are specially trained you should always refer any queries on topics such as these to an expert. Indeed, there is nothing worse than the untrained amateur giving advice on subjects he or she knows very little about!

In customer services, therefore, the staff need to consider certain factors when they are asked for advice.

- Is the advice required about a general, unimportant matter or a very important one?
- Could there be any adverse or serious consequences if incorrect information is given?
- Does the person dealing with the query know enough to answer it correctly?

In many organisations, a special function known as **technical services** exists to give specific advice. Industrial companies often have a technical services division and computer companies often have technical service staff who will answer detailed queries

Figure 1.61 Customers sometimes need technical advice

and give advice to users. In your college, you may have specialist staff who will give advice on grants and loans. You will also have careers advisers. In a sense, these are all customer service staff, in that they are helping to give advice that is appropriate to your particular needs and they are all specialists in their own particular fields.

Providing credit facilities

As you have already seen, business organisations routinely allow other business organisations to buy on credit. However, the credit terms that are agreed may vary from one customer to another, as you will see in Unit 3. Individuals also often require credit for expensive items, such as a car. Without this facility, they may not be able to buy the product and the business will not make the sale.

Credit and private individuals

Private individuals can pay for items they buy in cash, by cheque or on credit. Credit can be obtained in one of three ways.

1 Paying by credit card. The holder of the card can then choose whether to pay off the debt in full the following month or spread the payments over the next few months. This is not suitable for very expensive items which exceed the buyer's credit limit.

2 Paying in instalments on direct debit. Insurance can be bought in this way. Instead of paying for 12 months' insurance at once, you could arrange to pay over the course of the year. The insurance company will add an interest charge to your bill, so that you pay more using this method.

3 Borrowing the money by taking out a loan. This may be from a bank or from a finance company. Most car dealerships, for instance, operate as agents for finance companies and will arrange finance when they sell a car. Again interest is added for each year of the loan.

The more payment options offered by the company, the more likely it is able to meet the customer's needs.

Customer services staff need to know all the options available and to be able to give customers help and advice as to the most appropriate for their particular needs. They also need to be aware that some customers may be rejected for loans because they have a poor credit record, and be able to explain this tactfully to the customer. Such conversations, of course, should always be conducted in private!

Delivering goods

No customer wants to purchase a large, heavy item and then find the company either doesn't offer a delivery service, or delivery charges are extortionate, or delivery times are inflexible. In many cases, the customer may decide the whole transaction is too much trouble and go elsewhere.

Ideally a business will offer a range of services related to the transportation and delivery of goods.

- Physical assistance with packing and loading if the customer wants to take a heavy item home by car.

- An optional delivery service which:
  - is free or low cost
  - is to a wide geographic area
  - operates at times which suits the customer, not the firm.

- A postal service for ordered goods which are not immediately available.

- Delivery staff who are friendly and courteous and handle the goods carefully.

You may like to note that in the United States it is also common practice to offer to giftwrap items when they are bought – for no extra charge! It is also customary for airport staff on domestic routes to take heavy baggage from passengers immediately they alight from their coach or car. But they expect a tip – such is the price of excellent customer service!

After-sales service

After-sales service includes several types of activities:

- giving refunds on returned goods
- offering a repair service for faulty goods
- offering a maintenance service
- dealing with complaints
- dealing with technical queries.

Giving refunds

There should be a clear policy on returned items, so that customer service staff are not frequently having to ask their boss for assistance or clarification. Some organisations will accept any goods back within a limited period, providing the customer has kept the receipt, and will refund the money. Others will only exchange goods which are faulty, they won't exchange goods simply because buyers have changed their minds. Others will only allow items which are not faulty to be exchanged for other goods or for a credit note, so that the purchaser can select another item at a later date.

It is far better if the refund policy is clearly explained to a customer at the time the purchase is made, and the importance of keeping the receipt should be stressed. However, this is not essential legally if some other proof of purchase is provided, such as a bank statement showing a payment was processed or a credit card voucher which details the transaction.

Offering a repair service

This may be a small-scale operation, such as a small jeweller's shop, or a large-scale one. Makers of household appliances routinely have a service facility. Customer service staff

Figure 1.62 A special extra service

take the calls, check the customer's details on a database, find out details of the fault and arrange for a technician to call. Spare parts which are regularly needed will be carried in the technician's van so that the appliance can be repaired immediately.

Large business organisations will take out a service contract when they buy expensive technical equipment and this will be part of the sale terms. Administration will routinely have a service contract for equipment such as photocopiers, so that they can be mended promptly if they are faulty. Large computer organisations, such as IBM, have specialist staff on hand around the clock to deal with problems with computer installations, as the cost and consequences of 'downtime' is horrendously high.

Offering a maintenance service

Many organisations regularly check the equipment they have installed as part of the terms of the sale. A business organisation with a comprehensive burglar alarm system will expect the engineers to visit regularly to check the equipment. Fire extinguishers are regularly checked and inspected in all organisations – you can check when the last inspection took place on each one. Security equipment, such as CCTV cameras, is also checked and tested.

With some items, part of the sales package may be free maintenance or servicing for a specified period. This may be offered with a fleet of business vehicles and would certainly be part of a leasing contract.

Dealing with complaints

Consumer service staff will also handle any complaints received over the telephone or in writing, and most businesses have an official complaints procedure which all staff must follow. This also enables senior staff to check that all complaints are dealt with promptly and that no serious issues are left unresolved.

Dealing with technical queries

On page 85 you saw that customer service staff in a technical support function often give technical advice to customers. This is also a form of after-sales service. As an example, many people evaluate Internet service providers not just by their connection cost and transmission speed, but also by the speed they respond to customers with problems. The 'help' facility is a critical part of this service and some providers are far better than others. This is a good example of a service where excellent technical support attracts more customers.

Customer services and its affect on other functional areas

You should now have learned enough about the functional areas of a business to identify the links between customer services and all the other departments. Test yourself by doing the Activity below.

 **ACTIVITY**

Copy out the table below and complete the final column by identifying at least two links between customer services and each functional area shown.

Functional area	Links with customer services
Human resources	
Finance	
Administration	
Production	
Marketing and sales	

Other functions of the business

Functional areas differ between one business and another. Some businesses also give slightly different names to functional areas than others. This is particularly the case in the case of organisations such as a hospital, college or local council. Your college may have an estates function, which looks after the buildings and security; a student support function (which is really customer services) and a computer services function, which is similar to the IT function described on page 59. Your local council will have a housing department and a planning department. A hospital may have a large administration section and its reception areas may be split between those relating to inpatients and their families and those for outpatients.

You have already learned that:

- manufacturing organisations have a production function. In service organisations (and some manufacturing organisations) this may be known as their operations function.

- in some organisations human resources is known as personnel

- some businesses have a technical support function, such as large computer organisations or companies manufacturing complex industrial equipment

- many organisations today have an IT function, which may stand alone or be part of administration, or be called computer services or something similar.

There are three other functions you need to understand before you complete this section of the unit. These may be 'stand-alone' functions or they may be linked to another main functional area, as is often the case.

These are:

- quality control

- research and development

- design.

You should then have a good understanding of all the different types of functions you may encounter when you undertake your case study.

Quality control

Many organisations once employed quality controllers to check the quality of a finished product, either by examining each finished article or by random sampling. In some cases quality is checked by a machine linked to a computer, which will test that items have been manufactured within specified tolerances. Most organisations now prefer to 'build-in' quality at every stage of manufacture. This improves quality, given that some faults may not be noticed at the final checking stage.

Total quality management (TQM) is a system used by most organisations. Standards and methods are set for each stage of production. Each operator or team is responsible for checking the quality of its own work. Another name for this system is **right first time**. In many cases the system is extended to suppliers, who must conform to certain quality standards. This ensures that any components which are used in the final product are up to the standards set by the buyer.

Whilst quality is important for any product or service, in some cases tolerances and margins for error are very small. Electronic components, scientific equipment, drugs and aircraft parts need rigorous quality control, otherwise the products won't work or could

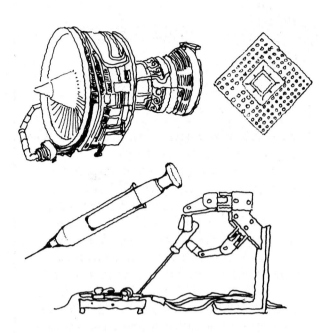

Figure 1.63 Sometimes there is no room for mistakes in quality

be dangerous. It would not be cost-effective for a company to spend as much on monitoring quality when making filing cabinets or wrapping paper.

Research and development

Research and development is usually known as R & D. It is usually the next stage after market research and aims to meet consumer needs or to translate the ideas of designers into usable products which can be manufactured at a reasonable cost. The type of R & D activities which are undertaken vary from one industry to another.

- Pharmaceutical companies spend millions of pounds on R & D, researching and testing new drugs.

- Food manufacturers employ technologists to develop new products, such as 'ready meals', chilled foods, sauces, etc. Many companies have extended their ranges

considerably over the past few years to meet our demand for more exotic dishes.

- Electronic companies are working on new technology products, e.g. digital televisions and cameras, DVDs (digital versatile disks), APS cameras, mobile phones which connect with the Internet and read your email.

- Some R & D specialists concentrate on developing new production processes or applying technological advances to production processes. Their general aim is to produce high-quality products more quickly and more cheaply.

- Most organisations aim to continually improve product performance – computers with more memory and greater operating speed, motorbikes that are faster but safer, washing machines that spin faster or use less water or power, more powerful microwave ovens. These are just a few of the developments which have been made over the past few years. Another term for this is **engineering design**, which is carried out in R & D. This contrasts with **industrial design**, which is the function of designers.

Design

Industrial design is increasingly important in many organisations. This determines how the product will look and the way consumers use it. If you look at an old style kettle and compare it with a new jug kettle you realise the effect designers have on our everyday lives. Cars, answering machines, telephones, televisions, household appliances, computers – design is important in all these and countless others. In organisations making fabrics, wallpaper or clothes new designs are produced each season as fashions change.

Figure 1.64 How products look can affect sales

Many organisations use **computer-aided design (CAD)** to help them to design new products – from a chair to an aeroplane. The designer can sketch basic shapes on screen and then vary the dimensions, angles and size of particular parts. The product can even be stress tested by computer. In some industries, CAD packages are linked to **computer-aided manufacturing (CAM)** or **computer-integrated manufacturing (CIM)**. Did you know, for instance, that it is possible to design a carpet on computer and then download the settings for the machine which produces the carpet? The carpet is then manufactured automatically to the exact design specified.

SNAPSHOT

Coming to a house near you . . . shortly

How well do your appliances communicate? You might think this is a strange question, but your children probably won't! Tested, developed and ready for release in the year 2000 is a microwave oven with a computer screen so you can manage your finances, a toilet seat that will raise itself and a fridge which incorporates a computer, television and radio in its front door. You can peer into the screen and, using your in-house video conferencing system, chat to anyone in another room. Your fridge will even monitor your eating habits and warn you when your food supplies are running low or passing their sell-by dates. And when you only possess half a sausage, an egg and a slice of cheese, your fridge will suggest a delicious recipe you can cook in minutes.

This, believe it or not, is only the beginning. By the year 2020 we should all be using a networking system being developed by Sun (who created Java) called Jini. This is a computer program which will link all your household appliances. Your washing machine and refrigerator will then have 'remote' servicing, and talk to one another. Presumably your fridge will also be able to check with your colour printer and electric toothbrush whether more cartridges or a new brush head should be added to your electronic shopping list!

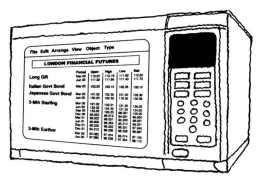

Microwave ovens can now do more than cook your food

CASE STUDY 1.7

The humble shopping trolley seems to be just a functional item. It has a use, full stop. But shopping trolleys are undergoing a revamp, in type as well as style.

There is now a fascinating variety of shopping trolleys. One large, deep trolley for everyone is not enough. Now we have 'zimmer' trolleys for the elderly to save bending, 'estate' trolleys to carry two young children, trolleys with crush proof sections for flowers – and nine other variations!

But many of these are now being discarded. A new bionic trolley has been introduced by Sainsbury's. Made of recyclable plastic, the trolley is lighter and easier to control. They will also last forever, unlike metal trolleys which have a lifespan of seven years.

The new trolleys are also supposed to be kinder – to users and cars. No more snagged tights, nicked ankles or scratched paintwork. Just one question for the designers. Will they be any better at going in a straight line?

Activities

1 Identify the benefits of the new trolley for:
   a   shoppers
   b   Sainsbury's.
2 Is the new trolley more, or less, environmentally friendly? Explain your answer.
3 Sainsbury's plans to produce the plastic trolleys in bright colours. Suggest at least two reasons for this decision.
4 What is meant by the word 'functional'? Use a dictionary to help you.
5 Why do you think the new trolleys are called 'bionic'?
6 As a group, brainstorm the different designs for trolleys you would suggest, in addition to the four which are mentioned. You could always research your answer by examining the various styles at a local supermarket or DIY store!

Section review

Refresh your memory of Section 1.2 by writing short answers to each of the following questions and activities.

1 *A charity aims to recruit more qualified staff next year. Describe three ways in which the human resources function could help them achieve this aim.*

2 *Many companies are keen to offer equal opportunities to their staff and are concerned that they comply with legislation in this area.*

   a   *Which legislation relates to equal opportunities in employment?*
   b   *What steps should be taken to ensure that equal opportunities are available to all existing and future staff?*

3 *Your friend has recently started work in the finance department of a large firm. She says that she is working in the most important area of the organisation.*

   Explain why many people in business would agree with her.

4 a   *What type of resources are needed by all businesses?*

b   *Identify three ways in which these resources would vary between a large factory producing furniture and a furniture retailer.*

5   *Purchasing is an essential function of all manufacturing organisations. Describe two modern methods of purchasing which reduce the storage space required.*

6   *Describe three ways in which the administrative function supports the work of other departments in an organisation.*

7   *A sportswear manufacturer has expansion as one of its aims. In what ways could the marketing and sales function help the company to achieve this?*

8   *Identify four ways in which you could assess whether customer service was effective in an organisation.*

9   *Explain the differences you would expect to find in the customer service function of:*
    a   *a large superstore*
    b   *a firm which sold household appliances.*

10 *Give two examples when each of the following functions may communicate with each other.*
    a   *Production with marketing*
    b   *Finance with marketing*
    c   *Human resources with production*
    d   *Administration with human resources.*

1.3 ORGANISATIONAL STRUCTURE

At the end of this section you should be able to:

- identify the role of an organisational structure in achieving aims and objectives
- understand and create an organisation chart
- compare a flat organisation structure with a hierarchical or matrix one and explain the differences
- identify how an organisation structure is likely to affect functional areas and communication methods.

Overview of organisational structures

Most of us know from experience that several people trying to do something together will end in chaos unless they are organised to do certain tasks. If there are only two of you, for example, making the lunch and feeding the dog, it's easy to divide up the tasks between you. If five of you are trying to make an elaborate meal without knowing who should be doing what, imagine the mess.

In an organisation with dozens of employees, it is important that each member of staff knows exactly what to do, and how this links up with work carried out by other members of staff. People are therefore grouped into functional areas which relate to their job, so that people doing similar jobs work in the same area. These areas are then linked in an overall structure. In a large organisation you are likely to find more functional areas than in a small or medium-sized one. In this case you may find that there are only a few departments performing a variety of functions.

The way in which an organisation is structured is shown on its **organisation chart**. This is a diagram which identifies the different areas and also shows the links between them. In

this section you will learn how to understand and draw organisation charts.

You already know that job roles vary between functional areas. Within a functional area, however, some staff will be more senior than others. In a large organisation there may be several levels of staff in each department from the most senior to the most junior. People would then be more likely to **specialise** in a particular range of activities. In a small organisation there may only be two or three levels of staff who may be expected to do a wider range of tasks.

Understanding why there are differences in structure, how they affect the people who work in the organisation, and how organisational structures change as businesses alter their aims or increase in size, is also covered in this section.

Investigating organisational structures

All businesses try to organise their activities in the best way possible to achieve their aims and objectives. They do this by grouping specific functions into functional areas. These areas are then linked together as parts of the overall organisation structure.

Having an organisation structure is important. Employees know where a particular job is done and by whom. New staff can quickly learn who they should talk to about a particular matter. They can identify the senior people in the organisation and they can see who else works at the same level as themselves.

For management, the organisation structure can be analysed to check that there is no duplication of work and that there are no key activities for which no-one is responsible. They can watch the size of different functions to make sure the amount of work they do is in balance with the organisation as a whole.

The most suitable organisation structure depends on several factors:

- the aims of the business

- the activities undertaken to meet these aims

- the size of the organisation

- the number of employees

- the 'culture' or style of the organisation

- whether the organisation produces goods or offers a service

- the geographical scope of its operations.

There is no 'right' or 'wrong' organisation structure. A structure works if it helps people to do their work efficiently, communicate with each other easily and assists the business to achieve its aims and objectives.

However, aims can change, and when this occurs a business may **restructure**, or reorganise, its structure to meet its new aims. An organisation which increases its range of activities or expands may introduce a new functional area or a new section within a functional area. If it contracts or refocuses its activities it may reduce or remove a section of its operations or even an entire area of work.

Grouping of activities

All organisations arrange staff into groups according to their activities. Those doing similar tasks need to work together. This reduces communication problems and enables staff to help each other. Groupings are usually made according to functional activities. So the main divisions or departments will be the type of activities you studied in Section 1.2.

Figure 1.66 Designers working together

You should be aware, however, that some organisations organise their groupings in other ways, e.g.:

- **By product or specialism**. A retail company or hospital could be arranged by product or specialism. A retail store may have a grocery department, a furniture department and a clothing department. A hospital may have a pediatric (children's) department, a geriatric (old people's) department and a surgical department.

- **By area**. A large national or international company may organise its activities geographically, with different sections dealing with the UK, Europe, South America, Australasia etc.

- **By customer**. An organisation which deals with both commercial and private customers may have two separate divisions, one for each type of customer. This could be appropriate for a service organisation, such as a bank, or for a business which produces goods, such as a telecommunications company. This separation enables each division to concentrate on the needs of their particular customers.

- **By operation or process.** Some organisations have departments based on the part of the process carried out by staff. If you studied a film company you would find it broadly grouped into pre-production activities (casting, obtaining finance, choosing locations), the production work (making the film) and post-production activities (advertising, distribution).

Organisation charts

An organisation chart is a diagram which shows the structure of the organisation. It shows the job titles of employees and their relationship with each. It does not usually include people's names as it would go out of date too quickly. At the top of the chart are the more senior staff. They have more responsibility than those lower down.

- **Horizontal links** on a chart show staff who work at the same level of each other and who relate to each other.

- **Vertical links** on a chart show the staff for whom a particular manager or supervisor is responsible.

As an example, we will examine the chart of a small web site design agency and then compare it with a medium-sized brewery. The two organisations are different in many ways. One offers a service and the other produces goods. One is new and 'high-tech' and the other is in a traditional industry. The number of staff is different and so is the style or 'culture' of the organisation which affects working conditions for employees.

A worked example

Cybernet Ltd

Cybernet is the creation of Tim Bevans. Tim has been a computer whizz-kid since school and, after working for a few years, set up in business himself, offering a web site design service. After twelve months it soon became clear that he could not design the pages quickly enough to keep all his clients satisfied. He needed more staff. He hired Catherine Sutton and Amjad Akhtar to help him. Catherine had substantial IT experience and is a very good graphic designer. Amjad is a superb computer programmer.

The organisation chart for Cybernet is shown in Figure 1.67. Note that we will use names at this stage, even though they are not usually shown on the chart.

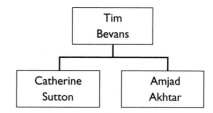

Figure 1.67 Cybernet Ltd – early stages

At this stage there are two levels at Cybernet. Tim is in charge and is at the top. Catherine and Amjad are on the same level, but not as senior as Tim, who is their boss.

Catherine and Amjad work hard and Tim starts to concentrate on generating more business. He is so successful that three years later he has taken on eleven more staff:

- four computer programmers who report to Amjad, who is now the technical manager

- four graphic artists who report to Catherine, who is now the creative manager

- an administration manager, who looks after the accounts and finance, the payroll and all the administrative needs of the business. He has two staff to assist him.

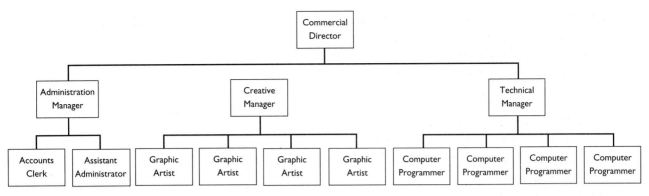

Figure 1.68 Cybernet Ltd – later years

Tim has also decided he needs a proper job title. As he is still concentrating mainly on developing the business and obtaining new clients, he calls himself commercial director.

The organisation chart for Cybernet now is shown in Figure 1.68.

Flat structures

Cybernet has a flat structure. Even though the number of levels has increased from two to three, the overall shape is still flat. A business with a flat structure is likely to

- be relatively small

- operate quite informally, in that everyone will know everyone else and there will be few formal procedures staff have to follow

- have good communications, in that it is easy to speak to other people and find out what you want to know

- be good at responding quickly to new ideas or specific customer requests

- be flexible, in that if the design team has a problem a programmer may be able to help, or if everyone has to work longer to meet an important deadline then this is unlikely to be a problem as everyone will work late and may take time off later to compensate.

Organisations have problems maintaining a flat structure as they expand. At present

Amjad is responsible for four programmers. If Cybernet continued to grow, and more programmers were hired, how many could he supervise properly? Five, ten, twenty? Eventually his job would become impossible and his subordinates would feel neglected.

The technical term for the number of people supervised is **span of control**. A manager may be able to supervise many people doing very routine operations (e.g. packing). If subordinates do complex work then the number which can be supervised properly is reduced. In Amjad's case, probably seven or eight would be the limit.

At this point either another technical manager could be employed or, more likely, the best programmers would be promoted to team leaders and work directly under Amjad. They would have their own staff. So the number of levels would increase by one. If some junior trainees were hired, then the number of levels would increase again. Therefore, the greater the number of staff, the less likely you are to find a flat structure, unless the operations undertaken by staff are very routine and the span of control is quite large.

Deputies and assistants

A deputy is someone who is linked to his/her boss vertically on the organisation chart. An assistant is not and is usually shown linked by a broken horizontal line. This is regardless of job title. So a PA, a secretary or an administrative assistant could all be shown in this way.

Figure 1.69 shows the structure if Guy, a store manager, has an assistant, Joel, and a departmental head, Harvinder. Harvinder is literally 'in line' for Guy's job, whereas Joel is not.

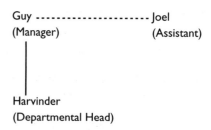

Figure 1.69 Organisation chart of deputies and assistants

ACTIVITY

1 Tim appoints a PA/administrator to assist him at Cybernet. He also adds another computer programmer and another accounts clerk. Draw the new Cybernet chart.

2 Cybernet's aims are to:
   • react swiftly to the challenge of new technological developments
   • continue to expand
   • continually improve the quality of their service to clients.
   Examine the benefits of a flat structure and identify how this structure can help Cybernet to achieve its aims.

3 Assume Cybernet decides to introduce multi-media operations next year. This means employing specialists in this field. As a group, discuss the changes that would most probably take place in the organisation structure.

A worked example

Kingsley Brewery

Kingsley Brewery was established in 1884 and is one of the few remaining independent breweries in the country. The Kingsley family are well-known in the town of Highbridge. Walter Kingsley started the brewery and his three sons all entered the business, as did their sons and one grandson. Today the company is still family-owned. Stephen Kingsley, Walter's grandson, is the managing director. His son and daughter are both directors of the company, which employs 400 people.

Stephen Kingsley is not interested in expanding the brewing business. He has, however, increased the range of operations. As well as brewing beer and lager the company also owns its own range of Kingsley Inns, which is managed by Sarah Kingsley. Sarah is keen to help the company compete against the brewing giants which dominate the market, and feels that owning their own food and drink outlets is the best way forward.

The structure of the company in terms of functional areas is shown in Figure 1.70.

However, each functional area represents a department, which undertakes activities as follows.

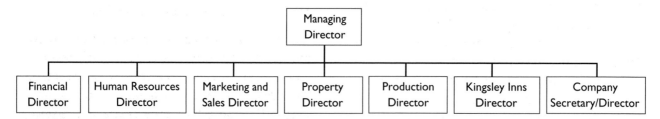

Figure 1.70 Functional areas at Kingsley Breweries

- The financial director is responsible for several accountants, the credit control section, sales invoicing and the recording of purchases.

- The human resources director is responsible for personnel activities, training and security.

- The sales and marketing director is responsible for a large number of staff, including retail sales managers. Advertising is undertaken by an agency.

- The property director is responsible for maintenance of existing properties, surveying and recommending new properties for purchase and refurbishing these.

- The production director (often termed the head brewer) is responsible for brewing operations, packaging, engineering, technical services, quality and distribution. Production is the largest department at Kingsley Brewery.

- Kingsley Inns almost runs as a separate business within the company, with its own operations manager, administration manager and human resources manager.

- The company secretary is responsible for all the legal affairs of the company. In addition his or her department includes the payroll, administration, cleaning, and the IT manager also reports to him.

The organisation chart for the largest department, production, is shown in Figure 1.71.

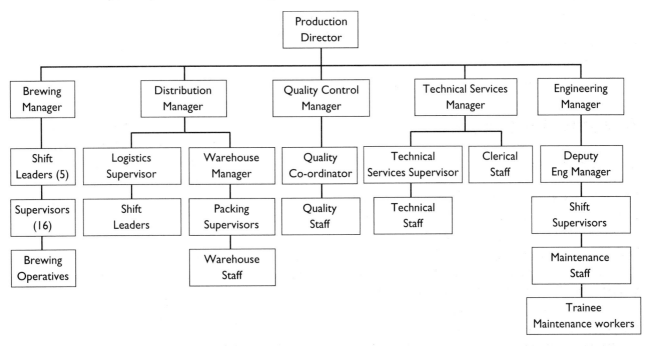

Figure 1.71 The production department at Kingsley Brewery

Hierarchical organisations

A hierarchical organisation is taller than a flat structure. It has many levels. The word 'hierarchy' means 'a system whereby grades or classes are ranked one above the other'. Kingsley Brewery is a hierarchy. If you count the number of levels in the production department (count the longest line) you will see there are **six** levels. And remember that above the production director is the managing director (as shown in Figure 1.70). So there are seven levels altogether.

Hierarchical structures are sometimes called **pyramid structures** because at each level downwards there will be more employees. If you draw this, you will make a pyramid shape. The more hierarchical the structure, the steeper the pyramid.

What differences does having a hierarchical structure mean to the way the organisation operates?

- Each functional area has many staff, each of whom do a particular task. They are more apt to **specialise** in their own job.

- Each person will have an official job title and will probably be on a specific salary scale for that level or grade of job.

- There may be a tendency for departments to operate in isolation unless there are systems and procedures in place for communication to take place *between* departments.

- There are likely to be written policies about hours of work, holidays, punctuality, health and safety, promotion, methods of working etc. This ensures that standards are the same throughout the organisation and no employee can claim that he or she is treated less fairly than anyone else. However, it does mean that there is likely to be less flexibility. You couldn't suddenly take a day off, for instance, without following the correct procedure.

- Communications can become 'distorted' as messages pass from one level to another, so staff at the bottom receive a slightly different message than the one the manager meant them to receive.

- Staff at the bottom may feel the manager at the top has no idea what they think or do.

- Many people may have to be consulted before an important decision is made. This means that the company may be slow to react to changes and challenges.

- The organisation is likely to be more formal, e.g. with a dress code, more traditional ways of working and greater deference to senior staff.

To reduce communication problems the organisation may set up special systems to improve the flow of information and ideas. These are discussed in the next section. However, if the disadvantages are still there, and they are interfering with the aims of the company, then the company may **delayer**. This means removing a whole level of staff from the structure. Today, the tendency is for large companies to reduce the number of layers as much as possible to improve communications and responsiveness – and, in some cases, to reduce staffing costs.

There are, however, benefits to working in a hierarchical structure. These are likely to include:

- a clear job role – you know what you have to do and how to do it

- good promotion prospects – to the next level upwards, and so on

- a clear pay structure

- specified holiday entitlement, pay scales, company pension scheme – you know where you stand

- a large number of colleagues

- a human resources function that will give you guidance and help on your rights as an employee, training opportunities, company benefits, and a whole range of specialist staff to deal with any problems

- a wide range of facilities, e.g. a company canteen, car park, rest rooms, staff social club etc.

- the opportunity to join a union.

An alternative type of structure – matrix

There is one other type of organisation structure which is neither flat or hierarchical. This is called a **matrix** structure. It is often found in organisations that deal with specialised 'one-off' projects, such as aerospace companies or civil engineering companies. For example, a civil engineering company may be working three projects at the same time – constructing a new motorway in the UK, building a bridge abroad and a high-rise bank in London. Think of these as projects A, B and C. In each case there is a project team of experts who see the project through. All these teams need the support of the main functions of the organisation such as finance, human resources, production. The project managers will be in constant contact with the major functional managers about costings, staffing and design. The project teams work on the project until completion, when the team will be disbanded and a new team formed to work on a new project.

In this case the organisation chart is drawn in a different way – see Figure 1.72. You can trace the dotted lines on this to see which person each project manager contacts regularly.

The advantages of this structure are that:

- everyone makes the best possible use of individual specialist skills

- departments such as finance and human resources can have specialist staff to support the project teams

- new teams can easily be formed and included in the structure

- old teams can easily be removed from the structure.

Disadvantages can include:

- possible communication problems between staff in all the different areas.

- drawbacks for staff just specialising in one area, with perhaps no opportunity to get wider experience.

SNAPSHOT

Who's who at the top

By now you know that job titles can vary considerably from one organisation to another. However, when you start work it is useful to know who is the most important person in the organisation! After all, this is the person you have to impress if you want to improve your career prospects.

In a college the chief person is the principal. But the titles are very different in large organisations. American organisations – and a few British – give their top people titles such as president or vice-president. British companies usually favour chief executive or managing director. The chairman of a company is also very important, but is less likely to be involved with the day-to-day operations. Some government-related organisations use the title director general. The government, of course, is headed by the prime minister. On a ship or an airplane the captain is in charge. Wherever you work, you should find out who is at the top, and what their correct name and title is, on day one!

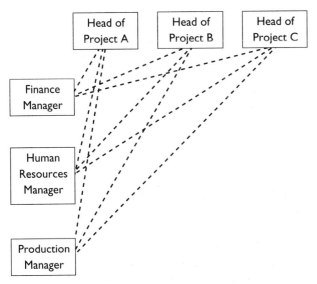

Figure 1.72 A matrix organisation chart

The benefits and limitations of organisation charts

Studying an organisation chart will give you an idea of the business – its size, how formal it is likely to be, how it is likely to operate. However, you should be aware that whilst organisation charts are useful, they also have certain limitations. They won't tell you, for instance, that the trainee manager in finance is married to the managing director's son or that your new boss was transferred from marketing and hates his new job!

Benefits

- You can immediately see the way the company is organised and the functional areas into which it is divided.

- The job titles within each functional area will show you the activities which take place and the type of work which is carried out.

- You can see which staff are:
  - the most senior
  - at the same level
  - managers of other staff
  - subordinates to other staff.

- You can see how many staff each manager has to supervise.

- You can see how many levels there are in the organisation, and you can draw certain conclusions from this. However, you would have to check the degree to which these apply in any organisation you studied.

Limitations

- The organisation chart may not be up to date. You only need one person to leave and not be replaced. Ideally, the chart should be updated regularly.

- You cannot see the informal links between different people and different departments – who is friends with whom,

SNAPSHOT

Ford 2000 – slimmer and fitter

In 1994, the Ford Motor Company announced a major restructure. Management felt that the way the company was organised was out of date, that there was overlap between different operations, high levels of wastage and poor communications. This was reducing profits.

In the 1980s and early 1990s Ford was made up of two similar organisations – one in North America and one in Europe. The American side concentrated on making cars the Americans liked – large, flashy and gas-guzzling. The European side concentrated on making cars for the more restrained Europeans with their smaller roads and expensive fuel.

Environmental concerns have meant that Americans are becoming more 'European' in the size of car they prefer. Europeans, in turn, have learned from the Americans and introduced some of their safety devices and other features into European cars. In other words, the two markets are becoming more similar.

Ford's aim is to merge its two operations to reflect these changes. Ford 2000 will consist of 7 levels, not the old 14 levels. Managers will report both to their geographically specific vehicle centre and to an executive from one of the functional departments of manufacturing, purchasing, marketing and finance.

which people meet socially, who is popular with the boss and who is not.

- You cannot see the **lateral** links between different functional areas. These are the links between departments which were stressed as so important in Section 1.2. None of these are included on organisation charts!

- You cannot tell from the chart whether the style of company is formal or informal, whether management is fair or harsh, whether the organisation would be good to work for, or not.

- You cannot tell who is the best worker, nor who willingly takes on additional

responsibility, nor who is most likely to get the next promotion.

- The chart ignores all informal methods of communication (see Section 1.4).

- The chart does not show the 'power' held by certain groups of staff in particular situations. For instance, the security staff can order the managing director to leave the building if there is a bomb alert. He would be very silly to ignore them! The IT staff can close down the computers in one section of the company if there is a virus – and not even the director in charge would stop them. You should not, therefore, assume that only people at the top of the chart can give instructions or orders!

CASE STUDY 1.8

Jane Richardson is a friend of yours and started work at Cybernet last year. She works mainly on sales administration and keeps a database of customers. Because she is interested in IT work she has started learning HTML, the programming language used to create web pages, and helping out with simple tasks when the programming team is busy.

You have always assumed Cybernet must be a marvellous place to work. There is no dress code – unless you count jeans, trainers and tee-shirts – and staff regularly go the local pizza place at lunchtime. Times are very flexible. Staff can arrive anytime up to 10.30am but they do work late – a 7pm finish isn't unusual. Many of the programmers and designers have computers at home and sometimes work from there, downloading their files onto the company system electronically.

When you next bump into Jane you are amazed when she tells you she is miserable and thinking of changing jobs. She hasn't

had a pay rise since she started and daren't raise the topic with her boss, Keiron Jenkins, the administration manager. She often works late and this has disrupted her social life. For the past three weeks she has also gone to work on Saturdays to help out with a large project with an urgent deadline – but hasn't been paid overtime or offered any time off as compensation. On top of that, Tim has started giving her work as she shows a flair for dealing with clients and Amjad seems to forget she is an administrator and keeps asking her to do programming work. This caused a row with her own boss, Keiron, yesterday, who said she should learn to get her priorities right.

Activities

1 Identify the benefits of working for a small, flexible organisation such as Cybernet.
2 List three disadvantages of working at Cybernet.

CASE STUDY (continued)

3   If Cybernet was larger, and jobs were more specialised, would this solve Jane's problems at all? Give a reason for your answer.

4   Larger organisations are more likely to have formal staffing procedures. How would this approach help Jane?

5   Tim is the commercial director of Cybernet and wants it to continue to expand. As a group:

a   suggest three measures he should take for this to be successful

b   identify three problems he may encounter as the business grows larger.

6   As Jane's friend, what would you suggest and why?

Section review

Check your understanding of this section by writing short answers to each of the following questions and activities.

1   *What do you understand by the term 'business structure'?*

2   *Identify three ways in which companies may structure their activities.*

3   *Clearly explain the difference between a 'flat' organisation structure and one which is 'hierarchical'.*

4   *You have recently changed your job and moved from a very large organisation, which was hierarchical, to a small organisation with a flat structure. What differences might you find as an employee?*

5   *What type of organisation is likely to use a matrix structure?*

6   a   *What is meant by the term* **restructure***?*
    b   *Why is this sometimes necessary?*

7   *Draw a pyramid and then divide it horizontally to identify the different levels at Cybernet. Then repeat the exercise for Kingsley Brewery. Explain the difference in shape you obtain.*

1.4 WORKING TOGETHER – BUSINESS COMMUNICATIONS

Overview of business communications

In any organisation people communicate in many different ways, every single day. They talk at meetings, have group discussions and negotiate over the telephone. They write memos and emails, draft letters and reports and send a faxes in emergencies. They have coffee with colleagues from other departments and exchange news. They chat in the corridor and over the photocopier and gossip with their close friends. They read the staff magazine to see what else is going on.

So what can we learn from communications? How important are they to a business and to the people who work there? How critical are they to the business's aims and objectives? What methods of communication are used and why?

Communication in a business can be both **formal** and **informal**. When employees are doing their jobs communications will be formal and concerned with work. These

include meetings, telephone conversations, writing memos and reports. When they stop for a chat or have lunch with colleagues the communications are informal. These may involve gossip or speculation about other colleagues or the organisation in general.

An effective organisation does not ignore informal communications, nor does it try to prevent them. Instead it uses them to its advantage, as you will see below.

Today staff have more ways of communicating than ever before, largely through advances in technology. Faxes, emails, computer file transmissions, satellite links, video conferencing were all unknown 20 years ago. However, increasing the range of communications does not necessarily increase their effectiveness. The right people have to receive accurate information at the right time, and in the best way, otherwise

Figure 1.73 Informal communication

much of the benefit of communicating will be lost.

This section therefore deals with the vital role communications plays in organisations today and what staff need to know to communicate.

Lines of communication

Formal communications

The way employees formally communicate can be drawn as lines on an organisation chart, which is where the expression 'lines of communication' comes from.

Vertical communications include:

- those which flow **downwards** from senior management. These are likely to include:
  - ○ information for employees
  - ○ instructions for staff
  - ○ encouraging messages or praise for a job well done by a person or team.
- those which flow **upwards** from staff to supervisors or from supervisors to their managers. These may be:
  - ○ feedback on new working methods
  - ○ responses to surveys or questionnaires
  - ○ information on the progress of work
  - ○ suggestion schemes.
- **quasi-vertical** communications, where staff representatives have direct dealings with senior management. Typical examples include trade union negotiations, staff associations and worker councils.

Lateral communications are those which take place between different functional areas – and

which you learned about in the last section, e.g.:

- a meeting between sales and production about the following month's production schedule
- an internal training event run by human resources
- a budget report from finance to production with a request for comments on overspends
- a meeting between all the managers in an organisation to decide next year's aims and objectives.

Informal communications

Lines of informal communication are much harder to draw! You would need to know about the informal network of friends and colleagues within an organisation and how often they may contact one another. The informal links between people is often known as the **grapevine**. News can travel very rapidly on the grapevine, often far more quickly than by formal methods.

Managers need to be aware of this when there is important news or information to tell staff. The danger is that information may 'leak' out and pass along the grapevine before the manager has a chance to tell the staff formally. The problem then is that the informal version may be different from the one management intended! By the time management tell staff formally, many staff will have formed their own views based on the informal version of events.

Managers, however, can use the grapevine to 'test' staff opinion on an idea. If staff react strongly against the idea, then managers can drop it or modify it! If staff are in favour, managers can go ahead. Politicians frequently do this. They leak information to the press about what they may do, and wait to see how the public react before either formally proposing the action they intend to take or rejecting it as something they never planned to do at all!

Lines of communication and organisation structures

In a hierarchical structure, the lines of communication from top to bottom will be longer than in a flat structure. It's likely there will be far less contact between those at the top and those at the bottom. In a small organisation the boss can 'walk the job' and chat to staff both formally and informally. This is virtually impossible in a very large organisation.

Some management experts argue that a good manager should always make a point of getting to know the different parts of an organisation and the people working in them – no matter how big it is. Many managers don't do this, preferring to communicate with colleagues at the same level and with those in their own department. This is

sometimes known as the **ivory tower syndrome**.

In a large organisation these are some of the problems that may occur.

- Senior staff only tell the boss what he/she wants to hear – rather than the truth. This is more likely to happen if managers get blamed for anything that goes wrong and if the boss never talks to employees to get their version. This happened with IBM, some years ago, and Marks & Spencer, more recently. Senior management in both companies lost touch with what the public wanted because they only listened to what those around them were saying, and this was usually what they wanted to hear – good news!

- Communications down the line become distorted by managers giving their own versions to staff. Sometimes this is deliberate, often it is accidental. It is just that each of us has a different version of the same events. If it's accidental, this may be just a case of the individual seeing things in their own particular way.

The links between communications, aims and objectives

It is worth refreshing your memory about the most common aims of business organisations. These are often focused on:

- making a profit
- providing goods or services
- expansion
- improving quality
- beating the competition
- the environment.

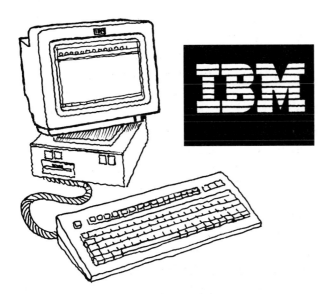

Figure 1.74 IBM is one of the biggest computer companies in the world

To achieve any of these aims it is vital that:

- staff co-operate with each other – within and between functional areas

- the organisation meets the needs of its existing customers and *listens* to what customers are saying – whether they like what they hear or not

- important information is available to all staff as and when they need it

- new developments are communicated to staff quickly

- important issues are discussed with the right specialists present, so that the eventual decision is the best possible one

- relevant information is obtained on topics such as future product developments by competitors and potential new customers

- relevant technological developments which would improve production or quality is passed to the appropriate staff who take action promptly.

It is worth studying one or two of these areas in more detail.

Staff cooperation

You have already learned (see page 72) that some departments may have problems dealing with one another because their internal aims are different. The relationship between sales and production is an obvious example. In an effective organisation differences should be overcome for the good of the organisation as a whole. This requires departments to understand each other's point of view – and this needs a good flow of communications. It's better to talk, as they say.

A constant flow of communication between departments is likely to result in greater cooperation between staff. Regular meetings give staff the chance to discuss problems and get clarification on matters they are not sure about. Views can also be aired. There should also be a regular flow of written communications passing on information staff should know about.

Customer needs

If you telephone a company for information you expect to get accurate information quickly. If you are promised information by post you expect to receive it. If you order something you expect it to arrive on time. You expect the invoice to be accurate and for your payment to be banked. You would not expect reminders to pay long after your cheque had cleared.

To achieve this requires a constant flow of information within the company. Staff handling telephone enquiries need to have good product knowledge. To have this, marketing and sales need to keep them informed about the current range and prices. They need catalogues and price lists to hand – or they need access to the information if they have to write to someone who has made an enquiry. When an order is received it needs to be passed to despatch for the goods to be sent and to finance for an invoice to be issued. Payments need to be recorded properly and this information should be available to credit control clerks.

In other words, the better the flow of information between departments, the more effective the company will be in meeting customer needs. And this is just for standard enquiries! Customer complaints need an exchange of information within a company during the investigation stage so that the issue can be resolved as quickly as possible.

Important information

Important information can relate to general issues or specific matters. A general issue would be the dates the company is closed over Christmas. A specific matter may be a customer change of address or a customer gone out of business. Unless this sort of information is communicated to staff then mistakes will be made. A member of the sales staff who is not told that the company will be closed on a certain day may arrange for a customer to call on that day. Finance, who are not told of a customer's change of address, may send dozens of payment reminders to the old address. This is hardly effective or efficient!

New developments

Situations can change very quickly. For example, a company producing industrial machinery for sale worldwide sends a technician to the Lebanon to repair a faulty machine. Within days war breaks out. The priority is to contact the Foreign Office and get information and help to enable the technician to leave the country as quickly as possible.

Figure 1.75 What's in the mail might make a difference

This is an extreme case, but there are many occasions when being unaware of the latest developments leads to taking the wrong action. This is one reason why most organisations insist on the mail being opened as early as possible – and staff not taking action until they have received their daily updates!

Important issues and the role of specialists

No-one knows everything and no-one is always right. This is why an exchange of information and opinions between several staff who are familiar with a topic usually results in a better decision than only one person would make.

Information needed for making a decision can be obtained in a variety of ways. Meetings can be held to decide a course of action. A manager may ask key staff to prepare a report giving their views. For speed, staff can be asked to give their opinions via email. The collection of information and opinions from different sources is beneficial for the organisation.

Relevant information for business aims

Business aims can only be achieved after several questions have been answered. For example:

- **Environmental aims** – what steps can be taken for the company to become more environmentally aware? How can packaging be changed? What items can be recycled? How can fuel and energy be saved? How will this affect production?

- **Expansion** – what methods of expansion would be best? To what regions or which new countries? Which products should be sold there? How can this best be achieved? What is the culture in that country, what are the preferences of the people, what features would they prefer?

- **Quality** – how can quality be improved? Should the company concentrate on product performance or durability or both? How do competitors' products perform? How much will improving quality affect price? How will this affect sales?

For those directly involved with achieving the aims the more information they have the better. However, it has to be the right information. It must be accurate, up-to-date and relevant to be useful. All key facts must be included. It must be factual and not interpreted to suit the presenter. It must be transmitted to other people in this way, so that they have the correct information to work with.

SNAPSHOT

Information overload

There was a time when a manager arrived at his or her desk, opened the mail, read it and then got on with work. Now there are also emails to read, faxes to look through, messages left on voice mail and computer print-outs. It leaves very little time to do anything else!

*The danger of too much information is that people become stressed or overwhelmed. You feel like that if you get too many handouts or course notes in a day. **Information overload syndrome** is what this is called. It can make staff (and students!) less productive rather than more productive.*

Too much information – particularly if much of it is irrelevant – can cause delays and errors. The wrong information may be included in an important document, simply because it is available and not because it is the right information. Remember this when researching for your case study!

Methods of communication

There are two main categories of communication – spoken (usually called **oral**) and **written**.

- **Oral communication** may be face-to-face (when we meet someone) or over the telephone. If we phone someone and they are unavailable we can leave a message on an answering machine or use voice mail, which is a type of electronic answering service. Many staff carry pagers or bleepers so that they can receive messages at a distance, security guards and engineers may use private radios and many business people and private individuals use mobile phones.

- **Written communications** may be sent by mail or transmitted electronically. They can include illustrations or graphics as well as text. A letter is the most obvious example of a business communication. Others include telephone messages, notices on noticeboards,

Figure 1.76 A range of communication

newsletters and reports. Brochures and catalogues advertising products are also a form of written communication. Documents accompanying a purchase or sale communicate information about the price and the product or service that has been bought.

The method of communication chosen will depend upon various factors:

- the reason for communicating
- the person receiving it
- the urgency of the situation
- the complexity of the message
- whether immediate feedback is required.

The reason

Written communication is usually used if the matter is important or serious. This gives formality to the communication and provides a record of what it contains. For instance, when you received your GCSE results you also got a printed record to use as evidence of your achievements.

The most formal type of written document is usually the business letter or a report. The least formal is an email message.

The recipient

Communication with people inside an organisation is said to be **internal**. Communication with people outside an organisation, such as customers and suppliers, is said to be **external**.

Internal communications include staff meetings, newsletters and internal telephone calls. A **memo** is the internal equivalent of a letter. Emails are often sent internally through a networked computer system.

External communications include business letters, telephone calls, fax messages, advertisements and meetings with customers and clients. Emails may also be sent externally over the Internet and many organisations have web sites carrying information to attract potential customers.

The urgency

Some methods of communicating are more rapid than others. It is quicker to telephone, email or fax someone than send a letter. When urgent documents have to be delivered rapidly many organisations may use a courier service. Another method is to download information from one computer to another. Many newspapers are produced this way – the pages being produced in the newspaper offices and then transmitted electronically for printing.

The complexity

Complex information that needs careful study must be in writing. Company accounts are typed out, as are legal documents. Conditions

Figure 1.77 Documents sometimes need to be sent rapidly

of employment must be written down, so that they can be referred to if there are any disputes between employees and employers involving these conditions.

Feedback

Communicating isn't just about passing on information, it's also about getting responses from whom you are communicating with. These responses are **feedback**. They tell you what someone thinks about something or they provide you with information you want. Feedback from talking to someone face-to-face is better than that from talking to someone on the telephone. You not only hear what they say, you can also see their expressions and gestures. It gives you a better idea as to whether they are being honest with you or telling you the truth.

You can write a letter or email someone you want feedback from – but there is a time delay.

This gives the person time to think about the matter and give a considered response. This has advantages and disadvantages. It is useful if we want someone to think about something carefully, or if they need to find out more information before they can respond. It is not useful if we want to 'test' their reactions quickly, before we say any more.

With other forms of written communication there is no feedback. I cannot tell if you are reading this with interest or half-asleep – and I doubt if you will write and tell me! A notice on a noticeboard is the same – you may read it or you may not – I do not know. All I can do in either case is to try to attract your attention and hope you will keep reading. Advertisements are similar. Unless customers are invited to respond by completing a coupon or form, a business can only use its sales to gauge whether customers are responding or not.

	Oral	Written
Advantages	Rapid Relatively cheap Voice can be used for emphasis or to show feelings Immediate feedback possible Can check listener(s) paying attention Body language (gestures, facial expressions) emphasise meaning and attitude	Has formal authority Provides a permanent record as evidence Can be retained for future reference Can be studied at leisure Can be copied for other people Creates a 'distance' between sender and recipient – useful for difficult communications (e.g. bad news) Can include visual information and colour to aid understanding/emphasis
Disadvantages	Clear speech essential Message must be clear and unambiguous to be understood Person must be able to hear the message without distractions Long or complex messages easily forgotten External factors may distract speaker or listener Can be difficult to handle if open hostility or disagreement shown by listener	Takes time to produce – particularly if long or complex Keyed-in documents need skill to be produced quickly and accurately Will be spoiled by poor command of language, spelling or punctuation Must be legible – may depend on handwriting ability of writer Delivery may take time Permanency may prove a disadvantage if contents are inaccurate, out-of-date or writer later regrets sending message

Figure 1.78 Advantages and disadvantages of oral and written communication

Oral		Written	
Internal	**External**	**Internal**	**External**
Telephone	Telephone	Memo	Letter
Voice mail	Voice mail	Email	Email
Pager or bleeper	Answering machine	Telephone message	Fax
Private radio	Face-to-face conversation	Report	Form
Face-to-face conversation	with caller or visitor	Summary	Catalogue, brochure or price list
with colleague	Meeting	Staff newsletter or magazine	Advertisement
Meeting	Interview	Notice	Invitation
Interview	Presentation	Meetings document	Purchase and sales documents,
Presentation		Business accounts (in a privately	e.g. order, invoice, statement
		funded organisation)	Business accounts (in a publicly
			funded organisation)

Figure 1.79 Methods of communication

Communication methods to which people can respond are known as **two-way** and those to which they cannot are called **one-way**.

A summary of the advantages and disadvantages of oral and written communications is given in Figure 1.78 and a full list of the types of communication methods you would be likely to find in business is given in Figure 1.79.

 **ACTIVITY**

I   Identify which would be the most appropriate method of communication in each of the following situations. Assume you have access to the full range of electronic equipment. You may think that more than one method is appropriate. This can happen, but be prepared to discuss the advantages and disadvantages of each approach.

    a   A hotel has asked you to confirm a reservation you have made over the telephone. It is urgent as your boss is staying there tonight.

    b   You work for a bank which wants to inform a customer that his account is seriously overdrawn.

    c   You urgently need to contact a colleague who is travelling between your office and a customer to tell him the meeting is cancelled.

    d   You wish to inform all staff of the date the new staff car park will be open.

    e   You need to make an urgent dental appointment.

    f   You have been asked to provide some customers with information on the products you sell and their prices.

    g   You want to ask your boss if you can have next Tuesday off work as a day's holiday.

    h   You need to let a colleague have the financial details relating to a customer's account.

    i   You work in human resources and receive a request for a reference for a previous member of staff.

2   Given the frequency of communications in business, excellent communication skills are essential. Electronic mail has increased the importance of this skill as a lack of ability to write well is on screen for anyone to see! A new employee at Cybernet has sent the following email to all staff.

    a   How many errors can you find?

    b   Rewrite the message as you think Paula should have worded it.

From: Paula Marshall
To: Everyone
Date: Wednesday, 31 January 2000
Subject: Missing paper

Can you all please look around for a peace of paper I lost yesterday? It became seperated from the file what I was carrying in the main office. It has information on everyone who payed they're bill last month. I need it quick for the reminder letters I have to sent out in Febuary.

Please help me to find it as its important. Thanks.

3 Check with your tutors that you understand all the different types of communication listed in Figure 1.79. If there are any forms of IT transmission systems you do not understand, remember that you can also check these with your IT tutor. Try to make sure that you see a real fax message, an email and find out how to transmit information electronically.

Section review

You have now reached the end of Section 1.4. Test your memory by writing brief notes on each of the following.

1 *Describe three types of oral communication methods and three types of written methods. Clearly explain an appropriate use for each one.*

2 a *Give two examples of formal communication methods and two examples of communications which are informal.*

   b *What factors would influence your decision in choosing whether to send a formal or informal communication?*

3 a *What do you understand is meant by the term 'grapevine'?*

   b *State one advantage and one disadvantage of the grapevine for the managers of an organisation.*

4 *Feedback is an important aspect of many communications.*

   a *Identify the methods of communication you would use if you needed immediate feedback.*

   b *Give two examples of situations when immediate feedback would be essential.*

5 *In what ways can*

   a *an appropriate organisation structure, and*
   b *a good communication system*

   help a business to achieve its aims and objectives?

1.5 BRINGING IT ALL TOGETHER – PRODUCING A CASE STUDY

At the end of this section you should be able to:

- understand what is meant by a case study
- understand what your case study must include
- research the information you need
- structure and organise your case study
- prepare an effective presentation.

Overview of business case studies

A case study is a type of report which provides an understanding of a business by looking at particular aspects of it. You are required to write a case study as your assessment for this unit. The aim is for you to show your understanding of the content of this unit through your case study. So, if you do not understand something, you should ask your tutor to clarify it.

You must use at least four different ways of presenting information in your case study. Here are examples.

- **Text** is an obvious way – and will comprise most of your written case study. It is obviously much easier if you can prepare your case study using a word processing package.

- **An organisation chart** should be included. If you can use a presentation package then you could do this on computer and integrate it into a word processed document. If integration on your system is difficult, you could include it as an appendix at the end and refer to the chart in the text.

- **An oral presentation** is required to demonstrate your findings on customer services (see page 118).

- A **graphic** would qualify for your fourth method, e.g. a **diagram, table, pie chart, graph, list** or **plan**. You could, for instance, devise a table showing the employees in a particular department and their job role. You could produce a pie chart to show the frequency with which different types of communication methods are used – and so on.

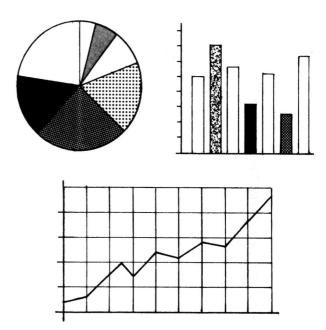

Figure 1.80 Samples of graphics

Organising your case study

First a few do's and don'ts:

DO

- make sure you are clear about the type of information you are meant to obtain.

- talk to your tutor about a suitable business to use for your case study. If you have a part-time job then this business may be suitable. If you are doing or will do work experience as part of your course, then the business you do it in may be better. Or you may be able to visit a business where your family or friends work.

- expect your tutor to discuss with you the resources which will be provided to help you, such as visits to businesses, talks by business people etc.

- select a medium or relatively large business, as you need an organisation which has functional areas/departments you can investigate. You can't do this if you are investigating your local grocery shop!

- talk to your tutor about using certain information from an accepted case study on another organisation if you can't get that kind of information directly from an actual business.

- expect all businesses to be different. Your investigations might produce quite different results from another person in your group – and both may be correct.

- make clear notes, with appropriate headings, and file them neatly. This is especially important if you have obtained the information after visiting a business or talking to someone who works there.

- assemble your information in sections, over time. Planning will be important – so will your time management skills.

DON'T

- expect to be able to produce the whole thing, from start to finish, in about two days and get a good mark!

- be tempted to work with someone else *unless* you have been clearly instructed to do so by your tutor.

- copy information from a book or from the Internet without clearly identifying your source (see page 118). This is known as plagiarism and is heavily penalised.

- panic when you find out you have to give a presentation. Read page 118 instead!

- confuse quantity of information with quality. The more you demonstrate your understanding of the topics and your ability to consider and analyse the information the better. You will also receive high marks if you can show you can work independently and produce original work.

- expect your tutor to do the work for you!

The content and structure of the case study

Your case study must cover all the main areas you have studied in this unit. It may be helpful to complete each of the following areas one at a time, and check you have included all the essential information. This will help you to present the information in a logical order.

Ideally, the sections should be joined together so that they 'flow' naturally from one topic to another. Aim to give your reader a comprehensive overview of the business, but also include detailed insights into specific aspects, such as equal opportunities, methods of communications, organisational structure and all the other key areas given below.

Aims and objectives

Start by describing the kind of business it is, what it does, why it is in business and what it aims to achieve. Even if there are no formal aims and objectives you should be able to find out what the business is aiming to do. If no-one knows then the business isn't going to get very far! It will help if you have covered business activities in Unit 2 when you are doing this, as this will extend your understanding.

Functional areas

You must describe the purposes and activities of four functional areas. One of these *must* be human resources. Customer services should *not* be selected as this is covered later. Bear in mind that human resources and administration may be decentralised in some organisations and carried out by each manager or within each department.

You have to describe the functions that are carried out, why they are carried out and how they operate. This includes identifying the product or service each area provides inside the business and how it links to the products or services available for customers or clients.

You need to be able to identify at least four jobs in each functional area and say what people do – and state which jobs are typical and which are, perhaps, only temporary or short-term. Remember to include information on employer and employee responsibilities.

Don't forget that all functional areas interact with each other *and* with external contacts. You will increase your chances of getting a better grade if you give examples of how and why interaction takes place and how this helps to achieve the aims and objectives of the business. Don't forget to identify the differences between the contributions of the functional areas you are studying.

Equal opportunities and employment legislation

You must be able to describe how the equal opportunities of the employees are safeguarded. Remember to link the legislation outlined in this chapter with the equal opportunities policies published by the business. Then try to find out how these are

put into practice – try to do this by including specific examples to illustrate the points you make. Don't forget that you have learned about four different Acts during your study of this unit (see page 19). Use these to highlight your examples.

Communication methods

You must explain how different functional areas communicate with each other and with external contacts. You must include at least six different types of communication and include both paper-based and technological methods (e.g. fax, email etc.). You must be able to show that you understand *why* different methods are used and when a particular method is the most appropriate. Ideally you could present this in a table and perhaps include some diagrams to show how the information flows from one person to another.

You may find there are differences between the types of communication methods routinely used by different functional areas, or departments. The more clearly you can identify *why* these differences occur, the better. For example, sales may need fast communication to customers whereas human resources may be more concerned with the confidentiality of information. This will influence the method of communication used. Remember to explain how the communications you are discussing help to achieve the business's aims and objectives.

Organisational structure

You need to find out how the organisation is structured. There may be an official organisation chart you can use. If this is too large you could obtain a departmental chart which will be easier to analyse and write about. You also need to compare this structure with a different one and say how these differences affect communications. So, if your chosen business has a hierarchical structure, your contrasting structure should be either a matrix or a flat structure – and vice versa. Don't forget to draw diagrams to show the structures, with lines linking the managers to the staff or the different functional areas. You will find it easier to make the comparison if your organisations are not too dissimilar in size.

Keep your comparison relatively short and concentrate on the main features. For a higher grade, you need to critically analyse the structure of the business you are studying. Are there any weakness or problems? Does the structure help good communications or hinder them? Look back at some of the points made in this chapter for ideas – but only apply those which are appropriate.

Sources of evidence

Your tutor will make various resources available to help you with your case study. You may be given a talk by a manager or employee who works in a particular functional area or department, you may visit a business and talk to the people who work there. Alternatively you may have access to specific business documents or even a specially written case study. You may form into groups and give presentations on specific areas of a business. Finally, you should have done your own research, in your local or college library and on the Internet. The information you gather must be clearly listed, so keep a detailed record of it!

If your source is a magazine or journal, state the title and date of publication. If you have used a book, give the title and author. If you visited a business, state the name of the organisation, the date you got the information and the name and position of the person you spoke to.

Your list does not have to be very long, but should include all the main sources you used.

Presentation on customer services

You will have to investigate a customer services facility and give a presentation on this. You may investigate an outside organisation or the customer services area in your college. You must be able to explain how the business meets customers' expectations. You need to think about what customers expect and to consider what are the major characteristics of good customer service. If you find that the business fails to meet the expectations of some customers then you should recommend improvements. Do make sure these are sensible and realistic – you can hardly suggest they double the staff without thinking of the cost implications! If you think the service is excellent, then find out how the business has achieved this.

Remember that good customer service helps to protect the consumer, who is also protected by laws. You do not have to know these laws unless you are studying the option unit on this topic.

Figure 1.81 Making a presentation

During your investigation you should prepare notes or prompts to help you and OHTs (overhead transparencies) to illustrate your main points. If possible you should prepare these on computer. You should also expect to be asked a few questions after your presentation.

---

10 Golden Rules for Presentations

1 **Check the details** – the exact topic, time, date and location, length of time allowed, whether written information or graphics are required, whether you will have time to answer questions, whether you are working in a team, how to dress, who will be there.

2 **Obtain relevant information** – from printed information, your own notes, asking people who know.

3 **Plan a beginning, a middle and an end** – and order your material accordingly.

4 **Only talk about topics you understand**. If you don't understand something that is essential, have a word with your tutor. Otherwise, leave it out.

5 **Highlight key points and put on 'prompt' cards. NEVER read from your notes.**

6 **Check the room and equipment before preparing visual aids** – and don't be over-ambitious. Three OHTs, produced on computer and printed in colour, are often more effective than an elaborate 3-D model which may fall apart!

7 **Always print OHTs – and check they can be read from the back of the room**. Check, too, how to put them on the machine. Don't leave the machine switched on when you've finished using it.

8 **On the day – start by introducing yourself and SMILE.** If you are the 'front' person for the team, then introduce yourself, then your team.

9 **Stand tall, keep your head up, speak slowly and clearly**. Bonus points if you can sound enthusiastic and interested. *Don't* be tempted to make jokes.

10 **Answer questions honestly**. If you are in a team then answer only when you are asked. However, if someone else is stuck you can justifiably help them out. If you don't know the answer to something, simply say so. No-one is perfect. Don't let it shake your confidence.

Good luck!

Figure 1.82 Golden rules for presentation

A final word – on presentations

The word 'presentation' strikes terror into the hearts of many students – yet it is a very useful skill to learn. In business you may be asked to give a presentation to your colleagues, your boss or to an important customer. You will learn about presentations in 'Communication'. To help, there are 10 golden rules listed in Figure 1.82. Keep these in mind when you are making presentations and you should give more than a passable performance.

Section review

Check you have clearly understood what will be required of you by writing short answers to the questions and activities below.

1   *State the four methods of presenting information you must use in your case study.*

2   *Identify how you see the role of your tutor when you are preparing and writing your case study.*

3   *At this stage, roughly how long do you think it will take you to do the work properly? Give a reason for your answer.*

4   *If you are quoting from any sources of information, what must you do and why?*

5   *Your sister works in a small solicitor's office with three other people. Would it be suitable to base your case study on this business? Give a reason for your answer.*

6   *Why is it sensible to use IT facilities and resources when you are preparing your case study?*

7   *What preparations would you make to ensure you could cope with some basic questions following your presentation?*

No business organisation stands still or operates in isolation. Businesses interact with each other, as well as with their customers. Some produce the components or raw materials that are used in manufacturing by other companies. Others specialise in services, such as transport, financial services, and waste removal.

Businesses are also affected by many external factors, some of them within their control and some of them not. A business may choose to locate in an area it thinks will be good for customer access or passing trade. A competitor may introduce a new product which is more appealing to customers or technologically superior, and this may affect sales.

Customers' needs and tastes change for various reasons – fashion trends, lifestyle changes, increases or decreases in income – and this affects the goods and services they buy. Financial events affect business – as do government policies. A rise in interest rates has two effects. It makes loans more expensive to repay – for both companies and individuals. It also reduces sales, which lowers the profits of many companies. If the pound is strong, foreign holidays and imported goods will be cheaper. This is good for travel companies and importers of raw materials, but not for exporters – because this makes British goods expensive overseas. Public opinion also affects businesses – environmental pressure groups, for instance, have forced some companies into developing environmental policies.

This unit examines all these issues. By the time you have completed it you will know the following.

- There are many different types of business ownership. You will understand why certain businesses have a particular type or ownership and will be able to identify the main features of all the different types as well as the different liabilities of the owners.

- All businesses operate in one or more industrial sectors. You will understand the differences between each sector and current trends in the UK.

- The type of activities carried out by businesses varies. You will know which are emerging and which are declining in the UK and how these trends affect particular businesses.

- Businesses are usually located in a particular place for a reason. You will understand the reasons which influence location and be able to identify why a particular businesses is in a certain location.

- Stakeholders have an influence on business. A stakeholder is someone who has an interest in the business. Customers are one group of stakeholders. You will be able to identify all the different types of stakeholders who affect a particular business and explain their main interests.

What is crucial in this unit is that you must be able to *apply* everything you learn to an investigation of two contrasting businesses. The last section gives you hints, tips and advice on how to do this.

2.1 BUSINESS OWNERSHIP

At the end of this section you should be able to:

- identify the different types of business ownership
- explain the main features, benefits and drawbacks of different forms of ownership
- explain the concepts of business risk and limited liability and apply these concepts to various businesses
- identify the reasons why particular businesses have a certain type of ownership
- apply your knowledge to two contrasting businesses to make effective comparisons.

Overview of business ownership

Many people in the UK own their own business. They include the hairdressers, newsagents, greengrocers, plumbers and decorators in your own area. The manager of your local Benetton or Pizza Hut may own the business, but as a franchise. All these are small businesses and the people who own them actively control operations day to day.

Other people own larger businesses. In some cases they may own and run the business, i.e. control its operations on a day-to-day basis. In other cases, they may never go near the business. Instead they have **shares** in the business and are called **shareholders**. In some organisations the owners leave it up to paid directors to run the business. Some people *jointly* own a business in partnership with other people, such as solicitors or accountants. Other people may set up in a business as a cooperative with no single boss or leader. In some cases, the business may be publically owned and controlled by the state, on behalf of the people.

All these types of ownership exist in the UK. All have particular features, certain strengths and some drawbacks. The type of ownership is often linked to the **scale** and **scope** of the operation. A business which operates on a small scale (i.e. is small in size) and only sells locally will have a different type of ownership than one which operates on a large scale and sells its goods all over the world.

If you were setting up in business yourself – and hoping to expand in the future – you would need to be aware of the options that exist. If you work for an organisation, you should be aware of who exactly owns the business which employs you and how this affects your working environment.

Understanding the different types of business ownership that exist – and why certain types are more appropriate to particular business activities than others – is the focus of this section.

Figure 2.1 A range of businesses

Private ownership

Most organisations in the UK are **privately** owned. This means they are owned by individuals rather than the state or government. In these cases an individual, often known as an **entrepreneur**, takes the **risks** involved with running the business. If the business is successful the owners make a **profit**.

Profit is the reward to owners for the risks they take and for their efforts in running the business. The owners can keep all the profit after paying the business expenses and paying any tax due.

There are four main types of privately owned organisation:

1 **Sole traders** – the smallest type of enterprise.
2 **Partnerships** – where two or more people jointly own the business.
3 **Private limited companies** – the smallest type of incorporated enterprise (see page 129).
4 **Public limited companies** – the largest type of privately owned business.

In addition, there are two other types which are rather less common:

5 **Franchises** – where a large organisation allows an entrepreneur to sell their goods and use their name, for a fee and a share of the profits.
6 **Cooperatives** – where a group of individuals collectively operate a business and share the profits or losses.

Each type of organisation differs in several ways.

- They have different benefits and drawbacks for the owner(s).

- Some are more appropriate for small businesses whereas others are better for large-scale enterprises.

- They obtain their finance from different sources.

- They have different opportunities for, and restrictions on, any potential developments.

- Their legal responsibilities vary.

- They may use and distribute their profits differently.

You need to be aware of all these differences. In each case you will find them outlined after a brief description of each type of enterprise.

Sole traders

This type of business is owned by one person – although he or she may employ other people to work in the business. A sole trader is someone who decides to own and run his or her own business and most probably uses personal savings as capital to start it up. There is therefore just one person taking all the risks. If the firm is successful then the owner's reward is the profit. The owner can

Figure 2.2 A sole trader

keep all the profit after expenses have been paid (called the **net profit**), although he or she must pay income tax on this to the Inland Revenue.

If the business is unsuccessful then the owner loses money. The concept of **unlimited liability** means that the owner may also lose his or her personal possessions and be made bankrupt (see below).

The sole trader can make all the decisions as to how the business is run and is responsible for keeping accounts to show how much profit (or loss) has been made each year.

Benefits for the owner

- Easy to set up – there are no formal procedures to follow, particularly if the sole trader is using his/her own name.

- Ideally suited for offering a personal service to customers.

- Decisions can be put into effect quickly as there is no-one else to consult.

- The sole trader is his or her own boss and does not take orders from anyone else.

- The sole trader can be flexible as to working/opening hours and which days to work.

- Bad (unpaid) debts can be avoided as the customers are usually known to the owner – and most transactions are usually for cash, rather than on credit.

- There is the minimum of paperwork – unless the business is registered for VAT (see page 252).

Drawbacks for the owner

- Long working hours.

- Illness and sickness cause problems – when the business is closed the owner makes no money.

- Highly dependent upon the skills and ability of one person.

- Difficult to raise capital to start up or expand the business.

- The owner has **unlimited liability** for any debts. This means that if the business is unsuccessful the owner may have to sell personal possessions to pay any debts. If some of the debts remain unpaid the owner may be declared bankrupt. It is for this reason that many sole traders prefer to set up a private limited company (see page 129).

- The owner's skills may only relate to his/her specialist area and be poor in relation to running the business and undertaking accounting, marketing and administration activities.

Important facts

1 In law, the sole trader and the business are one and the same. If your hair was ruined by a local hairdresser you would sue the owner, which may be the hairdresser him/herself. When the owner dies, the business ceases to exist.

2 Banks are often reluctant to lend money to sole traders. Usually the business is started with the owner's savings and borrowings from family and friends. Young people may be able to obtain finance through special schemes, such as the Prince's Trust (see page 227).

3 A sole trader can keep all the profit, after paying expenses and income tax. The accounts of the business are private. Always remember that a sole trader is **personally** liable for any unpaid debts. If he or she fails to pay then personal possessions may be taken and the owner declared **bankrupt**.

4 Opportunities for development are likely to be limited because it is difficult to

raise additional capital. The most usual way to expand is to plough the profits back into the business to extend the premises or open more outlets. However, this will depend on the ambition of the owner – many sole traders prefer to operate on a small scale.

5 Typical examples include newsagents, plumbers, hairdressers, beauticians, small retail shops, market traders, small catering outlets (e.g. Chinese restaurants and kebab houses). These do not need huge amounts of money to set up the business, most transactions are cash (i.e. paid at the time) – so there is little danger of large unpaid debts – and providing a personal service is important.

Partnerships

A business partnership is set up by at least two people and up to 20. The partners jointly own the business. This means that

Figure 2.3 A partnership of solicitors

responsibilities and risks are shared by the partners. Partnerships are often formed by people with different skills, so a greater range of services can be offered. In most partnerships, all the partners play an active part in the business. In some partnerships there may be one or more **sleeping partners** who have invested money but do not work in the business on on a day-to-day basis. They usually receive a smaller share of the profit than **active partners**.

It is sensible for the partners to sign a **Deed of Partnership** which sets out the details of the partnership agreement, such as the salary of each partner, the share of the profits each one receives and the procedure to follow if there is a dispute. Whilst this is not a legal requirement, it does save disputes later. All partnerships are governed by the **Partnership Act 1890** which assumes that all partners are equally liable for any debts, unless a Deed of Partnership with different terms has been drawn up.

Benefits for the owners

- Problems can be shared and discussed.

- New skills and ideas can be introduced.

- It is usually easier to raise capital as all the partners contribute.

- There are obvious benefits to be gained from combining the knowledge and expertise of all partners.

- The partners can specialise in their own particular area of expertise (e.g. in a legal practice, one partner may specialise in family law, another in litigation, a third in business law, and so on).

Drawbacks for the owners

- The partners may not always agree or contribute equally.

- The profits must be shared.

- All partners must be consulted before a major decision can be made.

- The partners have **unlimited liability** for any debts, and are therefore personally liable.

- The actions of one partner are binding on all the other partners.

- The death of a partner means the withdrawal of this share of the capital as the money must be paid into his/her estate. For this reason, it is usual to take out a life assurance policy on each partner's life.

Important facts

1 In law, the partners are 'jointly and severally' liable for the actions of each other. This means, for instance, that if one partner ran up debts and then disappeared, the others would be responsible!

2 Partners share the profits equally, unless a different arrangement is specified in the Deed of Partnership. They are all liable to pay income tax on the profits.

3 All the partners have unlimited liability for all debts but the accounts are still private. In a **limited partnership**, which is rare in the UK, the sleeping partners may only be liable for the amount they have invested in the business. In such cases at least one active partner **must** have unlimited liability for all the debts.

4 Financing the business is easier because all partners contribute towards the enterprise. Raising money for expansion is also easier. However, most partnerships are relatively small scale, though there are exceptions. The John Lewis Partnership is the largest in Britain, with its 34,000 employees classed as partners and receiving a share of the profits each year.

5 Typical examples of partnerships are accountants, solicitors, doctors, dentists, veterinary surgeons, estate agents. Many partnerships are in professions where the professional body insists that its members are personally responsible for their actions, e.g. accountants, solicitors and doctors.

SNAPSHOT

Breaking up is hard to do

Starting up in business may be like the start of an adventure – but it's a risky one. The rate of failure for small businesses is high – particularly those run by one person. Those run by at least two people working as a partnership are more likely to be successful than sole traders. However, a recent survey of entrepreneurship (carried out by Dr Thelma Quince at Cambridge University) showed that the level of partnership break-ups was as high as divorce – two out of every five – and just as traumatic for those involved. In every case of the partnership turning sour, the business suffered and often closed down.

Too often, partnerships are started without those involved working out the details. This might lead to disputes as to how profits should be shared out – particularly if one partner is providing the energy and ideas and the other most of the finance. Success is more likely to cause disputes about money.

The Federation of Small Businesses recommend a legal partnership agreement which sorts out profit splitting at the outset and deals with other issues, such as what will happen if one partner wants to leave. If partners think through the main issues from the outset, the partnership is less likely to end in bitterness and disaster.

CASE STUDY 2.1

The British government has been concerned about the relatively low numbers of entrepreneurs in Britain. In America 70 per cent of new jobs since 1993 have been created by new businesses and 1 in 12 people started a business; in Britain only 1 in 30 started a business in that time and only 16 per cent of people believe there are good opportunities to do so in the near future – as against 57 per cent of Americans.

Various reasons have been suggested to explain the difference. In America, it is argued, being an entrepreneur gives status. Ninety-five per cent of Americans respect people who run their own business, whereas in Britain this is as low as 30 per cent. The risk of failure and the shame of possible bankruptcy worry people and stop them taking a chance. Success is not admired in Britain as it is in America, and often arouses resentment in colleagues and friends.

The American Small Business Administration (SBA) is a powerful group which not only supports entrepreneurs financially but also represents their interests through its contacts with the American government – in preventing measures that will create difficulties for small businesses.

Britain is trying. The Small Business Service (SBS) has been set up to represent the interests of small businesses at government level – but is unlikely to be as powerful as the SBA for a long time. The Department of Trade and Industry is looking at changing bankruptcy rules to allow bankrupts to keep up to £20,000 of their money – enough to put down a deposit on a house – and to be discharged from bankruptcy (so they can start another business if they want to) in six months rather than the present three years. Entrepreneurship may be portrayed more positively in schools and colleges in the future.

The experts say that the most important thing is to reduce the amount of red tape which restricts small businesses and costs them money. The Federation of Small Businesses has estimated that employment legislation – such as the national minimum wage, the working time directive and Fairness at Work proposals – has cost small businesses about £220 million a year because of the need to keep more records.

Figure 2.4 Sir Richard Branson, one of Britain's most famous entrepreneurs

Activities

1   What reasons are given for the high success rate of small businesses in America?
2   a   What is 'bankruptcy'?
    b   Why would an entrepreneur fear possible bankruptcy?
    c   How does bankruptcy link up with the concept of unlimited liability?
3   a   What is 'red tape'?

CASE STUDY (continued)

b   What example is given in the case study of a government initiative which is costing small businesses money?

4   It is agreed that partners who have the same values and beliefs have a better chance of running a business successfully than those who do not.

a   What do you understand by the phrase 'values and beliefs'?

b   Can you give an example of some of your own values and beliefs about business?

c   Compare your values and beliefs with others in your group to see whose correspond – and whose do not!

5   As a group, discuss your attitudes to entrepreneurs. Are these positive or negative? How would you feel if one of your friends started a small business and either went bankrupt or made a fortune? Then decide how your views as a group might be different if you were students in an American high school.

Private limited companies

Many private limited companies start out as sole traders or partnerships. They are mostly small-scale operations, often with just family members running the business. They form a limited company to:

a   improve their financial security, as the owners (now called shareholders) are no longer personally liable for their debts. Instead their liability is **limited** to the amount of their own investment. The abbreviation 'Ltd' has to be part of the name of the business. If the business fails, the owners do not go bankrupt. Instead the company goes into **liquidation** (see below). So anyone who lends money or sells goods on credit should check that the business they are dealing with is financially sound.

b   provide a better 'image' to their customers, who are likely to assume the business is more secure (whether it is or not!).

Do remember that many professions will not let their members form this type of enterprise.

A private limited company issues shares to its owners. Each share represents a share of the company and each share equals one vote. Therefore a shareholder with more than half of the shares could always outvote the other shareholders. For this reason, the proportions held are often carefully thought out. Two

Figure 2.5 A garage may be a private limited company

people who wanted to have joint control, for instance, would need to have 50 per cent of the shares each.

Benefits for the owners

- The business can still stay small – many private limited companies have only three or four shareholders (the minimum is one director and one shareholder – there is no upper limit to the number of shareholders).

- The owners, or shareholders, usually work in the business every day and have a vested interest in its success.

- The shareholders are often directors also – and responsible for running the business.

- It is relatively easy to set up a private company (see below) – in some cases the owners may only invest £100 or £200 each to start with.

- Shares can only be transferred with the agreement of all shareholders, and cannot be sold to the public. This gives the owners direct control over the business.

- Banks are more willing to make loans to a limited company – particularly if it has a good financial track record in business.

- Because of **limited liability** the owners can never lose more than they have invested – no matter how much money is owed.

- The accounts are still private between the owners, their accountants and the Inland Revenue.

Drawbacks for the owners

- It is not possible to sell shares to the general public to raise additional capital.

- Limited companies have to comply with more regulations than sole traders or partnerships, for instance they have to register with the Registrar of Companies and have their accounts **audited** (checked) by an accountant. They also have to comply with the requirements of various Companies Acts.

- A limited company is not allowed to trade under the name of an existing company if this is likely to cause any confusion to suppliers or customers.

- If the company ceases trading it must be officially 'wound up' and if the company cannot pay its debts it will go into liquidation, which can be a time-consuming and difficult process.

Important facts

1   An enterprise must follow a set procedure to become limited. This includes drawing up a **Memorandum of Association** and adopting **Articles of Association**. The first relates to the structure of the new company, the second to the way it will operate. The process is quite simplified these days, and can be done by contacting a specialist company registration firm.

2   In a limited company, the organisation has a separate legal identity and is known as a **corporate body**. In other words the company is **incorporated**. You will often see the abbreviation 'Inc' at the end of American company names. The company owns property, employs and pays staff (including the directors), takes legal action and is responsible for its debts. In law, it is like a separate individual. If you break your ankle in Tesco you would sue the company – not the manager. Because the company is legally separate from the owners, it will continue after the death of the latter, until it is formally wound up. Companies are therefore issued a **Certificate of Incorporation** when they are set up –

this is rather like a 'birth certificate' for a company.

3   In a limited company, **corporation tax** is paid on the net profit. The company pays all staff a salary – directors and employees.

4   It is easier to borrow money from a financial institution, such as a commercial bank, particularly if the company has a good financial track record. This enables the company to grow more quickly. Other sources of finance may include local authorities (which control finance for regeneration schemes and European funds for development areas), specialist finance houses and investment banks. Remember, too, that a private limited company can offer shares privately – so additional capital may be raised by selling shares to family members, friends or employees.

5   Theoretically all the profit belongs to the shareholders. However, it is usual for a proportion of it to be ploughed back into the business each year to allow for improvements, replacement of old equipment and/or expansion. The profit is usually distributed according to the proportion of shares held.

Figure 2.6 A limited company can be sued for injury

Figure 2.7 Littlewoods sells through its stores and mail order catalogues

6   Typical examples of small private limited companies in your own area (look through the phone book or Yellow Pages to find examples) may be garages, garden centres, recruitment consultants, caterers, building and heating firms. However, some larger companies choose to remain private. One of the largest private limited companies in England is Littlewoods – famous for its stores, football pools competition and mail order catalogues. This is still a family run firm and privately owned.

Public limited companies

These are the largest type of privately owned enterprise in the UK. Many started as private limited companies and were then **floated** on the Stock Exchange. Floated is the term used when a public limited company is launched. Any person can buy shares in a public limited company – identified by the letters 'plc' after its name. The shareholders in these companies are different from the directors – who are usually free to choose whether or not to own shares. Many directors are simply salaried employees, paid to run the company.

A company must have more than £50,000 before it can 'go public' and must have a satisfactory financial track record. Also, there needs to be enough people interested in buying shares for it to have a successful flotation.

Benefits for the owners

- The major benefit is vastly increased capital as many thousands of people or organisations may buy shares in the company. This makes expansion much easier.

- Some public companies can be quite small – there only needs to be a minimum of two directors and two shareholders.

- Very large public companies can often operate more cheaply than small companies as they operate on **economies of scale**. For instance, they can mass-produce goods for sale and buy in bulk to save money.

- If the company is successful, the shares will increase in value, which will increase the overall value of the company.

Drawbacks for the owners

- A public company must be registered as such with the Registrar of Companies and has many external regulations to comply with. Any problems a company encounters may become news if the press run a story on it.

- An annual general meeting (AGM) must be held each year and all shareholders must be invited. Shareholders who do not agree with the way the company is managed may raise objections or vote against a proposal made by the directors.

- Specific accounts must be prepared each year and these must be audited. Moreover, the accounts must be published so that a 'problem year' cannot be hidden.

- Shareholders will expect to receive a **dividend** in return for their investment. They will also want their shares to increase in value. If the company has a poor year or if the stock market performs poorly and the shares fall in value, shareholders will be tempted to sell, further depressing (lowering) the price. This makes the company vulnerable to a take-over bid as it is then relatively 'cheap' to buy.

- The shareholders may have little interest in the long-term prospects of the company and simply be interested in quick returns on their investment. In these cases their interests are different from those of the directors, who may be looking at the longer-term security of the company.

- The original owner(s) may lose most of their control over the company, even if they retain a substantial number of shares. Sir Richard Branson bought his company back from public ownership because of this!

Important facts

1 Legally, a public limited company is owned by all its shareholders – so its ownership may be constantly changing as shares are bought and sold. Note that most shareholders in the UK are

institutions – pension fund holders, banks, insurance companies, etc. and not private individuals.

2   A public limited company must not only comply with all the requirements of the various Companies Acts, but must also abide by the rules of the Stock Exchange.

3   A public limited company can usually choose from a variety of sources of finance. It may decide to borrow money from a bank or other financial institution. Alternatively, it can raise money by issuing additional shares or by asking for special loans (called **debentures**). Much will depend on why it wants the money and for how long – money raised by selling shares never has to be repaid! However, there is a limit to the number of shares that can be issued, the number depending on the company's financial value.

4   A public limited company may decide to grow quickly by buying up shares in another (usually smaller) company. This is a **take-over**. It does not need to buy all the shares to do this – just enough to give it the controlling vote (theoretically 51%, but in reality often less). Or it may **merge** with another company of similar size to grow bigger.

There are several advantages to a merger. The increased size usually means the company can reduce its operational costs for each unit produced, e.g. if two building societies merge, they can close many of the branch offices they no longer need and save on staff costs. Bulk buying can also save costs. The company may be more financially secure by the pooling of the financial assets of both organisations.

5   The net profit (after tax) is paid out to the shareholders in the form of a dividend, although the company will also put a proportion into its **reserves** each

Figure 2.8 Sainsbury's is a public limited company

year. Some types of shareholders (e.g. preference shareholders) receive a fixed dividend each year. The dividend paid to ordinary shareholders will vary depending upon how much profit there is and how much is required for reserves and re-investment. Deciding on the balance can be critical. Too little dividend and shareholders may sell, too few reserves leaves insufficient money for reinvestment, e.g. to renew outdated machinery and equipment.

6   Typical examples include virtually all the household names you can think of – Marks & Spencer, Tesco, Sainsbury's, ICI, Rolls Royce, Barclays Bank.

ACTIVITY

1   Which type of business would you operate if you:

   a   wanted to give a personal service and there was little financial risk involved b wanted to give a personal service but there was considerable financial risk involved

c were a professional but didn't want to work alone

d have already run a successful company for years and want to expand rapidly?

2 Look through the financial pages of any national newspaper and find the shares that are quoted. You will find these are divided into different sectors. The current share price is shown and you can also check its highest price this year, the lowest, and its change from yesterday. Remember that these are all public limited companies.

3 The net profit of a public company is £11 million. It has 30 million shares. It decides to recommend a dividend of 20p for the year to shareholders, to be paid in two instalments.

a What is the total amount paid out as dividends?

b How much is left for reinvestment?

c Why is reinvestment important?

d As a group, discuss what might happen if the shareholders were dissatisfied with the performance of the company and many people sold their shares.

4 Suggest one reason why each of the following businesses are owned in the way they are and identify two drawbacks for the owners in each case.

a Peacock, James and Butler, architects – partnership

b John Birch, fishmonger – sole trader

c Hillside Garage Ltd – Ford dealership

d Orange plc – mobile phone company which floated in the late 1990s.

5 Read the article 'From entrepreneur to billionaire'.

a Why did Sir Richard Branson decide to float the Virgin group?

b Identify three reasons why Sir Richard did not like running a public limited company in the late 1980s.

SNAPSHOT

From entrepreneur to billionaire

Britain's most famous entrepreneur is Sir Richard Branson, who started in business running a magazine for students. Today, he has an empire, the Virgin Group, worth £3 billion, and covering a range of activities, from hotels and planes to cosmetics and cinemas, from cola and wedding dresses to trains and financial services.

Sir Richard's experiences with 'going public', however, have been chequered – and he details these in his book Losing My Virginity. *In 1986 he floated the Virgin Group to raise money to buy Thorn EMI, the largest record label in Britain.*

The flotation raised £30 million but Branson soon regretted the move. Board meetings had to have formal proceedings and include additional directors nominated by financial institutions. Decision making was slowed down as nothing important could be introduced until all the board had met and agreed. Branson also disliked the British way of paying out large dividends to shareholders rather than ploughing profits back into Virgin for further expansion. He felt his time could be better spent concentrating on running Virgin than pleasing City financial representatives. He also felt the City did not understand how record companies were run and this affected the share price of Virgin.

The stock market crash in October 1987 was the last straw and in July 1988 Branson announced a management buyout of Virgin. This meant borrowing the money so that Branson and his team could buy all the shares back from shareholders. The exercise cost him £300 million and a complete reorganisation of the company, but Branson felt it was worth it – just to retain control again.

Figure 2.9 The Virgin Group is involved in a range of activities

out on your own. It is little wonder, then, that it is so popular! Benetton, Prontoprint, Wimpy, Kentucky Fried Chicken, BSM and Body Shop are all examples of franchises. These are enterprises where a small shop or outlet is run by a **franchisee**, who has been given permission to operate the business by a **franchisor**, the organisation which owns and controls the product or service being sold.

The franchisee gets the benefit of the franchisor's expertise in marketing and operations. The franchisor will often supply the raw materials or stock for sale, provide shop displays and give help and advice to the franchisee, who usually has the exclusive right to operate in a certain geographic area.

The franchisee has the responsibility of running the business on a day-to-day basis and can keep most of the profits. However, he or she must raise most of the capital and pay an initial licensing fee to the franchisor. In addition, the owner must pay a share of the annual profits to the franchisor for the use of the trade name.

Other types of private ownership

Two other types of private ownership exist, but these are rather less common.

- Franchising – which is becoming more popular.
- Cooperative ownership – which is relatively rare in the UK.

Franchises

A franchise is a way of owning a business without taking the normal risks of starting

Figure 2.10 A franchise business

Franchises in Britain are overseen by the British Franchise Association (BFA) which operates a code of conduct for its members.

Franchises also operate in areas other than retail. These include:

- goods and services sold direct to the public, e.g. Tupperware and Dyno-Rod
- production plants, e.g. the bottling and canning of Coca-Cola, Pepsi and Seven-Up
- cable companies, e.g. CableComms
- care services for the very young and the elderly, e.g. Alphabet Zoo and Community Careline Service.

Another form of franchise is that where an individual or organisation is allowed to operate a business on the premises of someone else. A hotel or hospital, for instance, may give a florist permission to open an outlet in their building and charge rent plus a franchise fee (in effect, part of the profits).

Benefits for the owner

- Some authorities say there is less risk than starting in business as a sole trader and a higher survival rate over the first five years. Others say the figures for failure are broadly the same. Much seems to depend on the type of franchise – the most successful are famous names such as Burger King and McDonald's which sell well-known products.
- Selling a known name to the public.
- Advice, guidance and expertise from the franchisor.
- Fewer decisions to make in operating the business.
- Most of the profit is retained by the business owner.

- With a reputable franchisor, there is no competition within a specified area.

Drawbacks for the owner

- Some of the profit has to be paid to the franchisor.
- The owner is not free to make all of his/her own decisions, particularly as to the product range or the prices at which to sell the goods or service.
- Only the franchisor's product(s) or service(s) can be sold.
- The franchisee is largely dependent on the popularity of the franchisor's product or service and the amount of advertising undertaken by the franchisor.
- There is a danger that a franchisee will 'sign up' with a disreputable organisation which takes his/her fee and initial payments for little or no return.
- Long hours and few holidays.
- Business success is dependent on the skill of the franchisee and the strength and dependability of the franchisor. If either are lacking, the business may fail.

Important facts

1 Franchising is often called the 'half-way house' between working for someone else and working for yourself.
2 Franchising costs money which the franchisee needs to borrow or save. The franchisor's initial fee is between £5,000 and £100,000. The more well-known the name, the higher the fee. Franchisees also often need to pay for equipment and stock and to rent premises.
3 The franchisor normally charges between 6 per cent and 8 per cent of sales turnover a year in fees.

4 Banks offer special loan packages to franchisees which are more generous than normal independent start-up loans.

5 The franchisor provides initial training and on-going advice on issues such as staff, raw materials, stock levels etc.

6 A few 'big name' franchises are very successful. However, some disreputable organisations offer franchises to the gullible at a high initial price and with unfavourable contract terms, and some are 'fly-by-night' operations which last only a few months.

SNAPSHOT

Hats off to franchises?

Felicity Draper spotted a gap in the market when she realised her female friends often wanted a hat to wear for a special occasion only, and were unhappy at spending a lot of money for something they would only wear once. She hit on the idea of hiring hats – from basic styles to fancy creations suitable for Ascot and Buckingham Palace garden parties. She also decided to stock a range of accessories, such as handbags and gloves, for her customers.

She opened her first business in the late 1980s, using £1,000 of her savings to buy 80 hats – her first stock. Her business grew quickly and she opened a second shop. To expand quickly she hit on another idea – instead of trying to run dozens of shops she would open a network of franchises. Today she owns five shops of her own and controls 45 franchised outlets.

Cooperatives

What is the difference between Pulp and Oasis? You may give many different answers but it is unlikely that you would know that Oasis' songwriting royalties are split unequally (no prizes for guessing that Noel Gallagher has the biggest share!) whereas Pulp operates as a cooperative.

So, what would be the difference if you were a member of the band? In the case of Oasis you would receive about 13 per cent of the royalties (against Noel's 48 per cent share). If you were a member of Pulp you would receive a straight 20 per cent. Bear in mind there are five members in each band!

Jarvis Cocker, a member of Pulp, has been quoted as saying 'We grew up in South Yorkshire. It's important nobody is richer than anyone else, otherwise it's not going to last, is it?' Conversely, Noel Gallagher argues, 'It's me who is up until 7am writing the album, and a bassline or drum pattern never made a song better.' (Quoted from *Q* magazine).

The principle of worker cooperatives is that there is no boss, that profits are divided equally and that the business is run in the *collective* interests of the workforce.

Figure 2.11 A band can be run as a cooperative

This concept has often been more successful in Europe than it has been in the UK. There are famous and successful worker cooperatives in Spain, France and Switzerland – but few in Britain. People have often wondered why. After completing this section you may have your own opinions.

Benefits for the owners

- Each worker/owner has a share in the business and an equal voice in making decisions as each of them has one vote.

- Each person has an equal share of the profits.

- It is possible to form a limited company as a worker cooperative and to have the protection of limited liability.

- Jobs can be rotated so that everyone can have a turn at doing the pleasant jobs – as well as the less pleasant.

- The workers themselves are not forced to be owners – each worker can decide for him or herself.

Drawbacks for the owners

- Although special forms of finance are available for cooperatives, some organisations (banks, insurance companies etc.) may hesitate about dealing with cooperatives because there is no recognised leader who takes responsibility.

- Suppliers may be reluctant to sell goods on credit for the same reason.

- Job rotation means that some people will do jobs they are not trained, or ill-equipped, to do.

- Decision making can take a long time if everyone is involved.

- Disciplining (or sacking) a poor worker may be difficult if everyone is 'friends together'.

- Good leaders may be stifled and feel they cannot develop their full potential.

- Decisions which are made for the good of the workforce may not be the best for the firm, e.g. a new machine which will produce better quality goods but will make three workers redundant may be rejected.

Important facts

1   The most successful cooperative enterprise in Britain is the CWS (Cooperative Wholesale Society). This organisation has its origins in the days when workers united together to help each other.

2   The CWS is Britain's largest farmer, runs a vast funeral business, a large travel agents' chain, controls the successful Cooperative Bank and CIS financial services division, as well as managing the supermarket Cooperative chain. Its

Figure 2.12 CWS is Britain's best known cooperative business

financial results are not particularly good (apart from the bank), but it argues that it is not just in business to make money, but to do its best for its members (in this case, its customers).

3   Other types of cooperatives include producers who realise there are definite benefits in working together, e.g. dairy farmers. Milk Marque is a dairy farmers' cooperative which handles about 45 per cent of all milk produced in the UK. It buys from farmers and sells to the dairy industry, and is now interested in moving into processing milk for sale.

4   Interflora is another type of cooperative. In this case 2,700 florists are involved and collectively deliver about £80 million worth of flowers each year in the UK.

5   Worker cooperatives are those where groups of workers join together in an enterprise. Some successful mail order companies are worker cooperatives. Others are 'worker buyouts', where a group of workers collectively raised the money to buy a company from their bosses – often when it was being closed and their jobs were threatened.

CASE STUDY 2.2

In the late 1960s, Edmund Potter was an intelligent hippy living in a caravan. Being a hippy he didn't agree with the way conventional businesses were run. He felt that the owners took advantage of their workers, paid them low wages and kept the profits for themselves. He wanted to set up a company that would do two things. It would provide something beneficial for society and it would provide work for other people in the hippy commune.

Today, Delta-T, Edmund Potter's brainchild, is one of only six hi-tech worker cooperatives in the UK. It is owned and run by the staff who work in purpose-built offices outside Cambridge. Delta-T is a scientific instruments company which invented a device that measures the physical environment of growing plants. Thirty people work there and sales turnover is more than £1.5 million a year.

Delta-T has not forsaken Edmund Potter's philosophy. It is not just driven by the profit motive. It will only trade ethically and will not sell to defence or tobacco companies –

even if this means turning down profitable opportunities. It firmly believes in the well-being of its workers and will support them at all times. Needless to say, staff turnover is extremely low. Workers in cooperatives are renowned for sticking together when times are tough – even mutually agreeing a pay cut if this will help. Such tenacity means they

Figure 2.13 Delta-T is still run as a cooperative

CASE STUDY (continued)

should certainly survive and in a world where environmental and ethical issues are becoming more and more important, perhaps the day of the worker cooperative is about to dawn in the UK.

Activities

1 Who owns Delta-T?
2 Explain the meaning of each of the following words. Use a dictionary to help you:
   a ethical
   b forsaken
   c tenacity
   d conventional
   e brainchild
   f philosophy.

3 Identify two aims of Delta-T.
4 Compare Delta-T's stance on profits with that of an ordinary company, such as McDonald's or Virgin. Identify as many differences as you can.
5 Why do you think staff turnover is low at Delta-T? Give a reason for your answer.
6 If times are tough, why is it likely that Delta-T might survive?
7 Why might the future look bright for cooperatives such as Delta-T?
8 If you were particularly bright, hard-working and imaginative, what disadvantages do you think there might be if you worked in a cooperative organisation?

Public ownership

The public sector in Britain relates to all the institutions and organisations which are owned and run by the **state** and are overseen by the government. These include:

- central government offices
- local authorities
- public corporations.

In all these cases the finance, or funding, comes from the government and is raised through taxation. In Britain, the number of public corporations has fallen dramatically in the last 20 years as many of these organisations have been **privatised**, i.e. moved from public to private ownership. As a result the private sector has expanded and the public sector has declined.

The government does hold shares in a number of companies – known as **golden shares** – so that it can prevent them from being bought or taken-over. However, it does not interfere with the way the companies are run on a day-to-day basis.

Central government

There are many government departments, all dealing with different matters at a national level. Each department is overseen by a government minister and has its own budget. Ministers bid for money each year and the amount which is agreed forms part of the main government budget – which is raised from taxes.

The major government departments are listed in Figure 2.14 below.

Department	Responsibilities
HM Treasury	Plans and supervises the spending of all government departments, local authorities and public corporations. Advises the government on economic policy and puts this into effect.
Ministry of Defence (MoD)	Administers the armed forces and implements defence policy.
Department for Education and Employment (DfEE)	Co-ordinates full-time education for under-16s plus further and higher education. Supervises regional employment policies, Learning and Skills Councils (from 2001), employee rights, health and safety (through the Health and Safety Commission), pay and equal opportunities.
Department of the Environment (DoE)	Links with local authorities on local planning and inner cities. Responsible for conservation and environmental protection, including energy efficiency.
Department of Transport (DoT)	Responsible for overseeing airports, coastguards, motorway and trunk road developments, road safety legislation and vehicle licensing.
Department of Trade and Industry (DTI)	Promotes UK exports, gives information and advice to small firms, responsible for company legislation, consumer safety and protection and competition policy. Promotes the use of new technology.
Export Credits Guarantee Department (ECGD)	Assists UK exports by providing insurance to British exporters and guaranteeing repayment to British banks which provide finance for exports.
Foreign and Commonwealth Office	Operates diplomatic missions and embassies worldwide to promote British interests and protect British citizens abroad.
Department of Health (DoH)	Responsible for the operation of the National Health Service and the supervision of social services.
Department of Social Security (DSS)	Responsible for the operation of the social security and benefits system (e.g. child benefit, income support and the social fund).
Home Office	Responsible for the police, probation and prison services and immigration policy.
Ministry of Agriculture, Fisheries and Food (MAFF)	Responsible for agricultural policies (including EU policies), plants, fisheries and forestry as well as food regulations.
HM Customs and Excise	Responsible for the collection and administration of customs and excise duties and VAT.
Board of Inland Revenue	Administers and collects direct taxes – mainly income tax (paid by individuals) and corporation tax (paid by companies).
Department of Culture, Media and Sport	Responsible for broadcasting, films, libraries, sport and tourism. Oversees the National Lottery.

Figure 2.14 Major government departments

Local authorities

Government departments are responsible for overseeing the nation's public services, whereas local authorities are responsible for local public services. The type of local services required can vary a lot – those needed in an inner city or in an area with high unemployment are likely to be very different from those in a rural area or in the shire counties, which have their own needs.

In most areas of the country a two-tier system operates, with a **county council** running major services across a wide area and **district councils** running specific services to smaller communities. Social services would be provided by the county council and refuse collection by the district council. Other services provided by councils include: education, police, highways, fire service, libraries, probation and magistrates' courts, recreation and tourism, environmental health, economic development.

Since 1993, another type of authority has emerged, one with **unitary** status. Blackpool, for example, opted for unitary status, which meant that it was no longer responsible to Lancashire County Council for the services it provides.

The money to provide local government services is obtained mainly from the government through the **Revenue Support Grant**. This money is supplemented by the amount raised through **council tax** and **business rates**. Other income is raised from loans, council house rents and the sale of council services (such as swimming pool charges). The councils also have to publish a budget, which must be issued to every council taxpayer each year.

Public corporations

There are very few public corporations in Britain today. They were at their peak in the immediate post-war years, when many industries were nationalised. This brought them under state ownership, theoretically for the good of the people. Although the state was the owner, each industry operated separately with a chairman and a board responsible for the day-to-day operations of the organisation. An annual report was submitted to parliament and the accounts were published annually for scrutiny by the Public Accounts Committee. The organisation received subsidies and grants from the government (financed by taxation) but was usually expected to pay its way overall.

By the 1980s the burden of supporting many of the public corporations was thought to be too great for taxpayers to bear. Many corporations were then privatised, i.e. converted into public limited companies. Examples are British Telecom, British Aerospace, British Airways and British Gas. Regulatory bodies were appointed to act as 'watchdogs' to monitor their operations. For instance, Ofgem is the regulatory body for gas and electricity suppliers, Oftel for British Telecom.

The main organisations still owned by the state are:

- the Post Office
- the Bank of England
- the British Broadcasting Corporation (BBC).

Why does the state want to own anything at all? Those in favour of state ownership make certain points.

- Private individuals only operate with profit in mind. Therefore they would always want to provide goods and services for the better off and not the poor, and institutions such as the National Health Service would not exist, even if they were socially desirable.

Figure 2.15 The BBC is a public corporation

- Some public services benefit everyone, even though people may be unwilling to pay for them. Also, it would be difficult to charge people separately for their use. Examples include the police and prison service, the legal system and the armed forces.

- The government is the only institution which can effectively 'monitor' the damaging effects of big business's tendency to want to make maximum profits and keep costs to a minimum. This is done through the Department of the Environment (which monitors pollution), the Department of Trade and Industry (which monitors pricing and competition policy as well as health and safety), as well as the legal system itself.

There are certain arguments made in favour of the Post Office, the Bank of England and the BBC.

- If only private postal services existed, letters sent from or to remote areas would be very expensive. With a state system, the charges 'balance out' over the whole country. It is also worth noting that the Post Office is very profitable and the government has benefitted from this service.

- The Bank of England is responsible for the government's finances and implementing its monetary policy. So the government would not want to lose control of what the Bank does.

- The BBC is funded largely through a licence fee which is paid by anyone who owns a radio or television. This means that it doesn't have to compete with commercial radio and TV for the money it needs. There are however worries about whether this leaves the BBC open to interference by the government of the day.

ACTIVITY

1   Many people get confused between the terms **public limited company** and **public sector**. Always remember that *usually* a plc is privately owned but its shares are available to the public. The public sector, on the other hand, comprises those departments and institutions run by the state. Write a brief paragraph to explain the differences clearly and give examples in each case.

2   State two benefits and two drawbacks of public ownership (i.e. ownership by the state).

3   The BBC is publicly owned whereas ITV and BskyB are privately owned. As a group discuss whether this helps the BBC to produce quality programmes – which may be less commercially successful – or not. Or whether the days of quality programmes are really over, and the BBC should move with the times, produce

what the majority of viewers want and raise its money from advertising like everyone else.

4 Read the news article on 'The Post Office – a plc with a difference' and answer the following questions.

   a Why is the Post Office a 'unique' plc?

   b What is a monopoly?

   c Some people think it would be better to privatise the Post Office and sell the shares to the public. Can you think of any advantages and/or disadvantages of this?

SNAPSHOT

The Post Office – a plc with a difference

In the summer of 1999, the government announced that the Post Office would become a unique plc in Britain. It would be a publicly owned public limited company, with the government owning all the shares. The reason for this decision was two-fold. The Post Office wanted greater commercial freedom to operate and to reduce the amount of money it traditionally paid to the Treasury. At the same time, the government had announced that it would keep the PO in the public sector. The new type of plc was a compromise between the two.

Other differences would be the loss of the Post Office's monopoly on mail items costing 50p or less. The chairman of the PO said that being the only provider of this service had meant the PO could provide a next-day service even to remote locations at the same price. Losing the monopoly would open the market to courier firms. It was estimated the PO would lose £100 million of business a year with the change. There were also concerns that after 2003, when state benefits will be paid through bank accounts, there would be job losses in sub-post offices.

Section review

Refresh your memory on the previous section by writing short answers to each of the following questions and activities.

1 *In two or three sentences, explain exactly what is meant by the concept of **unlimited liability**.*

2 *Identify three benefits of being a sole trader and two drawbacks.*

3 *A sole trader decides to expand his business and takes a partner. State three benefits he will gain from this and two disadvantages.*

4 *What does the term **incorporated** mean? Give two examples of incorporated organisations.*

5 *State four differences between a private limited company and a public limited company.*

6 *Give two reasons why a person may be tempted to open a franchise rather than start as a sole trader. Identify three drawbacks of this course of action.*

7 *In two or three sentences explain the concept of a **cooperative** organisation. Identify two benefits and one drawback for the owners.*

8 *In two or three sentences clearly state the differences between private and public ownership.*

9 *In the case of one of the following organisations, state why public ownership is considered desirable:*

   a *the Post Office*

   b *the Bank of England*

   c *the BBC.*

10 *Many famous entrepreneurs started as sole traders – Sir Richard Branson, Anita Roddick, Shami Ahmed. Through what stages might their businesses have passed as they successfully expanded over the years – and why?*

2.2 INDUSTRIAL SECTORS AND BUSINESS ACTIVITIES

At the end of this section you should be able to:

- describe the different industrial sectors in the UK
- explain whether each is growing or shrinking at the present time
- describe the main business activities undertaken by business organisations and identify the core business activity of an enterprise.

Overview of industrial sectors

All industries can be described as belonging to a particular industrial sector. These relate to the stages of production of a particular item. A motor vehicle is a good example of such a product. This single item passes through all three stages of production.

- First, steel for the bodywork is made from iron ore and other minerals and these have to be extracted from the ground. Glass for the windscreen is made from sand and other minerals and these, too, have to be obtained. These activities are known as the **primary** stage of production, where natural resources are obtained from the environment.

- Second, steel has to be manufactured and so does glass. This will be done by manufacturers who then supply a car assembly plant. All these organisations operate at the **secondary** stage of production. This is concerned with manufacturing, processing and assembling finished goods, as well as constructing large items from raw materials (e.g. a bridge or a motorway)

- Finally, the vehicle is sold to you by a retailer. You may have needed a loan to buy it and obtained this from a bank. These organisations operate at the **tertiary** stage of production and provide a service to members of the public.

These three stages can be used to group all the different industries in the UK.

The facts on industrial sectors

The primary sector

The primary sector is concerned with producing or obtaining raw materials. This can often mean extracting natural minerals or natural products. It therefore includes occupations such as farming and agriculture, fishing, mining, forestry and oil and gas drilling.

Figure 2.16 Examples of the different industrial sectors

The secondary sector

The secondary sector is concerned with manufacturing, processing, assembly and construction. Mostly this relates to manufacturers of consumer and industrial goods. A paper mill, a carpet factory, a shipyard and a house builder are all found in this sector.

The tertiary sector

The tertiary sector is often called the **service sector**. It includes all the providers of services to businesses and to individuals, and can be divided into four sections.

- **Public services** (including administration, defence, health, education and personal services such as hairdressers).

- **Financial and business services** (including banks, insurance companies, advertising, law, accountancy).

- **Transport and communication** (including haulage companies, bus and train providers, radio, telecommunications and television companies).

- **Retailing, distribution, hotels and catering** (including shops, distributive services, inns and pubs, fast-food outlets).

Standard industrial classification

A more detailed division of industries is found in the Standard Industrial Classification, which was last revised in 1992. You will often see this listed as SIC 1992. From this you can more precisely break down statistics on employment and production to compare different types of industries over a period of time. You will find this invaluable

if you are trying to find out about trends in different industries. The broad divisions of SIC 92 are shown in Figure 2.17.

Primary sector	
Section A	Agriculture, hunting, forestry
Section B	Fishing (includes hatcheries and fish farms)
Section C	Mining and quarrying (includes coal mines, oil and gas extraction, quarrying, salt production)
Secondary sector	
Section D	All manufacturing industries
Section E	Electricity, gas, steam and water supply industries
Section F	Construction
Tertiary sector	
Section G	Wholesale and retail trade
Section H	Hotels and restaurants
Section I	Transport, storage and communication
Section J	Financial services
Section K	Real estate, renting and business activities
Section L	Public administration and defence, compulsory social security,
Section M	Education
Section N	Health and social work
Section O	Other community, social and personal service activities
Section P/Q	Private households with employed persons, extra-territorial organisations and bodies

Figure 2.17 The broad divisions of SIC 92

Trends in industrial sectors

In the UK today, more people are employed in fast-food restaurants than in all the shipyards, coal mines and steel mills combined. Yet 30 or 40 years ago no-one had heard of pizzas or burgers, and shipyards were booming. Twenty years ago a union activist called Arthur Scargill was fighting for the rights of the miners, ten years ago British Steel was boasting about how well it was doing and Britain still had a car industry. What has happened and what is happening in Britain?

In all countries sectors change. Some expand and others decline. Businesses will only produce goods, or offer a service, that customers want to buy and are prepared to pay for. In other words, there must be a **demand** for the product or service. Moreover, the selling price must be high enough to allow the supplier to make a profit *after* paying all the business expenses. This profit is then the entrepreneur's reward. No-one goes into business for nothing!

If demand increases an industry will expand. A good example today is the mobile phone industry. Because demand for mobile phones has increased more firms have entered the market because there is the opportunity to make a profit. In your own area, you may like to find out how many mobile phone outlets have opened in the last few months or years. If more goods are offered, competition is likely to mean prices will fall and the consumer will benefit.

The opposite also occurs. If demand falls, an industry will decline. Businesses can no longer make a profit and will close down or move into producing or selling other, more profitable, items. Britain used to have a thriving textile industry but foreign imports were cheaper and demand for British goods fell. Today many British manufacturers have closed because they have been unable to compete with cheaper foreign products – from motorbikes to electronic goods.

Factors which influence demand

There are various factors which affect demand for goods and services as well as the price of the product. Remember that if demand falls for an item then retailers will no longer stock it and because retailers no longer order it, manufacturers will stop making it and in turn will no longer need the raw materials they used before. Therefore changes affect all the different sectors of production.

- **Relative prices** – in competitive markets consumers will buy goods they consider to be good value. Someone buying a car, a foreign holiday or a household appliance will compare prices and will usually buy the one considered the best value for money. If a foreign product is much better value than a British one, it is likely to have higher sales.

- **Income and wealth** – if you are broke you may live on baked beans on toast, if you have money to spare you may buy fillet steak or go to a restaurant. The amount of money we have to spend not only affects *how much* we buy, but also *what* we buy.

- **Tastes** – your own personal tastes and preferences are individual to you. We all like different styles of clothes and shoes, for instance. But fashion and trends affect our tastes. So does clever advertising and brand names which promote an 'image'. In Coke vs Pepsi taste tests people preferred Pepsi when blindfold but bought Coke when they were not!

- **Technological developments** – technology not only affects our tastes and preferences, it can also mean that some products become obsolete. Word processors have replaced typewriters and calculators have replaced adding machines. Far fewer people buy firelighters or matches today than they did 50 years ago! Mobile phones are about a tenth the size today of the original versions, computers are faster and more powerful, widescreen and digital televisions are replacing traditional sets, mini-disc players are replacing Sony Walkmans – and so on.

Figure 2.18 Technology has changed our world

- **Population and lifestyles** – changes in population affect demand. An example is that more people are living longer so the demand for retirement homes and nursing homes has increased. People's lifestyles have changed – most people go out to work and fewer women stay at home. They therefore like to buy items which will help them, such as tumble driers, dish washers and pre-prepared ready-meals.

- **Seasonal factors** – few people buy fireworks in February or Christmas cards in June! Demand is also influenced by the weather – a poor summer can destroy trade in many British seaside resorts.

- **Location** – the convenience of obtaining a product or service may influence where you go. Most people prefer a local hairdresser yet many will travel several miles for a special visit to a theme park. Local shops often stock products which are basic necessities or which people don't

want to travel any distance to buy – such as food and alcohol. Hence the popularity of local off-licences and small take-away food outlets.

- **Associated products** (often called **complementary goods**) – if you buy a torch you need batteries, if you have a computer you need floppy disks to back up your work, if you are buying a car you would be sensible to check the price of spares, if you book a foreign holiday you need to order currency. Many goods and services have associated products which you demand because you have bought the first item.

ACTIVITY

1 Identify the most important factor(s) influencing the demand for each of the following products or services:
   a ice cream
   b video recorder
   c visiting the cinema
   d aftershave
   e camera films
   f pasta sauce
   g answering machine
   h diamond ring
   i paperback book.

2 The textile industry in the UK has declined dramatically over the last 30 years because of cheap, imported goods. As a group, identify two textile goods where price is a critical factor and two where you think it is not. How do you explain the difference?

3 There has been a surge of interest in fitness equipment and exercise machines, private gyms and keep fit centres. Thousands of people are on diets and virtually all food manufacturers today produce 'low fat' versions

of food products. People drink diet Coke and bottled water on a regular basis.

a As a group, how do you explain this trend in lifestyles?

b For which products might demand fall as a result?

Identifying trends in a sector or industry

There are two factors you need to consider if you are investigating a sector or an industry. The first is **employment**, the second is **output**.

The government produces a wide range of statistics on industrial sectors in general and industries in particular. The Office of National Statistics regularly produces information on employment in Britain in studies such as its quarterly *Labour Force Survey*. Information on the *Labour Market and Skills Trends* is produced by the Department for Education and Employment (DfEE). In addition, you can access the *Monthly Digest of Statistics* and the *Annual Abstract of Statistics* to find out more about a particular industry. The *Family Expenditure Survey* will tell you how people are currently spending their money. You will find all these publications in your school or college library.

Employment
It is tempting to think that if employment in a sector, or industry, is increasing that the industry is expanding. Equally, you may think that if employment is falling that the industry is declining.

Often this is the case – but not always. Fewer people *will* be employed if an industry is in decline. But fewer people will be employed if machines or computers can now do the work instead or if the individuals who work there are more efficient.

British Steel employs fewer employees today to make more steel than it did 20 years ago –

largely because of technological developments and computerisation. Therefore employment in the sector has been declining (because fewer workers are needed) whilst the amount of steel produced by each worker has been increasing – as you will see in Figure 2.19. This is known as **productivity**. If demand remains the same and productivity per person rises, then the number of workers required will usually fall.

Year	1977	1987	1997
Per employee (tonnes)	114	317	521

Figure 2.19 Productivity in UK steel, 1977–97 (approx. 80% made by British Steel)

Output
Output is the total value of goods produced by a sector or industry and its contribution to the British economy. Obviously if an industry is expanding its contribution should be rising. If an industry is declining its contribution will be falling.

Think of the British economy as a 'household' where each industry is a member making a contribution towards the country as a whole. Some industries provide a large contribution and are 'high earners'. Others contribute a much smaller amount. You also need to be aware of which industries are contributing more each year, and which are contributing less.

Putting employment and output together
These two factors together should give you a good indication of whether a sector is increasing or decreasing. As a starting point, the broad trends by sector are given below, together with a few tables to help you to get used to working with figures. But first, a word of warning about using statistics!

Using statistics

People who don't like working with figures may be nervous of statistics. However, statistics is just a set of numbers to record something specific. It could be the number of people attending a cinema each night, the number of people buying trainers or taking holidays abroad. Looking at the numbers recorded year on year starts to give you a picture of what is happening in Britain.

Some warnings, however!

1   Always make sure you are comparing like with like. Statistics are often given for the UK (Britain plus Northern Ireland) and for Britain (England, Scotland and Wales). Always check which set you are using and stick to them.

2   Statistics which show money can be a problem as you cannot just compare one year with another. This is because of inflation. If you ask your grandparents how much they earned at your age you would be shocked! As an example, the average daily rate for a Saturday worker in 1962 was less than £1 a day. Therefore, adjustments need to be made for inflation to take account of the rise in income over the years.

3   To help, the government often provides non-monetary tables with a **base year** in which an index was set at 100. As an example, the last base year for output was 1995. You then simply need to see whether the figure is greater, or less, than 100 in any year to identify whether the trend is up or down from 1995.

4   The government is constantly updating its figures. So if you are using a different source book from someone else, your figures may not be exactly the same. The same happens if you use a reference book printed in a particular year – as the government may have updated earlier figures as well as adding new ones. Usually, however, the differences are only small ones.

Employment trends

In April 1999 27.36 million people were in employment in the UK across all three industrial sectors – although some were also self-employed. By calculating the number of people in each occupation it is possible to find out the percentage working in each sector. This can then be compared with previous years to identify the broad trends.

Figure 2.20 shows the percentage of people employed in each sector between 1989 and 1997. Identify the trends in each case and remember these when you read the commentary on page 151.

Sector	1989*	1991*	1993*	1995+	1997+
Primary (%)	4.91	4.60	4.27	2.31	1.55
Secondary (%)	27.03	24.24	22.64	22.05	22.55
Tertiary (%)	68.96	71.16	73.09	75.62	75.9

* Based on Standard Industrial Classification 1980
+ Based on Standard Industrial Classification 1992

Derived from *Annual Abstract of Statistics* 1995 and 1999, ONS

Figure 2.20 UK employment by sector, 1989–97

Output trends

Figure 2.21 shows the output for each sector over the same period. This is how much each sector has contributed towards the nation's wealth. You should notice that:

*   output in the primary sector has fluctuated – although the general trend is downwards. However, its contribution is larger than you might expect, given the percentage number of people employed in this sector today.

*   the secondary sector also shows a few fluctuations but a general downward trend. Here the contribution is more in line with the percentage of people employed in the sector.

- the tertiary sector shows a steady increase, apart from a slight decline between 1993 and 1995.

If you have the time, you may like to project the increase in the service sector between 1989 and 1997 and see how many years it will be before the UK earns virtually all its money from the tertiary sector!

Sector	1989	1991	1993	1995	1997
Primary (%)	7.19	7.16	7.02	6.84	6.35
Secondary (%)	31.16	27.48	25.86	26.76	25.73
Tertiary (%)	61.65	65.36	67.12	66.39	67.92

Derived from *Annual Abstract of Statistics* 1995 and 1999, ONS

Figure 2.21 UK output by sector, 1989–97

Commentary on sector trends

Trends in the primary sector

Agriculture is one area where productivity has increased – and this is why the primary sector seems to contribute more than you might expect in terms of output per person. Technological developments have resulted in sophisticated equipment that can cultivate huge amounts of land. Crop seeds and animal husbandry have been improved and developed to give greater yield and fertilisers and pesticides have increased the amount of crops harvested each year. Small farms have virtually disappeared and been replaced by large farming enterprises, assisted by European subsidies. This has meant that Britain is far more self-sufficient in food than it was in the past.

The next development for these enterprises is genetic modification of seeds to improve crop yields still further, but the success of this may depend largely on public opinion, given that many people are opposed to genetic farming – Prince Charles for one – fearing there may be side-effects which are not clearly understood.

North Sea oil counts towards the primary sector and so does natural gas, also extracted largely from the North Sea. However, supplies of both of these will fall in the 21st century as such resources run out.

Coal mining has decreased sharply in Britain. In the last ten years 50,000 jobs and 48 collieries have disappeared. Coal is used to produce electricity but can be imported more cheaply from abroad. Other forms of electricity production are available, such as hydro-electric (from water), nuclear fuel and even wind farming. Gas-fired electricity stations are the most popular, because they are cheaper to build and considered cleaner to run. Coal has been a less popular source of natural fuel given environmental concerns relating to acid rain and clean air. Today fewer homes have coal fires or solid fuel central heating. Gas or electricity are usually the preferred options.

The great fuel question is what will happen when the oil and gas in the North Sea start to run out.

Figure 2.22 Wind power is an alternative energy source

Trends in the secondary sector

The secondary sector includes many different types of manufacturing industries, as well as construction. Both employment and output has shrunk in this sector and the trend has increased in the last 20 years. Many traditional industries, such as shipbuilding and textiles, have almost disappeared, unable to compete with cheap foreign imports. There was 43 per cent less output of textiles in Britain in 1999 than in 1979.

Production of coke, petrol and other fuels is largely unchanged, so too are outputs of food, drink and tobacco, whereas the production of electrical and optical equipment, including computers, has increased by 60 per cent. The paper industry is surviving with some increases in orders – mainly because of the demand from computer users. Engineering figures were boosted by some large aerospace orders in 1999. A further growth industry is UK film production, with the number of films rising steadily throughout the 1990s.

Many factories today are owned by foreign companies and nowhere is this more noticeable than in car production. There are no large-scale British-owned car producers today.

Construction performed well in the late 1990s but there are fears that this is temporary, with a number of 'one-off' millennium projects finishing at the beginning of the new millenium.

One of the problems for Britain is that many of its manufactured goods are sold abroad. If manufacturing continues to decline Britain will be selling fewer goods, and earning less money, in the global market place.

Trends in the tertiary sector

In contrast to the primary and secondary sectors, employment and growth in the service sector have been rising steadily.

Figure 2.23 The financial world keeps on growing

Business services and computing have shown the most dramatic increases, with finance, communications, catering and distribution industries also growing strongly.

In financial and business services, employment increased by an average of 4 per cent a year between 1981 and 1997. Growth is expected to continue but at an average rate of about 2 per cent between now and 2007. Between 1981 and 1997, 1.3 million new jobs were created in public services. The majority of new jobs in this area in the future are expected to be in education and health. Distribution, hotels and catering have grown in the 1990s and this trend is expected to continue as these services benefit when people have more money to spend.

The only tertiary sector area where growth is not predicted is in transport and communication. In the UK most people still prefer to travel by car rather than public transport – which may limit opportunities for growth unless the government introduces measures to force private car drivers off the road. In communications, the sector is increasing but is very keen to improve productivity through increased computerisation, which may affect employment. The growth in the communications industry, as in the spread of mobile phones, has been phenomenal, but experts believe this has now 'peaked'.

In the 1990s the trend in the service sector throughout the European Union was the same. Business services, health care, education, recreational activities and hotels and restaurants together accounted for more than 70 per cent of employment growth between 1994 and 1997.

 ACTIVITY

1   It is predicted that the manufacturing sector will account for less than 20 per cent of UK output by 2010. Do you think this is likely to be correct? Give a reason for your answer.

2   Figure 2.24 shows the output from 1989 to 1997 for all tertiary industries, from the 1995 base year of 100. Rank these services for 1997 in order of growth.

3   Services which employ large numbers of part-time staff, such as hotels and restaurants, may report a large increase in the number of people employed, yet to some people these jobs may not be as 'valuable' as some other jobs.
   a   Why do you think this is the case?
   b   As a group, discuss why you should consider the different types of employment that exist when you are finding out about trends in a particular industry.

4   The number of people employed in each sector for 1998 is given in Figure 2.25. Calculate the percentage in each case. Are the trends discussed so far continuing or is anything changing? Support your answer with numerical examples.

Sector	Employment 1998
Primary	494,000
Secondary	5,079,000
Tertiary	17,664,000
Total	23,237,000

Figure 2.25 UK employment by sector, 1998

	1989	1990	1991	1992	1993	1994	1995	1996	1997
Wholesale/retail	89.4	88.4	86.3	87.5	92.5	97.5	100	103.4	107.5
Hotels and restaurants	106.1	107.5	100.4	96.4	98.5	101.2	100	102.4	104.5
Transport and storage	88.2	87.9	84.4	87.5	89.3	96.3	100	100.7	106.2
Communications	76.8	80.1	79.6	79.5	83.6	90.7	100	110.8	127.6
Financial services	92.3	98.1	98.7	94.2	96.3	97.3	100	104.3	108.9
Real estate, renting, business services	84.1	86.4	84.1	82.6	84.7	93.5	100	106.8	117.4
Public administration/ defence	102.2	103.7	105.6	105	102.9	101.3	100	98.5	97.4
Education	87.8	89.2	92.2	95	95	98.7	100	101.6	103.6
Health and social work	79.7	80.6	86.1	88.6	92.6	95	100	104.4	107.9
Other personal services	81.1	81.5	81.4	83.2	89.7	92.5	100	103.3	108.1

1995 indices = 100

Figure 2.24 Tertiary sector's contribution to the British economy, 1989–97

5   The number of female workers in different industries is shown in Figure 2.26, together with the projected employment figures in 2007.

   a In which industrial sector are the majority of women employed? Can you suggest why this is the case?

   b Identify the industries where the change is forecast to be the greatest and see if you can suggest possible reasons.

	1997	2007
Agriculture	22.2	21.9
Mining and utilities	19.6	21.0
Metals, minerals and chemicals	19.4	19.9
Engineering	21.4	22.2
Other manufacturing	37.9	36.0
Construction	13.8	16.4
Distribution, hotels and catering	55.5	56.3
Transport and communications	26.1	25.8
Financial and business services	53.2	52
Mainly public services	67.5	67.3
Whole economy	**49.7**	**51.7**

Source: *Business Strategies* 1997

Figure 2.26 Percentage of female workers per industry in 1997 and predicted percentage by 2007

6   Check in your college library and find the employment figures for each sector for 1999 and 2000 by looking at the *Annual Abstract of Statistics* for these years. Then identify if any trends have changed and see if you can find out why.

Business activities

Every business has one, or more, business activity. The **core business** activity is the most important activity for the business – and usually generates the largest amount of income. Manchester United Football Club is a notable exception (see page 155) as its income from retailing, merchandising and several other activities is greater than its income from its core activity of playing football. This is very unusual. However, all of Manchester United's activities are concerned with providing a service. This is not the case with all businesses.

SNAPSHOT

The changing face of employment in Britain

In 1990, British Telecom employed 245,000 people. By 1996, that number had fallen to 134,000. Yet telecommunications is a growth industry – so why the fall in jobs? In 1990 the telephone exchanges in Britain were not computerised. Engineers were required to repair faults, switchboard staff were needed to handle directory enquiries, and all these staff needed managers. Computerisation made the vast majority of these staff unnecessary. Getting rid of them reduced BT's wage bills and enabled it to compete more successfully against other companies – such as Cable and Wireless.

BT is not the only organisation – and telecommunications is not the only industry – where such changes have occurred. Banks once employed tellers to count the cash and pay it out over the counter. They also used to close at 3 pm! Today you can take your money from a cash machine at any hour of the day and banks such as Direct Line offer a 24-hour telephone banking service. Retailers used to hire people to price the goods, weigh the produce and calculate the bill. Today barcoding has made these jobs obsolete.

Consumers benefit in several ways. Service is quicker, hours are more flexible, companies have fewer costs and so can reduce the price of their goods. Employment has also increased – even if some jobs don't seem to be very challenging.

Business activities and industrial sectors

You have already seen that businesses operate in the primary, secondary and tertiary sectors. Some operate just in one sector and others in more than one.

A business involved in agriculture, fishing, forestry or mining operates in the primary sector. But a farmer who sells farm produce to the public would also be involved in the service sector – he is both a farmer and a retailer. A bulb grower or fisherman who also sold to the public would be doing the same thing. However, the core business activity in each case is in the primary sector.

A manufacturer operates in the secondary sector. But many manufacturers today operate 'factory shops'. In this case the manufacturer is acting as a retailer and selling to the general public. The core activity is in the secondary sector but the selling activity is in the tertiary sector.

Retailing, transport and communications are all service sector activities. So, too, are other services, such as finance, health care, leisure and sport. However, a retailer producing and selling its own brands of goods also operates in the manufacturing sector – although it will usually pay established manufacturers to perform this operation on its behalf. Marks & Spencer is virtually unique in that it only sells St Michael's products – which are manufactured specifically for its stores. Tesco, Sainsbury's, Asda and other large supermarkets sell their own brands as well as other brands. So does Boots, which sells its own brand cosmetics and pharmaceuticals as well as other brands, whereas your local chemist only sells products made by other organisations. However, in all these cases the core business activity is still retailing.

Finally, some organisations actually operate in all three sectors – although this is unusual.

An oil company which operates rigs in the North Sea and has its own refineries and sells the output through its own chain of garages would operate in all three sectors – primary, secondary and tertiary. It extracts and refines the product and then retails it, which is a service activity.

Identifying the core business activity

It is important to identify the core activity in a particular business. Some businesses are easy – they simply concentrate on one activity – but many try to do other things as well, to maximise their income. For instance, a large supermarket such as Tesco has a core business activity of selling food and household consumable items. But is also sells flowers, newspapers and magazines, tobacco products, clothes, alcohol and, in some larger stores, pharmaceutical products. It also operates as a bank – you can open a savings account with Tesco and pay in or withdraw money when you visit a store. The aim is to provide 'one stop shopping' – where you can get everything you need under one roof. But the core activity is still food and household consumables. This is because changes in demand for the *other* items will affect the overall sales figures far less. If demand for the core activity falls, then the business is in serious trouble.

You can see if this works if you apply it to Manchester United Football Club. If team performance declined then fewer people may be interested in watching them play. If the team was demoted from the Premiership then the club would not be able to charge as much for its tickets so income would fall twice over – from declining sales and from revenue per ticket. There would be less interest in buying club memorabilia. Corporate sponsors may be harder to find. This is why the club's football manager, Sir Alex Ferguson, sees the

Figure 2.27 Manchester United's core business

performance of the team as paramount, as this is the core activity that drives everything else (see also page 73).

Changes to core business

You have already seen that although the primary and secondary sectors are shrinking and the tertiary sector is growing, *within* these sectors the trends may be different for individual industries, depending on changes in consumer demand, the price of imports, increased competition and changes in technology. This type of change can affect decisions made by businesses which may close down uneconomic parts of their operations to concentrate on the areas which are more profitable. This ability to respond to changes in demand is critical for business success and you will learn more about this in the next two sections of this unit.

A business can therefore sensibly decide to move from one core business activity to another. Initially, when demand for an original product or service starts to fall, the company **diversifies** and starts operations in

another area where it perceives increased growth. Over time, this takes over and replaces the first activity. As an example, many traditional fish and chip shops in Britain diversified into selling other foods – pizzas, kebabs, curries, to name but a few. If a particular shop found it was selling very few fish and chips but making more money from its other foods, it may decide to stop making fish and chips altogether. In this case its core activity will still be catering/retailing but it will have changed the type of goods it sells and provides within this area.

Moving from one core business activity to a completely different activity in a different sector would be very unusual, as the owners are unlikely to have much knowledge or expertise in this area. It is like imagining the Manchester United football team becoming farmers or manufacturers! Even Sir Richard Branson, who has expanded Virgin across a wide range of activities, from wedding shops to airlines, financial services to music and mobile phones to holidays, has concentrated on one sector – in this case the tertiary sector. He has also carefully structured the organisation so that each division operates separately and has bought in expertise when needed.

ACTIVITY

1   Define the term 'core business'.

2   A brewery produces beer which it sells in its own pubs.
    a   In which sectors does the brewery operate?
    b   What is the brewery's core business activity?

3   Tesco sold mobile phones in 1999. Is this part of its core business? Give a reason for your answer.

4 Boots plc announced in 1999 that it will start opening shops specialising in men's grooming products in large cities.

   a How would you define Boots' core business activity?

   b Why do you think Boots is interested in opening specialist shops?

   c Do you think this could ever become Boots' core activity? Give a reason for your answer.

5 List six businesses in your own area. Then identify the activities and the sectors in which these businesses are involved. Finally, identify the core business activity of each one and check your answers with your tutor.

Trends affecting business activities

In the previous activity Tesco started selling mobile phones and Boots is moving more strongly into men's grooming. Their activities are therefore changing as they try to perceive what customers now want and need that they can supply. All business activities are subject to change and are affected by various factors including:

- new legislation and standards introduced by the government

- levels of spending by households and businesses

- social trends – which affect *how* people spend their money and time

- technological changes and advances

- competitors entering/leaving the market

- the type of staff they can attract and wage rates.

There are literally dozens of factors which all have a different effect – depending upon the exact business activity in which the firm is involved, its location, type of customers and employees, size, and so on.

SNAPSHOT

Changing the business to meet a challenge

The chief executive at BAA, Mike Hodgkinson, is no stranger to change – which is a good thing. BAA (British Airports Authority) appointed him to steer the company through a difficult time. BAA's core business activity is running national and international airports. During that time capacity has risen from 72 million passengers in 1992 to over 112 million in 1999. At the time of his appointment BAA was facing problems from the loss of duty-free sales. In addition he wants to 'grow' the business by expanding the number of airports which BAA run. He believes BAA can offer its services in managing duty-free contracts across the world after the end of European duty-free.

Retailing is becoming an increasingly important area for BAA which has been at the forefront of developing retail space in airports. The company is also involved in factory-outlet shopping centres and is keen to expand this area, using the Internet as a pre-order service.

BAA also runs the Paddington to Heathrow Express rail service and is looking to sell tickets for that service on the Internet. But for 2006-7 Hodgkinson must also expand services at Heathrow's planned Terminal 5. Unless this is done, he feels that London's airports risk losing substantial amounts of business to foreign airports – both in terms of travel and retail business.

CASE STUDY 2.3

Jones' shoe shop was established in 1910. William Jones was a boot and shoe repairer who made working boots for the men who worked in nearby factories. They needed their boots to last – and often returned them to the shop time and again for repair, before finally buying a new pair. William also made fine Sunday shoes, for when folks dressed in their Sunday best and went to the local church or chapel.

William's son, Frank, worked there as soon as he left school, and took over the business when William retired in 1950. By now Frank's son, Derek, was ready to help out and spotted the new trend of ready-made shoes available through wholesalers. Derek started offering a wider variety of shoes – to men, women and children. As memories of the austerity of the war years started to fade, spending on footwear increased. By the early 1960s the shop was doing a booming trade in selling fashion shoes, and could afford to stop repairing shoes altogether.

When Derek's son, Andrew, started in the business in 1974 he was concerned that sales were steadily falling. Competition from large stores was increasing. People were no longer interested in buying shoes from a local outlet. A few large superstores were opening outside the town and Andrew saw this trend increasing. He could no longer compete against the 'big boys' on price, nor on variety. His own children no longer liked wearing shoes – all they wanted were trainers.

Andrew used this information to change his stocks. He stopped selling formal shoes and concentrated more on casual shoes and trainers. But people who wanted trainers started asking if he sold other items as well – from football shirts to swimming trunks to exercise bikes! Slowly Andrew began to stock more sports goods and reduce his shoe ranges. Today Andrew runs a flourishing sports shop which he is hoping his daughter, Natalie, will take over one day. He often thinks back to old William and wonders what he would think if he saw the shop today!

Activities

1   Identify the main changes that have taken place within Jones' since it was established.

2   How would you describe the core business activity:
    a   in 1915
    b   in 1965
    c   in 1995?

3   As a group, discuss and identify the factors which have influenced the changes at Jones'.

4   William Jones was a sole trader, and so was his son and grandson. Today the shop is run as a private limited company.
    Identify three reasons why Andrew may have decided to change the type of ownership.

5   The shop still operates on a small scale. If Natalie is very ambitious, how could she increase the scale of Jones' operations? Discuss your ideas with your tutor.

6   How many generations of the Jones family will have worked in the business if Natalie starts work there?

Identifying current trends in business activities

This section has been designed to help you to analyse business activities and identify common trends and factors which are influencing businesses today. However, you must remember that all businesses are different – and whilst one might be struggling another may be doing very well.

Social trends

Before you look at trends in different activities it is useful to find out something about the United Kingdom and its inhabitants. How many people work in each particular sector and each individual industry? How has this changed over the years? How do people spend their money? Do they have more to spend these days or less? How do people prefer to spend their leisure time?

 **ACTIVITY**

1   Figure 2.28 gives the average earnings of individuals in Britain. Has this increased or decreased? Now look at the change in retail prices. If you look at the two figures together what conclusions can you draw?

	1981	1994	1995	1996	1997
Average earnings (GB only) £ per week Jan 1990 = 100	124.9	325.7	336.3	351.5	384.5
Retail prices Jan 1987 = 100		74.8	144.1	149.1	152.7	157.5

Figure 2.28 Standard of living in the UK, 1981–97

2   Figure 2.29 shows you how consumers are spending their money. Match this with your

	1988 %	1991 %	1994 %	1998 %
Expenditure on commodities or services				
Housing	17.5	19.4	16.4	15.7
Fuel and power	5.1	4.7	4.6	3.9
Food	18.7	17.8	17.8	17.0
Alcoholic drink	4.5	4.2	4.3	4.1
Tobacco	2.2	2.0	2.0	1.9
Clothing and footwear	7.1	6.1	6.0	6.1
Household goods	7.3	7.8	8.0	8.2
Household services	4.8	5.0	5.3	5.4
Personal goods and services	4.0	3.8	3.8	3.8
Motoring expenditure	12.4	13.2	12.8	14.2
Fares and travel	2.4	2.2	2.3	2.5
Leisure goods	4.7	4.7	4.9	5.0
Leisure services	8.9	8.6	11.0	11.8
Miscellaneous	0.4	0.6	0.8	0.6
Durable goods in households				
Car	66.0	67.8	69.0	69.8
Central heating	76.5	80.5	84.3	88.6
Washing machine	84.6	87.2	89.0	90.6
Refrigerator	98.0	98.2	98.5	99.0*
Fridge/freezer or deep freezer	75.2	81.7	85.7	90.0
Television	98.0	97.9	99.0*	99.0*
Telephone	84.7	88.0	91.1	94.1
Home computer	16.9	18.1	21.5*	29.0
Video recorder	50.2	64.6	76.4	84.1

* estimated percentage
Source: Office of National Statistics

Figure 2.29 Percentage household expenditure in UK, 1988–98

own household and decide whether you think it is representative of your family. Compare your answers with suggestions put forward by other members of your group.

3   Figure 2.30 gives you information on the number of people employed in each individual category of industry in particular sectors. At this stage identify general trends. Where is employment rising the most? Can you think why? Where is it declining? Have you any suggestions to make as to why this is happening? Bear your conclusions in mind as you read the next few pages and look back at this Figure from time to time to refresh your memory.

	1993	1994	1995	1996	1997	1998
SIC 92 **Primary**						
A Agriculture, hunting, forestry	326	292	266	271	268	266
B Fishing		7	6	6	6	6
C Mining and quarrying	91	71	67	74	79	80
E Electric/gas/water	206	191	172	147	148	142
Total Primary	623	561	511	498	501	494
Secondary						
D All manufacturing	3,906	3,923	4,021	4,062	4,107	4,076
F Construction	865	864	838	813	888	1,003
Total Secondary	4,771	4,787	4,859	4,875	4,995	5,079
Tertiary						
G Wholesale/retail	3,562	3,653	3,707	3,767	3,913	4,037
H Hotels and restaurants	1,185	1,198	1,262	1,296	1,307	1,316
I Transport, storage and communications	1,317	1,314	1,307	1,302	1,332	1,389
J Financial services	975	980	998	971	1,028	1,064
K Real estate, renting, business services	2,470	2,484	2,635	2,846	2,930	3,007
L Public administration/defence	1,463	1,441	1,404	1,392	1,363	1,350
M Education	1,829	1,853	1,864	1,864	1,880	1,896
N Health and social work	2,453	2,469	2,511	2,539	2,569	2,582
O–Q Other personal services	965	960	970	995	993	1,023
Total Tertiary	16,219	16,352	16,658	16,972	17,315	17,664
Total all sectors	21,613	21,700	22,028	22,345	22,811	23,237

Where applicable figures have been adjusted for rounding to ensure totals match.

Source: Office of National Statistics

Figure 2.30 UK employment trends by SIC categories, 1993–98

4 The section which follows identifies several of the major changes currently taking place in business activities. Discuss with your tutor the feasibility of different groups studying particular parts of this section in detail and presenting an overview of the findings to the rest of the class – complete with visual aids. Each group should also be responsible for adding at least two new items of information of its own!

Trends and the primary sector

The primary sector comprises agriculture, fishing, forestry and mining. What type of businesses are involved in these activities? If you simply think of farmers and deep sea fishermen you will find this doesn't go far enough. The Standard Industrial Classification 92 includes all the following activities:

Section A   Agriculture, hunting, forestry, crop and vegetable growing, farming, animal boarding and care, forestry and logging.

Section B   Fishing – including fishing, fish hatcheries and fish farms.

Section C   Mining and quarrying – including coal mining, oil and gas extraction, quarrying and salt production.

Facts and figures on the primary sector

This sector includes organisations from very small to the quite large. Independent farmers and growers on their own are small-scale operations, but together they can form a considerable industry – England's apple growers for example produce nearly 200,000 tonnes of fruit a year. Medium-size operations include commercial growers and bulb producers, wheat producers, and organisations such as Highland Timber, a forestry and timber harvesting group which owns land in Wales and Scotland. Coal production used to be large scale but has declined substantially. Today the largest company producing coal in the UK is RJB Mining.

Quarrying can be small and large scale. In the Cotswolds, for instance, quarrying for the distinctive stone of the area is much smaller than it once was. The largest companies – such as Redland, Hanson, Tarmac and Minorco – are involved in quarrying aggregates for road building. Blue Circle Industries is also worth investigating. One of their operations, Blue Circle Cement, is a typical example of a medium/large-scale organisation operating in the primary sector. The largest operations of all are those involved in oil, gas and electricity, but do remember that most of these are not only involved in extraction but also in production and distribution. They do not just operate in the primary sector.

You may find the tables in Figure 2.31 useful in giving key data on the primary sector. However, if you are investigating an

Agricultural output – total value (£ million)

Activity	1981	1991	1995	1997
Farming	2,475	3,532	4,904	3,969
Horticulture	988	1,879	2,010	1,929
Livestock	3,685	5,354	6,502	5,741
Livestock products	2,604	3,280	3,990	3,655

Land held for agricultural use – '000 hectares

	1981	1991	1995	1997
	17,593	18,854	18,746	18,653

Workers employed

	1988	1991	1995	1998
Agriculture, horticulture, forestry, fishing	336,000	326,000	272,000	272,000
Coal mining	86,900	52,300	12,500	7,000
Mining and quarrying, supply of gas electricity and water	446,000	297,000	237,000	222,000

Fuel used for UK electricity generation – million tonnes of coal equivalent

	1991	1995	1997	1999	2001*
Oil	12.9	6.1	4.0	4.0	8.0
Gas	1.0	21.3	36.0	50.0	65.0
Nuclear	29.6	36.3	36.0	36.0	36.0
Hydro	0.7	0.8	0.8	0.8	0.8
Coal	83.5	66.1	52.8	42.4	27.2

*Projected usage

Figure 2.31 Trends in the primary sector

organisation in this sector you will need to find specific figures on that particular industry. A useful starting point is the Ministry of Agriculture, Fisheries and Foods (MAFF) which you can access via the Internet on http://www.open.gov.uk.

Trends to consider

You may like to bear in mind some of the following when you are examining trends in your chosen industry.

• The European Union operates the Common Agricultural Policy (CAP) which costs the EU about $45 billion a year. Under this system farmers receive payments for producing particular goods. In 1997 Britain received $4.99 billion. Not all farmers benefit, however – it depends what they produce. It is estimated that about 80 per cent of the money goes to only 20 per cent of farmers throughout Europe.

- Don't think of farmers as 'low-tech'. In a survey conducted by the National Farmers Union's *NFU Magazine*, one in four farmers rated the mobile phone as the best invention ever. They like it because they can contact their staff, machinery dealers and family from wherever they are. One in five farmers regard home computers a huge help, with 53 per cent owning their own, particularly because they can keep records more easily. 16 per cent yearn for tractor hydraulics and 1 in 10 longs for a baling machine. Many also desire a quad bike to get around more easily!

- Environmental issues are very relevant to the primary sector. In 1997 the government announced a £4 million research programme into problems caused by industrial fishing. Tighter controls have now been introduced to prevent fish stocks being depleted.

- In 1999, the House of Lords ruled that organisations seeking to mine or quarry in new or extended sites would have their applications environmentally assessed before permission was granted. Permission is likely to be refused if a rare habitat is affected or if mining or quarrying would damage the environment.

- Companies have to be careful how they affect the environment as the major pressure groups will take action against them. Useful information on environmental concerns can be obtained by contacting Greenpeace, Friends of the Earth, the Forestry Trust, the Marine Conservation Society, and other environmental organisations.

- Remember primary industries when you see all the Christmas trees on sale this year!

- The weather has a vital influence on primary production and you should look at how the weather has been changing in recent years. English apple growers suffered their worst season for over half a century in 1997 when severe spring frosts and summer hail storms damaged crops. Poor weather in late summer can ruin wheat and barley harvests.

- The British public has taken to gardening *en masse* thanks to the popularity of TV garden programmes. This has boosted the sales of various organisations in the primary sector – given the increased interest in wooden garden furniture, stone building blocks, bulbs and plants. If you want to investigate this further visit your local garden centre or B & Q and find out where all the products on sale actually came from!

- Because oil is still essential to the British economy the government has been concerned at the rising cost of oil exploration. The Treasury has therefore agreed to give tax relief to companies continuing to explore for few deposits of oil in the North Sea. The aim is to encourage exploration and protect jobs.

- In Britain, coal was once the main source of fuel used to produce electricity. Today it is only used to meet peak demands. Gas and electricity produced by hydroelectricity and nuclear energy are now more common. The future for coal is in 'clean coal' which produces lower emissions of pollutants to meet international standards for quality of air. Clean coal can be used in the newer power stations. However the government has so far shown more interest in moving to gas-fired power stations – but gas from the North Sea will not last forever. Many experts argue that the best way forward is to have a sensible energy 'mix' – generating energy from various sources rather than one source or predominantly one source.

- Expect increased investment in new forms of energy – such as solar power and wind farming. Renewable energy sources like these need to be developed in the future.

SNAPSHOT

The future is green and organic

According to the Corporate Intelligence on Retailing, consumption of normal food and drink in Europe is static, however sales of organic produce are booming. The reason? Consumer concerns about food safety, particularly following alarms such as listeria in cheese, BSE in cattle, salmonella in eggs and the scare stores about genetic modification. Intensive farming has never been less popular. There are concerns for the animals and concerns for food safety. One answer would appear to be 'go veggie', another 'go organic'.

Fresh fruit and vegetables, milk and dairy products, cereals and bakery goods are the most common organic products. Organic meat is now a reality – and organic salmon is being farmed in Scotland. Expect the word 'organic' to spread to frozen food, convenience foods, fruit juices and even baby food before too long.

Almost all British retailers are now developing their organic foods businesses – and calling on more and more growers for their produce. Unlike intensive farming methods, organic farming offers opportunities for small farmers. Although costs are higher, consumers have shown they are ready to pay between 20 per cent and 30 per cent more to ensure their food is natural, tasty and safe.

Trends and the secondary sector

The secondary sector includes all those business organisations which manufacture goods. These may be consumer goods or capital goods.

- **Consumer goods.** You might think these are the sort of things we all buy from the supermarket, such as toiletries and food, and use quickly. These consumables are said to be 'fast moving consumer goods' (FMCGs). But consumer goods, such as stationery and raw materials, are also bought by businesses.

- **Capital goods** are meant to last much longer. They are bought much more infrequently. Examples in your home include domestic appliances, furniture and the family car. In business they include machinery, equipment (e.g. boilers and cranes) and vehicles. Computers are technically a capital item – but need replacing regularly because old systems quickly go out of date.

The secondary sector includes two other types of industries. According to SIC 92, the categories are:

Section D	All manufacturing industries.
Section E	Electricity, gas, steam and hot water supply, e.g. production and distribution of electricity, manufacture of gas, water collection and distribution. All these industries are commonly regarded as the **energy** industries.
Section F	Construction, e.g. buildings for commercial and domestic use, highways, roads, sports facilities.

Facts and figures on manufacturing in the UK

The extent of manufacturing – and how it is classified – in the UK is shown in Figure 2.32. This also identifies the number of employees in each different type of manufacturing industry in 1993 and 1998.

You can see that the trends for different manufacturers are not the same. Some industries are increasing the number of people they employ and others are decreasing. If you broadly accept that this identifies the growth and/or decline in certain manufacturing industries, you can see, for

SIC sub-group	Category	1993	1998
DA	Manufacture of food products, beverages and tobacco, e.g. meat and poultry, fish freezing, vegetable preserving, dairy food manufacture, breakfast cereals, pet foods, bread, wines, beer and tobacco.	458	448
DB	Manufacture of textiles and textile products, e.g. weaving, finishing of cotton and woollen goods, carpets, knitted articles, leather clothes.	359	331
DC	Manufacture of leather and leather products, e.g. handbags, luggage and footwear.	47	33
DD	Manufacture of wood and wood products except furniture, e.g. wooden containers and veneer.	88	88
DE	Manufacture of pulp paper and paper products, publishing and printing and reproduction of recorded media, e.g. corrugated paper, cartons, paper stationery, wallpaper, book and newspaper publishing, sound recording, video recording, computer media.	445	473
DF	Manufacture of coke, refined petroleum products and nuclear fuel.	40	31
DG	Manufacture of chemicals, chemical products and man-made fibres, e.g. industrial gases, dyes, fertilisers, plastics, paints, soap, detergents, pharmaceuticals, perfumes, explosives.	257	241
DH	Manufacture of rubber and plastic products, e.g. rubber tyres, plastic tubes and packing goods, plastic floor coverings.	192	225
DI	Manufacture of other non-metallic mineral products, e.g. glass and glass products, ceramic goods and tiles, bricks, cement, plaster.	146	145
DJ	Manufacture of basic metals and fabricated metal products, e.g. iron and steel tubes, aluminium, lead, zinc, tin and copper production, radiators, boilers, cutlery, tools, wire products, chains and springs.	545	564
DK	Manufacture of machinery and equipment not classified elsewhere, e.g. pumps, compressors, furnaces, ventilation equipment, tractors, machine tools, weapons, domestic appliances.	387	394
DL	Manufacture of electrical and optical equipment plus office machinery and computers and electrical machinery, e.g. information processing equipment, lighting equipment, electric batteries, televisions, radios, videos, medical equipment, surgical equipment, watches and clocks.	433	508
DM	Manufacture of transport equipment including motor vehicles, trailers and semi-trailers, e.g. cars, coach bodies, caravans, parts and accessories, ships and boats, railway locomotives, aircraft, spacecraft, motorcycles and bicycles.	345	401
DN	Manufacturing not classified elsewhere, manufacture of furniture and recycling, e.g. chairs, office and shop furniture, kitchen furniture, jewellery, musical instruments, sports goods, games and toys, brooms and brushes, recycling of scrap metal.	165	191

Source: *ONS Statistics*

Figure 2.32 Employees in manufacturing (000's)

example, that textiles are declining (through cheap imports) whereas paper and printed media is increasing. This is said to be largely due to the demands of computer users printing out information. Global paper demand has tripled in the last few years. In 1998 the UK used 11.5 million tonnes of paper, compared to 8.7 million tonnes in 1988! So much for the paperless office dreamed about by computer boffins 20 years ago!

The scale of manufacturing varies enormously. Very large organisations operate on a global scale – these are most likely to be oil producers and refiners (Shell and BP, for instance), motor vehicle manufacturers (Ford, General Motors), drug companies (Glaxo, SmithKline Beecham). There are literally tens of thousands of medium-sized manufacturers in Britain, often producing machinery and equipment, and small-scale producers with fewer than 50 employees.

In some cases, smaller scale enterprises have been more successful than larger ones. In Scotland, the cashmere industry is thriving with a number of small manufacturing units. The days of the giant textile producers are over.

Methods of operation have also changed. Technology has altered almost everything – from the way in which televisions are assembled to the way in which sandwiches are produced. Only in a few specialist industries, such as watchmaking or bespoke furniture manufacture, are craftspeople still required.

Trends to consider

- In 1979, manufacturing in the UK accounted for 26.5 per cent of national output. In 1999 it was 22 per cent. Employment has fallen even more sharply because of computerisation affecting productivity.

- The structure of industry has changed. Heavy engineering, ship-building and textiles have given way to assembly line jobs, and much of the manufacturing is done overseas. As an example, in 1999 P & O, the shipping company, ordered five new cruise vessels at a cost of £1.24 billion – two from Japan, two from France and one from Italy. Cruising in Britain is growing by 20 per cent a year, so many companies are likely to be ordering new vessels. Whether these will be made in Britain is uncertain. P & O argues that UK yards lack the design capability – a claim the Confederation of Shipbuilding and Engineering Union rejects.

- Overall, engineering has been the worst performer in all the manufacturing sectors – except for companies which operate in a niche market. Rolls-Royce Motors reported sales up 13 per cent worldwide and up 36 per cent in Britain at a time when most engineering businesses were suffering. Most engineering companies are small and export most of their goods. They are very vulnerable to changes in currency rates – if the pound is strong then they find it more difficult to sell abroad as their products are more expensive.

- Mass market goods are produced more cheaply in the Far East. As a result successful manufacturers in Britain are those concentrating on innovation and high-tech products – or niche markets. Traditional Weatherwear, in Cumbernauld, makes mackintoshes and demand has been so strong that the company has quadrupled its employees in the last four years. The company is currently turning away customers because of a shortage of skilled labour, however a new taskforce of apprentices should be trained and ready to produce by now.

- The Silicon Sector is the name given to semi-conductor plants, such as Motorola, Philips and Fujitsu. These operate all over the UK producing 'chips' for the electronics industry. The future is debatable as their success is dependent upon the price of chips in the world market – and the Far East can make them more cheaply.

- Silicon Fen, on the other hand, is a hi-tech cluster of manufacturers and entrepreneurs operating in Cambridgeshire. Over 700 new technology companies have created over 30,000 jobs. There is collaboration between business leaders, academics and local councils in attracting hi-tech industries to the area.

- Traditional industries have had to rethink their product lines. The Silver Cross factory in Leeds closed after 122 years of making streamlined perambulators for the royal family, as well as for the offspring of the rich and famous, such as Madonna and Jerry Hall. To the horror of traditional beer drinkers, 'real ale' breweries have closed one by one – taken over by larger, national organisations.

Figure 2.33 Silicon Fen in Cambridgeshire

- The North and Midlands have been most badly hit, but London and the south-east have also been affected. Shell, for example, closed its headquarters in the Strand and made 2,000 staff redundant.

- Most jobs lost in manufacturing are full time, relatively highly paid and predominantly male. Employment losses have been the most severe in metals, minerals and chemicals, and engineering. Greater London has lost the most manufacturing jobs. In 1997 there were 170,000 fewer manufacturing jobs in London than in 1987. There was also a large fall in the rest of the south-east.

- Between 1997 and 2007 employment is predicted to fall by a further 23.3 per cent in metals, minerals and chemicals, by a further 24.9 per cent in engineering and by 4.7 per cent in manufacturing industries in general. At the same time, however, productivity is forecast to increase.

- Many traditional breweries have closed – Vaux brewery in Sunderland is an example. Since 1976 more than 20 breweries have gone out of business – and the pace is quickening. In some cases this is because 'traditional ale' is more expensive to brew, in others it is because the trend is often towards lager and wine rather than beer. The under-24s are reputed to drink more alcohol today than any other age group, but prefer well-known brands, and balance going to the pub with going to the gym! You may have your own views on this. You may also like to consider the effect of drink/driving laws plus the increased popularity of wine shops and supermarkets as sales outlets for alcohol.

- Britain no longer owns a mass production motor manufacturing company. However, there are niche market producers, such as TVR and Reliant – which makes the three-wheeler Robin. There is quite a long waiting list for the Reliant Robin these days – over twelve months. Apparently it is becoming popular with environmentally-aware young people.

- Digitisation is affecting consumer electronics, e.g. digital televisions, digital cameras, DVDs (digital versatile discs), mini-disc players. Philips claims that DVD video sales are ten times higher than those of the compact disc at the same stage of its life. Another advance is the flat-screen TV set. Such technological advances affect manufacturers and the retailers who sell the products. Do you think your local video shop will still be in business in 10 years if video on demand becomes more available?

- Many manufacturers make products for the home consumer market – such as kitchen and bathroom manufacturers, furniture producers, carpet firms etc. If consumer spending is high because employment is high and if consumers have confidence in the future, then these type of manufacturers generally do well. If consumers stop spending, they have serious problems. Find out by looking at the retail sales index and see if this is increasing or falling – then look at which manufacturers must be affected.

- The defence industry's fortunes can be estimated by looking at government expenditure on defence – which has been reduced substantially year after year. The cessation of hostilities with other countries also affects them. British Aerospace is working to boost earnings by saving £80 million annually on costs by using more advanced manufacturing processes to halve the time needed to build a Tornado from 3 years to 18

months. However, these advances will affect employment. In 1992 the company employed 63,600 people, in 1998 it was 47,900. Expect it to be nearer 45,000 (or less) by the time you read this.

- Drug companies making stop-smoking aids are doing well. Smokers currently spent £70 million on nicotine replacement therapy. Some companies are researching drugs which will help smokers stop their craving overnight.

- Finally, the number of trains being ordered by operating companies has tripled since privatisation. In the four years to 1997, only 1,043 were ordered. Currently 2,236 vehicles are on order for delivery by 2002. The value of the orders is up from £889 million to £2.3 billion. The most ambitious order is a £920 million request for new tilting trains and modern rolling stock for the west coast main line and cross-country routes between Aberdeen and Penzance – both operated by Virgin.

Figure 2.34 With fewer enemies to fight Britain's defence industry has declined

Trends in other secondary industries

- The energy industries have been merging because it makes their costs lower. Deregulation has opened up the market – you can now buy gas from your electricity supplier and vice versa!

- According to figures released by the Public and Corporate Economic Consultants, 383,000 people are employed in oil and gas in the UK, with 35 per cent of the jobs in Scotland and 24 per cent in the south-east. Offshore oil and gas companies are worried the government may increase their taxes – which would increase their costs at a time when oil prices are low. This may put at least 10,000 UK jobs at risk.

- Construction has been doing well but there are fears that this is because of the millennium projects (such as the Dome) and there will be a fall in activity after 2000 or 2001. This sector is worth £58 billion a year to the economy and employs 1.4 million workers, but is often criticised because of poor profits, failure to invest and its treatment of employees. Health and safety risks are high, with 90 per cent of injuries involving untrained staff. In some cases large 'purchasers', such as Tesco, have reduced the cost of new sites by controlling building sites more closely and ensuring the workforce is skilled and well-trained.

- House prices have been rising in some parts of the country. If this continues then private building firms, such as Barratts, will be encouraged to expand their operations.

- Motorway and road building projects are influenced by government spending plans and by transport policies. You can find out what the Department of Transport is currently thinking by accessing its web site (http://www.open.gov.uk). These days the government is also more aware of the views of environmentalists, who are opposed to more road building. Car owners are likely to pay more for running their cars, e.g. through increased road fund licences.

- Overall, employment in construction is due to fall by 4.2 per cent between 1997 and 2007.

Trends and the tertiary sector

The tertiary sector is the most disparate of all the sectors. It includes many different types of business activities, which are summarised in Figure 2.36.

Because the trends in each particular industry can be totally different each one is discussed separately below.

Figure 2.35 The Dome helped create jobs in the construction industry

Service section (SIC 92)	Business activities
Section G	Wholesale and retail trade, repair of motor vehicles, motorcycles and personal and household goods and wholesalers, e.g. sale of motor vehicles and accessories, repair of same, wholesalers and agents, retail sales.
Section H	Hotels and restaurants, including bars, licensed clubs, canteens, youth hostels and camping sites.
Section I	Transport, storage and communication, including railway transport, taxis, bus and coach rentals, freight transport, furniture removal, water transport, pipelines, air transport, cargo handling and storage, travel agents, postal and courier services, telecommunications.
Section J	Financial services, e.g. banks, building societies, credit agencies, mortgage companies, insurance companies, pension companies, financial advisers.
Section K	Real estate, renting and business activities, e.g. estate agents, car rentals, boat and air rentals, radio, television and video rentals, video tape rentals, computer consultancies, research and development activities, solicitors, accountants, tax consultants, auditors, architects, quantity surveyors, recruitment agencies, advertising agencies, security, industrial cleaners, photographers, secretarial services, credit collection agencies, conference organisers.
Section L	Public administration and defence, i.e. national and local government offices which operate social security, health care, law and order and the fire service.
Section M	Education, e.g. schools, colleges, universities, driving schools, private training providers.
Section N	Health and social work, e.g. public and private hospitals, nursing homes, doctors, dentists, vets, social workers.
Section O	Other personal services, e.g. religious and political organisations, trade unions, employers organisations, motion picture and video production, radio and television activities, theatres, fair and amusement parks, discotheques, news agencies, libraries, museums, zoos, sports arenas, ice rinks, gambling and betting shops, dry cleaners, hairdressers, beauticians, fitness clubs, funeral directors.

Figure 2.36 Business activities of the tertiary sector

Retail and wholesaling

Everyone understands the general term 'retailing'. Retailing refers to selling goods in outlets as different as a hypermarket and a market stall, as a factory shop and a high-class department store such as Harrods. If you study the option unit on 'Retailing' then you will learn about the differences between retail outlets and the range of strategies they employ to tempt customers to buy the goods on sale.

Do be aware, though, that there are many different types of retailers and that if you look up figures in the Standard Industrial Classification for the retail sector you will also find that this includes figures for a variety of wholesalers (who sell mainly to retail outlets), retailers of alcohol and tobacco, pharmaceutical goods, clothing and footwear, furniture, books, second-hand shops and repairers. Don't forget, too, that many retailers operate on a mail order basis, either as well as or instead of selling direct to the public. In 1998, over four million people were employed in the retail sector.

Trends in retailing

- Retailing is seriously affected by changes in consumer demand and this, in turn, is affected by two factors:

  ○ the disposable income of consumers

  ○ consumer confidence about the future.

Disposable income is the amount of money you have left after paying tax, National Insurance and essential bills, such as rent or mortgage, council tax, fuel and food. If you receive a pay rise, but your essential expenses do not increase, you will have more money to spend buying goods or on leisure activities. However, your confidence in the future is important. If you have a temporary job which will finish in a week or two, it wouldn't make sense to spend all your money this week, no matter how much you were earning. If, however, you were in a permanent job with good prospects you would feel 'safer' spending your money.

- Consumer demand is also affected by interest rates. If interest rates are high then mortgages and loans are more expensive so consumers have less disposable income. If interest rates fall, mortgages and loans are cheaper, so consumers may spend more.

- In 1997 there were 319,000 retail outlets in Britain employing over 2.25 million people. Sales were valued at nearly £200,000 million. Consumer spending had risen steadily over four years. However, during 1998 and early in 1999 some retail outlets were under pressure. Marks & Spencer shocked everyone by announcing a serious fall in profits. Other retailers also faced difficulties after poor summer sales and low consumer spending at Christmas in 1998. However by the middle of 1999 sales were starting to improve, mainly because steady cuts in interest rates gave consumers more to spend.

- Despite difficulties, many retail outlets have steadily expanded and taken on more staff. Tesco announced it intended to create 10,000 jobs during 1999. More large out-of-town shopping complexes were opened, such as Cribbs Causeway, Trafford Park and Bluewater Park, to add

Figure 2.37 Trafford Park shopping centre

to existing centres such as Meadowhall, Lakeside and the Metrocentre.

- Staff in retailing are often employed on a part-time, flexible hours basis and many are women. Superstores now open 24 hours a day and 7 days a week in many areas.

- Mail order shopping has also increased. Many small organisations find it more cost-effective to sell their goods by mail order than to have premises in expensive town and city centres. They can also target a wider market over a greater geographical area. Next Directory has been particularly successful. Burton owns the catalogue companies Racing Green and Innovations. Great Universal Stores has bought Argos (see page 70). Growth is also anticipated in e-commerce, i.e. retailing over the Internet (see page 83).

However, these developments have had a price. More out-of-town large shopping complexes and more goods bought by mail order or over the Internet, means that fewer people do their shopping locally, or in their own town centre. If sales fall and businesses close, town centre shops cannot be re-let because of the lack of trade. This can start a downward spiral with the area becoming more depressed, fewer and fewer people shopping there, more and more businesses closing and so on. Many councils have tried to stop this happening by offering free parking, organising special shopping weeks and reducing rents to small businesses and market traders.

SNAPSHOT

How far will you travel with a headache?

Local chemists are said to be on the decline. Supermarkets and grocery stores are making life so difficult for local pharmacists that retail specialists Verdict Research have forecast the closure of 2,000 community chemists over the next few years.

This is because the British public likes to buy as much as they can under one roof, and because we don't need a chemist's advice to buy toiletries, cosmetics or disposable nappies. A local chemist can't survive if customers only buy cough medicine and aspirin.

Another retailer with a headache is the charity shop. Their success in the early 1990s resulted in a huge increase in the number of charity shops in every town – too many to go round, in fact. Not only did this lead to a shortage of customers per shop, but also to a shortage of volunteers and a shortage of donated goods. Oxfam's profits fell by 6.7 per cent and the Children's Society, whose profits dropped by 27.2 per cent, was forced to close many smaller outlets.

ACTIVITY

1   Ask your parents or your tutor to describe retailing in your own town centre area 15 or 20 years ago. Or visit your local library and read about your town at that time. Then, as a group, discuss the outlets that exist today and identify how retailing has changed in your area over that time.

2   Some of the more specific trends are shown in Figure 2.38. Add to these from your own experiences. Discuss your ideas as a group.

On the up	Declining or struggling
Organic food/vegetarian/ health food shops	Charity shops
Home shopping (catalogue or Internet)	Local chemists
Supermarket 'own brand' products	Mid-range clothing retailers (Mothercare, Richards)
Out of town shopping complexes	Small off-licenses and tobacconists
Trendy kids wear	Small, local bookshops
Themed megastores (for records, trainers etc.)	Traditional fishmongers, butchers and greengrocers
Snacks, lunch foods, low fat foods, chilled 'ready meals'	National Lottery tickets
Bottled water	Laura Ashley clothes
Prepacked sandwiches	MFI furniture
Male grooming products	Expensive jewellery
DIY	Men's magazines
Garden products	Low alcohol lager
Bookshops with coffee shops	Fruit machines
DVDs	Filofax
Mini-disk players	Body Shop

Figure 2.38 The rise and fall of businesses in a nutshell

Other services

If you look at Figure 2.36, you will see that there are a variety of different services listed under the tertiary sector, in addition to retailing. A **service** is provided by any business which is involved in the following activities:

- catering, e.g. hotels and restaurants

- transport and storage of goods

- communications

- financial services

- real estate or business services

- public administration

- education, health care or social work

- community, social and personal services (this group includes leisure and sport).

As you look at the trends in some areas you will see the term **deregulation**. It is important that you know what this means. A regulation controls the way a business operates, whereas deregulation removes these controls. It normally means that more businesses can operate competitively in a particular activity, without any restrictions. As an example, since 1 April 1997 European airlines have had an 'open skies policy'. This means that all trade barriers have been removed and any airline can compete freely with any other in the domestic markets of the European Union.

Catering trends
- The number of restaurants has increased in Britain – so has the number of take-away food outlets. People have become more adventurous in what they eat (partly as a result of going on foreign holidays) and this has led to the opening of Sushi bars and other specialist restaurants.

- Niche markets are successful but only for a short period. The late 1990s saw a proliferation in coffee shops like the Seattle Coffee Company, Costa Coffee and Coffee Republic. In the 1980s the trend was wine bars. What will it be by 2010?

- The growth of business hotels has been static. Special weekend break prices have failed to tempt enough people to stay away during a time when business is low. Hotels are wary of possible government regulations to limit 'unforeseen extras', such as high telephone tariffs from hotel phones. A new trend is hotels catering for female business travellers. Many hotels use the Internet for marketing.

- Many businesses in this sector are governed by licensing laws. Changes, such as drink-driving regulations and extended licensing hours, affect their operations.

- Fast-food continues to be popular. McDonald's UK is still opening new restaurants at the rate of about 100 a year and creating 5,000 new full-time and part-time jobs – mainly for young people. Burger King opened 33 new outlets in 1998. The fast-food industry is one of the largest employers of young people in the country. McDonald's alone employs 55,000 with 35,000 aged between 16 and 20.

Transport, storage and communication trends
- Rail companies are complex and to be avoided for serious investigation. Britain now has many train operating companies (TOCs) running train services, as well as Railtrack, which provides the infrastructure to support these services.

- Deregulation has increased competition on bus services and between taxi companies. Private bus and coach companies compete to provide the most competitive fares on the most lucrative – and busiest – routes.

- Deregulation of the airlines has led to an increase in the number of airlines and the emergence of 'no frills airlines' such as EasyJet and Ryanair, which pare costs to the bone by operating from less popular airports, cutting out travel agents and charging for extras such as food and drink on board.

- Freight and cargo companies are affected by the number of goods exported each year and the number of people immigrating/emigrating. Goods are usually transported by container by train and by sea. Air freight is common for valuable, highly perishable and urgently-needed goods.

- The travel business is booming. Most people now see an annual holiday as a necessity, not a luxury. Prices are competitive and the number of major travel operators has been reduced – many smaller companies are often owned and controlled by the larger ones. The 'big' operators are Thomson, Airtours, Cooks and First Choice. Cruises are increasingly popular (see page 165).

Figure 2.39 Travel is booming

- Motorbike courier services are relatively new. The number of private companies delivering packages and parcels has been increasing rapidly. Those in your area can be found by looking in the Yellow Pages.

- More letters are being posted every year – despite the increase in the use of the Internet. In 1988 13,568 million letters were sent, by 1998 this had risen to 19,266 million according to the Royal Mail.

- Telecommunications is a growth area. Mobile phone ownership is currently 16.8 million. Ownership is said to be peaking. The main players are Vodafone AirTouch, Orange, BT Cellnet and One2One. A new innovation is pre-pay phones – though these are said to be more expensive in the long run.

- More people own a home computer than ever before and are signing up to Internet services – access to which is now offered free by many providers. BT is looking at new technological innovations which will make connections much faster for all Internet users.

Trends in financial services

- The number of local bank branches has been falling rapidly because of costs. Critics accuse banks of closing down in poorer areas and not providing facilities for local people. In 1999 Barclays announced plans to cut a quarter of its workforce by 2002 – industry experts stressed this was not a new trend. According to the Credit Card Research Group, 6,000 jobs have been created over the last five years.

- There has been a boom in the number of credit cards on the market. There are 37 million credit cards in Britain, on which over £1,744 is spent every second, the average value of a purchase being £49. Most spending is on entertainment, food and drink, travel, household items and clothing.

- Building societies have been merging since the 1980s to save costs. Many, such as the Halifax, have converted into banks and become public limited companies. This means they are now accountable to their shareholders. Critics argue that this means that savers (another stakeholder) will now take second place.

- Insurance companies have also been merging. When Eagle Star's owner merged with Zurich Insurance this resulted in a reduction of 540 jobs in the company. By the mid-2000s it is likely that only a few key players will remain.

- All financial providers are aware of the power of the Internet and the popularity of telephone banking and 24-hour banking. The Prudential's Egg account is now only available through the Internet

and more and more banks are investing heavily in this form of service (contact their web sites to see what's available).

- Be aware that financial providers are facing competition from other 'players'. Supermarkets are already involved in offering financial services – you can save money through Tesco or Sainsbury and borrow money from Marks & Spencer!

- The government is keen to encourage more people to save towards their own pension. The stakeholder pension scheme begins in 2001 and financial providers are looking to increase their business by selling these to lower paid workers who do not have a company pension scheme.

Trends in real estate, renting and business activities

- Estate agents are highly dependent upon the property market for their business. When property prices increase and interest rates remain low (so mortgages are cheaper) their business increases. You will find articles on the state of the property market in your local paper.

- The rental business as a whole is variable. Business people will always rent cars – as will holidaymakers – so it is unlikely national providers such as Hertz and Avis will struggle for business. An interesting investigation would be into a local firm which probably also provides van hire. Some people still chose to rent their television sets, however most people prefer to buy them outright, especially as they can negotiate a discount for cash or arrange credit terms which work out cheaper than renting. Video film rentals are popular but are likely to have to change to meet the challenge of DVD. Future generations may be able to

Figure 2.40 Many building societies are now banks

'download' videos by choice – so the video shop may be a thing of the past in another 20 years.

- Solicitors have changed in two main ways. Deregulation has meant that their charges for routine services such as house conveyancing have fallen. Competition has reduced charges for wills and probate and many solicitors offer free advice mornings for potential clients. Two areas where solicitors are benefiting from increased business are family law and litigation. The first is through the increase in the number of divorces in Britain and the second is because people are more likely to sue for damages in civil actions than in the past (such as injuries sustained in road accidents).

- Accountants have gained customers since the Inland Revenue introduced self-assessment. Many sole traders and partners no longer wish to take the risk of completing their own accounts and self-assessment forms and prefer to ask an accountant to do it for them. Conversely, the rules for auditing companies have changed so that they are less rigorous for small private companies.

- The remainder – in brief.

  ○ Consultancy work is generally popular – tax consultants, management consultants, computer consultants. Whenever there is constant, rapid change which affects business you will find that consultants are often used to advise how best to adjust to these.

  ○ Recruitment agencies and selection consultants depend on the job market. When unemployment is high they may struggle, when employment is good and people are looking to change jobs regularly they benefit

from increased business. Don't forget that recruitment agencies often specialise in temporary employment opportunities.

○ Security firms are becoming more and more popular. You may find that your college employs a security firm – a sign of the times! Certainly many retail organisations do. Security services are normally sub-contracted because this is more cost-effective than employing and managing specialised security staff.

○ Industrial cleaners are also sub-contracted. Your college probably buys in its cleaning services rather than employing cleaners. This has been a growth area for entrepreneurs in the past few years.

○ Secretarial services are generally less popular than they were several years ago. The use of computers and modern software packages means

Figure 2.41 Security companies have taken over some of the work of other organisations

that many people can now produce their own documents quickly and easily.

Public administration

- All these activities are in the *public* sector. Also this relates to the agencies (i.e. the civil service) rather than to the practitioners. So your regional health care agencies and education offices are included in this heading but not doctors, dentists and schools.

- Many uniformed public sector organisations now employ civilian staff for administrative operations, e.g. the police.

- Defence activities have been reduced in the UK and the defence budget has been cut drastically over the past 10 years.

Education

- Further and higher education is funded differently from schools – and is very complex, as are the changes which education has faced over the last 10 years. Tempting though it may be to investigate your own school or college, if it is a large institution, you may find it difficult to focus on the precise type of information you need.

- Driving schools today are either run by small operators (often sole traders) or are franchised operations, such as BSM. They now have to prepare clients for a written test as well as the practical driving test.

- Private training providers operate in all areas of business, and offer various training programmes. Some are run in conjunction with colleges for young people on National Traineeships or Modern Apprenticeships. These schemes conbine work and training over a specified period.

Health and social work

- Hospitals exist in both the public and private sectors. Public ones are funded through the NHS, the private ones take patients who are prepared to pay for their treatment or who are covered by medical insurance. In this case the insurer pays the fees.

- Nursing homes and residential care is a growth area because the number of elderly people in Britain is increasing. Elderly people are funded by the state on a sliding scale if their savings and assets are below a certain figure (currently £16,000). Above this figure they pay their own fees. Nursing and residential homes have to operate to standards set down by the government and controlled through the local social services offices. In some cases this has led to homes closing down because they cannot meet the requirements profitably.

Figure 2.42 Private hospital patients pay for their care

- Doctors may operate in health centres or in private practices. Some of these may be fund-holding – which means they control their own budgets. This system, too, is scheduled to change. More doctors now use computerised appointment systems, are keen on 'customer service' and employ preventative techniques, e.g. operating Well Woman clinics.

- The number of dentists taking on NHS patients is declining – many find it unprofitable and will only treat private patients. Some operate group practices and some operate alone. Cosmetic dentistry is a growth area – but mainly in city areas.

- Some vets specialise in small animals (cats, dogs etc.) and others in farm animals – it largely depends on the areas they operate in. Checking that animals are fit to travel and issuing them with the correct identification and certification is another source of income for vets. There are also 'spin off' products made by manufacturers – from cat food to dog leads – which vets sell for extra income.

- Social workers are employed within the public service. They are assigned to geographical areas in towns and cities and each has a 'case load', which may include children, single parents, elderly people. Specialist social workers are attached to hospitals.

Miscellaneous activities
- For details on trade unions contact the TUC on their website at www.tuc.org.uk (see also pages 42–44).

- It may seem strange to think of a religious or political organisation as a 'business activity' until you remember that many of them are very wealthy! All the main political parties have web sites, and if you are tempted to investigate a religious organisation check with your tutor to make sure you will be able to find the information you need.

- Motion picture and video production is, hopefully, returning in force to Britain. The British film industry has had some notable successes over the past few years, including *Four Weddings and a Funeral*, *Trainspotting* and *Notting Hill*. It has been lobbying the government and the Arts Council for additional funding.

- Radio and television activities. Besides the main producers, such as the BBC, there are many small independent producers working in radio and television. Their success and popularity is increasing every year as it is often cheaper for the BBC and ITV to buy programmes from them than to make their own. You can find out who produces a TV programme by watching the credits at the end.

- In brief.
  - Leisure organisations, such as theme parks, sports arenas and fitness

Figure 2.43 More and more people are trying to get fit

centres, are becoming more and more popular. Theme parks however need to be continually investing large sums of money to provide us with 'new thrills' on each visit. Increased leisure time and a greater interest in personal fitness has increased membership of most fitness centres and sales of fitness equipment. In 1999 the fitness business was worth nearly £1 billion.

○ Theatres have always struggled to be profitable. Grants from the Arts Council have been reduced in recent years. Those catering for minority interests, such as ballet and opera, have found it more difficult than those catering for popular tastes.

○ Gambling and betting shops are closely regulated and no one under 18 is allowed to participate.

○ Most funeral directors were once run on a small scale by private owners, with the main exception of the Cooperative Funeral Service. There are now fewer firms which operate more cost-effectively on a larger scale, over a wider area.

In conclusion

Hopefully this section has given you ideas about the type of organisations you could investigate for your unit assessment and the trends which are or have affected them. However, do be aware that these have only been broadly summarised. In your own investigations you will have to find out in more detail what factors have, or are, influencing their activities and how these are likely to affect business operations in the future (see pages 180–198).

SNAPSHOT

The revolutionary milkman!

The 'milkman' who now delivers to your door is just as likely to be a woman and may soon be armed with a hand-held computer terminal to order anything to be delivered to your door, from dry cleaning and disposable nappies to flowers or holiday photographs! At least, that is what may happen if Express Dairies have their way. They are looking at relaunching the local milk delivery person in a big way.

Another idea is to improve Britain's recycling record by using milk floats to collect household rubbish for recycling in the afternoon. Express Dairies have been talking to supermarkets about collecting waste paper, bottles and cans – as well as making deliveries for supermarkets to those who want to order by phone or over the Internet.

Milk deliveries fell throughout the 1990s, because of competition from cheaper supermarket milk which keeps fresh for longer. However, the fall is slowing and business continues to be profitable. The investment in hand-held terminals will cost £5 million and – if you live in London, the East Midlands or Yorkshire – one could be coming your way very soon.

Section review

Refresh your memory on this section by writing short answers to each of the following questions and activities.

1 *Identify four business activities which take place in the primary sector.*

2 *Is the primary sector, as a whole, expanding or declining? Give a reason for your answer.*

3 *Explain how it is possible for employment in an industry to be declining while output is increasing.*

4 *Identify one other activity which is found in the secondary sector, in addition to manufacturing.*

5 *Manufacturing activities, as a whole, are declining in Britain. Does this mean that all manufacturers are declining? Give a reason for your answer.*

6 *State five activities which take place in the tertiary sector.*

7 *The tertiary sector, as a whole, is growing. Can you identify one activity in this area which is not predicted to increase?*

8 *Explain the term 'core business activity'.*

9 *Explain how you would identify the core business activity in a business you were investigating.*

10 *Select **one** specific industry which you are interested in investigating further and summarise the changes that have taken place. Add **one** item of information which you have researched yourself and which has not been included in the previous section.*

2.3 INFLUENCES ON BUSINESS

At the end of this section you should be able to:

- identify the different influences on business
- explain the factors which influence a business's choice of location
- identify why a business may choose to relocate
- explain the term 'stakeholder'
- identify how stakeholders can influence business activities
- understand how the influence of stakeholders can vary
- identify the potential for conflicts of interest among different groups of stakeholders.

Overview of business influences

All businesses are influenced by the world around them. Even a small business, such as Jones' shoe shop (see page 158), has had to change to survive. It is unlikely that William Jones would have generated much business today with his original idea, although it was successful at the time. In 10, 20 and certainly 50 years, many of the business activities which we know today will have changed or ceased altogether, and new ones will have taken their place.

Over a long period of time it is easy to identify influences and their effects. It is more difficult to identify what is happening *now* in a particular industry – and whether that trend will continue or not. Yet business people have to be able to do this. Those who are 'ahead of their time' are the ones who are the most successful. Those who refuse to change or ignore important influences are the ones most likely to fail.

In this section you will be studying two key influences on business. You will study business location – where different types of businesses are to be found and why. You will also learn about stakeholders – those people who have either an interest in, or an influence on, the business, or both. You will also look at the trends which were noticeable when this book was written and will be able to identify those which have continued and, hopefully, extend the list with some new trends. Then you can start applying what you have learned to businesses in your own area.

The location of business

Businesses can choose where to locate. Sometimes choice of location is critical. In other cases it is less important. What is the difference? And what happens when a 'right choice' suddenly becomes the wrong choice?

Factors influencing location

Every business locates where it thinks it will be successful. If you remember that businesses need:

- staff to work there
- raw materials to produce finished products
- customers
- to keep their costs as low as possible

then their reasons for choosing a particular location start to make sense.

Local labour supply

All organisations need to be able to employ staff. So it makes sense to locate in an area where people live. A factory in a remote part of the Scottish Highlands would have trouble finding anyone to work there. Motorway service stations have to pay to transport staff from local towns and villages to the service station itself, a cost which other businesses can avoid. The factors which influence a particular location are often **local skills** and the **cost of labour**.

Local skills

In some parts of the country particular skills are a tradition. If you wanted to set up in business making pottery you would be sensible to locate in the Midlands, around Stoke-on-Trent. If you wanted to make cutlery, then Sheffield is the place. If you were making boots and shoes, then Northamptonshire is the area for you. Probably the most famous examples today are in the United States. Silicon Valley and Seattle are renowned for their computer industries, so this is where whizz-kid programmers head for. California is the home of the film industry, so if you were keen to work on special effects and digital technology, this is where you would go.

Figure 2.44 Formula 1 racing team headquarters are located close to suppliers

Britain's Silicon Valley is located along the M4. The area is also famous for Formula One motor racing firms. Scotland has its own Silicon Glen and Cambridge is building a reputation for high-tech skills and is now known as Silicon Fen. Firms wanting to specialise in these particular industries know that if they locate in these areas they will be able to recruit staff with the skills they need. The City of London is renowned for its financial skills and expertise, so this is where you will find large international banks, stockbrokers and insurance firms.

Other firms don't need particular skills – or may be willing to train unskilled staff. Firms doing light assembly work often locate where there is a ready supply of cheap (often female) labour. Many of these have set up where traditional industries, such as mining, have closed. Areas with high unemployment tend to have lower wage rates – the competition for jobs keeps pay rates down. At the North Celynen Colliery in Wales, Aiwa employs 1,000 people making videos, and in the Rhondda Valley – the heartland of the old Welsh mining industry – Taxdata employs 250 people making CD packaging. In the Dearne Valley in South Yorkshire, at a former colliery, over 2,000 people work for Ventura – part of the Next group of companies. Ventura is a call centre and mail-handling company which handles over seven million customer accounts for various clients, such as Cellnet and the Cooperative Bank.

Call centres employ operators equipped with a computer and telephone whose task is to answer telephone enquiries or telephone existing and potential customers to generate more sales for companies. Today approximately 150,000 people in the UK work in call centres. Most of these are located in parts of the country where wage rates are lower. However, in some places, such as Tyneside, Leeds and Glasgow, where many call centres have been set up, competition for experienced staff is now increasing and pay rates are rising. So the pool of skilled labour in the area is affecting the cost for firms.

The cost of labour will always be more important to businesses which are **labour-intensive** than those which are **capital-intensive**. A labour intensive firm is one which needs a high number of staff – such as call centres, or your own school or college. A capital intensive business is one where machines or technology do most of the work – as in a modern electricity generating plant. Here the cost of labour is less important in the choice of location.

The cost of premises

The cost of premises is determined by the forces of demand and supply. The greater the demand for premises – and the fewer there are available – the higher the cost. For that reason, premises in city centres – especially in London – are much more expensive than the cost of premises in the suburbs or in the regions. For example, the lease for a large store (60,000 square feet) in Oxford Street, London, was on sale for £12 million in 1997! This is because Oxford Street is a **prime site** – in a town a large high street store would be less, but not cheap. In 1997, Marks & Spencer bought 19 high street stores from Littlewoods for £192.5 million, paying 'over the odds' for the stores it wanted. They were actually valued at around £80 million. Premises on major town centre shopping routes are always more expensive than on secondary 'side' streets – simply because most shoppers stay on the high street. Areas of high employment with a surplus of skilled labour – Newbury, in Berkshire, is a typical example – are more expensive places to locate than areas where unemployment is high and the area depressed, as in some parts of the north-east.

The result is that companies which have no reason to locate in London or the south-east will move to other towns and cities. Those businesses which are not dependent upon passing trade will locate outside town and city centres in cheaper areas or on industrial estates.

Within Britain, many local authorities offer 'packages' to encourage businesses to locate to their area. They may offer financial assistance for large firms and reduced rents for small enterprises. Specialist rental and leasing companies will offer attractive packages enabling businesses to locate easily in special workspace sites, office complexes, business or retail centres. Some centres are 'managed' with a central reception area, business services and shared meeting rooms. Retail units may be available on short-term licence agreements, payable weekly. All these attract organisations to locate where costs will be lowest and where, hopefully, they will be able to expand the business without substantially increasing their costs.

Figure 2.45 London's Oxford Street

Financial help from the government

How prosperous is your area? If you live in London, the south-east, or the east of England (e.g. Norwich), then you live in an officially prosperous area. If you live anywhere else, the situation is different, although in Scotland, Northern Ireland, the West Midlands and the south-west, prosperity rose above the UK average between 1986 and 1996. However, the north-east, north-west, Yorkshire and Humberside, the East Midlands and Wales all declined below the national average.

The European Union and the government are concerned about such inequalities. They would like all regions to be equally prosperous. So what is being done to help?

For some time in the UK there have been **Assisted Areas**. These are areas of Britain where regional aid may be given under European Community law. **Regional Selective Assistance** (RSA) is the main form of such aid in Britain. This is a discretionary grant awarded to support a project which will stimulate employment opportunities, increase regional competitiveness and improve prosperity. Between 1985 and 1988 the scheme created 100,000 jobs, reducing employment by 0.5 per cent in the Assisted Areas, at a cost of about £130 million a year.

In 1998 the European guidelines on regional aid changed and all member states were asked to propose new Assisted Areas to operate from 1 January 2000. In July 1999 the Department of Trade and Industry put forward new proposals which included the following.

- Tier One (maximum) assistance for Cornwall, Merseyside, South Yorkshire and West Wales and the Valleys. Here grants of up to 40 per cent of the project cost will be available. The government has also proposed that Northern Ireland be treated as an exceptional case for assistance.

- Tier Two assistance for areas most in need of employment creation, investment and regeneration. For these areas a 20 per cent assistance grant will be available. This includes the Highlands and Islands and various areas in England, Wales and Scotland. Rather than designate towns or cities the government has used 'ward boundaries' (which denote voting areas).

- Tier Three assistance for Enterprise Grant Areas where assistance will be available to businesses employing up to 250 people. The aim is to encourage the development of small businesses as these are seen as vital for improving employment and prosperity long term.

It is estimated that total expenditure on regional industrial assistance in Britain between 2000 and 2003 will be over £785 million, with £45 million dedicated to small businesses.

Once the new Assisted Areas have been agreed by the European Commission, they will remain in force from 1 January 2000 to 31 December 2006.

 **ACTIVITY**

Divide into four groups. Each group is responsible for finding a specific piece of information and presenting its findings to the class.

1 Group one. Find out whether you live in an Assisted Area by accessing details on http://www.dti.gov.uk/assistedareas. You can also find the information on http://europa.eu.int/comm/dg04/index:en.htm. Also investigate which areas *near* to you are covered by Assisted Area status – and which are not.

2   Group two. Contact your local authority to find out what incentives they offer to firms wishing to locate in your area. If your local authority has a web page, you will be able to find the information there, but if they operate a regional development office it may be better to visit them.

3   Group three. Nominate a group representative to contact your local Business Link or Regional Development Agency to find out the costs of business premises in your own area.

4   Group four. Investigate the cost of retail sites in your shopping centre by contacting the company which operates the centre. Often there is an office within the centre itself. You could also add to your information by checking your local paper on the night it advertises business premises – and finding out how much it costs to rent office space or a manufacturing unit.

Note that you will find it useful to keep this information and use it when you are investigating business start-up costs in Unit 3.

Transport links for supplies and distribution

Many businesses need to be able to obtain supplies easily and transport finished goods quickly to their customers. An obvious answer is to locate on a motorway network. Many 'new towns' in the 1950s were deliberately developed in such locations, such as Warrington New Town in the north and Milton Keynes in the south. The next time you travel on a motorway, note the number of large organisations you see – retail superstores, large manufacturers, distribution companies. All of them need good transport links to operate profitably. Large superstores (e.g. Dixons, Comet, Sainsbury's, B & Q) have several large depots around the country where they hold bulk supplies which are then broken down for delivery to individual stores in the area.

Figure 2.46 Many companies need access to a motorway

However, not all businesses are dependent on road links. Heavy goods are often better – and more cheaply – transported by rail (on the European mainland they use rivers and canals, too!) A cement factory, for instance, may have its own rail sidings so that heavy bulk materials can be transported easily.

Some businesses locate near airports or seaports because their business involves storing goods waiting to go overseas or having arrived from overseas. Another suitable location for such firms is near the Channel Tunnel. They can be freight forwarding agents (which send goods abroad) and more unusual enterprises, such as kennels which specialising in sending animals abroad to join owners who have emigrated. A new venture in such locations may be 'pet passport' offices!

Suppliers and natural resources

Many businesses locate near their suppliers and raw materials. This is particularly the case if:

- they need a specific item which is only available in particular areas of the country

- the raw materials they use are heavy and costly to transport

- they are dependent on specialist suppliers for their product.

Cement companies are found near natural deposits of limestone or chalk, an essential raw material only found in certain parts of the country. Paper mills are found near water, because paper can't be made without it! This was also the reason for the location of cotton and woollen mills. Sheffield became a steel centre because it was near to coal, iron ore and limestone – all of which were required to make iron, from which steel is made. Whisky is made in the Highlands of Scotland because it needs peaty water. Cider is made in Somerset because the climate favours apple growing – and so on.

In many cases natural resources can't be moved, or are too expensive to move. If you wanted to set up in business making stone ornaments for gardens, you would be sensible to locate near a quarry supplying this stone – rather than pay a small fortune to have it brought to you, especially if the finished ornaments are small enough to transport easily.

If you were dependent on a few specialist suppliers you would probably set up in businesses near them. In the case of car making, suppliers tend to locate near a car production company, which needs fast, regular supplies of electrical components, tyres, windscreens etc. Another car manufacturer may be attracted to the same area, so that it can also get its supplies cheaply and easily. More suppliers then move in to meet the increased demand. This is one of the reasons that Japanese car manufacturers, such as Nissan, have located in the north-east of England.

The need to compete with businesses involved in the same activity

Imagine there is a large shopping centre in your area attracting all the trade – and you set up in business half a mile away. Or an organisation opens an airport hotel for business travellers on a site five miles from the airport. In both cases the businesses would find it harder to succeed because they are not in the right place to compete with their main rivals.

This is why you often find the same type of businesses clustered together. Look at the seafront in any popular British resort, such as Brighton or Blackpool. You will find many hotels and various traders – as well as amusement arcades and the like. A few yards down any side street there may be little activity. In large cities, you will find different types of restaurants clustered together – Chinese, Thai, Indian, Japanese. In some cities, such as Manchester, San Francisco and Sydney, there is a Chinatown where Chinese traders are grouped together and compete with each other. In cities there is a 'business district' where you find the offices of major companies, accountants, lawyers, stockbrokers. In the City of London there are many firms involved in financial services, including banks, stockbrokers, insurance companies – competing with each other but also often *depending* upon each other and interacting with each other on business matters. Estate agents also locate in one area – given that people looking to buy or rent property want easy access to information about a range of property handled by different estate agents.

Not all businesses, however, benefit from being close to their competitors. In some cases, they do better when they are well apart – as in the case of garden centres, bowling alleys, theme parks and cinemas. Too many in

Figure 2.47 Blackpool's seafront at night

one area competing for the same business is likely to end in some succeeding and others failing. Relocating to another area where there is less competition, or none at all, increases the chance of succeeding.

Nearness to customers

Being close to customers – individuals, businesses, or both – is important.

This is why most companies in Britain are located in the south-east, the largest consumer market in the country. It's also why Rotterdam is the world's largest oil terminal – as well as handling grain, iron ore and sulphur. The port is on the doorstep of the huge industrial market of Europe in general and West Germany in particular.

This is 'nearness to customers' on a grand scale. On a small scale you will find petrol stations located on main roads; doctors and dentists with their practices near to their

patients, small grocery shops in highly populated neighbourhoods and retailers with premises in shopping centres or with a market stall. If you don't have the means to make the customer come to you, then you must go to the customer.

Nearness to the customer is less important in industry if transport costs are cheap and customers are spread all over the country, and possibly all over the world. Being close to customers is important where smaller industrial companies service the needs of larger organisations in a particular trade. In Yorkshire, dyers and finishers of woollen cloth do many of the pre- or post-production operations for larger companies. In Northamptonshire leather tanners and distributors support the boot and shoe trade.

Assembly plants also tend to be near their customers. The small or light components of computers are relatively cheap to transport to the assembly plants, but the finished product is more bulky, so the plant needs to be near a motorway network or a large number of customers.

History and tradition

The reasons for the location of a particular industry may be a mixture of what is essential, history and tradition. It may have been because a particular entrepreneur liked the area. Joseph Rowntree had no other reason for starting chocolate production in York apart from wanting to live there! In other cases, the original reasons for a business locating in a place no longer apply, but the business remains where it is. Lincolnshire, for example, is renowned for its many horticultural firms and growers. This is partly for geographic conditions, including climate, fertile soil and promixity to ports, such as Felixstowe, where flowers and bulbs are imported from the Continent. Even

Figure 2.48 Horticultural centre

though the conditions for cultivating plants can now be simulated in greenhouses anywhere in the country, Lincolnshire remains a major horticultural centre.

Some firms prefer to remain in the same location because they have built up associations and supportive links. Local colleges may run industrial courses relating to these organisations. There may be a local trade association which benefits many of the owners. In such cases, there is little impetus for a business to relocate to be 'on its own' somewhere else.

In other cases, relocation becomes essential. Many years ago British Steel was located inland near to iron ore deposits (essential for steel manufacture). When the iron ore in Britain ran out, it had to be imported. As this was already expensive to ship, it made no economic sense to transport it from the ports to the inland sites of the steel works. So

British Steel relocated to coastal sites. This devastated many communities in parts of the Midlands but, in this case, tradition had to be sacrificed for the industry to survive against competition from other countries, such as Japan.

 ACTIVITY

1 Identify the main factors which each of the following businesses should bear in mind when deciding where to locate:
   a   a washing machine manufacturer
   b   a wine producer
   c   a firm making potato crisps
   d   a motel
   e   a leisure centre
   f   a frozen fish producer
   g   a brick manufacturer
   h   a large international bank
   i   a large importer from the Continent
   j   an employment agency
   k   a radio station.

2 Identify four factors which could make a business decide to relocate.

3 Explain why you might find a business in an area for no apparent reason.

4 Wages are generally cheaper in the north than in the south. Why, then, do so many companies still prefer to locate in the south-east of England, where wages are the highest?

5 Identify the major industries which were a feature in your own area in the past. Find out which still exist and which have either gone altogether or changed in some way. Talk to your parents or grandparents – or someone else you know who has lived in the area for a long time. As a group, and with your tutor, discuss the factors which have influenced the changing face of industry in your area.

SNAPSHOT

The perils of location

One firm didn't do its homework very well when it set up in business. Philip Gibbon is an oyster farmer. He grows oysters in the River Teign and runs a purification plant at his home in Stock Gabriel, near Dartmouth in Devon. To clean his oysters he brings in barrel-loads of sea water from Torbay twice a year.

In 1993, new hygiene rules demanded that the water must be changed fortnightly. So the Ministry of Agriculture, Fisheries and Food insisted that Mr Gibbon have a constant supply of fresh sea water to wash the oysters. This is essential because oysters are eaten raw.

Mr Gibbon was then in the unenviable position of owning an oyster farm too far from the sea. He had two choices. Close down, or relocate. At 75, it is unlikely Mr Gibbon will move his operations!

CASE STUDY 2.4

Cadishead, near Irlam, is not a place many people know. It is on the banks of the Manchester Ship Canal – and is the new location of a firm called Chemitrade, the UK's largest distributor of bulk and packaged solvents. Originally Chemitrade was running its operations from central London. Why did it move?

According to Chemitrade's business manager, James Kite, the expiry of the lease on its London offices triggered the change. Until then the sales and administrative staff were based in London. The chemicals, which mainly arrive by sea from Rotterdam, were stored at Cadishead. It made sense to combine the whole team together in the same place to improve communications and productivity.

Chemicals are a huge bulk item and Chemitrade sells 100,000 tonnes every year. So, it made sense to reduce product handling time by having its own jetty. It takes eight or nine hours to offload 3,000 tonnes from a ship whereas it takes 140 tankers to transport 3,000 tonnes by road and 2 hours to unload each tanker.

Other factors also played a part. The competition for workers in central London is intense and salaries are high. This meant that good staff could easily move on. The company felt that although its staff turnover rates were good, they could be improved. In the north-west jobs are harder to come by and salaries are generally lower.

It cost Chemitrade between £650,000 and £700,000 to move, the major costs being the construction of a new office and relocation allowances to the staff who decided to move with them. The company thinks it is worth it, and has no plans to move again in the foreseeable future.

Activities

1 What business is Chemitrade in?
2 Identify three reasons why Chemitrade decided to move.

CASE STUDY (continued)

3 a How many hours would it take to unload 3,000 tonnes of chemicals arriving by road?

  b If the cost of unloading was £50 an hour, what would be the total cost of the operation?

  c Assuming the cost of discharging the chemicals from a ship was the same per hour, how much would the company save using this method?

4 Why are salaries higher in London than in the north-west of England?

5 Irlam is situated near the M6. In what ways will this situation also benefit Chemitrade?

6 If you had worked in London for Chemitrade, would you have relocated with them? Discuss your answers as a group and try to decide the factors which would be important to the employees who were offered the opportunity to move.

The influence of stakeholders

Whether you realise it or not, you are a stakeholder in many businesses. This means you have an interest in a business and can influence the way it operates (even if only slightly). You are a stakeholder in your school or college, in the shops you buy from, the cinemas you visit – anywhere you spend money as a consumer. You have an interest in them because if they closed down or relocated – or don't stock the items you want – you would probably be inconvenienced. You have an influence on them because if you pass a remark, make a suggestion or register a complaint they may listen, and if they receive the same type of remark or suggestion or complaint from several customers, they would be wise to take some action.

Who else are stakeholders in businesses? Examples of stakeholders are:

• customers

• employees and managers of the business

• shareholders

• the local community

• the government.

However, the type of interest and degree of influence of each group varies between different types of stakeholders and different types of businesses – as you will see below. In addition, stakeholder interests may not only differ but conflict – which can cause problems. First it is important that you understand how individual groups of stakeholders relate to business organisations.

Figure 2.49 Cinema-goers are all stakeholders

Customers as stakeholders

All customers have an interest in the businesses they support – but the *type* of interest they have will vary, depending upon the business activity. If you are an avid collector of Boyz Own records then you may be devastated that they have disbanded. If you support Newcastle United or Blackburn Rovers then you may feel let down that your team isn't playing very well or if it is relegated. You also have an interest in how much season tickets are likely to cost in the future. If you are a car owner then you may be very concerned to read that the company is no longer producing your particular model and spares won't be available after the next two years. If you have spent years looking for a local hairdresser who really understands you then you may be annoyed and disgruntled if he or she decides to move a hundred miles away – and so on. In some cases, therefore, you want continuity, in others you want reasonable prices, performance, quality or convenience. At your school or college you no doubt have an interest in the quality of teaching and the results of previous students, but research shows that most students are more concerned about how friendly their tutors are and the type of facilities available!

The influence of customers will depend on the type and size of the business – and how receptive it is to the views of customers. If you change your buying habits and buy Virgin Cola rather than Coca-Cola, then Coca-Cola is unlikely to notice. This is because it operates on such a large scale it only knows something is wrong if many customers stop buying and sales fall. If you and your friends are regulars at the local sandwich bar and suddenly stop going there, the owner is likely to wonder why – and may ask you if you suddenly call in again.

Some organisations are particularly interested in getting the views of their customers.

Holiday companies issue questionnaires, Boots operates a consumer panel, others pay telephone marketing companies to telephone people to find out their views, supermarkets operate customer service desks and log comments and requests made by customers. If you are irritated that your local store doesn't stock a particular item then you can make enquiries. Smaller shops will often obtain a specialist item for you. A local shop will provide goods in small quantities for the old lady who lives alone – a large supermarket is unlikely to offer the same service. Your corner shop may allow you to owe them money if you have no change – it is not advisable to make the same request in Dixons or Boots!

There is therefore a different type of interaction between customers as stakeholders and different types of businesses, depending on the type of business activity, the size and scale of the business and its attitude to individual customers.

Figure 2.50 Boots uses a consumer panel to get the views of its customers

Employees and managers

As an employee you have a different kind of interest in a business. It may be pleasant to work for an ethical company which offers value for money to its customers and is responsive to customer complaints, however your *main* area of interest will be in:

- the way staff are treated

- the rates of pay

- whether the business is secure – or likely to close down any day.

You will want your employer to treat you fairly.

- To allow you time off for emergencies, when these occur.

- To pay you sick pay when you are ill and holiday pay when you take a holiday.

- To comply with the law in health and safety and employment protection.

- To employ managers who treat their staff with respect and courtesy.

- To give you interesting work to do – which matches the job description.

- To support you if you want to improve yourself and study for more qualifications.

You will want to be paid a fair rate of pay in relation to other people in the same type of job. You would not expect the company to pay more to a new member of staff doing the same type of work but who is younger, has less experience and fewer qualifications. You will expect your pay to be reviewed at regular intervals.

You will want some job security – even if you don't want to stay there forever. You will not want to work for a company with a 'hire and fire' philosophy or a company in danger of closing down because business is so poor. You will hope that the business is flourishing so that there are promotion prospects if you work hard.

Managers have similar expectations. They, too, like to be treated fairly, paid well and to have job security. Employee needs do not change just because you climb the ladder! However, managers also like the opportunity to make decisions, to prove that they can do the job well and to be given responsibility. But then all the best employees do!

The influences of employees vary from one business to another. If there is a recognised union, then there is likely to be more formal discussion between employee representatives and management. This means that the views of employees are discussed by union representatives and managers and taken into account where appropriate. However, this is not always the case. Some organisations virtually ignore the unions and in smaller non-unionised firms there may be an informal arrangement between boss and staff which works very well. There are no hard and fast rules on this subject! What you are likely to find, however, is that businesses which listen to their employees have more motivated and happier workforces. Even if suggestions cannot be implemented, the fact that someone is listening is often the key to good employee/employer relationships.

Shareholders as stakeholders

Shareholders are people who invest money in a company. The general public and institutional shareholders can only invest in a public limited company. An institutional shareholder is a large company, such as a pension fund or insurance company, which invests on the stock market. However, if you had the money, you could own shares in hundreds of companies in the UK. You could, for instance, buy shares in large football clubs, in travel companies, electricity suppliers, retailers, telecommunications companies and manufacturing companies.

If you are a shareholder you have two main interests. The first is that the company will do well and the value of your investment will increase. The second is that the company will pay a good dividend twice a year. This is your 'return' for investing your money – it's like putting your money in a building society and receiving interest.

If the managers of the company make decisions which you think are inadvisable, or against the company interests, then you may protest. All shareholders are invited to attend the company's annual general meeting (AGM). They can also vote at this meeting. You have one vote for each share you own. So, if you own 500 shares you have 500 votes. But if the shareholder next to you owns 500,000 shares then he or she can outvote you every time. This is why many small shareholders do not bother to attend meetings. If they are dissatisfied with the performance of the company they simply sell their shares. This action *can* have an influence on the company. If a large enough number of shares are sold in a short space of time the share value will fall. The company will then be worth less money, which can make its future uncertain – and

Figure 2.51 An AGM meeting

directors like job security just like every other employee! Institutional shareholders – who own hundreds of thousands of shares – have far greater influence on the directors of a company. If they all vote against the company, then their actions can have a far-reaching effect – in an extreme case they may even vote that the company is taken over by another organisation or that all the executives are replaced.

The local community as stakeholder

The local community has a vested interest in the type of business activities in the area. You may be uninterested in events 50 miles away, or in the change of ownership of a local shop, but you would certainly take an interest if a large factory was built next to your house and operated 24 hours a day.

Fortunately, planning restrictions are unlikely to allow this. Industrial and residential areas are usually kept separate. However, there are many issues that concern communities and which they may object to. These include:

* the building of new ring roads and motorways which will spoil the countryside

* objections to air-borne pollution from factories and nuclear processing plants – and fears about long-term medical effects

* concerns when prisons or remand centres are planned in semi-residential areas – because of worries about escapes.

* worries about 'socially undesirable' activities being established where there are young people. In one town a major protest was sparked by an amusement arcade being given planning permission near a school and college.

People also may be concerned about business activities and operations that could reduce the value of their properties. A new motorway or a new airport close to where you live could drastically reduce the value of your home. You could also be seriously worried about other issues, such as air pollution and noise levels.

Some people feel strongly enough about these issues to take direct action. Some chain themselves to trees, build tunnels and form barricades to stop developments such as the second runway at Manchester Airport. Most people don't act in this way, but they can object in other ways.

If a local community does not agree with what business is doing, what can it do? First, it can boycott the company and its products. But this would only be effective if the business depends on local trade. Second, it can make its objections known to the press to try to increase pressure on the company – no organisation likes bad publicity. The company, in reply, may simply express its

own views and do nothing, particularly if it doesn't depend on local sales. Third, local people can lobby their counsellors – given that all local politicians depend on the people's votes to remain in their jobs. Fourth, they can lodge a formal appeal. This is the most likely course of action if a community objects to a proposed business plan.

Decisions relating to business plans are made by the local planning authority (LPA) in an area. An example could be an application by a supermarket to build a new store on land outside a town centre. If the local community disagrees with the decision then it can appeal. Usually someone will set up an action or protest group to coordinate local efforts. All appeals in England and Wales are dealt with through the Planning Inspectorate at the Department of the Environment and the Welsh Office. If the appeal is complex then a hearing may take place or an inquiry might be held. At the end of the investigation the inspector in charge of the case makes a decision and submits it to the Secretary of State for the Environment. The Secretary of State does not have to agree with the inspector's decision and can overrule it – but this is rare.

Finally, those who bring a complaint may be able to challenge any decision they disagree with in the High Court. This is also rare, and would need to involve some irregularity in the way the appeal was heard for it to be allowed.

The government as a stakeholder

The government has a very positive interest in all businesses – otherwise it would hardly be trying to encourage them with initiatives such as regional aid. Businesses create employment opportunities. They pay tax. People who are employed pay tax and don't claim benefits – which means the

Figure 2.52 Local action against plans to build a bypass

government gains revenue. British goods can be sold abroad which brings money into this country. People who are employed and earning a wage are more likely to save for their retirement – so are less of a burden on the state when they are older. They spend money which helps the economy. They are generally happier and healthier people. If the economy is doing well and individuals feel prosperous, they are less likely to vote for a different political party at the next general election. These are all reasons why the government takes an active interest in business.

However, the government is aware that without any regulation some undesirable business activities may take place. Smaller businesses would be at the mercy of more powerful enterprises. Consumer rights may be ignored. Dangerous products may be offered for sale. People may be cheated on price. Some executives may embezzle money or defraud the company. Employees may be treated shabbily. This is why legislation is needed to control the way businesses are run. The government therefore has a significant influence on businesses – as it can make an activity unlawful (illegal) and therefore effectively control business operations. The government also monitors operations (through watchdog bodies such as Ofgas and Oftel) and sets standards, e.g. trading standards, safety standards and environmental standards, which businesses should follow.

However, as you have already seen, governments do not just try to restrain and control business activities. They also want to encourage businesses. To do this they introduce supportive (such as regional aid) or protective measures. Competition legislation, for instance, protects smaller businesses (and consumers) by making it an offence for large businesses to collude and fix prices. Health and safety legislation not only protects employees but also gives employers legal

protection against unsafe actions by workers, or workers who disregard safety instructions. The government also promotes business abroad – as at Trade Fairs and British Weeks – to try to help exporters. The government publishes information and statistics on business trends to help business planning. You have seen examples in this unit, taken from statistics produced by the Office of National Statistics.

SNAPSHOT

Order, order!

Some business chairpeople have been taking lessons from the Institute of Chartered Secretaries and Administrators on how to keep order when an AGM starts to get out of hand. This can happen if protest groups attend AGMs or if shareholders are extremely unhappy about the way a company is run. In 1997, directors of British Aerospace had to barricade themselves behind plastic shields when they were besieged by groups campaigning against the arms trade. RTZ, the mining company, struggled through interventions from Friends of the Earth and other protesters. Shell, castigated for its human rights record in Nigeria, had protesters burn the company's flag at its AGM. The World Development Movement drove a tank to HSBC's AGM to protest over claims that Midland Bank helped to finance arms sales to Iraq.

In Japan, companies are more devious. Those expecting trouble arrange to hold their AGMs on the same day, forcing protesters to divide their action. UK utility companies were accused of using this strategy when six meetings of electricity companies took place on the same Friday at locations as far apart as Manchester and Dorset, and the following Wednesday three water companies held their AGMs on the same date!

ACTIVITY

1   As a group, discuss how much interest and influence you think you have as a stakeholder in your school or college. What systems are in place to obtain your views? What happens if you make a suggestion? How interested will you be in the institution once you have left? How much notice should a college take of its students if, each year, their needs and wants change? Talk through your ideas with your tutor.

2   Find out about government departments and information by accessing the government web site on http://open.gov.uk. It's a large site, so allow some time to do this!

3   As a group, and with your tutor, discuss the type of issues relating to business activities which have been reported in your local press – particularly when the local community has objected to something. What type of issues in your area generate strong feelings? Have you, personally, ever been involved with a planning decision – or anyone you know? If not, what type of issues do you think you would feel strongly about – and what would you do?

4   Which do you think would have the largest number of stakeholders – a large business or a small one? Give a reason for your answer.

CASE STUDY 2.5

Peter was absolutely furious. They had only moved to the area two years earlier, to get away from the town. Their brand new house was in a small country lane, only a hundred yards from a busy road, but looking out of the window you could believe you were miles from anywhere. Then, out of the blue, he discovered that the little garage workshop at the end of the lane was closing down – and being sold to developers. The workshop was rather an eyesore, run by two elderly brothers, but they serviced his car cheaply and everyone was used to them. Now there were plans to turn the site into a large service station.

Word spread around the district and an action group was formed – with Peter at the helm. As a businessman he felt he had the ability to lead the group and make a formal appeal. He organised a petition and collected signatures. He filled in the forms. He attended the hearing. The appeal was dismissed.

Three years later the little lane is still a backwater but at the end, on the main road, is a large service station selling petrol, sandwiches, newspapers and general supplies. The people in the area seem to have got used to it. One says it is useful when they run out of bread or milk! Peter isn't interested – he and his family moved when the result of the appeal was announced. They live three miles away, hoping there are no changes planned in their new neighbourhood.

Activities

1   Why did Peter form an action group?
2   How effective were members of the action group as stakeholders?
3   Why did the service station want to locate on this site?
4   How concerned are the local community about the change now, three years later?
5   Who are the stakeholders in the new service station?
6   Out of all the stakeholders you listed in 5 above, which group do you think has the most influence? Give a reason for your answer.

CASE STUDY (continued)

7   Do you think local communities should have more or less influence in planning decisions? And can you identify any trends in the UK in relation to community or pressure group interests? Decide your answers as a group.

8   Do you think the shareholders in the service station chain would agree with protesters in a local community if another new site was being developed? Give a reason for your answer.

Competing interests amongst stakeholders

The type of interest shown by different groups of stakeholders is different. The number of stakeholders in a business also varies. The more varied the stakeholder groups – and the more active they are – the more likely that there will be competing interests among these groups.

This is easier to illustrate by example. Take two different businesses. One is a small veterinary practice, the other is a large public limited company which operates entertainment complexes.

The vet has a limited number of stakeholders.

*   His patients (the animals) and their owners. The animals are unlikely to be very argumentative stakeholders!

*   A few employees – perhaps a partner, a veterinary nurse and a receptionist.

*   The local community – who largely ignore him unless anything goes wrong.

*   The government – but in this case the vet simply checks that he is abiding by the laws which relate to his practice.

The vet is more likely to listen to the views of his customers and suggestions from his staff. These two groups of stakeholders have the greatest influence on his business.

The potential for conflict is relatively limited. Let us say that one night a sick dog at the surgery keeps the neighbourhood awake by howling and the vet receives complaints from local householders. He can hardly turn the dog out in the street as the owner – another stakeholder – would be upset. He can install double glazing or sound proofing to prevent the problem occurring again. He could even relocate to a less residential area – though this would be extreme. He can hope that the case is an isolated one. He could sedate the dog or arrange for it to be cared for elsewhere.

Now let us look at the case of the entertainment complex. It has a lot more stakeholders. These include:

*   existing customers who use the complexes in different parts of the country

*   potential customers who would like to use the complexes but cannot – because there isn't one in their area

*   existing employees and managers

*   potential employees who could be offered jobs if a new complex opened

*   shareholders who have invested in the company – both private and institutional. They want the company to expand and develop so that it earns more profit and is more valuable

*   local communities – in areas where the complexes are already situated and in areas where future complexes are planned

- the government – the local planning authorities, local councillors and national government.

The list is quite long and the potential for conflict is greater because of the type of operations in which the business is involved and its scale.

The company wants to expand to a new site where it believes there is a lack of entertainment for young people. It wants to open a multiplex cinema, bowling alley, restaurant and amusement arcade. However, the most obvious site for development is one mile from an exclusive residential estate. What might be the result? It's up to you to decide!

to such developments and so are local councillors, who want to protect town centre shopping areas. Small business owners in town centres are also fearful of their livelihood in this situation.

Yet many people are in favour. Customers like a variety of goods to be available in their area and they like the superstores because they are cheaper than local traders. Some councillors may be in favour because it increases employment in the area.

Whose side are you on? Debate the issue as a group and decide what you would do if you ran your local council!

ACTIVITY

1 Identify those stakeholders who would be:
   a indifferent to the idea
   b for the idea
   c against the idea.

2 Assume each group of stakeholders wants to 'win the battle'. What action might they take to further their cause?

3 The local paper becomes involved. How might the views of the editor influence the type of press coverage the dispute receives?

4 Is the outcome likely to be any different if unemployment is quite high in the region? Give a reason for your answer.

5 What factors will have influenced the company's choice of location?

6 Assuming there are no other suitable sites for development, what do you think should be the outcome, and why?

7 In many areas of the country there is conflict about the growth of superstores in out-of-town locations. Environmentalists are opposed

SNAPSHOT

Vodafone – where are you now?

At the 1999 AGM of Vodafone Airtouch their chief executive, Chris Gent, informed shareholders that the company would review its location if the government bowed to pressure from environmentalists. Vodafone's headquarters are in Newbury and it wants to develop a new £100 million, seven-building complex for almost 3,400 employees on the edge of the town. But environmentalists have protested about the new development, planned on a green field site. Although Vodafone has got local authority approval, Friends of the Earth are arguing that the proposed development would cause new traffic headaches. Mr Gent disputes this. He says that currently staff make over a thousand journeys a day between the 57 offices currently in existence around the town and that the new development would reduce road usage, rather than increase it.

Reading and Swindon local authorities are watching developments with interest. Both have offered alternative sites if the Newbury development is blocked.

Section review

Refresh your memory of the previous section by writing short answers to each of the following questions and activities.

1 *Give two reasons why business location is important.*

2 *Identify two types of business activities where it is important the business is located near to its customers. Say why this is important for each activity you identify.*

3 *Some types of businesses prefer to be situated near to their competitors. In other cases this may be a disaster. Can you think of two examples of:*
   a *businesses which locate near to their competitors*
   b *businesses which do not.*
   In each case give a reason for your answer.

4 *When would a business choose to locate near its major supplier?*

5 *What type of businesses are located near motorways – and why?*

6 *Some businesses locate where labour is cheap. When would this be an important consideration to a company?*

7 *Explain the meaning of the term 'stakeholder'.*

8 *Some stakeholders are more powerful than others.*
   a *Why does this difference occur?*
   b *Give an example of a stakeholder with a great deal of influence on business. Give a reason for your choice.*
   c *Give an example of a stakeholder with little influence. Again, explain your choice.*

9 *What factors influence the number of stakeholders who have an interest in a business?*

10 *Give an example of a situation where stakeholders may have competing interests. Try to think of an alternative to the ones which have already been outlined in this section.*

2.4 INVESTIGATING BUSINESS ORGANISATIONS AND ACTIVITIES

At the end of this section you should be able to:

- organise your own investigation into two contrasting businesses
- identify the information you need to collect or research
- research the information you need
- identify the current trends affecting that particular type of business activity.

Overview of the investigation

Your assessment for this unit involves investigating two contrasting business organisations. Studying two very different businesses means that you don't repeat yourself! It also gives you the opportunity to contrast the two.

The aim is to demonstrate that you understand how the businesses you are investigating fit into the wider business world and which influences have the most effect on them.

It is a requirement of the GNVQ award that one organisation **must** be small (a sole trader or a partnership) and the other **must** be larger (a company, cooperative, franchise or in the public sector).

However, you need to ensure that:

- each operates in a different industrial sector
- they carry out different activities
- the scale and scope of their operations are different.

This gives you greater opportunities to contrast their operations. It can be beneficial to investigate *different* businesses from any you chose for Unit 1. This not only broadens your own experiences, it also reduces the number of visits you have to make to one particular organisation.

Figure 2.53 Contrasting businesses

Organising your investigation

Re-read the do's and dont's at the end of Unit 1 (page 115–16). Virtually all of these also apply to this investigation!

Talk through your choice of business organisations with your tutor. If you are unable to investigate two actual businesses then it may be possible to investigate one and to use a case study for your other investigation. However, this is less satisfactory than finding out about a real enterprise.

At this stage, you may wish to consider the range of industries and businesses which operate in your own region and discuss these with your tutor. You also need to decide which businesses you can find out about easily and which would be more difficult. If you work part-time then your employer is an obvious option – provided the business is suitable. Alternatively, you may be able to use a business where you are having work experience or where your family or friends work.

A word of warning! It is usually very difficult to get the right type of information about a very large national or international organisation. You may also find that you gather a lot of irrelevant material on its operations which you may not understand. It is very difficult to sort this out to focus on the correct area. In many cases, students have problems if they choose organisations with more than about 250 employees.

Structure and content of the investigation

You need to obtain information on five different aspects of each business:

- The type of ownership – and how appropriate it is for each business.

- Whether each business is expanding or declining – and why.

- Current trends which are affecting each industrial sector in general.

- Current trends which are affecting the business activities of the organisations you are studying.

- Other influences on the business – such as location and stakeholders – and how the business is responding to these.

We will now look at these in more detail.

Type of ownership

You already know there are different forms of business ownership and that you have to study one business which is a sole trader or partnership and one business which is a company in the private sector, a franchise, a cooperative or an organisation which is publically owned.

You need to be able to show you understand the main features of the types of ownership which apply to the businesses you are investigating. Describe any type of ownership agreement – whether formal or informal – then explain the legal status. Remember that formal legal requirements are needed to form a company but not to form a partnership – though this would be useful. There will be a formal agreement between a franchisor and franchisee. The legal status of ownership is quite straightforward unless you are investigating a cooperative which may have unlimited or limited liability. You will have to find out which applies in your investigation.

Next describe the liability of the owners. This is not *financial* liability but a description of the responsibilities and drawbacks of that form of ownership.

Try to relate your description of ownership with the size of the business. You are unlikely to find a public limited company with 5 employees or a sole trader with 500! So there is an obvious link and you must find out how this operates for the businesses you are investigating.

Industrial sectors

You need to find out which industrial sector each business belongs to. This part is easy. Remember that some businesses operate in more than one sector – so check if this applies in your investigation. You must then:

Figure 2.54 Which industrial sector does this company belong to?

- describe the major trends that have applied to that sector over the last few years (up to ten years is quite sufficient)

- describe the different industries and business activities that comprise that particular sector.

Remember that graphs and tables show trends and changes and will help you to produce a more professionally finished document.

To achieve a higher grade you need to apply your knowledge of sector trends to at least one of the businesses you are investigating. You can do this by explaining how sector trends are affecting (or have affected) one of the businesses you are studying.

Business activities

You need to describe in full the main activities carried out by each business. Also, try to identify the core business activity. Is the business concerned with retail services,

transport or manufacturing, for instance? Does each business deal with products, services or both? What is the scale (i.e. how large) and scope (i.e. range of products/geographic area) of their operations? Then explain the trends of growth or decline for that particular activity in the UK. How are these trends affecting the businesses you have selected?

If you are studying a local organisation regional figures will probably be most appropriate. If you are studying a large national company, then national data will be more relevant. Guidance on sources of information is given on pages 205 and 206.

Location

Think about where the business is located. Why did it choose to be there? Is there a specific reason? Has the business always been there or has it moved from somewhere else? Try to find the reason for its original location and the reason for any moves. Is the current

Figure 2.55 Which part of town would you expect to find an estate agent?

location good or are there drawbacks? How does the location meet each business's need for resources? What influences are significant now and might affect its location in the future?

You should consider the influence of competitors at this point. If you are investigating a retailer or an estate agent, for instance, you may find that they are located in a certain district of the town. In a local community, business districts and shopping districts may change over time and businesses may move to 'stay with' the competition – or to stay separate. Find out if the competition has changed over the years and, if so, in what ways. Find out if this has had any influence on location or not.

You could illustrate this part of your investigation with a map or diagram of each locality. This should show important connections to resources, such as the location of the workforce, location of competitors, suppliers and transport routes. Don't forget to add explanatory notes so that your map or diagram is clear to the reader. A brief commentary is useful so that the reader knows what you were thinking and what conclusions you came to when you drew your map.

Stakeholders

You already know that all businesses are influenced by different groups of stakeholders and that some have more influence than others. You also know that stakeholders have an interest in the business because they are affected, in some ways, by its activities. In this section you will need to identify the stakeholders for *each* business (remember these will be different) and describe their main interests in full. Remember that different aspects of the business affect different stakeholders and that stakeholders' interests may vary, depending on different features of each business, such as the scale of its activities and the ownership of the business.

Find out if there have been any changes to stakeholder interests and expectations over the past few years – and how much influence each group has on the business. You need to show you understand why some stakeholders are more powerful than others and how they express their views. And what the business does in response.

To achieve a higher grade you will need to explain why the influence of stakeholders is different in each business. You also need to consider why there might be conflicts of interest among different stakeholders in a particular business. Even if there have been no conflicts so far, the fact that you have explained how they might arise in the future will help your grade.

Putting it all together

If you meet these criteria and obtain the correct information you will pass this unit. However, higher grades will be awarded to students who have:

- investigated each area thoroughly
- assembled the information in a logical order
- selected appropriate information (and discarded what is not relevant)
- identified their sources (see Unit 1, page 118)
- included relevant regional/local/national data on business and industry trends
- effectively compared both businesses. It is this last point which is often the most difficult.

Making comparisons

You may think it is hard enough to find out information on one business, let alone two. However, *comparing* two businesses is an even greater skill.

First, it is not necessary to compare each business, line by line, from every point of view. No-one will expect to read statements such as 'John Brown employs 4 staff but Telsor Engineering Ltd employs 50 staff, John Brown is a sole trader whilst Telsor is a private limited company, John Brown started in 1965 but Telsor was established in 1928'!

You need to decide what the main areas are for comparison, i.e. what are the key features that show some similarities and important differences. There are several options. Choose which one suits you best.

1   Describe one business, then describe the next, then do your 'comparative' section on *relevant* points only.
2   Cover each section at a time, e.g. ownership. Cover one business then the other, then compare the two but only on points that are appropriate. Then move on to the next section.
3   Cover your comparative sections with a table showing the similarities and differences – or two tables, one for each.

There are advantages and disadvantages to these approaches that you can discuss with your tutor. However, to get a good mark, the 'comparative' section always needs to be the most carefully written.

You may find it helpful to do this in the following way.

1   Start by gathering your information. You can't compare anything until you have all (or most of) the facts at your fingertips.
2   Draft your information sections – first for one business and then for the other.
3   Print out a draft copy. Go through this with a highlighter and identify interesting points of comparison. For instance, both businesses may have been located in the same area originally, but John Brown has had to move to replace his lost customers when the area declined,

whereas Telsor, with a broader customer base, did not need to.
4   You may find you have a possible point of interest for one business but do not know enough about the other business to compare it properly. It is always useful to leave yourself enough time to contact a business further if you need to – you can then telephone your contact to get the details you need.
5   Group your comparative remarks in sensible clusters. Use paragraphs. In this way you will deal with one item properly before moving on to the next.
6   Don't leave people guessing! In the above example, it's no use simply saying John Brown had to move but Telsor did not. Remember you need to say *why*. This is probably the most important question you should answer constantly throughout your work.

Researching your information

You can divide the information you need into two types:

a   that which you can only find out from visiting the business and talking to someone
b   that which you can research yourself, either from the Internet or from your library.

Visiting the business

To do this properly you have to plan well and be organised. Otherwise you might have to repeat a visit to check on things you forgot to ask the first time (which can be embarrassing) or you can lose valuable information you spent hours obtaining!

Figure 2.59 has a checklist you may find helpful. It might be useful to send it in advance to the person who has agreed to help you – so they know the type of information you are looking for. You should also anticipate making a few visits to find out everything you need – certainly expect to make at least two visits. You should make the business aware that you may have to make more than one visit or that you might have to phone them for extra information.

Useful hints and tips.

- Personal contact is always very helpful. It is always easier to arrange a meeting with someone you know, or if someone has mentioned your name in advance, than with a complete stranger in an unknown firm. If you are dealing with a stranger then introduce yourself properly.

- Explain *clearly* why you need the information, i.e. you are doing a case study on two comparative businesses for your GNVQ Intermediate Business award.

Figure 2.56 You need to be well-prepared when you visit the business you are studying

- Give a positive reason for choosing their business (not because it's the only one you could think of!). For instance, you think their business would be particularly interesting to study.

- Stress that you are not required to ask about financial information or anything confidential.

- Ask if you can meet the person who has a good, overall view of the business so you can talk to them about your case study.

- Agree to give the person who helps you a copy of your final work if he or she would like one (it's the least you can do!).

- If you are offered a tour around the business accept with gratitude. It will heighten your awareness of the business and how it operates.

- Arrange a meeting at a time, date and place to suit *them*. If this is during normal class time, make sure you tell your tutor in advance.

- Confirm the meeting in writing, if you can. A large firm, especially, will be impressed with your efficiency – provided your letter is well written and set out.

- Turn up about five minutes before the time scheduled. *Never* be late. If an emergency occurs at the last minute, telephone them, apologise and explain.

- Prepare your questions in advance and treble check you haven't forgotten anything.

- Note any useful facts and figures you have already researched and which you may want to mention during the discussion.

- Take an A4 pad containing lined paper, on which you can make notes.

- If you are hopeless at listening and writing at the same time, you could take

Figure 2.57 Make sure you thank those who help you

a tape recorder as well. But if the person to whom you are talking prefers not to use it, then you will have to go along with their wishes.

- When the interview ends, make sure you thank the person properly for helping you. Anyone in business is usually busy, so if they have given up their time to help you they deserve your gratitude.

- If you know you will need to revisit them, try to arrange the next visit before you leave. This saves you having to telephone and – more importantly – will help keep your time schedule on track.

- Write up your notes as soon as you return to college or – even better – as soon as you get home. Even professional interviewers do this!

Researching information

Do get to know your college library and how it is set out. You will find a wealth of information there if you know where to look.

Talk to your librarian if you are stuck – you will normally find library staff very helpful and knowledgeable. Don't forget that a lot of information can be found on CD-Rom or on your college Internet site.

You will find it invaluable if you can use the Internet. All government statistics are available on www.open.gov.uk and these are continually updated. There are some useful notes of guidance for students on the Office for National Statistics (ONS) web site – including a warning not to leave your research to the last minute! There is also a list of resources you may find helpful. These include:

- Free pamphlets from ONS libraries including:
  - government statistics – a brief guide to sources
  - UK in figures
  - ONS publications catalogue
  - labour market statistics – a guide to sources

Figure 2.58 Use the library for research

○ guide to services of the ONS.

- Major ONS economic publications, which you should find in your local or college library, including:

  ○ *Family Expenditure Survey*

  ○ *Retail Prices 1914–1990*

  ○ *Business Monitor MM23 – Retail Prices Index*

  ○ *UK National Accounts – The Blue Book*

  ○ *Economic Trends* (monthly)

  ○ *Labour Market Trends*

  ○ *Regional Trends*

  ○ *Key Data*

  ○ *Annual Abstract of Statistics*

  ○ *Monthly Digest of Statistics.*

- Social statistics – again many of these will be in your local or college library, including:

  ○ *Social Trends*

  ○ *General Household Survey*

  ○ *Social Focus Series*

  ○ *Birth Statistics*

  ○ *Marriage and Divorce Statistics*

  ○ *Housing in England*

  ○ *Key Population and Vital Statistics.*

- Census data – every 10 years in Britain there is a census which provides a huge amount of statistical information. If you are studying this award after 2002 you are fortunate, as the 2001 census figures will be published that year. Otherwise the latest set is for 1991.

The ONS can be contacted on the Internet but the information you get will be more limited. Remember that all the major newspapers have Internet sites. The TUC can be contacted on www.tuc.org.uk and has a link to the biz.ed site which has useful information. Do develop the skills to use a good search engine properly, e.g. www.altavista.com or www.yahoo.com. If you then define your search properly you can get a variety of useful information – just make sure it applies to the UK and not to the United States!

Finally, if you need statistics your library doesn't appear to have, you must ask for help. Library staff are knowledgeable and helpful. Giving advice is why they are there – and a key part of their job. They can also obtain almost any publication you need on an inter-library loan service. However, remember that many of the books you will be studying will be 'reference only' copies which you can't remove – so take enough money to pay for photocopies.

A final word of warning. Don't overwhelm yourself with pages of figures and tables, none of which you understand. It's better to work with, say, three or four sets of figures and analyse these properly. If you obtain data you can't understand, have a word with your tutor.

Organising and selecting information

Storing your information safely, labelling it clearly and keeping it well organised is essential. Nothing is more frustrating than trying to write up an investigation, case study, assignment or project and not being able to find what you need. Make sure you put everything in a folder, clearly marked. It is useful to date your research notes, then you know which 'version' is the most recent.

If you haven't enough material and are genuinely stuck, ask your tutor for guidance. If you have a great deal of information you may be tempted to include everything, whether it is relevant or not. Do make sure that you only use what is required. Otherwise you will be doing extra and unnecessary work. Your final assessment is judged on quality – not the number of pages you submit!

 **ACTIVITY**

Go through the checklist in Figure 2.59 and talk to your tutor about anything you don't understand. Discuss with your tutor whether you could extend the list in any way.

Now mark each item (a) or (b). Items marked (a) are those you have to find out from someone at the business. Items marked (b) are those you can start researching now. Often this is useful because it gives you a greater understanding of, say, the industrial sector, employment in the area, current trends affecting that type of business. This knowledge is useful when you talk to someone in the business and makes them realise you are taking your work seriously.

Section review

Refresh your memory of the previous section by writing short answers to each of the following questions and activities.

1 *Why is the Internet useful for researching information?*

2 *What steps should you take before contacting any business about your investigations?*

3 *What is meant by 'two contrasting businesses'?*

4 *You want to investigate a sole trader and a partnership. Is this permissible?*

5 *List three publications in your college library which will be helpful in your research.*

6 *How should you prepare for an interview with a business person about your investigation?*

What is the name of the business?

What size and scale is the business (e.g. number of employees/scope of its operations)?

Who owns it?

What is the legal status of the business?

What are the liabilities of the owners?

How does the ownership of the business link to the size/scale of the business?

In which industrial sector does it operate?

Is this sector increasing/decreasing?

What other industries and activities are included in this sector?

What types of activities are carried out by the business?

What is the core business activity?

Has the business changed in size over the last few years?

Does the business expect to change in size in the near future?

What trends are affecting the business activities?

Where is the business located?

Why was it located there?

Has the business ever relocated – and if so, why?

What factors could cause it to relocate in the future?

How many employees are there?

Is the business dependent on highly skilled employees?

Is employment high/low in the area?

Does the business find it easy to recruit the staff it needs?

Who are its customers?

What factors affect the buying decisions of the customers?

Who are its competitors?

How does the business ensure it competes successfully?

Who are its stakeholders?

Which stakeholders have the most influence – and why?

What measures does the business take to listen and respond to important stakeholders?

Have there ever been any conflicts of interest between stakeholders?

In what type of situation could this occur?

Figure 2.59 Business investigation checklist

7 *State three factors to bear in mind when you are organising and selecting information.*

8 *What is the best way to go about comparing two businesses?*

9 *Why is it useful for your business contact to see your checklist of questions in advance?*

10 *What fundamental courtesies should you observe so that business people think you are a pleasant and efficient student to deal with?*

A successful business owner, who spent many years building up his organisation from scratch, asked all job applicants one critical question at interviews: 'Why am I in business?' He would accept only one answer – so you may like to consider how you would respond. Any other response and the interview was promptly terminated and the applicant rejected for the job, no matter how qualified or experienced they were.

The answer he wanted was: 'To make a profit'. He didn't want to employ anyone who didn't understand that finance was the lifeblood of his business and that making a profit was critical to survival.

This illustrates the importance of this unit. If you have a key role to play in helping make your organisation successful you need to understand business finance. This unit has all the essential information you need.

By the time you have completed the unit you will know:

* the different types of costs involved in starting up and operating a business

* the different types of revenue (income) received by different businesses

* how costs and revenues may vary for particular types of products

* how businesses can forecast future revenues and payments so that they can make sensible decisions for the future

* how businesses can work out how many sales are required for a particular product or service to be profitable

* how to estimate the profit (or loss) of a business over a particular period

* the financial documents which are used when goods and services are bought and sold, and how these are completed

* the role of computers in forecasting, recording and monitoring business finance today.

This unit is externally assessed. You will be set questions in an assessment paper by your awarding body. Questions will be set at pass, merit or distinction level. This means that even if you answer some pass grade questions wrongly, but answer some merit or distinction grade questions correctly, you could still achieve an overall pass grade for the unit. However, it is important you cover and learn **all** the content of this unit to give yourself the best chance possible of achieving a good grade – preferably a merit or distinction – for the whole unit.

The best way to do this is to get plenty of practice in each of the topic areas. However, you will also need to understand the importance of the different techniques and documents used, why and how they help businesses and, above all, why they must always be accurate!

In this unit, you will find many practical activities. You are recommended to do **all** these – and to ask your tutor if you do not understand anything. The answers to all of them are given at the end of the book – but please don't look at them unless you are absolutely stuck. Finally, you should supplement these activities with additional exercises, particularly on the topics you find more difficult rather than those you find easy!

3.1 THE IMPORTANCE OF COSTS AND REVENUE

At the end of this section you should be able to:

- identify the start-up costs which must be met before a new product or service can be provided
- identify the running costs with which businesses are involved on a day-to-day basis
- explain the difference between fixed and variable costs
- identify the revenue which businesses receive from selling goods and/or services
- calculate profit (or loss) from given information on costs and revenue
- apply your knowledge of costs, revenues and profit to a particular business.

Overview of costs and revenue

You probably go into a shop almost every day of your life and buy something. Have you ever wondered **why** you pay the price you do for a particular item? A Mars bar, a file folder, a pair of jeans, this book, a hair cut, having a suit dry cleaned, going to see a film – why do these items cost what they do? And what about workmen either in your home or around your college – how do they know what to charge for a particular job? If you wanted to pay someone to paint the house, or tile a floor or build a wall – how much would that person charge – and why? How much does it cost to teach you, for one hour in college?

One obvious factor in calculating the price to charge a customer is the **cost** of producing the item or performing the service. If Mars charged less for a Mars bar than it cost to make it, then very soon Mars would stop producing them – or go out of business. The same applies to your local hairdresser and cinema and to any local painter or builder you employed. The painter, for example, needs to charge enough to pay for the materials he uses and for the time he spends doing the job.

However, there are often more costs involved in making a product or offering a service than you may think – and a person going into business for the first time has the additional task of finding the money to start up the enterprise. How much will they need to save or borrow? What sort of expenditure is sensible – and what is not? What items are essential – and what can be bought later? Can premises be rented or a vehicle leased to save paying out large sums of money at the outset? A useful way to start is to imagine that you are considering going into business and then look at all the different types of costs you may meet – before you start putting in any actual figures.

Figure 3.1 Starting your own business involves costs

Before you do this, look at the example below. This should give you some insight about the financial situation of many people in the UK who run a small business on their own.

Practical example – 1

Steve trained as a plasterer when he left school. He now works for himself. He is good at his job and is friendly with all the local builders – who often find him work. Steve works, on average, 5 days a week for 45 weeks a year.

He charges customers £120 a day. Out of this he pays for plaster (on average, he uses 2 bags a day at £5 each), his van and petrol. On average, he spends £1,300 a year on motoring costs (tax, insurance, repairs) but his van is getting old. He also classifies his mobile phone as a business expense and this costs him about £400 a year. He has also recently started a private pension scheme and pays £50 a month into this.

1   How much does Steve earn each year?

2   What are Steve's total business expenses each year?

3   How much will Steve have left from his earnings after paying his expenses and his pension payments?

4   Assume Steve pays no tax on the first £5,000 he has left after paying his expenses, but pays tax at 23 per cent on the rest, how much money will he have left each year?

5   If Steve is saving £100 a month towards a new van, how much will he have left to live on each month?

6   a   If Steve increased his charges to improve his income, what negative effects might this have on his business?

    b   How could Steve minimise these problems?

Answers are given on page 277.

Starting a business

Starting a business is a big step for anyone. It usually means leaving a job with a regular salary and taking the gamble that they will make more money in the long run by working for themselves. However, before they take this step they have to make sure their idea will work. It must be more than a hunch – it must be well thought out and costed carefully. Most new entrepreneurs start by making out a **business plan** – often with the help of a specialist adviser. This is essential for borrowing **capital** – money used in setting up the business. No bank or financial institution would ever consider lending money to a new business without scrutinising a business plan first.

There are various issues involved in preparing a plan – and some of these add to start-up costs. If you remember the six steps below, this will help you to bear in mind the stages in starting up a business from scratch.

Figure 3.2 You will need a business plan if you want to borrow money to start a business

Step 1 – the idea

Anyone with a 'good' business idea needs to step back and think about it critically. What are the strengths and weaknesses? What opportunities are there for the idea – and what problems (or threats) might be there be? This is often known as the **SWOT approach**. For instance, if you decided to set up a business designing web pages you may identify your technical skills in this area as a strength and your lack of experience running a business as a weakness. You may see an opportunity in advertising your service cheaply through the Internet and a threat in the high number of competitors in this business.

Often a business adviser will help a budding entrepreneur to think about the idea objectively and to identify all the problems and opportunities at the outset.

Step 2 – identify the market

It is one thing to think of a product to make or a service to provide – but will anyone want to buy it, and at what price? At this point it is important to identify potential customers as precisely as possible in terms of their customer profile, e.g. sex, age, income, spending habits. Very few businesses can afford to provide an overall service to all its potential customers. Usually they have to choose between offering a general service to a restricted number of customers – as in a particular geographical area – or offering a specialist service more widely. This is often known as **niche marketing**. For example, bread is a general product which may be produced and sold by a local baker in a town or village. Whereas speciality breads, such as those that accompany Thai, Indian or Italian meals, may be made by a specialist and distributed more widely.

At this stage, the entrepreneur must be able to identify:

- the key features of the goods or services
- the advantages of these over any competitors
- the **USP** – unique selling point – of the product.

Start-up costs are kept down if an entrepreneur does his or her own market research – through the local library, Internet, contacting government information services (such as the Office of National Statistics). However, many prefer to pay an expert to do this – and expert market researchers can charge up to £400 a day for their services. They will identify potential customers and their profile. From this you can predict potential sales, as well as appropriate advertising and where to sell the product or market the service.

Once the market is identified, you need to prepare a marketing plan showing how potential customers will be told about the product/service and how much will be spent on marketing and advertising at the outset.

Step 3 – consider prices and profits

The price charged for a product or service is usually more than it costs to make or provide. That is obvious. But if you think about brands such as Armani, Versace, Ferarri and Lambourghini it is obvious that not every business simply adds a small surplus for profit on top of the cost! At this stage our entrepreneur must consider what the market will pay for the goods – and this will be part of the market research investigation.

Everyday products, for which there is a lot of competition, are likely to be priced low. Otherwise they wouldn't sell. However, pricing too low can make potential customers think the product or service is inferior. Competitors' prices are a good indication of what the market will pay.

Specialist products, such as designer clothes or jewellery, are deliberately priced much higher, and this helps to compensate for fewer sales. A high price can make customers think a product or service is exclusive and high quality.

The general rule is that the lower the price (within reason) the more goods will be sold, the higher the price the fewer goods will be sold.

Step 4 – financial forecasting

If the market research survey shows what initial sales are possible and what price can be charged, the revenue for the first year can be predicted. This is usually done for various levels of sales – low, average and high.

At this point it is important to identify all the costs involved in making the product or providing the service. The total costs involved for each level of sales can then be worked out (see page 228).

Finally, the difference between the two will indicate potential profit for each level of sales.

Step 5 – thinking the unthinkable

At this stage more critical thinking is required. In business nothing is certain and nothing lasts forever. Our entrepreneur needs to consider what he or she would do if:

- advances in technology make the product or service out of date

- a competitor starts a price war

- they received an unexpected order for a large number of goods to be produced in a very short time.

The entrepreneur needs to think about these issues and make a **sensitivity analysis**. In

other words, he or she needs to identify those areas where sales are 'sensitive' to change.

Step 6 – obtaining the finance

By now our budding entrepreneur has thought through his/her business idea in some detail. Assuming the idea is still viable, the items required to start up the business need to be listed and costed. These may be funded through savings, obtaining a grant or loan, trade credit (see page 217) and renting/leasing. If any money needs to be borrowed, the **cost** of the borrowings, i.e. the **interest** charged, is another cost item.

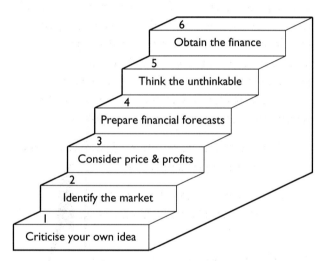

Figure 3.3 First steps to starting a business

Practical example – 2

Three students in a college decide to produce a quarterly newsletter/magazine. It will contain articles on local events; record, film and video reviews and topics of particular interest to students, such as financial advice and renting/sharing a flat. The revenue will come from sales of the magazine plus advertisements from local traders.

The students do their own market research. They aim to sell the magazine to 16–25 year olds. In their own town there is a college with

7,000 full-time students in this age group and two sixth form colleges each with about 800 students. Their research tells them that at least 1 in 5 students will buy the magazine, possibly 2 in 5 and, if they are very lucky, 3 in 5.

They can advertise cheaply by putting up their own posters. They have investigated potential advertisers and think that they could initially charge £12.50 for a quarter page advertisement, £25 for a half page and £50 for a full page. If the magazine is successful they could increase these charges.

They have asked students how much they would be prepared to pay for the magazine. At £1 only 1 in 5 would buy it, at 75p perhaps 2 in 5 would and at 50p perhaps 5 in 10. This is a point you should note – with most goods the higher the price the fewer the sales. So, if you want to sell big quantities, the price must be low. This however does not mean that the most profit would be made at that price – as you will see.

1   What is the total number of students in the area in the right age group?

2   1 in 5 students say they will buy the magazine at £1. How much revenue would this earn?

3   Now repeat this calculation for:

   a   2 in 5 students buying the magazine at 75p, and

   b   5 in 10 students buying it at 50p.

4   If it was your magazine,

   a   what price would you charge and why?

   b   at this price, how many magazines would you hope to sell?

5   You have five pages available for advertising. What would be your maximum quarterly revenue, initially, from this source?

6   What would be your total revenue from advertising plus sales?

7   The college will charge you for the paper you use and for photocopying (in black and white). You have calculated that each magazine will cost you 30p to produce and distribute if you do all the work yourselves.

   What would be your total costs of production if you made the quantity you selected in question 4b above?

8   If you can keep as profit the surplus from your revenue from sales and advertising, less your production costs, how much will you have made from your first sales?

9   As a group, do a sensitivity analysis of this idea. What changes could occur or what miscalculations might there be which may affect your predictions? In other words, what could go wrong?

Answers to this activity are given on page 277.

SNAPSHOT

A risky business!

Despite the importance of insurance, the Federation of Small Businesses estimates that 400,000 small businesses in the UK have inadequate insurance cover. All businesses are required by law to have employers' liability insurance (which covers employees as to injury, death or disease) and some professionals need to take out cover against malpractice. All vehicles must have third party insurance as a minimum. Ideally, the business should also have the building fully insured, as well as the contents (including stock), against risks such as fire, flood, accidental damage and theft. Vehicles may be best insured as fully comprehensive – and the premium is higher if goods are carried.

The one risk that retailers cannot insure against is shoplifting. Theft to an insurer involves breaking and entering.

Understanding start-up costs

The college students had very few start-up costs as they were using the equipment and facilities in their college to produce and distribute their magazine. However, this is very unusual. Even someone working from home needs basics such as a computer, telephone, printer and printed stationery!

The types of costs vary from one business to another. A list of likely types of expenses is given in Figure 3.4 on page 218. Before you look at this list, brainstorm some ideas yourself, as a group and make out your own list. Then see how many you thought of!

Quite a list, isn't it? Let's look at this in more detail, again through a practical example.

Practical example – 3

Jacqui Fallon has worked as a hairdresser for several years and knows she is good. She has clients who return week after week to her. She dislikes working for someone else and feels she could do better on her own. A few months ago her grandmother died and left her £10,000. Jacqui is seriously considering using this money to start up her own business.

She has seen some premises she likes which would cost £4,000 a year to rent – and she would have to pay three months' rent in advance. Business rates in the town would add another £2,000 a year. These are payable in 10 monthly instalments. She wants to redecorate the premises and has obtained a quotation of £500 for this. The installation of sinks and hairdryers will cost £2,500 and furniture (chairs, reception desk etc.) will cost a further £2,000. She needs to take out insurance – the minimum payment for essential liability insurance is £250 but she also wants to insure the building and contents and this will cost her a further £200 a year. She wants to use specialist products and also to offer these on sale to her clients. She estimates she will need to spend £850 on supplies and stock at the outset. She also needs sundry items – an appointments book, telephone, towels, overalls and protective gloves, cleaning materials and supplies and has allocated £750 for these. Power is connected to the premises, there is an existing telephone point and she has purchased a simple telephone answering system for £150. She thinks that most of her advertising will be by word of mouth through her current clients, but has allocated £500 for local advertising and printing posters.

1 Itemise all Jacqui's start-up costs and calculate how much her total bill will be.

2 Jacqui sensibly realises that she will need a 'contingency fund' of about £1,000 to cover any unexpected items and also to give her some money to live on while the business starts to generate some income. Allowing for this, how much money will Jacqui have left from her inheritance?

3 Jacqui is expecting to receive revenue from **two** sources. Can you identify each of these?

4 Jacqui needs to decide how much to charge clients. As a group, discuss what factors she needs to consider when reaching this decision.

5 Jacqui's colleague, Sara, is also thinking of starting up on her own but she likes the idea of being a mobile hairdresser. Draw up a list of start-up items that Sara will need, using Figure 3.4 as a guide, and discuss the likely cost of each with your tutor.

6 Who do you think would be able to generate the most revenue each week, Jacqui or Sara? Give a reason for your answer.

Answers are given on page 277.

Understanding running costs

Running costs – often known as **operating costs** – are the costs which must be met on a day-to-day basis. Several of them are simply extensions of the type of costs involved in starting up a business, but you will also find several new types of costs. A full list of typical business expenses is given in Figure 3.5 on page 218. Again, test yourself before looking at this – see how many regular expenses you can identify for an average business.

The type of expenses will always vary from one business to another. A manufacturing unit will need packaging materials and/or to pay for the distribution of goods to its customers, a retail shop will spend money on wrapping paper or carrier bags, an office may have higher communication charges for telephone, fax and Internet access.

Running costs can be divided into two types – **fixed costs** and **variable costs**. It is important that you understand the difference between these.

- **Fixed costs** do not vary with output. No matter how many items are produced or sold these costs remain the same. They therefore include all the general business **overheads**, such as rent, rates, insurance, heating and most staff salaries.

- **Variable costs** vary with output. The more goods are produced or sold the higher the variable costs. They include raw materials, packaging, sales commission payments, wages paid to people who are hired for a specific production job.

Adding the fixed and variable costs together gives you the **total costs** of running the business.

SNAPSHOT

Sale or return?

Stock can be a major item of expenditure for many new business owners. For a moment, try to estimate the cost of stocking a jeweller's shop or a record shop from day one!

*For most new entrepreneurs, however, help is available from manufacturers and wholesalers who allow a retailer to purchase goods now and pay for them later. This is known as **trade credit**. The goods are ordered and delivered and are paid for over a period of time (often between one and three months). The seller, of course, hopes that by then most of the initial stock will have been sold to cover the payments. The amount of money a customer is allowed to owe is known as their **credit limit** and this will vary from one customer to another. Customers who are financially sound and have a good*

record for reliability and prompt payments will usually have a higher credit limit than a smaller firm or a new customer.

*An even better deal, which some lucky retailers get, is goods supplied on **sale or return**. This means that unsold goods can be returned, free of charge, after a period of time. The retailer only pays for the goods he or she sells. Usually, this type of offer is only made available by manufacturers on obsolete lines or when they are desperate to sell off overstocks at the factory or warehouse. Some market traders specialise in buying and selling these items and will change the goods they sell to take advantage of such opportunities. In some businesses, sale or return is the custom. Most newspapers, for example, are sold to newsagents on this basis.*

Note that this is a very comprehensive list and very few businesses would need all these items!

- market research
- premises (purchase price or rent deposit or lease premium)
- any building alterations required
- fixtures and fittings
- legal/professional fees
- furniture
- equipment
- communications equipment, e.g. computer, phone, fax etc.
- advertising/promotional materials
- initial stock supplies or raw materials
- utilities and power, e.g. electricity, gas, heating, water, telephone etc. (if not already installed/connected)
- insurance (first premium)
- production machinery and tools
- protective clothing and equipment
- transport/delivery vehicles
- packaging materials
- business stationery
- licenses/permits (required by certain businesses only, such as pubs, children's nurseries, nursing homes, pet shops, gambling establishments)
- interest on any loans.

Figure 3.4 Business start-up costs

Business running costs are likely to include:

- owner's salary
- staff salaries
- insurance premiums
- rent or lease payments
- business rates
- advertising and promotions
- accountancy fees
- raw materials or stocks for resale
- utility payments – gas, electricity, water rates
- communication charges – telephone, fax, Internet links
- vehicle running costs (tax, insurance, fuel)
- depreciation on vehicles and equipment
- repairs and maintenance
- loan repayments
- interest on loans
- business stationery
- packaging materials
- postal and distribution charges
- miscellaneous supplies (e.g. cleaning materials, magazines for reception etc.)
- miscellaneous expenses (e.g. window cleaning, printing, photocopying etc.)
- professional subscriptions and fees
- tax

Figure 3.5 Business running costs

The type of costs incurred will vary depending upon the nature of the business. A manufacturing company will need production equipment which will have to be maintained and serviced but may spend little on decorations or fixtures and fittings. It will buy raw materials and packaging and pay for distributing the goods to its purchasers. A high-class department store may have deep pile carpets, escalators and elaborate displays. It will buy stock for resale and may pay sales commission to some of its sales people. So don't expect the type of costs you meet to be identical for all businesses – they will vary for specific types of businesses.

ACTIVITY 1

1   Your own household has fixed and variable costs, too! If you go on holiday then your fixed costs still need paying, but your variable costs do not.

As a group:

a   make a list of the normal average expenses incurred by a household such as your own

b   decide which you would still have to pay if you were on holiday and label these fixed costs

c   now check all the other items. These should clearly be variable costs.

You may find it hard to categorise some items. Your telephone, for instance, is partly fixed (the line rental) but partly variable (the number of calls made). Costs like this are sometimes called **semi-variable**, but at this stage of your studies you should classify all these items as fixed costs.

2   Go through the list in Figure 3.5 and check which would be fixed and which would be variable for a business. Compare your answers with other members in your group.

3   Go through this list again and decide which costs would apply to each of the following:
    a   a motor cycle courier
    b   a sportswear shop
    c   an estate agent.

Understanding revenue

Revenue is the income generated by the business. Businesses make money by selling goods or selling services or both – as you saw with Jacqui on page 216. Like costs, the type of revenue received will vary from one business to another.

In some businesses, such as retail trades and hairdressing, most sales are **cash**. This means that customers pay when they make a purchase. However, businesses selling to other businesses will be selling goods on credit. This means they allow the buyer some time to pay – usually one or two months. In these cases the revenue arrives after the sale is made. Here the seller must guard against two things.

a   **Running short of money** in the bank (because suppliers have demanded payment before customers have paid).

b   **Bad debts**. These are debts which remain unpaid because the buyer has defaulted on the deal. It is for this reason that most businesses carry out credit checks on new customers before allowing them to buy goods this way.

Having insufficient money in the bank is a far more common problem than bad debt. This is known as **cashflow** (see Figure 3.6) – and getting this right is critical to business survival. So, you need to understand this concept thoroughly.

Money flows in through sales – but flows out again as payments are made. Imagine a large tank of money. If the flow 'out' is greater than the flow 'in', the tank will run dry. This would mean no more bills – or wages – could be paid. If the flow 'in' is greater than the flow 'out' – as it should be – then the

The principle of cashflow

Cash in Bank

Revenue from sale of service or product →

→ Wages and salaries
→ Stock/raw materials
→ Expenses/overheads

_ . _ . _ . = Too much cash – transfer excess to interest bearing account

————— = Cash amount correct

. . . . = Shortage of cash – cannot meet current commitments

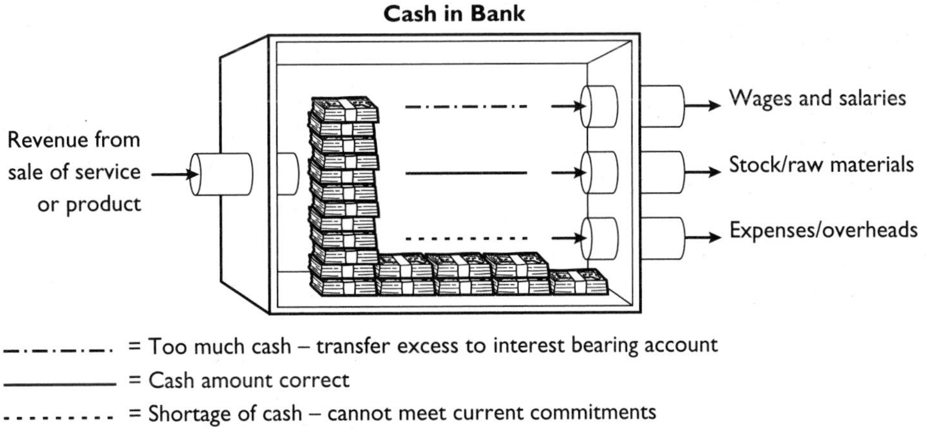

Figure 3.6 The principle of cashflow

amount in the tank would get higher and higher. The amount of cash needs monitoring carefully and any surplus transferring to an account which is earning interest, so that too much money is not lying idle in the firm's ordinary bank account. Surplus funds are known as **reserves** and are often used to expand the business by reinvesting the money as additional **capital**.

ACTIVITY 2

In groups of two or three, consider:

1   the types of costs, and
2   the types of revenue

you would be likely to find in each of the following businesses. Then compare your answers with other members of your class.

a   A motor dealership which sells cars and also repairs and services them.
b   An estate agent.
c   A mail order company.
d   Your own school or college.
e   British Telecom.
f   A supermarket such as Tesco.
g   A bank.
h   A doctor.

Understanding profit

How does a business calculate its profit? First you should be aware there are two types of profit – **gross profit** and **net profit**.

The formula for working out gross profit is:

$$\textbf{sales} - \textbf{cost of sales} = \textbf{gross profit}$$

The formula for working out net profit is:

$$\textbf{gross profit} - \textbf{expenses} = \textbf{net profit}$$

Let's look at this in stages.

1   **Sales.** This is the amount of money received by selling the goods. Another word sometimes used for the total value of sales in a year is **turnover**.

    If you sold 500 pairs of trainers at £100 each then the value of your sales (or turnover) would be £50,000.

SNAPSHOT

David versus Goliath?

The largest single reason why small businesses do not survive is because of cashflow problems. And these are caused, mainly, by larger companies not paying their bills on time. In cases where a very small firm is highly dependent upon a large and powerful company, just one large unpaid bill can be enough to force the business to close because it can't pay its own debts.

To help, the government introduced a new law – the Late Payment of Commercial Debts (Interest) Act, which came into effect in 1999. Under this law, all small businesses with fewer than 50

employees have the right to claim interest from large companies on late payments. However, some people think that very few small companies will use it. Why? Because they are worried that charging interest may destroy the relationship – and their key customers could go elsewhere. Even worse, some small businesses are worried that large suppliers will levy interest on them – once they have the power to do so in November 2002. But the banks are keen that small firms will use the law to help themselves – especially if the alternative is shutting up shop altogether.

2 **Cost of sales**. This is the same as variable costs as it comprises any expenditure which has been made specifically to produce or sell the product. The most usual item, therefore, is **purchases** – of raw materials and stocks. There are sometimes other items of expenditure involved in the cost of sales, which you will meet if you continue your studies to a higher level.

Let's assume the trainers you sold in (1) above cost you £50 each. In this case your purchases would be 500 × £50 = £25,000.

3 **Gross profit**. This is the difference between revenue from sales less the cost of sales. You can now calculate your gross profit by substituting the figures in the formula:

£50,000 – £25,000 = £25,000

4 **Expenses**. These are the costs of running the business – your operating costs. Let's assume these amounted to £8,000.

5 **Net profit**. You can now calculate your net profit by deducting your expenses from your gross profit:

£25,000 – £8,000 = £17,000.

Bear in mind that in real life you may now owe the Inland Revenue some money. However, for the purpose of your external test you may be pleased to know that you won't be tested on tax and how this affects profit figures!

Practical example – 4

Shahid is trying to earn some money in the holidays by selling T-shirts on a local market stall. The stall costs him £25 a day. Shahid is very lucky – he got his T-shirts on sale or return from his brother – so he really feels he can't lose, provided he can pursuade people to buy them.

His brother tells him he wants £3 for every T-shirt that is sold, and suggests to Shahid that he

Figure 3.7 Shahid aims to sell more T-shirts by making the price more attractive

sells them for £6 each. However, Shahid thinks he might do even better if he sells them for £6 each or £15 for a pack of three. He thinks this might tempt people to buy more.

Over the holidays Shahid works Wednesday, Friday and Saturday for 6 weeks. He sells 840 single T-shirts and 275 packs of 3.

Calculate Shahid's gross and net profit by working through each of the questions below.

1 What is Shahid's income from selling single T-shirts?
2 What is Shahid's income from selling packs of T-shirts?
3 What is Shahid's total sales revenue?
4 How many T-shirts has Shahid sold in total?
5 How much does Shahid owe his brother?
6 What is Shahid's gross profit, i.e. the amount he has left after paying his brother?
7 How much has he paid to rent the market stall?
8 What is his net profit for all his work?

Check your answers with the key on page 277.

Practical example – 5

Shahid decides to keep up this lucrative work as well as going to college. He has no classes on a Friday so he continues to take his market stall on Fridays and Saturdays. In November, because Christmas is approaching, he also starts to sell socks – at £2 each or £5 for three pairs. His brother wants £1 for each pair of socks sold.

Between September and the end of December Shahid's sales figures are as follows:

September (4 weeks) 340 single T-shirts
                     84 packs of 3

October (4 weeks)   210 single T-shirts
                     62 packs of 3

November (5 weeks)   320 single T-shirts
                     92 packs of 3
                     180 single packs of socks
                     68 packs of 3 socks

December (3 weeks)   420 single T-shirts
                     230 packs of 3
                     275 single packs of socks
                     184 packs of 3 socks.

Work out how much Shahid has made by calculating both his gross and net profit.

Check your answers with page 278.

And for potential distinction candidates – a final question. When you calculate the figures you will find that Shahid has made **less** than his brother – even though he has done all the work! *Quickly* – can you say why?

Financial terms

You have already encountered several financial terms. A list of these with their definitions is given below. Check that you fully understand each one and ask your tutor to explain any you are uncertain about.

Term	Definition
Bad debts	An unpaid debt.
Capital	The money invested in a business.
Cashflow	The movement of cash in and out of the business. Cashflow allows for not all buyers paying on time. Cash receipts are also included.
Credit	When goods or services are provided and there is a delay before the account is paid.
Depreciation	The fall in value of a vehicle or item of equipment. Depreciation is a cost because the item must be replaced at some stage in the future.
Fixed costs	Costs that do not vary regardless of the amount produced.
Gross profit	The difference between the revenue earned from sales after the costs of sales (purchases less unsold stock) have been deducted.
Net profit	The amount of profit remaining once expenses have been deducted from gross profit.
Overheads	General costs of operating the business. Overheads are always fixed costs.
Reserves	Profit which is retained and then usually reinvested in the company.
Revenue	The income obtained from selling the goods or providing the service.
Total costs	Fixed costs plus variable costs.

SNAPSHOT

Saving time, money and energy!

Many towns and cities try to encourage entrepreneurs to start up in business, but costs often deter people. To help with this, new 'managed premises' and purpose-built units are often available on much better terms than buying or renting a property from a landlord. 'Flexible terms' may be offered so that premises can be rented weekly, with no down payment required. If the business has to close down quickly, there are no expensive agreements to cancel or final payments to make.

The cost depends on the situation and the size of the premises. A provincial town is cheaper than a city. A town centre is more expensive than an industrial estate. A large, spacious office is dearer than a small one.

In some managed premises £60 a month would buy you 100 square feet of office space, £120 a month 200 square feet and so on. This will include all power and services and business rates. Building security (which reduces insurance premiums) and standard cleaning are likely to be included. There may be shared toilet facilities with other offices and even a central reception area to take messages when the office is closed. This is one answer for anyone who wants to set up a business and minimise start-up costs.

Turnover	The value of sales income over a financial year.
Variable costs	Costs which vary depending upon the amount produced – the more that is produced, the higher the variable costs.

Section review

Refresh your memory of the section you have just completed by writing short answers to each of the following questions.

1 *Give four examples of the start-up costs which would be incurred by a person starting up in business as a newsagent.*

2 *Explain the difference between fixed costs and variable costs and give one example of each.*

3 *Explain the term 'running costs'.*

4 *Describe how you would calculate the net profit of a business if you knew the value of the sales, the cost of all the expenses, and the cost of sales (i.e. purchasing the stock).*

5 *What is meant by the term 'bad debt'?*

6 *How would you describe the term 'depreciation' to someone who had never heard of it?*

7 *What is 'cashflow'?*

8 *Explain clearly why cashflow is so important to a business.*

9 *What is the correct term for the value of sales income over a financial year?*

10 *Explain why costs and revenue differ from one business to another.*

3.2 FORECASTS AND PREDICTIONS

At the end of this section you should be able to:

- explain why forecasts are important
- draw a break-even chart for a business from given data and identify the break-even point
- calculate the break-even point from given data using a given formula
- understand and explain how changes in costs, revenue and sales will affect the break-even point
- calculate total and average costs
- create a profit and loss forecast from given data
- explain the difference between inflows and outflows of money
- create a cashflow forecast from given data
- understand the importance of a cashflow forecast and interpret the data correctly
- understand why costs and revenues might change – and why actual data may differ from forecast data
- prepare forecasts using a computer spreadsheet package
- identify the advantages and disadvantages of using a spreadsheet package for preparing forecasts.

Overview of forecasts and predictions

If we want to know what the weather will be like tomorrow, we will probably watch the weather forecast on TV. The forecasters make a prediction about tomorrow – but they don't use a crystal ball! Instead, they take all the data they can find about wind speeds, barometric pressure and other relevant factors to produce an *informed* forecast about future weather. Often they are right, but sometimes they are wrong – particularly if they are giving a long-range forecast – as many things can happen in the meantime which upset their predictions.

Business forecasts aren't much different in that:

- forecasts are prepared to give an idea of what will happen in the future

- the forecasters use as much relevant data as possible – the more information they have, the better

- short-term forecasts are apt to be more accurate than long-range forecasts, because so many things can change over time.

Business forecasts do have one definite advantage over weather forecasts, however. If you prepare a business forecast and don't like the result, you can make some changes. Unfortunately, at this point in time we don't have the ability to do that with the weather!

There are three types of forecasts which you need to know. All of these are excellent techniques for forecasting whether or not a potential business idea has any real chance of success.

1 Break-even analysis.
2 Profit and loss estimates.
3 Cashflow forecast.

You will learn about these through a case study concerning Max – and you are recommended to read the following background notes on Max very carefully.

CASE STUDY

Max Jennings is a 21-year-old student who left art college last year. He lives at home with his mother, sister and younger brother. Max's specialism has always been computer graphics, but he also enjoys making models and has spent many hours trying to develop resins which would mould into realistic characters. When his brother, Sam, became interested in a new television programme called Starworld, which incorporated superb visual effects using digital technology, Max enjoyed trying to recreate some of the characters he saw on screen. After some trial and error he developed a material which would mould almost precisely to each character's features, and could be bent and moved and stayed in a chosen position.

Max has had a variety of part-time and temporary jobs over the past year. Two weeks ago he had £50 to his name. However, for his 21st birthday he received some money – £1,500 in all. He also met up with several of his friends and received some interesting news. One of them, Anya, works for the television production company which produces Starworld. She tells him the programme is being piloted just in this area but has been so successful they are hoping it will be networked sometime next year – and be transmitted nationwide. Max shows Anya the characters he has made and she is so impressed she asks if she can borrow them to show her boss.

A week later Max receives a telephone call. Anya's boss, Jack Noble, suggests to Max that he might like to consider producing the characters for sale. Jack is fairly confident that he will be able to get orders from several big stores in the region, especially if Max can produce several for the Christmas trade. He says that if Max is interested, he would have to pay Jack's company £200 for a licence to produce Starworld characters so that he is not in breach of copyright. He tells Max to let him know his decision.

Max checks his finances. He has £50 in the bank plus £1,500 birthday money. He will need to create his master moulds and buy raw materials to make the figures plus paints. He will need to package and market them. He will need somewhere to work. He decides that he will have to ask someone for advice and decides to speak to his mother's friend, Sue, who has a successful business of her own.

Sue thinks the idea is an excellent opportunity. She even says she might be interested in investing some of her own money into the enterprise. However, before she is prepared to do that, she says that Max and his business venture have five tests they must pass.

Figure 3.8 Max plans a business making models of TV characters

Case study – test 1

Sue tells Max that the first thing he must do is identify all the costs involved in starting up his business, as well as all the running costs. Max must then divide his running costs into fixed and variable costs.

She tells Max that when he has done this – and if he has done it properly – he will have passed the first test.

Max hasn't much of a clue about business costs but knows you have been studying the subject. You agree to help him. When you meet him a few days later he has drafted out a list after making a few enquiries.

1 Check Max's list of projected start-up costs in Figure 3.9. One essential item given in the background notes is missing. Add this to complete the list and then total Max's start-up costs.

2 Study Max's list of running costs in Figure 3.9 and divide these into fixed and variable costs.

3 Obtain three totals:
   a average fixed costs each month
   b average variable costs each month
   c total costs (i.e. fixed + variable costs) each month.

4 For Max's benefit write a brief description of the difference between fixed and variable costs.

Check your answers with your tutor or with the key on page 278. If you are correct then you can give the list to Max with confidence!

Case study – test 2

Max triumphantly takes his lists to Sue who is quite impressed. She then asks Max on what production figure he based his variable

Max's projected start-up costs
Deposit on workshop unit – £1,260 (£5,040 per year. I must pay 3 months' deposit – all rates are included plus building insurance and a phone line is installed plus all main services, i.e. gas/electric)
Contents insurance – first monthly premium £20
Workbenches and stools – £500 (Other production equipment, tools, paintbrushes etc. I already have)
Desk lights (to supplement flourescent lights) – £100
Moulds – will cost about £200 to make
Overalls (already have)
Packaging materials – don't need these for a couple of months, so have put them under running costs.
Office furniture (second-hand) – £120
Telephone (free – spare one at home I could have)
Stationery – £100
Computer/printer for designs etc. – I'll use mine.

Max's projected running costs	
Rent	£420 a month
Insurance	£20 a month
Advertising	£100 a month
Stationery	£100 a month
Telephone	£150 per quarter
Salary	£400 per month to start
Raw materials	Average £1,000 a month
Gas	£50 a month
Electricity	£30 a month
Accountant	£480 a year
Packaging	Average £800 a month
Distribution costs	Average £200 a month
Miscellaneous supplies (cleaning materials etc.)	£480 per year
Miscellaneous expenses	£240 per year
Contingency fund for emergencies	£360 per year

Figure 3.9 Max's projected start-up costs

SNAPSHOT

Angels and mentors

One of the most valuable assets for someone starting in business is a mentor who can give advice based on experience. The Prince's Youth Business Trust, a charity founded by the Prince of Wales, aims to help young people convert their business ideas into reality, provides a mentor for every new business. These are volunteers who offer advice and moral support.

The Prince's Trust, however, offers more than this. It offers loans to help young people (18–30 year olds) set up in business and grants for test marketing – to help applicants assess if there is a demand for their service or product. In certain circumstances a special bursary may be offered.

Figure 3.10 The Prince of Wales helps young people get started in business

The average start-up loan is £2,500 – although the ceiling is higher – and the interest rate is much lower than bank loan rates. There is a 'payment holiday' of six months whilst the enterprise tries to get on its feet.

The Prince's Trust has been an invaluable source of finance for many young entrepreneurs who, because of their lack of experience, have trouble persuading banks and other institutions to lend them money. Anita Patel had this problem. She failed to persuade banks to lend her money to start up in business but received a grant of £500 and a £2,000 loan through the Prince's Trust. Her business, Tania-Tapel Promotions, organises Asian weddings and is going from strength to strength.

Banks have also been criticised for being reluctant to lend to high-tech industries because of the risks involved. In this case a 'business angel' may come to the rescue – a larger firm which is prepared to help finance a new business in the early stages in return for a share of the profits later. However, at a seminar involving government representatives, the Federation of Small Businesses and the British Chambers of Commerce identified the need for a business-angel network offering experience and advice – rather than cash – for **all** new businesses, not just those started by young people.

The Prince's Trust aims to raise £50 million and wants the government to double this. It anticipates it will then be able to help 30,000 new businesses to get under way between 2000 and 2005. If you want to know more, contact the Trust on Freephone 0800-842842.

cost estimates. Max has thought of this, thanks to your explanation, and says that this figure is based on making 800 characters each month.

'Right,' responds Sue, 'then your next task is to undertake a break-even analysis to see how many characters you need to make to cover all your costs. Come back when you've done it.'

Max has no idea what a break-even analysis is, so decides to investigate further. He also needs your help again!

Break-even charts and forecasting

Break-even analysis is a useful technique for decision-making which involves both predicted costs and predicted sales. It identifies the **break-even point** at which the revenue from sales is just enough to cover the running costs of the business. Anything above the break-even point adds to profit. Producing fewer goods than indicated by the break-even point means the business will make a loss.

Break-even analysis is based on the fact that some costs are fixed and others are variable. When the fixed and variable costs are added together, the result is the **total cost** of production for that item.

Break-even charts

It is possible to draw a break-even chart quite easily from given data using the following steps. In the example below, a local, popular band, Archie & Co, want to hire a recording studio to produce their own CD, which they intend to distribute themselves. Shops in the area have agreed to take some supplies because they think the disc may sell well as the group have a large local following. The band is carrying out a break-even analysis to find out how many CDs they need to sell to cover their costs – then they can decide how many to have duplicated from the master produced in the studio.

(Note: you will find break-even charts much easier to do if you use graph paper, rather than ordinary lined or unlined paper.)

1   Start with a basic 'x' and 'y' axis. Label these. The 'x' (horizontal) axis is for **quantity sold** and the 'y' (vertical) axis is for **sales/costs (£)**.

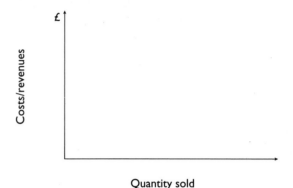

Figure 3.11 Break-even chart, stage 1

2   Decide the scales to use on each axis. Do this as follows:

Quantity sold. The lowest quantity sold is obviously zero. The highest level possible will depend upon the product. If you were selling custom-built sports cars then you might have a top figure of 50, but if you were selling ballpoint pens it might be nearer a million!

In our example, the band thinks it could distribute a maximum of 5,000 CDs – so this is the top figure. It would therefore be sensible to have a scale in thousands on the 'x' axis.

Costs/revenues. Concentrate on likely sales revenue when you are deciding your scale on this line. Again this will depend upon the product. Fifty custom-built sports cars might sell for over £2 million whereas a million ballpoint pens at 10p each would only be £100,000! Therefore you need to multiply your top sales figure by the estimated revenue you think you will receive for each item. Then divide the 'y' axis into suitable divisions.

In the example our band is supplying the CD to the shops at an agreed price of £2. (The shops will sell them for £4 – but this is the shop's profit margin). Multiplying £2 by a quantity of 5,000 would give a maximum sales revenue of £10,000. Again, a scale in thousands would be appropriate.

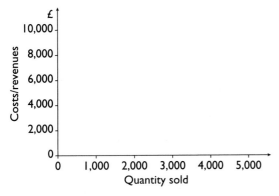

Figure 3.12 Break-even chart, stage 2

3   Average the estimated fixed costs. For instance, if a business expected to spend £36,000 on overheads over 12 months, the average would be £3,000 per month. Remember that this *never changes* – otherwise it wouldn't be 'fixed' – so you are really drawing a straight, horizontal line.

Our musicians have a fixed cost for hiring the studio – the charge is £500 a day and they will use the studio for 3 days. Their fixed costs are therefore £1,500. Draw in this line and label it **fixed cost**.

4   The next line to draw is the total cost line. This *starts* at the left hand-side at the fixed costs point. At this position there is no production so variable costs would be zero – the only costs involved would be fixed costs.

The band has found out that its variable cost for each CD will comprise three items. Duplicating the CD (50p), printing the sleeve (30p) and distribution costs (20p). The total is therefore £1 per CD.

If the band produced the maximum CDs (5,000) its total variable costs would be £5,000. However, this would be *in addition* to their fixed costs of £1,500.

The total cost line will therefore run from £1,500 at the left-hand side (the fixed cost line) to a maximum of £6,500 if 5,000 CDs were sold.

You now need to label this line. However, because this line is variable costs *on top of* the fixed costs, you must label it **total cost**.

It is the difference between the two lines which is the **variable cost** – as you will see on the diagram below. The gap always widens to the right as variable costs increase per unit of production.

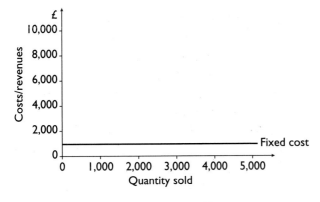

Figure 3.13 Break-even chart, stage 3

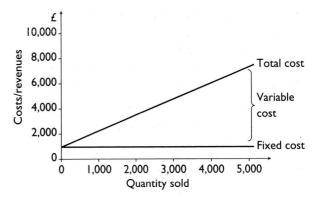

Figure 3.14 Break-even chart, stage 4

5 The final line to draw is **sales revenue**. This obviously starts at zero (if you don't sell any, then you obviously don't receive any revenue). The more you sell, the more you make – so this line also slopes upwards. The maximum our band could receive if it sold all 5,000 CDs at £2 each would be £10,000 – so this is the extent of the line.

At this point you can identify the **break-even point**. This is the point at which the total cost line *crosses* the sales revenue line.

Mark this point. If you now draw a line downwards to the 'x' axis you can read off the quantity required to break-even. From this you can see that our group must sell 1,500 CDs to break-even.

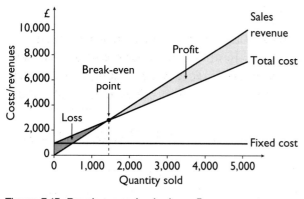

Figure 3.15 Break-even chart, stage 5

Practical example – 6

Nixa Hire Cars is a firm in Jersey which specialises in supplying holidaymakers with cars. Its average sales revenue is £150 per car. Its fixed costs are high – £4,550 each month – because it is constantly trying to upgrade its fleet and the costs of buying new cars are included in its fixed costs. However, its variable costs (mainly car cleaning and servicing) average out low at £20 per car hired.

How many cars must it hire out to break-even?

You are going to do this in two ways now – and, if you are good with computers, you can do it a

third way later. Using computers to do break-even analysis is the best and easiest way of all!

Drawing the chart

1 Start off with your 'x' and 'y' axes. Label these as follows:

x axis = cars hired
y axis = sales/costs line

2 Do your sums before you start putting in any scales. It would be sensible to count up the cars in 'tens', say from 0 to 60. If Nixa hired out 60 cars at £150 per car then their total revenue would be £9,000. If you wanted to work up to 100 cars then the maximum revenue would be £10,000.

Now mark off your horizontal and vertical axes appropriately.

3 Draw in your fixed costs line and label it.

4 Your total cost line will *start* at £4,550. If you are working up to 60 cars, then your variable costs will be 60 × £20 = £1,200. These must be added to the fixed costs. Therefore your total cost line will end at £6,750. Draw this in now and label it.

5 Draw in your sales revenue line. Remember this starts at zero and, if you are working up to 60 cars, will end at £9,000.

Label your line.

6 Mark off the break-even point and note the number of cars which must be hired. You will be able to check below if you are correct.

Using the formula

There is a simple formula to use to work out break-even, without having to draw the chart. This formula may look complicated at first, but don't worry about that. It's easy once you understand it.

$$\text{Break-even point} = \frac{\text{fixed costs}}{(\text{selling price per unit } less \text{ variable cost per unit})}$$

Let's look at this in stages, and apply it to Nixa Hire Cars.

1   We know that Nixa's fixed costs are £4,550. That takes care of the first part of the formula.

2   We know that Nixa's selling price per unit is £150 – the average cost at which they hire out the cars. That is the second figure we need.

3   The variable cost per car has been given to us – £20. That is the final figure we want.

Therefore our formula for Nixa is

$$\frac{4{,}550}{(150 - 20)}$$

4   All we have to remember now is that we *always calculate figures in brackets **first***.

Therefore:

a   (150 – 20) = 130
b   4550/130 = 35

That should be the answer showing on your chart. Nixa Hire Cars must hire out 35 cars to break-even. More than this and they make a profit, fewer than this and they make a loss.

You may wonder why people bother drawing a chart when they can work it out so easily with the formula – but often it's useful to see all the information you get on the chart, such as the potential profit (or loss) for different levels of sales, as well as the actual break-even point.

Incidentally, you don't have to learn the formula by heart (though it isn't hard to remember). In the external exam you will be reminded of it – but you must be able to use it!

Using a computer spreadsheet

If you can use a spreadsheet package then you have several advantages. You can prepare a break-even analysis very quickly. You can alter and change costs and revenues to see what happens to your break-even point and your profits. You can use the graphics

component to draw your chart, quickly and easily. Note that on a spreadsheet you cannot 'label lines' as such – you will have to create a key or legend to identify them.

Unfortunately, you won't have a computer with you in the external test, but you should still understand how to apply your skills – as this is the system used in most businesses today.

An example of a break-even spreadsheet for Nixa Hire Cars and the associated graphic is shown in Figure 3.16. Work through this carefully with your tutor to see how it has been compiled. You can then copy this model if you do one yourself.

 **ACTIVITY 3**

Practise using the formula. Archie & Co's fixed costs were £1,500, their variable cost per unit was £1 and their selling price per unit was £2. Use the formula to check your break-even figure of 1,500.

Case study – test 2 (continued)

This time you are on your own!

Max has asked for your help in preparing his break-even chart. He has contacted Jack who has advised him that he should charge shops £5 for his characters as they will add their own profit to that – and will probably sell them for about £10 each. Jack suggests Max sells the characters for £10 to private customers.

Max thinks that the highest number of characters he could produce by Christmas would be 3,000. You already have the figures for his average fixed costs – £1,300. Max has estimated his variable costs each month would be £2,000 for every 800 figures he produced.

1   Assuming Max sells 50 per cent of his output to shops and 50 per cent to

REVENUE

Sales volume (A)	0	10	20	30	40	50	60
Selling price per unit (B)	£150	£150	£150	£150	£150	£150	£150
Total revenue (AxB=C)	£0	£1,500	£3,000	£4,500	£6,000	£7,500	£9,000

COSTS

Fixed costs (D)	£4,550	£4,550	£4,550	£4,550	£4,550	£4,550	£4,550
Variable cost per unit (E)	£20	£20	£20	£20	£20	£20	£20
Total variable costs (ExA=F)	£0	£200	£400	£600	£800	£1,000	£1,200
Total costs (D+F=G)	£4,550	£4,750	£4,950	£5,150	£5,350	£5,550	£5,750

BREAK-EVEN POINT (D/(B-E)=H)	35	35	35	35	35	35	35

Break-even point
Nixa Hire Cars

Figure 3.16 Break-even spreadsheet for Nixa Hire Cars

private customers, calculate his average selling price.

2   Calculate Max's variable costs per unit.

3   Calculate his break-even point:
    a   by drawing a chart
    b   by working it out using the formula
    c   on a spreadsheet – if you have the facilities.

Check your hand-drawn chart and spreadsheet with your tutor. You can see if you have used the formula correctly by checking the key on page 278.

Case study – test 3

Max is delighted with the result – he can't see how he can fail to make money with such a low break-even point. He shows the chart to Sue, who is quite impressed and considers he should have few problems breaking even, given the quantity involved. However, Sue stresses that a break-even chart assumes the goods are *sold* – not just produced and standing in the stockroom! She also warns Max that in the 'real world', break-even points are only a rough guide – costs and revenues may vary considerably once the business gets under way.

She therefore suggests he does a little work to see what would happen if certain things occurred.

1   Fixed costs increase. Sue thinks Max would be very stretched to produce *and* distribute 800 characters a month on his own. So he might want to employ

Figure 3.17 Max has a problem

someone to help him, but this person's salary would add to the fixed costs.

2 Sue tells Max that he should try to reduce his variable costs. She suggests Max contacts his raw material suppliers to see if he can have a discount for buying in bulk – and the same with packaging suppliers.

3 Finally, Sue asks Max to consider whether his average selling price of £7.50 is realistic. He is likely to sell more to shops than privately, therefore Sue thinks £6 would be a more accurate figure.

Max asks you for help again. He wants to calculate three more break-even points.

1 Assuming the fixed costs increased to £1,800 – but his variable costs and his selling price stay the same.

2 If the fixed costs were £1,800 but the variable costs fell to £2.20 a unit. His average selling price is still £7.50.

3 If the fixed costs remained at £1,800, the variable costs were £2.20 a unit and the average selling price was £6 a character.

You have certain tasks to do.

a Calculate each break-even point by using the formula:

$$\text{Break-even point} = \frac{\text{fixed costs}}{(\text{selling price per unit } less \text{ variable cost per unit})}$$

If necessary, round out the break-even point to get a whole number.

b Produce a break-even chart for (3) above.

c If possible, prepare a spreadsheet from Max's original data and then vary your figures to get different print-outs. If you produce a related graphic, this will change automatically!

d Write a commentary for Max on your observations. What has happened in each case and why? You think Sue will expect him to know!

Check your answers with the key on page 278.

Case study – test 4

Sue thinks Max now has a much better appreciation of the factors which will be involved in his enterprise. She tells him always to watch his costs carefully, because it is not always easy to raise the selling price to compensate – business may be lost if he does.

Max's next task, Sue informs him, is to forecast his profit (or loss). She suggests Max does this for the next six months and brings her the results.

Profit and loss forecasts

You have already been involved in calculating profit (or loss) when you calculated Shahid's profits on page 221. When you are producing a forecast you have to *estimate* the sales, purchases and expenses over a given period in the future, rather than working with actual figures. Shahid was lucky – he made a good profit without forecasting. Usually, new businesses make an initial loss and only make a profit once they become established. In this case they need to have enough capital to survive the early months. This could well happen to Max, as he will have an initial production period without any sales. His profit and loss forecast will show him how bad this might be – and how long his 'non-profit' period is likely to last.

The break-even chart shows how many units must be sold to make a profit. However, to make an overall profit this level of sales must be *sustained* over a long period. The break-even chart assumes this level of sales is constant – which in the real world it never is! Hence, the value of a profit and loss forecast.

Remember that you first have to calculate the **gross profit** (sales revenue minus cost of sales), then **net profit**. If you have forgotten this, look back at page 220 to refresh your memory.

Practical example – 7

Let's return to Nixa Hire Cars – whose break-even analysis you saw on page 232. Nixa supplies holidaymakers, so it is likely it will make very little money early in the year – all the main earnings will be in the summer.

Nixa's boss, Jeanne, averaged out her figures for the break-even analysis. She has now been more precise, and has tried to predict what the average sales, cost of sales and expenses will be for each month from April to September. Based on the break-even point of 35, and her predicted sales figures, she has a total hire car fleet of 55. Her forecast figures are as follows.

Sales revenue

In the break-even chart, Jeanne averaged her hire charges at £150 per car. In reality, she charges less for small cars than large cars, or cars with air-conditioning. She also charges less in the quieter months of the year than the busy ones. Her more precise averaged figures are:

*   £110 for cars hired in April
*   £130 in May
*   £150 in June and September
*   £185 for July and August.

She estimates that she will hire cars at the following rate:

April – 20 cars	July – 55 cars
May – 32 cars	August – 55 cars
June – 45 cars	September – 40 cars.

Cost of sales

This is the same as Jeanne's variable costs – £20 per car hired.

Expenses

Jeanne averaged her fixed costs for the break-even chart, but has changed them a little for the month-by-month analysis as she hires additional staff in the summer.

April – £3,400	July – £6,400
May – £3,800	August – £6,800
June – £4,700	September – £4,200.

She now prepares her profit and loss forecast based on this information, using the template shown in Figure 3.18. Jeanne does this on a spreadsheet package. You can either copy the template on to paper and complete it with the appropriate figures *or* produce a spreadsheet. It is easier this way, but you will need to be able to prepare one on paper in the external test – so it is a good idea to get used to writing one before you start producing a spreadsheet.

Now complete your template with the appropriate figures and answer the questions which follow.

	April	May	June	July	August	September
Sales revenue						
Cost of sales						
Gross profit						
Total expenses						
Net profit						

Figure 3.18 Template for profit and loss forecast

1 Calculate and enter Jeanne's sales revenue each month.

2 Calculate and enter Jeanne's costs of sales per month.

3 Calculate her gross profit for each month.

4 Enter her expenses and calculate her net profit per month.

5 During which months does Nixa Hire Cars make a loss?

6 Can you explain *why* this happens?

7 During which months does Nixa Hire Cars make a profit?

8 What is the overall profit/loss made over the six months April–September?

9 What do you think the profit/loss forecast is likely to be in the remaining six months? Give a reason for your answer.

10 Seasonal businesses have to try much harder during their busy times to make enough to keep them going through the quieter times. Bearing this in mind, what do you think the profit/loss pattern would look like for:

   a a company making Christmas decorations

   b an ice-cream manufacturer

   c a package tour operator?

11 Jeanne is considering opening another branch and concentrating on top-of-the-range vehicles which would appeal to business visitors. She thinks the revenue will be more steady from this type of trade.

   a If she stocked four models which were hired at £150 a week, £180 a week, £200 a week and £230 a week, what would be her average sales revenue per week if all the cars were hired out?

   b If her fixed costs for 12 months were as shown below, what would be the average fixed costs?

January	£3,000	February	£3,500
March	£3,600	April	£4,200
May	£4,500	June	£5,600
July	£6,000	August	£6,000
September	£5,400	October	£4,800
November	£4,000	December	£3,400

Check your answers with the key on page 278.

Case study – test 4 (continued)

You are now ready to help Max prepare his profit and loss forecast. Max has deliberated long and hard and has given you the following figures.

1 **Sales.** Max has estimated he can produce about 200 characters each week – starting from the first week in September. He will close over Christmas. His estimated production figures are:

September (4 weeks) = 800 figures
October (4 weeks) = 800 figures
November (5 weeks) = 1,000 figures
December (3 weeks) = 600 figures
January (3 weeks) = 600 figures.

Max appreciates that although he might *make* the figures one month, he may not sell them during the same month. He therefore thinks his sales figures for his profit and loss account should be:

August   = 0 sales
September   = 300 sales
October   = 800 sales
November   = 1,000 sales
December   = 900 sales
January   = 400 sales.

This will leave him with 400 figures in stock at the start of February.

2   **Cost of sales/variable costs**. Max has estimated he will spend about £2,000 on materials in each of the first four months – as he needs to make advanced stocks for Christmas. He can reduce this to £500 in December and January.

3   **Expenses/fixed costs**. Max thinks he can keep to £1,300 for the first month – August – whilst he gets established and makes his moulds. He intends to hire someone to help him from September to November so he wants to increase his costs to £1,800 for these three months. In December he thinks the costs could return to about £1,600 and to £1,300 in January.

From this information, prepare Max's profit and loss forecast. Draw a template (as in Figure 3.18) and then carry out the tasks below.

a   Calculate Max's estimated sales revenue for each month, assuming he will receive an average £6 for each figure he sells.

b   Enter Max's estimated cost of sales figure for each month.

c   Calculate Max's gross profit.

d   Enter Max's expenses for each month.

e   Calculate the net profit for each month.

f   Calculate Max's overall profit or loss over the six-month period.

Check your answers with the key on page 279.

Case study – test 5

Max is quite triumphant when he takes his forecast to Sue – he was hoping the figures would be good – as this will mean he could pay himself a more realistic salary once the enterprise was underway. Sue studies the figures for a long time.

'I've just one or two concerns,' she comments. 'First, you need to have enough money to set up the business and support yourself until the enterprise makes a profit. You told me your start-up costs would be £2,500 and you had £1,500 saved. Now you say you need an extra £1,500 or so between September and November. That means that overall you need about £4,000 to start in business. If you borrow £2,500 then you will have to pay interest on the money, but you haven't allowed for this.'

'Second,' she continues, 'a profit/loss forecast shows when you think you will make the sales. But it doesn't show when you will receive the money. The two may be quite different if you are selling on credit. If the

Figure 3.19 Make sure you cover everything before getting excited about your forecasts

stores don't pay you until November or December for the figures you sell in September and October then you will have several months without any income. Have you thought about that?'

Max's euphoria was disappearing by the minute. 'Don't look too upset,' says Sue. 'Task 5 is the most important of all – and when you've done this we can make some proper decisions. You must now prepare your cashflow forecast – which shows when you think you will *actually* receive and pay the money. When you've completed it, come back to me.'

Max is disappointed there is still more work to do but heartened that he has nearly done all the projections required of him. He realises he has learned a lot – even at this stage.

He contacts you to see if you will help him with cashflow.

Cashflow forecasts

Cashflow forecasts are the most critical and the most important of all business forecasts. The problems of cashflow – especially for small businesses – were outlined on page 219. Max has already seen that in August and September he will make a loss. If no-one pays him any money for his figures until December he might have to close his business.

A cashflow forecast shows when the *money* will be received and paid – rather than when the goods will be made or sold. Again it is a 'best guess', but it does enable business people to adjust their ways of working if they can see a problem looming, such as a **negative cashflow** for a month or two. This is when the business is spending more than it is earning. The bank may agree the business can have a bank overdraft for a short period. This is when the bank agrees more money

can be spent than is held in the account. Overdrafts are usually a temporary measure and the charges are reasonable provided the overdraft is agreed in advance. Banks do not like a business to run up an overdraft without telling them first – and will charge much more in such cases.

If a business thinks it is likely to have a long-term cashflow problem then it may need to borrow more money. When it is starting up it may be eligible for special start-up help – such as the grants and loan given by The Prince's Trust to certain new enterprises (see page 227). From its cashflow forecast a business should know whether it will need financial help before it starts trading. Borrowing at that time will take much of the pressure off the owners.

Any loans that incur interest charges will affect the fixed costs – both in terms of the actual repayments and the interest which is added on.

A cashflow forecast concentrates on the **inflows** or **receipts** which will be received by the business each month, and the **outflows** or **payments** which will be made. It then looks at the effect of these transactions on the firm's bank account.

Practical example – 8

Jeanne of Nixa Hire Cars recently decided to improve and extend her current fleet of cars so that she can hire out cars to both holidaymakers and business visitors to Jersey. She needed a bank loan to help support these purchases, so she made out a cashflow forecast. She knew the bank would want to see this.

Jeanne has had few cashflow problems in the past, because holidaymakers pay for cars when they are hired. However, she knows that organisations which pay for car hire may make her wait for the money. She will have to offer at least one month's credit to get business trade, and this had to be included in her calculations.

Jeanne wanted to buy three good quality cars at a cost of £60,000. She has £50,000 in her reserves but needed to borrow the remaining £10,000. She intends to charge £250 a week for these cars. She has carried out some market research and knows that she can hire out two of them virtually from the outset.

Jeanne uses the template in Figure 3.20 to complete her cashflow forecast. The months are, of course, variable – depending upon the period over which the forecast is being calculated.

	April	May	June	July	August	September
INFLOWS/RECEIPTS						
Cash sales						
Credit sales						
Loans received						
Owner's capital						
Sub-total – all inflows (A)						
OUTFLOWS/PAYMENTS						
Variable costs (purchases, stock etc.)						
Wages/salaries						
Capital items						
Rent and rates						
Light/heat/power						
Repairs and maintenance						
Loan repayments						
Company vehicle(s) running costs						
Stationery and printing						
Telephone and postage						
Professional fees						
Insurance						
Advertising/promotions						
Miscellaneous expenses						
Sub-total – all outflows (B)						
Net cashflow (C)						
MONTHLY SUMMARY						
Opening bank balance						
Plus total receipts						
Minus total payments						
Closing Bank Balance (D)						

Figure 3.20 Cashflow forecast master

Stage 1 – inflows

1 Jeanne starts by entering her sales revenue from her profit/loss forecast under her cash receipts. These are the payments she can expect from the hire of her holiday cars.

2 Jeanne has estimated that she will be able to achieve two weeks' rental for two cars – but she won't receive the money until May. By May she is hoping to be renting all three cars most weeks – but again she expects to receive the money the following month. She doesn't expect to hire out the cars constantly throughout the summer to businesses – as some executives will be on holiday. Her estimates for her credit sales are therefore as follows:

April – no revenue	July – £2,500
May – £1,000	August – £2,500
June – £2,000	September – £3,000.

Jeanne enters these figures in the credit sales section.

3 Finally, Jeanne enters her own investment in April and totals her inflows for each month.

The first section of her cashflow forecast is shown in Figure 3.21

Stage 2 – outflows

4 Nixa's variable costs are £20 a car. The figures in Nixa's profit/loss forecast on page 278 did not include the new cars, so Jeanne has increased these figures slightly. Jeanne continues to enter all her fixed costs under outflows. Her new cars will be 'capital items' as they are used as part of the business (rather than stock or 'purchases' which is a consumable for resale).

Although some of the amounts are estimates, her entries are based on when payments will be made.

- Salaries and wages are paid in the month they are due.

- Where possible Jeanne pays bills monthly by direct debit.

- Other items will not be paid every month – her own car insurance is paid in July, for instance, which increases her vehicle costs during that month.

- Her accountant is paid twice a year.

- She spends most on advertising at the start of the season.

- She starts to repay her bank loan in May.

- She spends money on maintenance in September as she normally has the office painted at the end of the season.

Jeanne then totals her outflows. These are shown in Figure 3.22. Go through them with your tutor and check any entries you do not understand.

Jeanne then deducts her outflows from her inflows to get her net cashflow.

INFLOWS/RECEIPTS	April	May	June	July	August	September
Cash sales	2,200	4,160	6,750	10,175	10,175	6,000
Credit sales	0	1,000	2,000	2,500	2,500	3,000
Loans received	10,000	0	0	0	0	0
Owner's capital	50,000	0	0	0	0	0
Sub-total – all inflows (A)	62,200	5,160	8,750	12,675	12,675	9,000

Figure 3.21 Nixa Hire Cars – forecast inflows

OUTFLOWS/PAYMENTS	April	May	June	July	August	September
Variable costs (purchases, stock etc.)	480	880	1,140	1,340	1,340	1,040
Wages/salaries	2,000	2,000	2,000	3,000	3,000	2,000
Capital items	60,000	0	0	0	0	0
Rent and rates	650	650	650	650	650	650
Light/heat/power	50	50	50	50	50	50
Repairs and maintenance	0	0	0	0	0	500
Loan repayments	0	500	500	500	500	500
Company vehicle(s) running costs	80	80	80	480	80	80
Stationery and printing	200	50	50	200	50	50
Telephone and postage	80	80	80	80	80	80
Professional fees	0	0	0	0	600	0
Insurance	40	40	40	40	40	40
Advertising/promotions	500	0	0	0	0	0
Sub-total – all outflows (B)	64,080	4,330	4,590	6,340	6,390	4,990
Net cashflow (C)	(1,880)	830	4,160	6,335	6,285	4,010

Figure 3.22 Nixa Hire Cars – forecast outflows

From this you should be able to see that Jeanne has a positive cashflow for every month except April – when she has a negative cashflow of £1,880. A negative result can be shown in brackets as in Figure 3.22, or with a minus sign, i.e. –£1,880.

Stage 3 – bank balances

5   Nixa's bank balance at the start of April was £6,500. Jeanne enters this figure and calculates the closing balance for April by *adding* her inflows and *deducting* her outflows.

The result is shown in Figure 3.23.

ACTIVITY 4

1   Calculate Nixa's bank balance for each month from May to September. Check your answer with the key on page 279.

2   Jeanne knows that she can quickly check if she is correct by adding her **total** inflows (receipts) to her original opening balance and then deducting her **total** payments. This should give the final closing balance figure.

Check your own figures by copying out and completing the quick-check table that is given

Monthly Summary	April	May	June	July	August	September
Opening bank balance	6,500					
Plus total receipts	62,200					
Minus total payments	64,080					
Closing bank balance (D)	4,620					

Figure 3.23 Nixa Hire Cars – projected bank balance for April

immediately below:

	Opening balance	£6,500
Plus	Total receipts	
Minus	Total payments	_____
	Closing balance	_____

This system not only checks your figures quickly but also gives immediate guidance on the business – as overall receipts should obviously be greater than overall payments.

3   Jeanne's bank account is increasing rapidly. What action do you think she should take? Discuss your ideas with your tutor.

4   Jeanne could have chosen to have an overdraft for just three months.
   a   How could she tell she would only need an overdraft for three months?
   b   What is the difference between an overdraft and a loan?

5   Check how easy it is to prepare a cashflow forecast on a spreadsheet. Use the template on page 238 to set up Jeanne's spreadsheet and discuss the formulas you should use with your tutor. You will find this is far easier than writing it out – and it is very easy to adjust any figures if you need to.

Case study – test 5 (continued)

You are now ready to help Max to prepare his cashflow forecast. This will be for the months August–January.

Stage 1 – inflows

1   Max has had to rethink his sales revenue. Although he still thinks his overall receipts from production between July to the end of January should stay the same, he thinks he has to adjust his monthly figures.

   a   He thinks that only 20 per cent of his total revenue will come from private

sales but he will receive cash for these, so the money will be paid in the same month as the sales are made. He therefore expects to receive the following income from cash sales:

August – 0
September – £360
October – £960
November – £1,200
December – £1,080
January – £480.

   b   The remaining inflows will be from credit sales. Max will allow one month's credit to stores, so he expects to receive payment the month after he has sold his figures. He estimates his income from credit sales will be as follows:

August – 0
September – 0
October – £1,440
November – £3,840
December – £4,800
January – £4,300

2   Max's own capital is £1,500, which must be included in his inflows.

Your task

Using the same layout as that shown in Figure 3.20, enter all Max's inflows (receipts) on a cashflow forecast from August to January and then total them for each month.

You may also find it useful to calculate Max's total inflows – to help you undertake a 'quick check' later.

Stage 2 – outflows

1   During August, Max's start-up costs were as follows. These need entering under his outflows (payments) for that month:

Rent – £1,260 (3 month's deposit)

Stationery – £100
Royalty licence fee – £200
Insurance – £20
Capital items – £920

2   Max's variable costs were identified in his profit/loss forecast. He estimated £2,000 a month for the first four months and then £500 a month for December and January. He forgot he will receive one month's credit from his suppliers – so he needs to move each of these amounts back one month.

3   Max's fixed costs are as follows:

Rent – £420 a month (starting August)
Insurance – £20 a month
Advertising – £100 a month
Stationery – £100 a month
Telephone – £50 a month (starting August)
Lighting/power – £80 a month (starting August)
Other (miscellaneous) – £60 a month

For emergencies Max also wants to keep a contingency fund of about £30 a month, which should be added to his miscellaneous expenses.

Finally, he has decided to pay himself and his employee £900 a month in salaries as he wants someone to help him from the outset.

Stage 3 – bank balance

Max's current bank balance is £50.

Your task

1   From this information enter all Max's outflows on his cashflow forecast and calculate his net cashflow for each month. Again, you will find it useful to calculate his total payments for your 'quick check' later.

2   Work out Max's opening and closing bank balances for each month.

3   Do a 'quick check' of your final closing balance by adding the total receipts and deducting the total payments from Max's opening balance.

4   Advise Max on how much you think he will need to borrow to survive the first few months. Give a reason for the figure you choose.

Check your answer with the key on page 280.

Interpreting cashflow data

Max looks at his cashflow forecast in utter horror. He rechecks the figures over and over again. 'This is crazy,' he says. 'I'm going to work like an idiot until Christmas to get into debt. I must be mad. I'm going to tell Sue the whole idea is stupid and then ring Jack.'

With that he rushes off, his forecast under his arm.

Sue listens to Max's outburst without saying a word. Then she quietly studies the forecast for a few moments.

'You have three basic problems,' she says. 'First, you are not interpreting the data correctly, second you are under-funded at the outset – which I've already warned you about – and third there are one or two alterations we can make to improve the picture.'

'Tell me,' she continues, 'what *trend* do you identify with your net cashflow line?'

Your task

Look at Max's cashflow forecast again on page 280. Identify the line to which Sue is referring and see if you can answer her question before you continue.

Max studies this for several moments. 'Well, upwards, I suppose. Each month my debts get less and in November it's OK – I mean it's positive, not negative.' He panics again. 'But it's only £1,280 – that's nothing is it? And by then I'll owe – let me see – nearly £5,000! It'll take me years before I'm in profit properly.'

'Yes, but the outlook is good if we look long-term,' replies Sue. She takes the forecast back, makes some changes and extends Max's cashflow to cover February–April. Then she hands it back to him. Sue's amendments are shown in Figure 3.25.

Sue talks Max through the forecast.

'First,' she says, 'it is not unusual for a new business to struggle at the beginning. You can't start a going concern with £50 in the bank and £1,500 savings – not when your start-up costs alone were £2,500. The fact you need raw materials quickly and there is a time lag before you receive your payments makes things worse. That is why you seemed to be getting further and further into debt.

'Second, in February you are still owed nearly £2,000 from your January credit sales which you seem to have forgotten about. However, you have assumed that every debtor will pay you promptly each month, whereas some may not. You mustn't forget to remind debtors to pay you promptly – otherwise your cash flow will suffer.

'Third, I've guessed a few figures from February to April as it's always better to look at a cashflow forecast over the long term – preferably 12 months. By then you should be seeing a noticeable difference. I also think you can save money by working on your own in August when you are quieter. But this is up to you. I've also reduced your stationery next year – you'll be drowning in paper by then at the figures you've entered! The net effect at the end of April is that you'll have over £9,000 in the bank *and* you have all the assets of the business. Plus, by then, you will have built up a reputation and some regular customers. This is known as the goodwill of the business and is valuable. You are going to be producing characters that people will want to collect. A useful marketing strategy might be to start just with three or four of the most well-known characters and, once people have started to collect them, you can extend your range. This may mean you can produce more in the early days.

'Fourth, I am quite happy to accompany you to the bank to see if you can get a loan – though you will have to pay bank charges. I would therefore suggest that you contact The Prince's Trust first, as they specialise in giving loans to young people and I've assumed in the forecast they would give you a short 'repayment holiday' of about six months. You may be able to get a grant which doesn't need repaying – I've been optimistic and pencilled in £500 for this. I think you need to borrow £8,000 altogether – but this may be more than their ceiling for start-ups. Their interest rates are much lower than the bank. I am also prepared to invest £3,000 in the enterprise. You could also

Figure 3.24 Business angels may want a share of the profit

	Aug	Sept	Oct	Nov	Dec	Jan	Feb	Mar	April
INFLOWS/RECEIPTS									
Cash sales	0	360	960	1,200	1,080	480	550	850	1,000
Credit sales	0	0	1,440	3,840	4,800	4,320	1,920	3,000	3,500
Loans received	7,500	0	0	0	0	0	0	0	0
Grants received	500	0	0	0	0	0	0	0	0
Owner's capital	1,500	0	0	0	0	0	0	0	0
Sub-total – all inflows (A)	9,500	360	2,400	5,040	5,880	4,800	2,470	3,850	4,500
OUTFLOWS/PAYMENTS									
Variable costs (purchases, stock etc.)	0	2,000	2,000	2,000	2,000	500	500	1,000	2,000
Wages/salaries	500	900	900	900	900	900	900	900	900
Capital items	920	0	0	0	0	0	0	0	0
Rent and rates	1,260	0	0	420	420	420	420	420	420
Light/heat/power	80	80	80	80	80	80	80	80	80
Loan repayments	0	0	0	0	0	0	500	500	500
Stationery and printing	100	100	50	50	50	50	50	50	50
Telephone and postage	50	50	50	50	50	50	50	50	50
Insurance	20	20	20	20	20	20	20	20	20
Advertising/promotions	100	100	100	100	100	100	50	50	50
Licence fees	200	0	0	0	0	0	0	0	0
Miscellaneous expenses	90	90	90	90	90	90	90	90	90
Sub-total – all outflows (B)	3,320	3,340	3,290	3,710	3,710	2,210	2,660	3,160	4,160
Net cashflow (C)	6,180	(2,980)	(890)	1,330	2,170	2,590	(190)	(690)	340
MONTHLY SUMMARY									
Opening bank balance	50	6,230	3,250	2,360	3,690	5,860	8,450	8,260	8,950
Plus total receipts	9,500	360	2,400	5,040	5,880	4,800	2,470	3,850	4,500
Minus total payments	3,320	3,340	3,290	3,710	3,710	2,210	2,660	3,160	4,160
Closing Bank Balance (D)	6,230	3,250	2,360	3,690	5,860	8,450	8,260	8,950	9,290

Figure 3.25 Max's final cashflow forecast

contact Jack Noble to see if his company would be a 'business angel' – but be aware that, in this case, he'll probably want a share of your profits at a later date.

'Finally, always remember that these are forecasts and not reality. They are useful because they focus your mind on the important issues, stop you making silly mistakes and they give you targets. But targets are there to be beaten! You can work harder and produce more. You can try to reduce your costs and you should make a constant effort to keep these down. You need to be aware that costs have a nasty habit of going up unless you are very careful! Now, I think it's time you decided on a suitable name for your business and rang Jack and told him 'yes', don't you? After all, you've a lot of work to do, haven't you?'

ACTIVITY 5

Go through Max's final forecast shown in Figure 3.25 with your tutor.

1 Identify the changes Sue has made and their effect.

2 To what extent does Max's business appear seasonal? Explain your answer with reference to his net cashflow trend.

3 If Max suddenly found he might have a minus balance in the bank at the end of one month, what action should he take? Give a reason for your answer.

4 Sue has told Max always to remember two key facts:

- Make sure all debtors pay promptly.
- Watch all costs carefully.

With reference to cashflow, why are these so important?

5 Write a short paragraph explaining why a cashflow forecast is so valuable.

6 As a group, discuss whether Max's cashflow forecast could be improved still further. Implement the best ideas and calculate the resulting net cashflow and bank balances.

A final note – spreadsheets and accurate forecasting

Hopefully you will have had the opportunity to use a computer spreadsheet to produce some of your forecasts as you worked on this section. There are several obvious advantages to using these. But there are also some disadvantages of which you should be aware.

Advantages of spreadsheets

1 Spreadsheets enable you to manipulate, calculate and analyse numeric data easily.

2 Lengthy and tedious manual calculations – with figures having to be changed and recalculated – are avoided.

3 A spreadsheet can be set up to analyse any type of numeric data, e.g. budgets, sales analyses, recording profits, forecasts, stock movements.

4 There are no errors in calculations – providing the figures and the formulas have been entered correctly.

5 Recalculations are carried out automatically when data is changed.

6 The spreadsheet user can spend more time analysing the results of the spreadsheet, rather than doing the actual calculations.

7 Spreadsheets give an accurate financial picture so that problems can be identified, solutions considered and the best decisions made.

8 The results of possible solutions can easily be seen, simply by changing the data on a 'what if?' basis.

9 Graphic representations (line graphs, pie charts and bar charts) can be produced from spreadsheet data, so that the overall picture and trends are quickly identified.

SNAPSHOT

Have you got what it takes?

About 330,000 new businesses start up each year in Britain. According to a survey by NatWest bank and Warwick University, 81 per cent disappear within six years – though only a quarter of these were because of financial difficulties. In most cases it was because the owners found the commitment too great. On average they were working a 51-hour week and, in some cases, up to 69 hours a week.

Some of the entrepreneurs had given too little thought to their financial and market analysis. A NatWest bank spokesman said, 'I insist on seeing a cashflow forecast and want to know where the break-even point is, covering all the costs. Many potentially profitable start-ups get into difficulties because they simply run out of cash. They're not collecting their debts fast enough or they're holding too much stock or they simply don't work out how much cash they need.'

The general message seems to be 'never give up'. One entrepreneur, Will King, who set up his

own business producing a range of shaving oils and gels expected to be profitable in six months. In the first year his sales were actually £300 and his costs were £30,000. In 1999 sales by his company, KMI, were expected to reach £4 million.

In another survey by Warwick University, business failures were usually caused by trying to grow too quickly, taking too many risks, being under-capitalised at the start, lack of management skills or experience and pure chance, such as the unforeseen closure of a key customer or supplier. Those who succeed have been identified as having a strong desire to work for themselves, who are prepared to put in long hours and work alone at the outset and who are good at identifying niche market opportunities. They must be prepared to lobby relatives, friends and banks to obtain additional finance when needed in the early days. They must be strongly motivated to create personal wealth – which kept the survivors going when the going was tough. And, it would appear, lucky!

10 Spreadsheets can be 'imported' into other packages, e.g. word processing packages, so that they can be included in reports or other documents without the need for retyping.

Disadvantages of spreadsheets

1 If a spreadsheet is very large, it is difficult to print out on A4 paper without reducing the text size to become virtually unreadable. Similarly, it can be too large to be seen on screen, which can make working on it tedious.

2 A mistake in a spreadsheet can be catastrophic – as it may have 'spin-off'

effects if it is in a cell which is part of a formula. Therefore 100 per cent accuracy is vital.

3 On some packages, there is no facility for attaching notes to explain a cell entry.

4 The layout is important if a spreadsheet is to be easy to understand. New users may have difficulties planning how to set out a new spreadsheet.

5 Changing data in a spreadsheet may mean there is no historic record unless the updated spreadsheet is resaved under 'Save As'.

6 Inexperienced users may have difficulties working out how to enter formulae for complex calculations.

7 Copying formulae from one spreadsheet to another is easy, but copying figures may not be possible if they are derived from formulae calculations. In this case, the figures may have to be re-entered.

8 There is a limit to the number of variables that can be included in one spreadsheet, which works on the basis of rows and columns. Sometimes several spreadsheets have to be prepared to analyse the same data in different ways.

9 Errors may be made if you enter a cell reference in a calculation as an absolute reference when it should be a relative reference – and vice versa. If you do not understand this point, your IT tutor will explain it to you.

10 Sometimes it would be just as quick to do a calculation using a calculator – rather than go to the trouble of setting up a spreadsheet. However, you may want the calculation to be part of a longer report and it would *look* more professional as a spreadsheet.

11 Probably the most important of all. With all IT work it is possible to lose a file or corrupt it – and lose hours of work. Remember to save your work regularly and keep back-up copies.

It is worth discussing these advantages and disadvantages with your IT tutor – and see if you can extend either of these lists.

Section review

Before you complete this section, re-read Sue's comments to Max again. Then answer the following questions.

1 *What is a 'debtor'?*

2 *Why is it important that businesses make sure that their debtors pay promptly?*

3 *What is the difference between a 'grant' and a 'loan'?*

4 *What is 'goodwill'?*

5 *Why is it important to keep costs as low as possible?*

6 *Why does it help a new business if it can obtain supplies on credit?*

7 *What is the difference between inflows and outflows?*

8 *How would you explain the term 'net cashflow' to someone who had never heard of it?*

9 *Suggest reasons why each of the following costs may increase or decrease:*
   a *rent on premises*
   b *wages and salaries*
   c *raw materials*
   d *loan repayments*
   e *telephone charges*
   f *advertising.*

10 *What marketing strategy does Sue suggest to Max? State whether you agree with this or not. Give a reason for your answer.*

11 *What do you consider are:*
   a *the benefits, and*
   b *the limitations*

   of financial forecasts and predictions?

12 *Why are cashflow forecasts usually considered the most important type of financial forecast?*

13 *Why is it important to be able to interpret the data in a cashflow forecast properly?*

14 *Identify two advantages and two disadvantages of using a spreadsheet to prepare business forecasts.*

3.3 FINANCIAL DOCUMENTS FOR PURCHASES AND SALES

At the end of this section you should be able to:

- explain the use of financial documents
- describe the sequence in which financial documents are used
- complete financial documents accurately from given data
- check financial documents to ensure they have been completed accurately
- explain the problems that can be caused by inaccurate financial documents and describe the steps a business would have to take in this situation
- explain the advantages and disadvantages of using a computerised accounting system to generate financial documents.

Overview of financial documents

Almost every business transaction is accompanied by a financial document. If you pay to enter a cinema you receive a ticket in return. If you buy a bar of chocolate you are given a receipt. If you pay for something by debit or credit card then you have to sign a printed slip or counterfoil which confirms the transaction. All of these are classed as 'cash' transactions – because the supplier receives payment at the time the item is purchased.

You already know that an alternative to 'cash' transactions exists. Businesses buy and sell goods and services on credit. This means that payment is made at a later date. In this case, there are special business documents which accompany each *part* of the transaction.

At one time, all business documents were specially printed and completed either by

hand or on a typewriter. Today, computers can print out financial documents automatically, as they are needed. The computer at the same time adjusts the company's accounts to show the transaction has taken place.

Understanding the financial documents used in business transactions is important for several reasons. First, you are unlikely – ever – to work for an organisation that does not issue and receive such documents. Second, in your personal life you may receive such documents – particularly if you buy goods on mail order. Knowing how the documents have been compiled, why they are used – and how to check them – gives you an advantage.

In this final section we will return to Max's organisation. Two years have elapsed since Max set up his business. He has done quite

Figure 3.26 Max has now converted his enterprise to a limited company

well. He still operates a fairly small organisation, which is sensible. He knows that enterprises that grow too fast can run into difficulties. Max has called his enterprise 'DigiTech Characters Ltd'. Although he started out as a sole trader, Max converted the enterprise to a private limited company last year. If you have completed Unit 2, you should understand why he made this decision. One reason was that more suppliers were prepared to sell him goods on credit when he had limited status and more stores were prepared to buy from him. Max feels the company has a higher status now with its customers, and prefers the security of having limited liability.

Max was concerned that if Starworld characters lost their appeal his sales would fall dramatically. Sue counselled him about 'not having all his eggs in one basket'. He is currently working on the idea of producing football figures and is negotiating with a number of clubs about producing 'players' under licence. However, Max needn't have worried too much. Last year, Starworld was launched on national television. It was a huge success and the figures are now in demand nationwide. There is now talk of it being shown in other countries, which opens up the opportunity for Max to export his figures.

When Max started the business he had one person to help him – his sister Karen. Last year, a friend of Karen, Shazia, joined the company to run production and at the same time Max moved to larger premises. Since then he has appointed three other members of staff. Max himself concentrates on the overall business finances, generating more sales and new developments – as he considers these to be the main activities with which he should be involved. You are now the latest addition to his team.

The organisation chart at DigiTech is shown in Figure 3.27.

The first job you have been asked to do is to 'shadow' some of the staff and learn all about financial documents linked to business transactions.

The sequence of financial documents

On the first day you are working with Matt. He explains to you that although there are several financial documents involved when an item is bought or sold, there is a specific sequence in which they are issued, because they all have a particular purpose. Obviously DigiTech deals with both types of documents because it sells goods to customers and buys items from suppliers. The main financial documents you need to be able to issue and check are described briefly below.

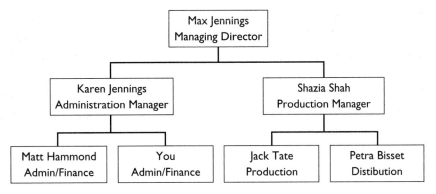

Figure 3.27 DigiTech organisation chart

Purchase orders

When an item is required, it must be officially ordered. No organisation will allow employees to order goods without permission – otherwise there would be chaos and the firm would be lucky to have any money after a few months! A purchase order is the official order for an item. DigiTech issues orders for items it requires, and receives orders from stores and football clubs which want to buy figures. Goods are never sent out until an official order has been received, though in an emergency an order may be transmitted by fax.

Delivery notes

When an item is despatched, a delivery note is sent to the customer. At DigitTech Petra sends out delivery notes in the packages. The delivery note states the contents of the package (but not the price) so that the person receiving it can check that the correct items have been enclosed. At DigiTech all items received are checked against the delivery note immediately and the checker then signs the delivery note. The carrier who delivers the goods usually requires a signature and then retains a copy of the delivery note to prove the package arrived intact.

Goods received note (GRN)

A goods received note (usually referred to as a GRN) is issued by the person who has checked in an incoming package and a copy is sent to the accounts department. This is now a written record of the actual goods which were delivered and their condition on arrival – sometimes it may differ from the delivery note. At DigiTech, Jack checks the supplies or raw materials he has received. He then issues a GRN and sends a copy to Matt. Matt can then keep this on file as a record that Jack has confirmed that the items were actually received.

Invoices

An invoice is a bill for payment. It states the goods that have been sent and includes details of the price. At DigiTech, Matt checks all the invoices that are received against the GRNs to make sure nothing is charged for what has not been received. Matt and Karen both issue invoices to customers – but Karen wants you to take on this job with Matt.

Credit notes

Occasionally an item is returned for some reason or because the charge on an invoice is too high. In either case a credit note is issued. This is the opposite of an invoice. It is confirming that the amount on the credit note will be deducted from the customer's account.

Statements of account

At the end of the month a statement of account is prepared. This shows all the invoices and any credit notes that have been issued during the month and the balance of money owing. It is, in effect, a summary of all the different transactions that have taken place between two organisations and a reminder of the total amount which must be paid. DigiTech allows its customers 28 days to pay, after receipt of the statement. After this time a reminder is sent. Karen is responsible for deciding when statements which DigiTech receive should be paid, as too many payments in one month can adversely affect the firm's cashflow.

Remittance advice slips

Not all organisations issue these, but DigiTech does, as it considers that they help people to pay more promptly. A remittance advice is sent with the statement and is returned by the customer with the payment.

This means the customer doesn't have to worry about writing a letter or copying the statement when payment is made. From a slip DigiTech can easily identify from whom the payment came and against which statement.

Cheques

DigiTech pays its suppliers by cheque and receives dozens of cheques a month in payment. Max and Karen both sign all large cheques, for security. Karen is allowed to sign cheques on her own if they are under £2,000. Matt, Shazia and Jack aren't allowed to sign any. All cheques received must be examined carefully as sometimes mistakes are made in filling out a cheque, which would be rejected by the bank.

Receipts

Very few businesses expect a receipt, as a cashed cheque is legally recognised as a receipt. DigiTech rarely asks for receipts for this reason. However, minor items are often bought by employees – Matt had to buy some milk in an emergency last week and Karen insisted on a receipt so she can balance the petty cash. This is the small amount of cash kept by the firm for sundry items and emergencies. Matt remembers a time when he had to go to the stationer's for some velcro which cost him a small fortune and lost the receipt on the way back! He still remembers the lecture Karen gave him, about how accountants insist that all purchases – no matter how small – have to be supported by a financial document.

Matt tells you that DigiTech occasionally issues receipts to private customers who buy figures, but very few now are sold in this way.

Finally, Matt draws a diagram for you which clearly illustrates the sequence and use of each document – in summary (see Figure 3.28).

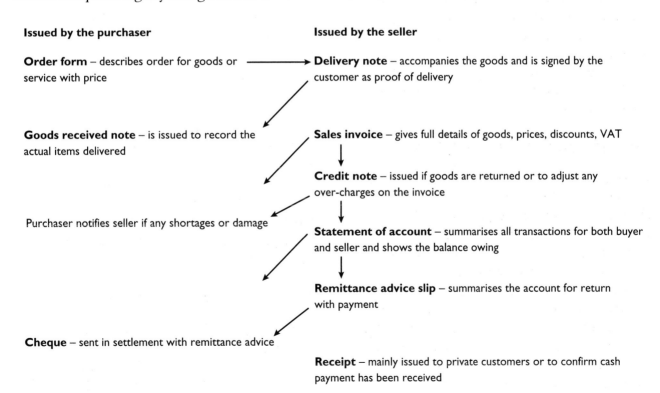

Figure 3.28 The sequence and use of documents in sales and purchasing

SNAPSHOT

The world of VAT

VAT is a tax which is added to the price of most goods every time they are sold. The timber merchant who sells to the furniture manufacturer charges VAT on the wood, the manufacturer who sells to the retailer charges VAT on the table, the retailer who sells to the customer charges VAT on the final selling price. The current rate of VAT is 17.5 per cent, but the government has the power to change this if it wishes.

HM Customs and Excise oversee VAT collection in the UK. Businesses do not owe all the tax every time an item changes hands – they pay the **difference** between the tax they collect and the tax they have paid out. However, only firms which are registered for VAT can do this. All firms must register for VAT if their annual turnover is £51,000 or more (as at 1 April 1999). However, this figure, too, is often changed. A small firm, which isn't registered for VAT, cannot reclaim VAT paid on its supplies or expenses – neither can it charge VAT to its customers.

Not all goods are liable for VAT. Some goods are zero-rated – food (but not meals in restaurants or take-aways), books and newspapers, children's clothes and shoes, prescriptions and exported goods. Some services are exempt from VAT, including insurance, education and medical services provided by doctors and dentists. Businesses which only deal in zero-rated or exempted goods are not required to register for VAT, regardless of their turnover.

VAT registered firms have to comply with certain regulations. For instance, they have to issue VAT invoices, which show their registration number and the amount of VAT charged. They have to keep records and complete a VAT return (usually quarterly) which summarises the total amount they owe HM Customs and Excise. Sometimes a firm may be able to claim a refund – if it has paid out more than it has collected. VAT inspectors can call to check a company's accounts and VAT records at any time. There are also penalties (fines) if VAT payments are late. Businesses therefore are very careful indeed to keep their accounts and records up to date and to send in their returns promptly.

Completing financial documents

The layout of financial documents varies considerably from one organisation to another. You only have to ask your parents for copies of delivery notes or invoices they have received to see this. As an example, look at your electricity, gas and telephone bills for the last quarter and see how they vary!

What you will find is that some headings are common to particular types of documents – even if the order in which they are printed is different. In this section you will be looking mainly at how DigiTech prints its documents, but you will also see other examples as well. Because of the common features, if you understand the reason for the document and the key items which are included, you will soon learn to follow different layouts.

At this stage Matt impresses just one thing on you – accuracy. He tells you that he has heard several horror stories about the results of errors made in documents. One supplier they used was so inaccurate Max stopped dealing with them any more. It turned out most of the errors had been made by a new employee who was later dismissed – but during her time at the company she probably lost them thousands of pounds worth of business. Because the problems can be so serious, Max stresses you must check your work carefully – even when the work seems easy. According to Matt, you are probably more likely to make a mistake when you are not concentrating properly than when you are working on something complicated!

Before you start, Karen has a quick word with you. She explains that all DigiTech financial documents today are produced by computer, as the company has a computerised accounts package which is also linked to its stock control system. The way in which this benefits everyone will soon become clear to you. However, keying in figures in a computer is no use unless you *understand* what you are doing – what the document will be used for, how the calculations are carried out and so on. Otherwise you will be unable to answer customer queries, solve simple problems yourself or check your work properly. She therefore tells you that for the first week or so, she wants you to practice by studying and completing some paper documents – then you will be shown how to do the same thing on computer.

Purchase orders

Completing purchase orders

Matt shows you a DigiTech order form he sent recently (see Figure 3.29). He tells you that this order should be of interest to you because it was for your desk and chair – amongst other things – which is due to be delivered later today. He explains that on the computer system, each order is allocated a specific number by which it is identified. If you make a mistake on one you cannot just tear it up and throw it away – you have to tell Karen as this would upset the accounts records. He also tells you that only Karen or Max can sign the orders for security.

Figure 3.29 DigiTech purchase order form

Matt informs you that he has to enter:

- The supplier's name and address. He tells you that DigiTech has a list of preferred suppliers – so you can't just contact a completely new supplier without permission. This is done to try to keep costs to target levels.

- Supplier's reference code – each supplier has a unique reference number, again allocated by the computer. This is also reflected in the files – all copies of financial documents relating to that supplier are filed under that number.

- The order number. The order number is useful as it helps to identify a particular transaction in the files. The order number is also quoted on many subsequent documents relating to the same transaction.

- The date.

- The quantity required. At this point it is important to check the unit in which goods are sold. For instance, shoes and jeans are sold in pairs, paper is sold in reams (500 sheets), pens may be boxed in 10s, 12s or 50s and envelopes in 100s or 1000s. These details are obtained from the supplier's catalogue.

- A description of the item – copying the catalogue description is usually the safest method.

- The item or reference code. This is usually shown alongside items in catalogues.

- The price per unit.

- The date delivery is required.

- Whether carriage is paid by the supplier or will be added as an extra. On orders received by DigiTech you can expect to see the phrase 'carriage paid', as the cost of delivery is included in the price.

You then have to check the order before you pass it to Karen or Max for signing. Orders are always printed in duplicate, as DigiTech keeps a copy for its records. Orders awaiting delivery are kept in a special file so that Matt can check quickly and easily which items are still outstanding.

Checking completed purchase orders

The most usual mistakes include.

1 Entering an incorrect or incomplete description of the goods.
2 Ordering the wrong amount because of confusion about the unit size. For instance, if pens are sold in boxes of 10 then you can only buy in multiples of this amount. If you order 15 then you will receive 150 pens, not 15!
3 Copying down the wrong reference or item code.

4 Entering an outdated price – if the catalogue is old you should contact the supplier to check the current price.
5 Not checking special terms for delivery, such as the required date, or whether carriage (postal) charges will be added as an extra or are paid by the supplier.

ACTIVITY 6

1 Check each item on the order shown in Figure 3.29. Ask your tutor if you are unsure of any entry.

2 See how quickly you can (accurately) state the total value of the order.

3 If Swift Office Supplies found it could not provide the desk and chair by the required date, what action do you think it should take, and why?

4 Why can only authorised individuals in an organisation sign order forms?

5 a What do you think would have been the result if Matt had inadvertently ordered 200 reams of paper – and no-one had noticed?

   b Suggest what action DigiTech could have taken in this situation.

6 Matt has told you that Max has agreed you should have your own computer and printer. There is a spare computer which is rather old, but which will do for the time being, but there is no spare printer. He asks you to make out an order yourself to Swift Office Supplies for an Omega ink-jet printer. The catalogue reference is 508-JP and the price is £124.20. He also asks you to add 24 ring binders. These cost £0.42 each and are sold in boxes of 6. You can choose the colours yourself. Matt tells you the order number will be 7470 and the order should be dated today, for delivery a week from today.

Ring binders:

Red	4001-RB	Blue	4002-RB
Black	4003-RB	Green	4004-RB
Orange	4005-RB	Yellow	4006-RB
Purple	4007-RB	Yellow	4008-RB
Navy	4009-RB		

a Your tutor will provide you with a blank order form. Complete this from the details above.

b Calculate the total value of the order.

7 a Matt shows you an order DigiTech received last month from Beacon Toy Stores and asks if you can spot the errors on it (see Figure 3.30). He tells you that all DigiTech characters are supplied in boxes of 10. Those suffixed 01 in the code are £60 a unit and those suffixed 02 in the code are £70. Can you spot the three main errors?

Beacon Toy Stores – Head Office
15 Musgrove Hill
FAIRFIELDS
Berkshire   Tel: 01412 839728   Fax: 01412 893709
RG8 4PL   Contact us at: www.beacon.co.uk

VAT Reg No 3879 9278 73

Purchase Order No: NZ20398   **DigiTech Characters Ltd**
                                        Unit 5, Brampton Industrial Park
                                        BRAMPTON
                                        Newshire
                                        BR4 9DK

Date: 28 August 2000

Item code	Quantity	Description	Unit price
8SW/01	12 boxes	White star knight	£60
5SW/02	15 boxes	Black star demon	£70
10SW/01	8 boxes	Red star princess	£60
7SW/02	6 boxes	Cyberbug	£84

Delivery: A soon as possible; carriage paid

Authorised signatory: _____ Title _____

Figure 3.30 Purchase order received by DigiTech

b If DigiTech receives an order and spots an error, what action do you think it should take, and why?

Check your answers with the key on page 281 and check your completed order form with your tutor. If your tutor approves the form he/she will sign it.

Delivery notes
Completing delivery notes

At DigiTech, Petra is responsible for despatching the figures and producing most of the delivery notes – but you may be asked to help out if she is very busy. You go to see her to find out what happens when an order is received.

Petra tells you that Karen receives all the orders. The vast majority are passed to Petra immediately but some are not. The exceptions are when a new customer sends in a large order and their credit worthiness needs to be checked before the order is processed. Orders are also held back if customers are over their credit limit because they still owe money for goods previously supplied.

Petra shows you the delivery note which she sent to accompany the order you have just checked (Figure 3.31) – after she had

DigiTech Characters Ltd
Unit 5
Brompton Industrial Park
BROMPTON
Newshire
BR4 9DK

Tel: 01232 788488   VAT Reg No 830/38473/99
Fax: 01232 601090
Website: www.DTcharacters.co.uk   Email: orders@DTcharacters.co.uk

DELIVERY NOTE

To: Beacon Toy Stores   **Delivery address** (if different):
     15 Musgrove Hill
     FAIRFIELDS
     Berkshire RG8 4PL

Date: 4 September 2000

Your order No	Customer Account No	Despatch date	Invoice No	Delivery method
NZ20398	7801	5 September 2000	10013	TDL Express

Item code	Quantity	Description
8SW/01	12 boxes	White star knight
5SW/02	15 boxes	Black star demon
10SW/01	8 boxes	Red star princess
7SW/02	6 boxes	Cyberbug

Thank you for your order. Please retain this delivery note for your records

Received in good condition (or comment here)
....
....

Signed .... Date ....

Please print name ....

White copy: customer   Pink copy: carrier   Yellow copy: DigiTech

Figure 3.31 DigiTech delivery note

contacted the firm to inform them about the unit price error and obtain authorisation. She tells you that she checks all orders quickly before processing them – just to make sure there are no errors.

She goes through each of the entries with you.

- The name and address are copied from the order. On the computer system, putting in the customer account number will automatically insert the customer's name and address in this section.

- If the delivery address is different to the address to which the account is to be sent, this is entered alongside. This occurs when orders are sent by head office and deliveries to be made to a particular branch.

- The date the delivery note is completed.

- The customer's order number – copied from the order.

- The customer account number. All customers are allocated an account number. Their records (both on paper and on computer) can then be identified quickly and easily. The account number can be accessed from the files or from the computer system.

- The despatch date is the date the goods are actually sent. Petra aims to send all orders on the day after the date the order is assembled and the delivery note completed.

- The delivery method is identified – in this case the carrier used was TDL Express. Petra explains that some carriers are more reliable than others and Digitech monitors which firms are the best, and which are not.

- The invoice number. This is to help the customer link the delivery note to the invoice which will follows. On the computer system the next available invoice number is automatically allocated.

- Item code – the code from the catalogue. When you enter this on the computer system, the description is inserted automatically on the delivery note.

- Quantity. The amount the customer has ordered is included so that the customer can check the correct quantity has been sent.

- Description. The catalogue description of the goods is added so that the customer can check the correct goods have been sent (without having to look up the original order). This can be done by computer or by writing it in.

- The received box – which the customer must sign. TDL Express asks the customer to complete this and then returns a copy of each delivery note to DigiTech. DigiTech does not expect the delivery people to wait until the box has been unpacked and each item checked individually. It does expect the customer to write a note in the box if the package is received damaged and to inform them promptly if there are any problems once the items have been unpacked.

Petra tells you that before they computerised the stock control system her worst problem was dealing with orders for goods that were out of stock. In these cases she marked 'O/S – to follow' on the delivery note. With the computerised stock control system, every order fulfilled automatically deducts the items from the stock list. A daily computer print-out shows Jack which items are highly active and warns him when stocks are running low, so that he can schedule production accordingly. This has solved the problem of being out of stock – Petra cannot remember the last time an item was out of stock. She thinks this has improved customer relations, as there are no delays to delivery because there is no stock. If they were out of stock she would ring the customer to say when the delivery would be.

Checking completed delivery notes

The following are the most serious errors.

1 Mistakes copying the order number, so that the customer cannot reconcile the delivery with his records.

2 Mistakes copying the customer account number or, manually, the customer's name and address. When this happens the document gets filed in the wrong file and the goods and the invoice are sent to the wrong customer!

3 Errors copying the item code and quantity, so that the wrong goods or the wrong quantity of goods are sent.

ACTIVITY 7

Check your understanding of delivery notes by answering the questions below.

1 What is the main purpose of delivery notes?

2 A customer has to check the contents of the package before signing for receipt. True or false? Give a reason for your answer.

3 How can a computerised stock control system help to avoid delays in deliveries?

4 What are the advantages of allocating all customers with their own account number?

5 Why is the description and quantity repeated on the delivery note, given that the customer has specified this on the order?

6 Complete a DigiTech delivery note yourself from the following information.

An order has been received from Hemple's Department Store, 15 Quay Street, Manchester M5 4PM, number 28903. Date the delivery note 10 September – the goods will be despatched tomorrow by Parcel Force. Hemple's order is summarised below. Their customer number is 5001 and the invoice number will be 10025.

12 boxes	Sky blazers	6SW/01
10 boxes	Black star demons	10SW/02
15 boxes	White star mechanoids	4SW/02

Check your answers with the key on page 281 and your completed delivery note with your tutor.

Goods received notes

Completing goods received notes

At DigiTech, GRNs are mainly made out by Jack Tate although those for office supplies are completed by Matt. Jack Tate receives all the raw materials used in production and all the materials Petra uses for packaging. He makes out the GRN as a check that all the items are correct – and this is only completed when the package has been unpacked and every item checked.

You go to see Jack. He warns you that the first step is to check whether the package is undamaged on delivery. Then it must be opened carefully – careless opening can cause damage, making it DigiTech's problem. Each item is then unpacked carefully, making certain it is as described and that the quantity is correct. The GRN is then completed. Jack tells you that goods ordered are correctly delivered in most cases, but then hunts through his files to find one which

Figure 3.32 DigiTech goods received note

wasn't. He shows you the example illustrated in Figure 3.32 and explains each entry to you.

- The first entry is the supplier's name and address – which must match the one on the delivery note.

- Each authorised supplier has an account number – in the same way that each customer has a customer number. All supplier records are filed under that number. On the computer system, the name and address is entered automatically once the supplier number has been keyed in.

- The carrier is recorded – so that DigiTech can also check if there are problems with a particular carrier.

- The GRN number and date is entered next. GRNs are issued in sequence and the computer automatically allocates the next number.

- Details of the delivery note number and date are copied from the delivery note.

- Jack enters his initials under checker. He tells you that in larger firms people may be allocated a code number or have to write their full name.

- The order number, quantity ordered and description is copied from the *order* – not from the delivery note, which may be incorrect. On a computer system this information is transferred automatically.

- The quantity delivered is entered. Usually this is the same as the quantity ordered. If not, an entry is made on the right-hand side.

- The condition of the goods is checked and the right-hand box is either ticked or details entered. Jack says that he normally notifies the firm immediately if there is a problem and arranges for damaged goods to be collected.

Jack tells you that, just occasionally, a mistake by the packer can mean that too *many* goods are delivered. He once had a student working with him one summer who thought DigiTech should just keep these goods and say nothing! She couldn't see that this would be tantamount to theft and that DigiTech was an honourable business with a good reputation – and wanted to stay that way.

- Jack tells you he prints out two copies – one for the purchases file and one for Karen. She keeps this and checks it against the invoice when this is received.

Checking completed GRNs

The most common mistakes.

1 On a manual system, miscopying details from the order or the delivery note.
2 Not checking goods properly and missing a problem or a fault.
3 Writing insufficient information to explain problems or discrepancies. The quantity damaged must be noted as well as the type of damage. Whether the goods have already been returned or still have to be collected should be noted.

ACTIVITY 8

I How would you explain the purpose of a GRN to someone who has never heard of them?

2 Is a GRN a document which is used internally or sent outside the company? Give a reason for your answer.

3 Why is it important for the checker to be identified on a GRN?

4 Why is it not acceptable for checkers in a large firm to simply enter their initials on a GRN?

5 When you return to the office you find a large package beside Matt's desk. This is the delivery of the order Matt sent to Swift Office Supplies. You help Matt unpack your desk and chair and put them into position. Now you really feel you belong at DigiTech as you sit down and try out the chair.

Matt won't let you rest long, however! He asks you to help unpack the filing cabinet and to unpack the box containing the stationery items. Then you have to check the delivery note and make out the GRN.

Swift Office Supplies Ltd
15 Cheyne Road   BROMPTON   Newshire   BR2 7PT
tel: 01232 879787   Fax: 01232 688092

DELIVERY NOTE

Customer name:

DigiTech Characters Ltd   Order No: 7458
Unit 5   Date: 20 September 2000
Brompton Industrial Park   Customer No: 60898
BROMPTON   Taken by: JL
Newshire BR4 9DK

Quantity	Item code	Description
I	530-D4	4-drawer metal filing cabinet
I	670-DL	L-shaped desk unit
I	2548-DC	Swivel task chair – navy
20 rms	200-MP	A4 multi paper – white
3	5078-OM	Laser cartridges – Omega laser OM452

Received (date): ....

By (please print) ....

Signed ....

Any damage or discrepancies must be notified immediately

Figure 3.33 A goods delivery note

The delivery note is shown in Figure 3.33. When you check the parcel you find that only two laser cartridges have been sent, and not three as ordered.

a Complete a GRN for the order you have just unpacked.

b What action will you take as to the missing cartridge?

Check your answers with the key on page 282 and your completed GRN with your tutor.

Invoices

Completing invoices

You are slightly nervous this morning as Karen, Max's sister, wants to tell you all about invoices. Mistakes on invoices can lose the company money. Invoices also involve calculating how much money customers owe the company, and mistakes can be made, particularly if the calculations are being done manually.

Karen explains that invoices are sent after the goods have been delivered. The layout of invoices varies from one organisation to another but the DigiTech invoice is fairly standard for computerised systems. Karen shows you an example of a DigiTech invoice (Figure 3.34) and goes through each entry with you. Then she asks you to compare this with a DigiTech delivery note (see Figure 3.31) to see what you notice about the layouts.

When you look at the two together, you can see that the same form is used, with slight changes to headings and extensions to the columns on the invoice. Karen tells you it is usual to use the same design on many financial documents so that the same information is printed in the same way each time. She tells you that the invoice will be automatically printed from the order when you use the computer system, and that you must understand each entry and how the

SNAPSHOT

Fast reactions = better business

The mail order business is growing rapidly. Today you can order goods by phone or over the Internet. Many businesses pride themselves on their speedy and efficient responses – which has been helped by advances in computerised systems.

If you phone Next Direct or Marks & Spencer Direct, you may first hear a computerised voice giving you a range of options which you select from by pressing a key. This gives you contact with a sales operator who is equipped with a telephone and a computer.

You are asked for your name and postcode. From this the computer automatically generates your full address, which is then checked with you. Your customer account number – if you have used the firm before – automatically appears on screen. As each item code is entered, the description appears on screen, the unit, unit price and total cost and when delivery of any item will be delayed. From this you are told the status of each item. The sales person will check the order details with you immediately and confirm the final cost of your order, including any postage charges. You are then asked to state how you will pay. Once these details have been entered and verified the order is then 'live'. Finally, the delivery date will be checked with you. If there are any special instructions, such as 'leave goods next door at number 35' these will be entered, too.

Computerisation has meant that items can be 'picked' automatically from warehouse stores and the stock figures adjusted. These details will inform sales and production operations the following day. The distribution section will automatically print out delivery notes from the details which have already been entered against your name. This is how the delivery person knows where and when to deliver your goods! Invoices are often printed out in huge batches overnight from the previous day's business transactions. Statements are generated automatically at the end of the month. At the same time, the company's accounts are adjusted. Sales and bank accounts are updated every time a customer places an order and pays an account.

Purchases are handled in the same way. Purchase orders generate GRNs which are matched against incoming invoices and the purchases account is updated. When invoices are paid the money is automatically deducted from the bank account. The accountants can see the daily financial position at the touch of a key.

The next time you place an order for an item from a mail order company, you may like to consider all the systems busily at work, automatically processing it!

---

calculations are carried out. This is in case a customer contacts you querying the invoice they received. She goes through the details of each entry with you.

- The customer's account number is entered first on the computer system and the name and address are checked. This is always the 'account' address, not necessarily the delivery address.

- The order number, customer account number, date and invoice number are similar headings to those on the delivery note. Only the entry under the date will be different if the despatch date is different to the invoice date. On a computerised system the documents will be printed at the same time, and the invoice sent out as soon as the goods have been despatched.

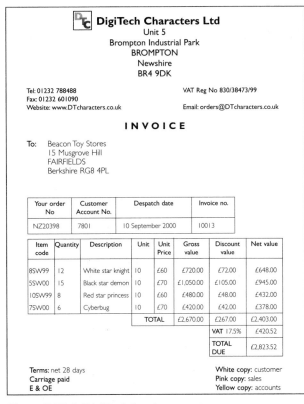

DigiTech Characters Ltd
Unit 5
Brompton Industrial Park
BROMPTON
Newshire
BR4 9DK

Tel: 01232 788488
Fax: 01232 601090
Website: www.DTcharacters.co.uk

VAT Reg No 830/38473/99

Email: orders@DTcharacters.co.uk

I N V O I C E

To: Beacon Toy Stores
15 Musgrove Hill
FAIRFIELDS
Berkshire RG8 4PL

Your order No	Customer Account No.	Despatch date	Invoice no.
NZ20398	7801	10 September 2000	10013

Item code	Quantity	Description	Unit	Unit Price	Gross value	Discount value	Net value
8SW99	12	White star knight	10	£60	£720.00	£72.00	£648.00
5SW00	15	Black star demon	10	£70	£1,050.00	£105.00	£945.00
10SW99	8	Red star princess	10	£60	£480.00	£48.00	£432.00
7SW00	6	Cyberbug	10	£70	£420.00	£42.00	£378.00
			TOTAL		£2,670.00	£267.00	£2,403.00
					VAT 17.5%		£420.52
					TOTAL DUE		£2,823.52

Terms: net 28 days
Carriage paid
E & OE

White copy: customer
Pink copy: sales
Yellow copy: accounts

Figure 3.34 A DigiTech invoice

- The item code, quantity and description are the same as on the delivery note.

- The unit is the quantity in which the goods are sold, the unit price is the price of each unit.

- The gross value is calculated (unit price × quantity).

- DigiTech allows all its major trade customers a 10 per cent discount. Private customers are not allowed discounts and so zero would be entered in this column. Max determines the amount of discount allowed to trade customers (called **trade discount**). The maximum is 10 per cent. New customers or those who usually place small orders are only eligible for 5 per cent.

- The net value is the gross value minus any discount.

- Each of the columns is then totalled to give total gross value, total discount and total net value.

- VAT is then calculated at the current rate and entered.

- The total due is the total net value plus VAT, and this is entered in the final box.

- The terms specify that the invoice must be paid in 28 days and that DigiTech will pay the carriage charges.

- E&OE stands for 'errors and omissions excepted'. Note the spelling of 'excepted' – this does not mean the same as 'accepted'! E&OE means that if an error is made on the invoice, and the customer is undercharged in error, the supplier has the legal right to adjust the account to make it correct and send an additional invoice to the customer.

Checking an invoice

Karen informs you that all invoices must be checked carefully. Whilst DigiTech can legally correct mistakes and issue a supplementary invoice, mistakes give people a poor impression of the company. There is also the cost and inconvenience of having to adjust the account and send out another invoice.

When an invoice is received by DigiTech this, too, must be checked carefully against the GRN – to make sure that all the goods on the invoice have been received in good condition. Then the calculations must be checked. Only after doing this is the invoice stamped and 'passed for payment'.

Karen shows you an invoice received from Parkway Computer Systems (Figure 3.35) which was passed for payment. She draws your attention to the fact that the computer supplier allowed DigiTech 2 per cent **cash discount**. A cash discount is allowed for immediate payment and the invoice is calculated to allow for this. Karen tells you

261

that she pays invoices which offer cash discounts immediately, whenever she can. However, DigiTech does not offer cash discounts to its customers, so you will not have to work out invoices which include this – but you may be asked to check incoming invoices which include it. If DigiTech had not taken advantage of the cash discount, then the invoice would have been based on the full price, less trade discount, and Karen would have had to pay VAT on that price, not the discounted one.

Parkway Computer Systems Ltd
Parkway Drive
BROMPTON
BR6 4JK

Tel: 01232 280280
Fax: 01232 300192

Email: http//www.Parkway.com

I N V O I C E

DigiTech Characters Ltd
Unit 5
Brompton Industrial Park
BROMPTON
Newshire BR4 9DK

Invoice No: 155571
Invoice date: 13 April 2000
Your ref: 280
Sales Order No: 0153197

Product	Description	Qty	Unit	Gross	Disc	Net	VAT code
01240	Parkway 430 System including Symantec Anti-Virus Parkway internal modem PS/2 keyboard PS/2 mouse	1	1	£720	5%	£684.00	1

NET TOTAL		£684.00
Cash Discount 2%		£13.68
SUB-TOTAL		£670.32
VAT		£117.30 *
Invoice Total		£787.62

Terms: 2% cash discount/7 days
* Based on cash discounted price
E&OE

VAT Reg No GB 250 38833 82

Figure 3.35 An invoice from Parkway Computer Systems

Karen tells you what the most common errors on invoices are.

1 Entering the wrong quantity sold.
2 Entering the wrong unit price.
3 Inaccurate calculations.
4 Forgetting to include the discount.
5 Forgetting to include the carriage charge.

ACTIVITY 9

1 What is the purpose of an invoice?

2 a Why is accuracy on an invoice very important?
  b What could be the consequences of *regularly* sending inaccurate invoices to a customer?

3 What action do you think a supplier should take if it *overcharges* a customer on an invoice by mistake? You may wish to look back at the sequence of documents shown in Figure 3.28 before you answer this question!

4 In Figure 3.36 is the invoice received from Swift Office Supplies for the items Matt ordered – including your desk and chair (Figure 3.29)? Would you pass this for payment? Give a reason for your answer.

Swift Office Supplies Ltd
15 Cheyne Road   BROMPTON   Newshire   BR2 7PT

I N V O I C E

Customer name:

DigiTech Characters Ltd
Unit 5
Brompton Industrial Park
BROMPTON
Newshire BR4 9DK

Order No: 7458
Date: 20 September 2000
Customer No: 60898
Taken by: JL
Invoice date: 24 September 2000
Invoice No: 16194

Qty	Item No	Description	VAT	Unit Price	Value
1	530-D4	4-drawer metal filing cabinet	17.5%	£123.50	£123.50
1	670-DL	L-shaped desk unit	17.5%	£105.80	£105.80
1	2548-DC	Swivel task chair – navy	17.5%	£98.40	£98.40
20 rms	200-MP	A4 multi paper – white	17.5%	£5.19	£103.80
3	5078-OM	Laser cartridges – Omega laser OM 452	17.5%	£138.20	£414.60

Gross Value	Discount	Net value	VAT	Amount Due
£846.10	£84.61	£761.49	£133.26	£894.75

Terms: one month, carriage paid
E&OE

Figure 3.36 Invoice from Swift Office Supplies

5 Karen asks you to make out an invoice. She tells you to look back at the order you processed from Hemple's department store (page 257). She reminds you that figures which are coded 01 have a unit cost of £60 and those which are coded 02 have a unit cost of £70. Hemple's orders from DigiTech infrequently, so is only entitled to 5 per cent trade discount. The invoice number is 10025 and should be dated 14 September. Karen doesn't think you need any more information to do this correctly, however to help you accurately calculate the totals on your first few manual invoices, she gives you a reminder card (see Figure 3.37).

Complete a DigiTech invoice from the information on your order form and from the additional details given above.

1 Gross Value = unit x unit price

2 Discount value = gross value minus trade discount

3 Net value = gross value minus discount

4 Total all these columns

5 VAT = net value x 17.5% (Note: this can be rounded down to the nearest penny)

6 Total due = total net value plus VAT

Figure 3.37 Reminder card for invoice calculations

6 You are due to receive the invoice for the ink-jet printer and files you ordered from Swift Office Supplies (page 253). Calculate the amount that will be showing on this invoice, assuming all the items are in stock and delivered as ordered. Note that Swift allow DigiTech 10 per cent trade discount.

Check your work with the key on page 282 and your completed invoice with your tutor.

Credit notes

Completing a credit note

A credit note entitles a customer to a refund on their account with their supplier. There are several reasons for issuing one.

- A mistake on the invoice.

- Faulty goods that have been returned.

- The wrong goods were sent and have been returned.

- The customer made a mistake on the order and the supplier has agreed the goods can be returned.

If you return faulty items to a shop you may be offered a credit note. However, in such a case you can insist on being repaid your money. In business if a supplier makes a mistake in invoicing an infrequent customer and that mistake is more than the amount the customer owes, then the supplier has to refund the difference.

Matt is proud that very few credit notes are issued by DigiTech. He says Shazia makes very few mistakes when she is completing orders and all invoices are checked carefully when they are sent. However, he manages to find one for you (Figure 3.38). This was made out after a batch of faulty Starworld characters were sent out in error.

He goes through the content with you. You notice the layout is very similar to an invoice.

- The customer account reference and name and address is entered.

- Most customers send the goods back with a returns note or letter explaining the problem. There is usually a reference and this is quoted in the returns reference.

- The date and invoice number are added next.

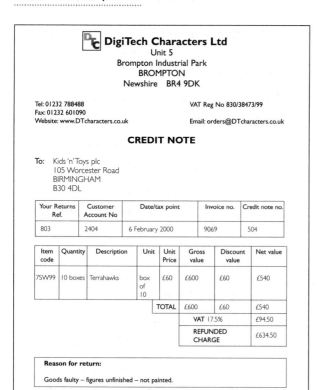

DigiTech Characters Ltd
Unit 5
Brompton Industrial Park
BROMPTON
Newshire   BR4 9DK

Tel: 01232 788488   VAT Reg No 830/38473/99
Fax: 01232 601090
Website: www.DTcharacters.co.uk   Email: orders@DTcharacters.co.uk

CREDIT NOTE

To: Kids 'n' Toys plc
      105 Worcester Road
      BIRMINGHAM
      B30 4DL

Your Returns Ref.	Customer Account No	Date/tax point	Invoice no.	Credit note no.
803	2404	6 February 2000	9069	504

Item code	Quantity	Description	Unit	Unit Price	Gross value	Discount value	Net value
7SW99	10 boxes	Terrahawks	box of 10	£60	£600	£60	£540
			TOTAL		£600	£60	£540
			VAT 17.5%				£94.50
			REFUNDED CHARGE				£634.50

Reason for return:

Goods faulty – figures unfinished – not painted.

White copy: customer
Pink copy: sales
Yellow copy: accounts

Figure 3.38 A DigiTech credit note

- The credit note number is then entered.

- The description of the goods and the unit is the same as on the original invoice.

- The calculations are done in the same way as on the invoice, except that instead of 'total due' the credit note totals the 'refunded charge'.

Checking a completed credit note

Matt tells you that credit notes being sent out are checked like invoices – for content and for the calculations. Credit notes which are received are related back to the GRN and the original invoice – to check that all items returned or missing have been credited accurately.

The most common errors.

1   Incorrect details – especially quantity.
2   Some returned items missing.
3   Discounts don't agree with the invoice.
4   Faulty calculations.

ACTIVITY 10

1   How would you describe the purpose of a credit note?

2   What steps would you take to check a credit note you had prepared?

3   Although Matt has boasted that very few credit notes are ever sent out by DigiTech, the following day you receive an apologetic telephone call from Beacon Toy Stores. They had only meant to order 10 boxes of the Black Star Demon but 15 were ordered in error. Karen agrees these can be returned. Two days later Petra confirms that the goods have been sent back and can be credited. Make out a credit note, number 510, for the amount due and date this for 29 September. Refer to Figure 3.34 for the discount details you need.

4   What checks do you think Petra made before she confirmed the items could be credited – and why?

5   Matt tell you that a credit note from Swift Office Supplies for the missing laser cartridge was in this morning's post. Before he shows it to you, he asks you to tell him the amount which should be showing on it. Refer back to the invoice (Figure 3.36) to help you.

6   If a credit note is incorrect, what action should be taken and why?

Check your answers with the key on page 282 and your completed credit note with your tutor.

Statements of account

Statements of account are produced by DigiTech at the end of each month. These summarise all the transactions that have taken place between DigiTech and each customer. The customer will not pay until the statement has been received – as this means sending one cheque rather than several.

Karen has just produced the statement for Beacon Toys which she now shows you (Figure 3.39). She points out the main entries and explains how the statement is calculated.

- The customer account number and name and address details are entered first.

- DigiTech prints the credit limit on statements – not all companies do this. Max thinks that this helps remind customers when they are nearing their limit and they will then pay promptly. He also thinks that it is easier to refuse to process orders if a customer is over the limit – as they have no excuse for not realising they had gone over!

Figure 3.39 DigiTech statement of account

- The date of the statement is included. This is usually the last working day of the month.

- Karen then explains the meanings of the different headings.

  - The date is the date on which a transaction took place.

  - The details column relates to the type of transaction, e.g. whether an invoice or credit note was sent, or whether a payment was made.

  - The debit column records money owing to the supplier.

  - The credit column records money received by the supplier.

  - The balance column is a *running* balance. This means it changes with each transaction – as you will see below.

- Karen tells you to read each line on a statement *horizontally* – not vertically.

  - Line one states any balance owing from the previous month. This is the first entry made at the beginning of the month. On some computer systems the line is still included even if no monies are owing and a 'nil' balance is recorded in the final column.

  - The next entry is for the invoice sent on 10 September, number 10013 (Figure 3.34). £2,823.52 is now owing to DigiTech, so this money is entered in the debit column. It is added to the initial balance to give a running total of £3,624.04.

  - On 15 September Beacon Toy Stores paid their end of August statement. The type of payment (cheque and cheque number, in this case) is recorded and the amount recorded in the credit column. The running balance is now adjusted – with the amount subtracted from the money due.

 ○ On 29 September a credit note was sent to Beacon Toy Stores for £370.12. This is also a credit item as it reduces Beacon's account balance. The running balance is adjusted accordingly.

• The total balance (i.e. the last figure in the running balance column) is repeated in bold at the bottom of the statement. This is the amount Beacon now owe DigiTech.

Checking a completed statement

On a computerised system, the statements are produced automatically – although they still need checking in case transactions have been omitted for some reason. This will happen if a wrong account number has been keyed in for a transaction – and the details then appear on someone else's statement!

Manual statements have to be checked to ensure that all items have been included and that the calculations are correct. Statements received by DigiTech are always checked carefully, particularly to see if all payments and credit notes have been included. If DigiTech has paid an account which is not recorded on a statement, it first checks its own records and its bank statement. If the cheque has been processed, it then contacts the supplier immediately so that the account can be adjusted.

Karen warns you about the most usual mistakes.

1 Carrying forward an incorrect balance.
2 Omitting a transaction.

3 Manually recording a transaction in the wrong column because of confusion between debit and credit. In this instance, a payment would actually increase the balance, rather than reduce it!
4 Manually miscalculating the running balance.

ACTIVITY 11

1 Identify two reasons why companies send statements at the end of the month.

2 What is the difference between a 'running balance' and a 'total balance'?

3 What action should be taken if a payment you made has been omitted from a statement you receive?

4 If Beacon Toys' statement amounted to £4,950 and they rang with a large order tomorrow, what do you think would be the result? Give a reason for your answer.

5 You have been asked to prepare two statements, one to Hemple's department store and the other to Kids 'n' Toys. Hemple's address and customer number is given on page 257 and the Kids 'n' Toys address and customer number is shown on Figure 3.38. Hemple's credit limit is £5,000 and Kids 'n' Toys' is £10,000.

   At the start of the month Hemple's had a zero balance. You prepared an invoice to them, number 10021, on 14 September for £2,757.13. On 20 September another invoice was sent, number 10032 for £1,300. However, part of this order was damaged in transit and a credit note was sent on 25 September for £82.50, number 508.

   Kids 'n' Toys had a balance at the start of the month of £4,694.20. They paid this on 16

September, cheque number 70092. They bought goods on three occasions: on 4 September for £4,723.60, invoice 10005; on 17 September for £1,520.00, invoice 10028; on 26 September for £1,280.50, invoice 10035. On 21 September a credit note was sent, number 506, for £210.60.

Make out both statements and check these with your tutor. For the time being do *not* complete the remittance advice forms shown at the bottom of the statement forms.

Remittance advice slips

Completing remittance advice slips

Some organisations issue a remittance advice to the customer so that it can be returned with the payment. Accounts staff can then see why the payment has been made because all the main information relating to the transaction is printed on the remittance advice. The most usual system is to print the remittance advice as a tear-off form attached to the statement. The customer then completes and detaches this and returns it with the cheque. This is the type of remittance advice slip which is issued by DigiTech (see Figure 3.40).

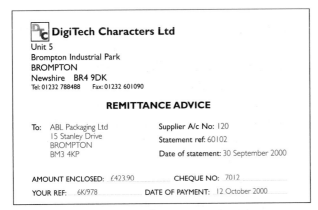

DigiTech Characters Ltd
Unit 5
Brompton Industrial Park
BROMPTON
Newshire   BR4 9DK
Tel: 01232 788488   Fax: 01232 601090

REMITTANCE ADVICE

To: ABL Packaging Ltd
      15 Stanley Drive
      BROMPTON
      BM3 4KP
	Supplier A/c No: 120
	Statement ref: 60102
	Date of statement: 30 September 2000

AMOUNT ENCLOSED: £423.90   CHEQUE NO: 7012
YOUR REF: 6K/978   DATE OF PAYMENT: 12 October 2000

Figure 3.40 DigiTech remittance advice slip

Some firms send invoices without a remittance advice slip attached. In this case DigiTech sends a copy of its own remittance advice forms with the cheque (see Figure 3.40).

Checking remittance advice slips

On some slips the customer can complete the amount to be sent, on others the amount is pre-printed as the total balance.

With incoming remittance advice slips you need to check that the amount on the cheque is the same as the amount written on the slip, and that the amount sent is the total owing. Otherwise Karen will want to know why!

With outgoing remittance advice slips the amount should be entered carefully to ensure this tallies with the amount which is being paid and which is shown on the cheque. This will normally be the same amount as the figure shown on the last statement, unless there is a query about a particular invoice, when part of the payment may be withheld.

 **ACTIVITY 12**

1   Identify the advantage of issuing a remittance advice slip attached to a statement.

2   What are the key items of information which must be included on a remittance advice slip?

3   You are instructed to make out a remittance advice slip for less than the total payment shown on the statement. Can you think of one reason why you might be asked to do this?

4   You receive a remittance advice slip which shows £840 owing, yet the cheque enclosed is for £480. What action would you take?

5   Why does DigiTech send its own remittance advice slips with its cheque payments if a slip hasn't been received with a statement?

6 Complete the remittance advice slips attached to the two statements you completed to Hemple's and Kids 'n' Toys.

Check your answers with the key on page 283 and your remittance advice slips with your tutor.

Cheques

Despite credit and debit cards and automatic payments through the banking system, the cheque is still one of the most common ways of paying suppliers. A cheque is a written instruction, which tells a bank to transfer the amount stated into another person's account.

There are several advantages to paying by cheque. A *counterfoil* is the written record retained in the cheque book which states to whom each cheque was paid, the date, why the money was paid and the amount. When the cheque is paid in by the recipient, the transfer is shown on the *bank statement*. This means there is a complete record of the transaction without the need for a receipt.

Every cheque has a unique serial number, which is also printed on the counterfoil and is

listed on the bank statement against the transaction. This is why a bank statement is legal proof that a bill has been paid – as the transfer of money can be traced back through the banking system.

Karen shows you a cheque she made out yesterday and explains the main components of it (Figure 3.41).

Printed information

1 The first item is the **name of the bank** and the **address of the branch** at which the customer has the account.

2 The numbers at the top right-hand corner, which are repeated again at the bottom, are the **bank sort code**. Every bank branch has its own sort code by which it is identified.

3 The longest number at the bottom is the customer's **bank account number**.

4 The final number at the bottom is the **cheque number** and this is repeated on the counterfoil.

All the numbers on a bank cheque are machine readable, which is why the

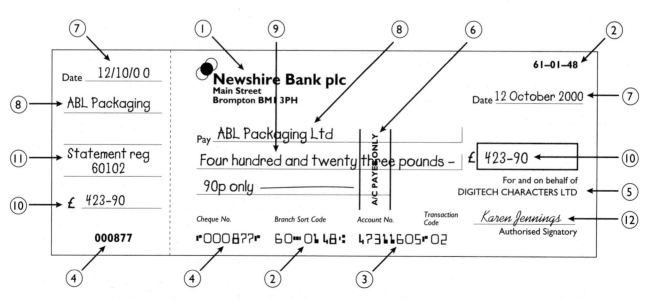

Figure 3.41 An example of a cheque. See text for an explanation of the different parts of it

figures look unusual on the cheque itself (though not on the counterfoil).

5 The **account holder's name** is printed on the cheque. In the case of a company, the words 'for and on behalf of' precede the name. This denotes that the signatory is signing for the company rather than on their own behalf. Often the words 'authorised signatory' or the person's official title is printed at the bottom, e.g. Director or Company Secretary.

6 All cheques today are **crossed** with the words 'Account payee only' – sometimes abbreviated to 'A/c payee only'. This means that the cheque can only be paid into the account of the person whose name is written on the cheque. They are known as 'crossed' cheques

Inserted information

7 The **date** is written on the cheque. This is usually the current date. Sometimes a person waiting for funds may wish to make out a **post-dated cheque**. This means writing a future date on the cheque. Most companies will not allow this as it means the cheque cannot be presented to the bank for payment until that date.

8 The **payee** is the person or organisation which will receive the money. Banks prefer the full name to be written, therefore a cheque to a woman, for instance, should not be made out to 'Mrs J Smith' (where the initial may be her own or her husband's) but to 'Janet Smith'. This name is also written on the counterfoil.

9 The **amount** being paid is written in **words** for amounts in pounds and in figures for amounts in pence. Some people prefer to end with the word 'only',

particularly if the amount is for pounds only. If this word is *not* written, then any spare spaces on the lines must be made unusable – normally by drawing one or two horizontal lines – to prevent anyone inserting an amount after the entry has been made.

Banks also prefer you to start writing at the left-hand side of the first line, again as a security measure.

10 The **amount** is then written **in figures** in the box. The £ sign is already printed. The amount in this box *must* agree with the amount written in words and this amount should be copied onto the counterfoil.

11 The **reason for payment** is written on the counterfoil. In the case of the cheque to ABL Packaging, Karen has entered the statement reference number as a quick method of linking the cheque to the accounts documents.

12 After all the entries have been checked to make sure they are correct, the cheque has to be **signed by** an authorised signatory. The official term for the account holder on whose name the cheque is drawn is **the drawer**. It is usual for more than one signature to appear on business cheques for large amounts as a security measure.

Large organisations which make out hundreds of cheques a month usually have these printed to their own design that they have agreed with the bank. The cheques may be in continuous format, with perforations, or printed out attached to a remittance advice. They are processed and printed automatically in batches – often known as a 'cheque run'. The signatures are stored in the system and also printed on the cheques as they are processed. Needless to say, only certain individuals are authorised to carry out a 'cheque run' and, before this takes place, the computer system will already have calculated the total amount being paid out and checked this against the current bank balance.

Checking cheques

If a mistake is made on a cheque, then it is likely the bank will reject it. This can be embarrassing for the drawer – as the payee then has to notify him or her that there is a problem. So it is important that all cheques – both incoming and outgoing – are checked carefully.

The following are the most usual causes of problems with cheques.

1   The wrong date. People may write the incorrect date by mistake – especially on the 1 January when people enter the previous year, rather than the current year. Cheques are only valid for six months, after which they are classed as 'stale'. So, if you wrote 1 January 2001 when you meant to write 1 January 2002, the bank will treat the cheque as being 12 months old and will reject it.

    Another 'date-related' problem is accepting a post-dated cheque without realising it. If you try to bank it before the date written on the top, the bank will not accept it.

2   A mismatch between the amount in writing and the amount in figures. If the discrepancy is only a matter of pence then the bank may telephone you and ask you to clarify the amount. But it does not have to do this and certainly will not if the difference is any larger. It will simply reject the cheque.

3   An amendment on a cheque. Banks do not like you to make alterations, as they cannot be sure that it isn't someone else trying to alter your cheque – which would be forgery. If a small alteration *is* required then the signature of the drawer must be written alongside to verify the change.

4   An unsigned cheque will not be accepted by the bank.

5   The drawer has insufficient funds in their account to cover the withdrawal. The bank will reject the cheque.

If a cheque is rejected it is sent back to the payee with an instruction to **refer to drawer** (abbreviated to R/D). This will also happen if the cheque is 'stopped'. In this case the drawer has instructed his bank to 'stop' payment. An example would be if you had your cheque book stolen and could not specify exactly which cheques were left in the book. You may agree it would be safer to stop the payment of all the cheques which had not yet been cashed.

Finally, Karen tells you that if private individuals buy Starworld characters then any cheques must be supported by a valid **cheque guarantee card**. The card must be checked to ensure:

• it has not expired

• that the account numbers on the cheque and card are identical

• that the amount printed on the card is not less than the total amount of the cheque.

If everything is in order, the number of the card is written on the back of the cheque and the signatures on the cheque and the card are checked to make sure it is the same. Bank guarantee cards are important, as they guarantee the bank will honour the cheque, *even if the drawer has insufficient funds in the account.*

ACTIVITY 13

1 In bank terminology, what is the person called who:
   a   receives a cheque
   b   signs a cheque?

2 State three reasons why a cheque may be rejected by the bank.

3 There are three numbers printed on the bottom of a cheque. What do these numbers represent?

4 State four details which should be written on a cheque counterfoil.

5 How does a business know that a cheque it sent to a supplier has been processed by the bank?

6 When will you see the words 'For and on behalf of' on a cheque?

7 Make out four cheques for Karen. If they are correct your tutor will sign them. Date them all with today's date.

   a   Swift Office Supplies   £165 – against their statement 80043
   b   John Martin   £450 – for decorating the offices
   c   Chandler's Property Services   £780.40 – for this month's rent
   d   Marshalls Ltd   £1,248.25 – for raw materials against their statement K64810

Check your answers with the key on page 283 and your completed cheques with your tutor.

SNAPSHOT

The future is . . . plastic?

In 1998 a significant event took place – which you probably knew nothing about! For the first time since cheques were invented (in about 1770), the number of payments made by credit cards and automated payments systems was higher than the number of payments made by cheques.

Personal cheque use in the UK has been falling for some time. Most people prefer to pay their bills either by credit or debit card or through the bank automated payment system (e.g. direct debit or credit transfer). They obtain their cash from cash machines, rather than make out a cheque to themselves. In 1998 the number of cheques used by companies also fell by 2.5 per cent to 1.2 billion.

The result was that in 1998 fewer than three billion cheques were cashed, compared to a peak of four billion cashed in 1990. Bankers are predicting that by 2008 only one payment in ten will be made by cheque. APACS, which operates the UK cheque clearing system, thinks that new innovations, such as 'smart' cards using chip technology, e-commerce, telephone and Internet banking and digital television, will make cheques obsolete in the future. Businesses, as well as private individuals, will prefer to use automated payment systems to settle all their bills.

Receipts

A receipt is essential for a cash payment, as it is the only evidence that the transaction took place. Unlike a cheque transaction, which is easily traceable, it would only be your word against someone else's if there was a dispute about a cash payment.

The amount of detail on a receipt varies a lot. A printed till receipt is produced for items bought in a wine shop. On some occasions the receipt may be hand-written and contain far more detail. Tradesmen doing household repairs usually have a pre-printed receipt book to record payments received from householders. They enter the details of the work and payment and give a copy to the householder. For the person paying, the engineer and the engineer's employer this is the proof that the transaction took place.

Most people know of the term 'expenses'. This is the money you are authorised to spend on behalf of the company, which will pay you back. If you travelled on business and paid a taxi fare or a hotel bill, the company would reimburse you. To claim expenses you must have receipts for the amounts you spent.

Finally, small items can be bought for a business and reclaimed through the petty cash system. A receipt is essential, even for inexpensive purchases, as Matt told you (see page 251).

Matt shows you the type of receipt you should make out if you *receive* a cash payment for purchases. He says this is relatively rare today as most DigiTech items are sold to stores. It is mainly used for staff and their friends who buy figures at a staff discount rate of £5 each. Matt says there is a limit to the number of figures Max expects any one member of staff to purchase this way. In this case, the money must be paid to Karen who

then issues a receipt. Matt shows you a receipt she made out for him when he last bought something from the company (see Figure 3.42). The receipt is produced in duplicate. One copy is given to the person who paid and Karen files the other copy in her accounts files.

Checking a receipt

How often do you check a receipt you receive? Most people never bother – however mistakes do happen. It is particularly important to check that the receipt is correct if you are spending someone else's money – as you can hardly reclaim a different amount! It is also important to *keep* receipts – particularly for non-consumable items – in case they later prove to be faulty. Many shops insist on seeing a receipt before they accept returned goods. This is not a legal requirement for faulty goods but you may be asked for some proof that the transaction took place. With a cash transaction, you are likely to have problems if you have lost the receipt.

A receipt should contain the date, a reference number, a list of the items purchased and the amount of each, together with the total paid. If VAT has to be paid this must also be shown.

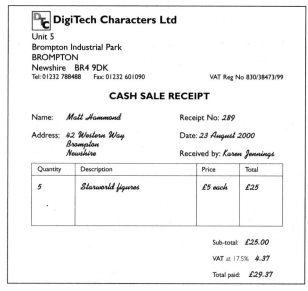

Figure 3.42 DigiTech cash sale receipt

A handwritten receipt should include the name of the person who paid and should be signed by the person who received the money – but these practices are not always followed, particularly if the receipt is on headed paper.

 ## ACTIVITY 14

1 Why are receipts an important document?

2 What are the advantages of using a cash register, if you have to issue a lot of receipts?

3 a Save the next receipt you receive and list the information it contains.

   b Compare your list with other members of your group and see how receipts differ. Then identify the common items on *all* the receipts.

4 Why do you think Max expects there to be a limit on the number of figures purchased by staff?

5 Petra wants to buy three figures for her nephew. She is not allowed to make out her own receipt and Karen is busy, so she asks you to do it. The receipt number is 314. Petra's full name is Petra Bissett and she lives at 14 Westcombe Road, Bromley. Use today's date.

Check your answers with the key on page 283 and your completed receipt with your tutor.

Financial documents and computerised accounting systems

DigiTech uses a computerised accounting system. This section and the Snapshot on page 260 have already told you a little about how this operates. Such a system must seem a welcome development for those accustomed to making out financial documents by hand.

However, there are advantages and disadvantages to it. Before we summarise these, check that you understand how a computerised accounting system works.

A computerised accounting system:

- records all credit sales to customers

- records all cash sales to customers

- produces invoices, credit notes and statements

- lists outstanding payments (usually called an 'aged debtors report' – this doesn't mean the debtors are old, it means the accounts are old!)

- records all purchases made – both by supplier and type of goods

- records all accounts which have been paid or still have to be paid to suppliers

- records all bank transactions

- updates the company's accounts every time a transaction takes place

- produces a variety of 'reports' or summaries, e.g. a balance sheet, VAT return, bank analysis, profit and loss account, audit report (which lists all transactions for checking).

Advantages

1 Many routine and tedious jobs are done automatically.

2 Fewer mistakes are made – the computer calculates perfectly provided the correct details are entered.

3 A huge amount of current information is available for managers at the touch of a key. They can see instantly, for instance, how much money is owed to the company or how much profit they are making in a month.

4 Accountants and auditors (who check the accounts of limited companies) prefer computerised accounts information as it can often be checked more easily and quickly (through the audit report) than a manual system.

5 The system can be linked to stock control packages (as you saw on pages 256 and 260) and payroll packages.

6 A list of all customers or suppliers can be obtained at the touch of a key. This can be used to print off address labels, for instance, or linked to a word processing package if the company wants to contact all customers or suppliers about a certain matter.

7 The aged debtor's report means that overdue accounts can be identified and chased up more easily.

8 Account numbers are allocated automatically by computer. There will be no mistakes made on allocation (e.g. missing out a number by mistake).

9 In a paper system documents may get lost or be misfiled. This cannot happen in a computerised system.

10 Access to specific sections of the package can be restricted to designated executives or managers, for security.

Disadvantages

1 The system takes time to set up as all the existing accounting information must be keyed in and checked, as well as all the customer and supplier names and addresses.

2 Setting up the system can be complex as the existing manual system may have to be readjusted to fit the way the package operates.

3 Staff have to be trained how to use the system and it will take some time before they can use it efficiently.

4 There is usually restricted access to parts of the package. On many systems only one person can access it at any one time unless a multi-user licence is purchased, which is more expensive.

5 If there is a computer failure then the system is inaccessible and no information can be accessed or documents produced.

6 A mistake can be difficult to correct. On some software packages it is impossible to cancel a wrong entry – the entry must be adjusted by making an opposite entry. This is required for the audit report which you should think of as a type of security check on all the entries that have been made.

7 The computer allocates every customer with a number. This is useful if there are a few regular customers, but may be inconvenient if there are thousands of casual customers.

8 Staff using a computer system may fail to check their work. For instance, someone might key in 230 units instead of 23, and not notice. They assume it will be correct!

9 It is easy to mis-key or transpose figures. The computer will simply accept the information on most systems – and process it.

10 Printing out very large numbers of documents, e.g. invoices, can tie up a printer for several hours, causing inconvenience to other users who share it.

11 An incorrect instruction can be processed many times before it is noticed – at best this results in reams of spoiled paper, at worst it may upset and annoy hundreds of customers.

SNAPSHOT

The other side of computerisation

You might fantasise about your bank cash machine paying you twice as much as you keyed in. However the machine's computer makes a record of every transaction, so the bank will know who you are and can ask you to return the overpayment!

Computers, it is often said, go wrong. They do silly things like sending invoices for 1p. But not on their own! Behind every computer disaster is an operator who got it wrong. One large mail order company with some retail outlets had two nightmares in one week. The company had computerised its stock control operations and its invoicing facility. Two developments to these programs caused the problem. The first involved the idea that fresh flowers for retail sales outlets should be added to the stock control automatic re-ordering system. The second was that mail order customers who had not settled their accounts after two months should receive a sharp reminder letter, and that customers who settled promptly should be sent a sales letter to encourage them to purchase more goods.

At the start of the week introducing these ideas a computer operator keyed in the wrong command for the flowers. This resulted in the ordering system adding the flowers required each day together. So on Tuesday the shops received Monday's order, but on Wednesday they received both Monday and Tuesday's orders and on Thursday . . . you get the picture? By Friday no-one could move for flowers – which are a perishable item. By Saturday the shops were giving the flowers away free.

On Wednesday the operator keyed in the commands for the reminder letters and the sales letters. Only he got them the wrong way round. So, the late payers were asked to buy more goods and the good payers were sent stern reminder letters.

12 Data corruption of an entire accounts system is every company's nightmare scenario. So computer files are backed-up on a regular basis. Ideally back-ups are stored off-site as part of a formal recovery process. This means that in the case of a disaster (e.g. fire or flood) at the company's offices the back-ups would be safe and the system could be re-activated with minimum delay.

ACTIVITY 15

The market leader for computerised accounting systems in the UK is Sage – who operates a wonderful web site. Access it on http://www.sage.com and find out about:

a their accounting packages – especially details about their instant accounting products and the case studies. You should be able to write an advantages list of your own, after this!

b their forecasting package – and why they think this is better than a spreadsheet (after Section 3.2 of this unit, you might agree)

c other information on their site. You may be particularly interested in the link to The Motley Fool UK site – particularly if you are doing the option unit on Personal Finance.

Print out the articles and information you find most useful and compare your findings with the rest of your group.

Section review

Refresh your memory on this section by writing short answers to each of the following questions.

1 *What is meant by the term 'trade discount'?*

2 *What factors would influence the credit limit allowed to a customer?*

3 *Give three examples of entries you may find on a statement of account.*

4 *Why is 'cash discount' sometimes given by organisations?*

5 *Explain why only certain organisations are VAT registered.*

6 *Describe three reasons why a credit note might be issued.*

7 *Give two advantages of using a computerised accounts package.*

8 *Why are receipts normally issued only for cash payments?*

9 *Why would a bank send you a cheque with the instruction 'R/D' attached – and what should you then do?*

10 *Identify two disadvantages of using a computerised accounts system.*

This unit covers the different job roles and working relationships in organisations. It builds on the knowledge you gained in Unit 1 about your employer's responsibilities to individual employees and your responsibilities to your employer. It looks at the different positions of individuals and how these affect working relationships and it examines the factors that encourage and motivate individuals in the workplace.

This option unit should also help you to understand how to relate to your colleagues at work. This aspect of work is often critical when deciding to promote staff – when 'people skills' are crucial.

This unit is externally assessed and all the important facts you need to know to take the assessment are covered in this chapter.

4.1 Job roles in the workplace

Every employee has a formal job role which determines the jobs and tasks they are expected to perform. The content of a job is usually specified in a job description (see page 279). This determines what is expected of the employee. A receptionist is expected to deal with visitors in a professional and pleasant way, managers are expected to organise their own work load *and* be responsible for the people they manage, a caretaker is expected to keep a building clean, and so on.

A job role is also about how the employee does the work. For instance, a manager is expected to be good at organising the work, motivating staff and passing on information. Different job roles also have different responsibilities. Generally, the more responsibility a person has, the more difficult and important the decisions they have to make – and the more they are paid to take those responsibilities. So, you would not expect to make your boss's decisions if you were working in a junior role.

You can analyse all job roles by identifying:

- the tasks which must be carried out by the job holder

- the skills required to do each task

- the degree of responsibility for each task

- whether the job holder is responsible for any subordinates

- the additional attributes required by the job holder

- the degree and level of previous experience required.

You can broadly differentiate between three different types of job roles in most organisations.

Managerial level

There may be three levels of management – senior, middle and supervisory – or just one. It depends on the size and structure of the organisation. Your own line manager is responsible for you and your colleagues. Managers need technical expertise to give advice and solve departmental problems. They also need good 'people' skills to coordinate the work and motivate staff. Managers have deadlines and targets to meet, and usually the more pressure they are under, the harder they find it to deal with 'people' problems.

Operational staff

These are the 'grassroots' staff who carry out the operational aspects of the business (see Unit 1, page 64). In a manufacturing organisation they are employed in production; in your college they are your tutors; in a restaurant they are the chefs and waiters; in an airline they are the pilots and cabin crew; in a hospital they are the nurses and doctors.

They all need technical skills – although the level of skills obviously varies. An airline pilot or surgeon needs several years more training than a waiter! Some need a high level of 'people' skills – for example, teachers, nurses, social workers, shop assistants – because their jobs involve direct contact with other people, such as students, patients, customers.

Support staff

These staff support the main operations of the organisation. In your college they include

Figure 4.1 A range of operational staff

those working in administration, finance, student services and computer services. They include all the administrators, clerks, secretarial staff and technicians in hospitals, in town halls and in private sector organisations. Support staff need to have specialist technical skills – which vary depending on their job – and 'people' skills – particularly when dealing with customers face-to-face or on the telephone.

The meaning of 'line' management

An organisation chart links people and shows 'lines' between them. Your own line manager is further 'up the line' than you are and is the person who is directly responsible for you and above you in authority. A deputy is said to be 'in line' for a particular job and is shown to be so because of the line linking a deputy to his/her manager – with no-one else in between.

Lines can also indicate communication flows. Communications are passed 'down the line' when they are passed from a manager to his/her staff, and 'up the line' when they travel in the opposite direction.

 ACTIVITY

In the external assessment you can expect to answer questions on organisation structures and organisation charts.

1   Reread Section 1.3, pages 94–104, to refresh your memory. Check you understand the Snapshot on page 101 and can answer all the questions in the Section Review on page 104.

2   Why are organisation charts often described as pyramids?

3   Obtain a copy of your college's organisation chart. Identify

a your own tutor's line manager

b the person who is next 'in line' for the principal's job.

4 What do you think would be the differences, both in relation to the organisation chart and working there, between

a a very large college with a hierarchical structure

b a small sixth-form college with a flat structure?

5 Just because a person is 'in line' for a job doesn't mean to say he or she will get it! As a group, discuss reasons why this may be the case.

Job descriptions and person specifications

Job descriptions

A job description or job outline contains basic information about the job itself and/or the role of the job holder. It is usually prepared or revised when a vacancy is created and before this is advertised. A copy may be sent to all the applicants. This may include:

- the job title or a summary of the job role
- the purpose of the job
- the main duties of the job holder
- the main responsibilities of the job holder
- the place or department where the employee will work
- the physical conditions
- the social conditions
- any special features of the job
- any special skills or qualifications required
- the person to whom the job holder reports

- anyone for whom the job holder is responsible for managing
- the appraisal arrangements (see page 285).

Don't expect every job description to include all this information! Some will be very brief and others more comprehensive. For instance, you could expect a manager's job description to include detailed information on the purpose of the job, their duties and responsibilities and the staff for whom they are responsible. Figure 4.2 is an example of a comprehensive job description. Note that information about the place of work and the working conditions is at the top, before details of the job itself.

Person specification

This identifies the skills and abilities required of the job holder. It is usually

---

Job description

Dataplan Corporation operates from a purpose-built, modern building in the centre of Hightown. The human resources department is on the ground floor.

The human resources department comprises six members of staff, all of whom report to the human resources manager, Jane Griffiths. The department works as a team, with all members of staff giving mutual support to each other. They are supported by Dataplan's legal adviser, Peter Farnham. The company operates an appraisal scheme whereby all staff are appraised on their performance annually, usually by their own line manager.

Dataplan operates a subsidised canteen and all staff participate in an annual bonus plan and receive a company-paid travel card or free parking. Other benefits include a share save scheme and pension scheme.

The job holder will be encouraged to work towards recognised human resource qualifications, such as the Certificate in Personnel Practice offered by the Institute of Personnel and Development.

Title	Human resources assistant
Department	Human resources
Hours of work	37 per week
Responsible to	Human resources manager
Responsible for	Not applicable
Job purpose	To provide support for the human resources team in dealing with job applications, scheduling training and staff development events, and maintaining a computerised staff database.

Duties

1. Answer enquiries and take messages from prospective and current employees both face-to-face and over the telephone.
2. Place job advertisements in the press on request.
3. Log applications for jobs and despatch job descriptions and application forms.
4. Log receipt of application forms and forward to appropriate line manager after deadline date.
5. Notify shortlisted candidates and make all appropriate interview arrangements.
6. Despatch appointment letters as directed and liaise with payroll section over start arrangements.
7. Assist training coordinator to organise induction programmes for new staff.
8. Log applications for staff training and staff development on staff database.
9. Schedule staff training events as requested.
10. Maintain computerised staff record system.
11. Undertake any other duties commensurate with the position as required by the human resources manager.

Figure 4.2 A comprehensive job description

JOB SPECIFICATION

JOB ROLE: Human Resources Assistant

1.   Experience

Essential
12 months work experience in
a commercial environment

Desirable
Previous experience working
in a human resources or customer
service environment
Familiarity with email and voicemail

2.   Qualifications

Essential
Communications qualification
IT qualification (e.g. CLAIT)
Good numeracy skills

Desirable
Keyboarding skills/WP qualification
Experience of PowerPoint

3.   Attributes

Essential
Able to deal effectively with a wide
range of people
Able to work unsupervised
Able to work as a member of a team
Neat and tidy appearance
Willing to study for additional
qualifications

Desirable
Able to cope under stress
Calm and patient
Good health record
Neat handwriting

Figure 4.3 Job specification

---

divided into **essential** requirements and **desirable** ones. Both should be included in the advertisement. Usually only applicants who have all the essential requirements are invited for an interview. Person specifications tend to cover:

- experience
- qualifications
- personal attributes.

An example of a person specification to match the job description in Figure 4.2 is shown in Figure 4.3.

Benefits of job descriptions and person specifications

There are several benefits for both employers and employees of issuing such documents – particularly if they are sent to job applicants.

For employers

- writing the documents means greater thought is given to the best type of person for the job

- the advertisement is likely to identify essential and desirable qualities more clearly

- applications can be assessed more easily for suitability

- the job description will help to decide a fair salary for the job, in relation to pay rates to other employees

- training needs for the newly appointed person can be more easily identified.

For employees

- the applicant can see exactly what the job entails

- there is less chance of unsuitable applicants applying

- although employees will be expected to be 'flexible' about what they do (no-one is likely to last long if they will only do the duties listed on the job description), an employee can identify if a task would be 'unreasonable' to be asked to perform. For instance, an accounts clerk should not be expected to clean the windows each morning! However, you should note that most job descriptions include a final phrase: 'Any other duties required by the manager which are commensurate with the position' (see Figure 4.2). This is to prevent people interpreting a job description too literally!

 **ACTIVITY**

1   Check the content of the job description shown in Figure 4.2 against the items listed in the bullet points on page 279. Try to identify an example under each bullet point heading.

2   Figure 4.4 shows an advertisement for a finance trainee for the same organisation. It

clearly identifies the essential and desirable requirements of the job. Work in pairs to draw up a comprehensive job description and job specification. Then compare your final documents with other groups in your class.

3   Using the advertisement in Figure 4.4 as a guide, draft an advertisement for the human resources assistant from the information you were given in Figures 4.2 and 4.3. Check your finished work with your tutor.

4   As a group, discuss why a manager's job description is likely to be more detailed than other job descriptions.

DATAPLAN CORPORATION

Finance Trainee

required for busy data communications company.

The successful applicant must have excellent numeracy skills and a flair for, and interest in, financial matters. A minimum of GNVQ Advanced Level Business (with financial options) or AAT level 3 is required. The ability to work as a member of a team is essential, together with a good knowledge of spreadsheets and a related IT qualification.

Although college leavers will be considered, preferably applicants will have gained one or two years' experience in a commercial environment or have a good track record of work experience. Ideally, applicants will also possess good communication skills and be able to demonstrate their ability to deal effectively with a wide range of people at all levels.

The successful candidate will be required to work towards higher level financial qualifications and career prospects are excellent.

Hours 9 – 5.30. Salary negotiable, depending upon age and experience.

For full details including a job description and application form contact Nikki King, Human Resources Assistant, on 02837-809010. Completed application forms should be returned to the Human Resources Department, Dataplan Corporation, 14 Riverside Square, Hightown, HG1 8EG, quoting reference 839.28.

Dataplan Corporation is an Equal Opportunities employer and welcomes applications from all sections of the community.

Figure 4.4 Job advertisement

4.2 Employer responsibilities to individual employees

If you have completed Unit 1, you will have already covered the concept of employer responsibilities under employment law and in Figure 1.11 on page 17. This section broadens your understanding of this concept and introduces you to the effects on the employee and on the business if the employer fails to meet these responsibilities.

You need to understand the concept of employer responsibility in relation to:

•   contracts of employment

•   induction programmes

•   appraisal schemes

•   training programmes.

First, however, you need to understand why it is in everyone's interests for employers to fulfil their responsibilities in these areas.

The rationale behind employer responsibilities

It is common sense for employers to ensure that new staff are supported so that they can perform their jobs effectively and productively as quickly as possible. If you ran a shop but couldn't be bothered to train your assistant then you would only be able to ask her to do a limited number of tasks and would be paying her a wage but doing most of the work yourself! There is simply no point in employing someone if they are not given the opportunity to do their job properly. In addition, if they become bored and leave the employer has to find a replacement. This costs money and the new person, too, would leave if the situation is no better.

You would also find that if you totally ignore your employee's needs you will be flouting employment law. Various Acts have given both employers and employees rights and responsibilities.

•   The Employment Protection (Consolidation) Act 1978, now amended by the Employment Rights Act 1996, states that all employees must be given written details relating to their employment within two months of starting work.

- Under the Sex Discrimination Act, the Race Relations Act and the Disability Discrimination Act all employees must be treated fairly and equally.

- Additional rights and responsibilities are covered in other legislation, such as the Employment Relations Act 1999, the Working Time Regulations and the National Minimum Wage Act.

In summary

There are therefore three main reasons why it is in the interest of employers to meet their responsibilities.

1 **Legal implications** – all organisations must abide by the requirements of current employment law and must be careful to avoid discrimination.

2 **Financial implications** – staff who are well trained are more productive and therefore *save* the company money (because they work more quickly and make fewer mistakes) and *earn* it money (as they are more capable of pleasing customers and generating more business). Staff will be motivated, will stay longer and this will reduce the cost of replacing them and retraining new staff.

3 **Ethical implications** – an employer genuinely interested in the welfare of all staff must treat each person fairly and equally.

Contracts of employment

Under the terms of the Employment Rights Act 1996, all employees with one month's service are entitled to a written statement about the terms and conditions of their employment no later than two months after their employment starts. This means that:

- if you work somewhere for less than one month you are *not* entitled to any written statement

- if you work for more than one month you must receive *something* in writing. The correct term is 'written particulars of employment'. This does not necessarily mean you receive a written contract of employment

- after one month you have this right, whether you work on a full-time or part-time basis.

Most permanent staff are given a written contract either before or upon starting work. This may be a letter rather than a written contract.

Key items

The following must be included in the main document:

- the hours of work

- the place of work

- terms and conditions of employment

- entitlements (pay and benefits, including holiday pay).

In addition, the names of both parties (employer and employee), the date on which employment commenced and the job title must be stated.

Secondary information

The following information *must* be given to the employee but can be given in a separate document.

- If the job is only temporary, the date on which the employment will end or the length of time for which the employment will last.

- Details of any collective (union) agreements which affect the terms and conditions of employment.

- Any specific conditions requiring the employee to work outside the UK for longer than one month. In this case details have to be included as to the length of the time spent abroad, any additional pay and benefits, the currency in which the employee will be paid and any terms relating to the employee's return to the UK.

- Details of the employer's grievance and the appeals procedures.

Reference information

The employee should also be informed of the following, or told where to find the information.

- Sickness benefits and sickness entitlement.

- Pension scheme details.

- Notice entitlement, i.e. the length of notice the employee should give and is entitled to receive to terminate the employment.

- Details of the employer's disciplinary rules and procedures.

Note that if you are starting work with a firm with fewer than 20 employees, then you do not need to be supplied with information on disciplinary rules and procedures and only limited details are required on the grievance and appeals procedures.

Benefits of issuing contracts of employment

There are several benefits to both parties if a contract of employment is issued:

- The employer is complying with the requirements of employment legislation.

- The employee knows he or she is working for a reputable organisation which observes legal requirements.

- The contract gives full details of the employment – so there is less likely to be any misunderstandings.

- The relationship between the employer and employee is defined in law – so both have legal protection if anything goes wrong.

- If a dispute arises, the contract will help to define what can be reasonably expected of each party.

 ACTIVITY

1   Look back at Figure 1.12 on page 19, which identifies the main rights of employees under the Employment Rights Act 1996. Then reread the Snapshot on page 22 which covers other relevant legislation.

Now make a list of six rights you have as an employee.

2   If an employee fails to observe the terms of the contract of employment what action can an employer take? Equally, what action could you take if your employer treated you unfairly? Refresh your memory of both grievance and disciplinary procedures by rereading pages 18–30 in Section 1.2.

3   Your friend, Sam, has got a part-time, permanent job in a computer store. He shows you the text of a letter he has received (Figure 4.5.) and asks you if it includes all the essential

Dear Sam

PART-TIME SALES ASSISTANT – HIGHTOWN STORE

Further to your recent letter, confirming your acceptance of the above position, I have pleasure in writing to confirm your appointment. Please note that the terms and conditions of your employment are detailed below.

1. Your appointment will commence with effect from Saturday, 30 October, 2000.

2. Your starting salary will be £4.50 per hour, payable each month in arrears, direct to your bank account. It is normal for the company to review all salaries annually.

3. Your appointment will be subject to two weeks' notice in writing on either side.

4. Your hours of work will be 8 hours Saturday and up to 4 hours Sunday, but you may be required to work extra hours to suit the needs of the business. Your hours of work cannot be permanently guaranteed because these will also depend upon the needs of the business. Your supervisor will notify you as far in advance as possible if changes are required. If no advance notification is possible you will be offered a minimum of three hours' work.

5. All employees who work on a day designated as bank holiday will be paid double time for actual hours worked.

6. You will be responsible to the Store Manager.

7. Your first four weeks comprise a probationary period, during which time your performance will be evaluated. If it is rated as satisfactory during this time you will be taken off your probationary status.

8. In the event of sickness, you must telephone the Store Manager within one hour of the time you were due to commence work, on the day in question, or arrange for someone else to telephone on your behalf. Any period of sickness in excess of 3 days requires the submission of a doctor's certificate. Payment for self-certificated periods of sickness will be at the discretion of the company. You will receive statutory sick pay, if appropriate, which is payable up to twenty eight weeks in any year. Any entitlements after that period are paid by the DSS.

9. From the commencement of your employment you will start to accumulate paid holiday entitlement. This entitlement starts to operate when you have been in continuous employment for 13 weeks. Any holiday taken within the first 13 weeks will be unpaid. On the completion of 13 weeks' continuous service you will be credited the paid holidays for that period. Between 13 weeks and 26 weeks you are entitled to one weekend with holiday pay. Between 26 weeks and 1 year you are entitled to two weekends with holiday pay. After 1 year you are entitled to four weekends with holiday pay.

10. If you have any grievance relating to your employment you should approach the Store Manager and try to reach a satisfactory resolution. If there is a failure to agree, the matter should be referred, in writing, to Ms J Sharrack, Human Resources Manager. Thereafter, if there is still a failure to agree you have the right of appeal, either verbally or in writing, to Mr P Benson, Managing Director.

11. Detail of the company pension scheme and disciplinary procedure will be given to you during your induction on your first day of employment.

I should be obliged if you would please sign and return the enclosed copy indicating your acceptance of these terms.

Finally, I should like to welcome you to DataComm and hope that we will both benefit from a long and happy working relationship.

Yours sincerely

Jane Sharrack
Human Resources Manager

Figure 4.5 Sam's letter from DataComm Computer Store

information he should receive in his 'particulars of employment'.

Give a reasoned argument in support of your answer.

Induction programmes

Sam's letter refers to an induction programme on the first day he works in the store. Most organisations have an induction programme of some kind – although the length and content may vary considerably.

What is an induction programme and why are they useful for new employees *and* the organisation as a whole?

As a new student you probably underwent an induction programme at your college. The aim was to make you familiar with the college and your course, so that you could find your way around, understand how the organisation operates and give you the key information about the course. This helps you become 'effective' as a student as quickly as possible. In the same way, induction programmes in business introduce the new employees to the organisation as a whole and the job in particular. The aim is to make the employee effective as quickly as possible. A further benefit is that because all new employees attend induction together people have the opportunity to meet other new staff and start to make friends.

Most induction programmes have three elements:

- **a personal element**, which includes details of company policy and procedures; conditions of employment; knowledge of the building and layout, environment and people; individual responsibilities in relation to health and safety. A handbook is often given to all new staff which details this information.

- **an organisation element**, which relates to the history of the organisation, the structure of the departments and job titles, and information on products and markets (e.g. British, overseas, types of customers etc.)

- **a health and safety element**, so that new employees know how to respond if there is an accident or an emergency situation

- **a job element**, which relates to the job itself and the duties required.

Very large organisations tend to have more comprehensive induction programmes. The first part may be 'off the job' – in a separate training area. In Sam's case, it may be far more informal. He may get a short talk from the manager, a quick 'tour' around the store,

INDUCTION PROGRAMME

Monday, 17 November 2000

Please report to room 243 at 9 am

0900	Introduction and welcome	Geoff Barnes, Human Resource Manager
0915	Terms and conditions of employment	Rehana Kauser, Personnel Officer
0945	Health and safety and fire training	Peter Gibbons, Health and Safety Officer
1030	*Coffee*	
1045	Company overview and structure	Ken Johnson, Managing Director
1100	Current markets, plans for the future	Jack Chang, Marketing Director
1130	Guided tour	Geoff Barnes, Human Resource Manager
1230	*Lunch*	
1330	Company IT network and computer system (hands-on session)	Kate Price, IT Manager
1445	*Tea*	
1500	Mentoring, training, staff development and appraisal system (plus allocation of mentors)	Rehana Kauser, Personnel Officer
1545	Departmental induction Transfer to own working area	Departmental Heads
1615	Introduction to mentor and colleagues	

Figure 4.6 An induction programme schedule

and told to 'work shadow' an experienced employee for the rest of the day. He will be given tasks gradually, so that he will be able to serve customers on his own in two or three weeks and will be able to use the cash register in five or six weeks or after he has had special training. In this case most of his induction is 'on the job'.

In large companies, new employees are often assigned a **mentor**. This is a colleague to whom they can turn, informally, for help, advice, information, and to stop you making mistakes.

Figure 4.6 is an example of an induction programme in a large organisation.

ACTIVITY

1 As a group, discuss what aspects of your college induction programme you found useful

– and those you didn't. Your tutor may be interested to hear your views!

2 If you have worked in an organisation (either part-time or full-time) and been involved in an induction programme, discuss its content with the rest of your group to see the extent to which inductions may vary. If you were issued with a handbook, bring this to class to show people who haven't seen one.

3 Your brother has his own business but doesn't believe in induction programmes. What arguments would you use to persuade him to change his mind?

Appraisal schemes

In many organisations, reviewing staff performance and identifying staff development and training requirements is done through an **appraisal scheme**. If you have worked part-time for McDonald's, for instance, you will have been appraised as part of your job.

Appraisal interviews are usually held annually, between the employee and his/her manager. These are confidential. A good appraisal scheme will allow employees to nominate a different person to appraise them, if they believe they will not get a fair appraisal from their line manager.

Key features of good appraisal interviews

- The person being appraised (known as the appraisee) is given advance warning of the date of the appraisal by the person doing the appraising (known as the appraisor).

- The appraisee clearly understands what will be discussed. The normal content is:

  ○ review of past performance to date, often linked to success in meeting previous performance targets

○ a review of job performance overall, including difficulties encountered by the appraisee

○ new aims and objectives for the employee set for the forthcoming year (linked to the aims and objectives of the company – see Unit 1, page 2)

○ an assessment of training and development requirements – linking the needs of the employee to future performance objectives

○ a discussion about future career aims and progression opportunities to help employees to plan their careers.

• In a good appraisal, the appraisee should do most of the talking and should be encouraged to make suggestions to improve performance or develop career ambitions.

• Many companies have a policy of financially supporting training linked to improving employee skills and promotion prospects. If you wanted to do an advanced IT course this may be supported if IT is a key part of your job. You would be very fortunate if the same company agreed to pay for your Italian lessons to improve your holiday conversational skills!

• The aim of appraisals is to give the employee and manager time together to focus on the appraisee. Many appraisees may find this motivational and satisfying. However, it shouldn't be the only time that the manager comments on performance or reviews key issues with staff. Appraisal is just *one part* of satisfactory employee relations.

Appraisals handled badly can be disastrous. If you find yourself with a highly critical boss who never lets you get a word in edgeways, comfort yourself that this is *not* the way appraisals should be run – and look for an alternative career opportunity!

The benefits for the employee and organisation

Successful appraisals aim to:

• enable the organisation to identify who most deserves future rewards (e.g. promotion opportunities)

• discover the future potential of employees

• identify the training needs which are required and link these to the organisational aims and objectives

• control and monitor staff performance

• give individual employees the time to talk about their hopes, aspirations and problems, with their own boss in private

• assist individuals to identify areas where they would like to develop their skills and expertise

• bring past successes to the attention of their boss, if these seem to have gone unnoticed

Figure 4.7 Appraisals benefit employees and employers

- improve employee motivation (see page 298) by understanding and recognising their own needs
- to check the effectiveness of current practices in relation to recruitment and training.

ACTIVITY

1   As a group, find out if any members have been appraised in a part-time job. If any have, ask them if they are prepared to tell you about:
   a   the content
   b   the outcome
   c   their view of appraisals from their own experience.
   If not, suggest what might happen if an organisation *didn't* have an appraisal scheme.

2   Some organisations have proposed one, or more, of the following types of appraisals:
   a   appraisals relating to the performance of a *team* rather than an individual person
   b   appraisals where high performance is linked to a pay award
   c   360-degree appraisals – where managers' appraisals are influenced by the views of their staff and colleagues.
   As a group, identify the benefits and drawbacks of each approach from the point of view of *both* the employee and the organisation. Ask your tutor to arbitrate on contentious issues!

3   Your friend Paul has just taken part in a disastrous appraisal. His boss, Jamilla, was negative and only focused on problem areas, hardly let him speak and threatened to demote him if he didn't improve. Paul tells you that Jamilla's appraisals are random and she seems to 'pick out' members of staff she doesn't like.
   a   What is likely to be the effect on employees who are appraised like Paul?
   b   What action should Paul's organisation take to stop this situation continuing?

Training programmes

Most organisations expect their employees to take an active role in their own professional development. This may be through the appraisal system (where the employee is expected to make a few suggestions!) or through employees identifying areas of experience they want to develop and suggesting these to their manager.

The organisation itself may identify where there is a lack of skill or expertise. This can be overcome by employing new staff or, more often, developing the skills of existing staff. Employees who turn down their boss's suggestions are unlikely to appear at the top of any promotion list!

Training programmes can be carried out for a variety of reasons.

- To provide new employees with the skills and knowledge required to perform their jobs effectively, in the minimum of time (e.g. induction programmes, basic training on company equipment or IT systems).

- To satisfy a skills shortage, either overall or in a particular department (e.g. PowerPoint training because few people can produce professional materials for presentations).

- To improve performance (e.g. customer service training to help staff deal with customers more effectively)

- To develop the particular job role (e.g. by taking a professional qualification to improve expertise, such as a personnel or accounting qualification).

- To enhance the role – to give the job holder additional skills to enable him/her to take on a broader range of tasks (e.g. training an accounts assistant to use financial accounting packages on a computer). This also helps staff to 'cover' for each other in the case of absence.

- To facilitate secondment, transfer or promotion.

  ○ Secondment is when an organisation allows a member of staff to work somewhere else temporarily. This may be for another department or another, allied, organisation, or another branch office. An example is an excellent administrator working in Britain being loaned to the French division of the company to set up a new office and being given language training beforehand.

  ○ Promotion is moving up one level or more. This usually only happens if the employee proves they can handle the additional work and responsibility. To do this they often need training. Potential managers, for instance, may do a part-time management course to improve their prospects.

  ○ Transfer is permanent. A member of staff may apply for transfer at the same level to another branch or another department. This may only be possible if the person concerned is multi-skilled.

Training can be **on-the-job** or **off-the-job**. On-the-job training takes place in the normal working situation (e.g. learning to use a switchboard or photocopier). This is appropriate when the training is job specific and a benefit is that training can be scheduled flexibly around the employee's working day. Disadvantages are that the trainer may be inexperienced or poor at passing on his or her skills and training may be postponed or interrupted if there are urgent work deadlines to meet.

Off-the-job training is so specialised that it can only be done separately from doing the job itself. This can take place in a company's own training facilities or at a college or at a

Figure 4.8 Off-the-job training

specialist training centre. The benefits are that the employee is away from work and there are no distractions – so he or she can concentrate on learning something new. It is also possible to study for a higher level qualification or receive specialist training which needs a tutor or trainer with particular skills or expertise. A disadvantage may be that sessions are inflexible and held at certain times each week. During the day it may be difficult to attend if there are pressures to complete urgent jobs. During the evening many people are tired and find it difficult to concentrate.

ACTIVITY

In each of the following examples identify:

a the reason(s) for the training

b whether it would be more likely undertaken on or off the job

c the benefits for the organisation *and* the employee.

1 Bill Scott has recently been appointed to the health and safety committee. He asks if he can 'work shadow' the health and safety officer for two days to gain a better insight into health and safety issues.

2 Imran Saddiq is interested in IT and knows his company is developing electronic shopping over the Internet, but few people understand this very well. He asks if he can learn about web page design.

3 Karen Sinclair is a junior in the marketing department. She reads about Institute of Marketing courses and asks if she can study for the first level examination.

4 Michelle Hope has just started work as a trainee administrator at your college. She is told she will have to learn how the college computer system operates.

5 Barry Martin is a junior manager who has just found he has to use a computer. Barry's background is production and he decides he needs to learn keyboarding skills and improve his communication skills and written English as quickly as possible.

6 Debbie Sayers is employed as a graphic artist but wants to become more involved in computer-aided design and 3D multi-media packages. She asks if she can learn about these after reading details in a computer magazine.

4.3 The employee's responsibility to the employer

The employer has a responsibility to each employee, and in return each employee has certain responsibilities to the employer. This unit expands on the responsibilities discussed in Unit 1 and also identifies the consequences for both parties if these responsibilities are not discharged.

Before starting this section, you should refresh your memory by referring back to the chart in Figure 1.11, page 17, identifying employer and employer rights and responsibilities.

In Unit 1 you learned that there are two types of employee responsibilities:

1 **Express terms**, which are specified in the contract of employment, such as your working hours, place of work and holiday entitlement.

2 **Implied conditions**, such as obeying reasonable instructions, acting in good faith, using reasonable care and skill and respecting your employer's property.

This means that you have to follow the company procedures, conventions (the way things are usually done) and instructions you are given – whether you agree with them or not – on issues such as:

- time-keeping
- accepted mode of dress (often called 'dress code')
- accepted standards of behaviour
- care of your employer's property
- your legal responsibilities in relation to health and safety.

Time-keeping

Anyone can be late on the odd occasion because of an unavoidable problem – the buses or trains are on strike, there was a domestic emergency or an accident meant you were stuck in traffic. Hopefully you won't be late because you forgot to set your alarm or ignored it when it went off!

If you *know* you are going to be late and can phone your employer, it is sensible to do so. Simply leave a message that you have been unavoidably delayed but will arrive as soon as possible – giving an estimate of the time. Otherwise, apologise when you arrive and explain why you are late. This is basic courtesy and it's unlikely to count against you.

However if you are frequently late you will get a reputation for being unreliable. Your employer's disciplinary procedures may involve giving a verbal warning and, if the lateness persists, a written warning. This would be because you had breached the terms of your contract of employment by not being present for the hours you agreed to work.

Mode of dress

There are three main reasons for a specific dress code where you work:

1   There is a specific uniform which employees must wear (from overalls to suits).

2   There are certain 'conventions' in the company which determine what type of dress is allowed and what is not (e.g. suits and ties for men, smart suits for women).

3   There are health, safety or hygiene reasons (e.g. safety boots, protective clothing, hair tied back or covered in the case of employees involved in handling food).

Figure 4.9 A range of dress codes

Unless you can prove that your employer is discriminating against you on the grounds of gender or race, then you cannot argue with the dress code. Even if no specific rules are laid down, there is an implied duty that employees should wear suitable and acceptable clothes for work. The clothes that are suitable for a representative who is regularly visiting customers will be different from those of a security officer or a production worker.

Your appearance and even the jewellery you wear can be part of a dress code. An employee who turns up looking scruffy, with hair unwashed and face unshaven, can be disciplined under the dress code. As for jewellery, the requirements of a production or canteen worker are very different from those of a sales assistant in a jewellery store! A cook with the Royal Fleet Auxiliary was sacked after he refused to remove a stud from his eyebrow. He claimed unfair dismissal but lost his appeal. The employment tribunal ruled that the dismissal was fair and that, 'There is nothing inherently wrong in employers imposing a dress code on their employees.' It dismissed the former cook's claim that the stud did not affect his ability to do the job.

Accepted standards of behaviour

At college or school you may find there is a code of conduct which identifies the type of behaviour to which all students must conform. You are unlikely to be given a code of conduct when you start work – although some employers, such as McDonald's, do issue guidelines for new staff. Instead you are expected to understand what is covered by the term 'acceptable behaviour'. Broadly this means:

•   abiding by any rules and regulations, such as not parking in visitors or disabled spaces, not smoking in 'no smoking' areas, not lending your ID badge to anyone or disclosing your computer password

- respecting other people who work in the organisation – at all levels – and treating them courteously

- not disclosing confidential information about your organisation or your job to outsiders

- respecting your employer's property – not taking stamps or pens home, not sending your private mail from work, not doing personal jobs at work

- cooperating over minor amendments to your job description or over requests to be flexible about the time you work (e.g. to help out in a busy period).

The law does protect you against having to obey 'unreasonable' instructions but basically defines these as orders which would be asking you to:

- commit a crime (e.g. falsify an expense claim)

- be placed in a position of danger (e.g. use a machine with a broken protective guard).

Care of your employer's property

You have an implied condition to look after your employer's property. This includes:

- taking care of equipment

- reporting equipment faults

- making sure that required stock and equipment are available.

Taking care of equipment

If you are 'taking care' of equipment, you are not only using it correctly and not damaging it, but also helping to maintain it. This can be as fundamental as keeping something

Figure 4.10 Being a messy worker can cause accidents – as well as making you unpopular

clean to making sure it is repaired when it goes wrong (see below). This means:

- finding out how something works *before* you start to use it

- using it properly, and in accordance with instructions and company procedures

- referring to the manual (or asking for help) if something goes wrong

- keeping your working area – and the equipment you use – neat and tidy.

Items of equipment used regularly in business include computers, printers, fax machines and photocopiers. Photocopying four sheets of paper and leaving the area in a mess, or covering a page with liquid paper which then smudges on the glass, will make you very unpopular with your colleagues. This is one case where it is far wiser to be 'Mr Neat' or 'Miss Tidy'.

Reporting equipment faults

Unless you know exactly what you are doing, and have received specific training, *never* try to mend a fault in a complicated machine, such as a photocopier. You are more likely to make the problem worse and may hurt or even injure yourself in the process.

Most organisations have a specified procedure for reporting faults. Make sure you follow this and report problems *promptly*. Don't let subsequent users discover the problem later. According to a survey carried out by the recruitment consultancy Office Angels, one of the most unpopular employees is the person who deserts the photocopier as soon as there is a paper jam – without attempting to fix it, or telling anyone or even leaving a note to let other people know that help is on the way. Don't let this be you!

Making sure stock and equipment are available

If you borrow something, return it immediately after use. If you need stationery or equipment then use the correct procedures to obtain it. If you are *responsible* for stock or equipment then make sure it is stored safely and that stocks of regularly used items are checked regularly and reordered in good time. Don't issue any items to colleagues without the proper paperwork (usually a signed order form or requisition).

And don't help yourself to items on a colleague's desk, such as scissors, a punch or stapler because you have lost your own – and *never* help yourself to items from the stock or stationery cupboard without specific permission. This isn't borrowing, it's theft of your employer's property.

Legal responsibilities

In Unit 1, you studied your legal responsibilities under the health and safety legislation. You should have noted that you have a responsibility to your employer to:

- take reasonable care of your own health and safety and that of others who may be affected by your activities

- cooperate with your employer and anyone acting on his or her behalf to meet health and safety requirements.

This means that if you are involved in any of the following activities you may not only find you are dismissed but also prosecuted:

- acting recklessly, so that you are in danger (e.g. by using the lift after the fire alarm sounds)

- encouraging other people to act recklessly with you (e.g. telling your friends it's only a drill, and getting them to enter the lift with you)

- fooling around or engaging in horseplay which could endanger other people (e.g. setting off fire extinguishers 'as a joke', pulling a chair away from someone about to sit down)

- ignoring a specific health and safety instruction (e.g. not wearing protective clothing, continuing to work after a fire alarm sounds).

Remember that failure to comply with health and safety legislation not only means that you have breached your contract of employment, it also means that you have been criminally negligent – and legal proceedings could be taken against you.

 ACTIVITY

1 John Miller plc has a dress code which covers three main groups of employees:
   a production workers
   b canteen workers
   c office workers and representatives.
   From the following, identify which group(s) of employees would be affected in each case.
      i Nail varnish and jewellery is not permitted, apart from wedding rings.

ii   A tie must be worn when visiting customers' premises.

iii   Safety boots must be worn at all times.

iv   No dangling jewellery (e.g. bracelets, earrings or chains) is permitted.

v   Hair must be clean, covered by a hat and away from the face. It must be kept short or tied back. No hair ornaments are permitted.

vi   Male employees should preferably be clean shaven. Beards are not permitted. Moustaches must be short and regularly trimmed.

vii   Low-heeled, comfortable shoes should be worn. No stiletto heels are allowed.

viii Jeans and trainers are not allowed.

ix   Skirts should be no shorter than five centimetres (two inches) above the knee.

2   An employee may be given a verbal warning, a written warning, a final warning or instantly dismissed. Much will depend on the previous conduct of the employee and whether this is a 'first offence', the seriousness of the offence and whether any previous warnings have been given (see also Section 1.2, pages 29 and 30).

Classify the actions below into those you think may result in instant dismissal and those where the employee should receive a warning. Discuss your suggestions with your tutor.

a   Theft of a computer.

b   Using a computer to search the Internet for information on the local football team.

c   Leaking confidential information to a friend who works for a rival organisation.

d   Hacking into computer files.

e   Using another person's ID card.

f   Taking drugs at work.

g   Pilfering stationery.

h   Being continually absent from work without explanation.

i   Taking holidays without obtaining permission beforehand.

j   Being insolent to the boss.

k   Being insolent to a colleague.

l   Being so tired (through constant late nights) that it is impossible to do the job properly.

m   Coming back drunk from a lunchtime celebration.

3   Employers and employees also have obligations under the Health and Safety at Work Act. These were described in Section 1.2 on pages 35–42.

a   Reread these now and list both your responsibilities and those of your employer under this Act.

b   A female employee is asked by her line manager to remove a charm bracelet as she operates machinery as he is concerned it may become trapped. She fails to comply with the request and her manager does not ask her again.
     If the bracelet jammed in the machine one day and she hurt her arm, who would be responsible and why?
     i   the employee
     ii   the manager
     iii both of them.
     Discuss your ideas as a group.

4.4 Working with others

In the survey by Office Angels, referred to earlier, other behaviour which irritates work colleagues include mobiles ringing in meetings, gossiping, not returning items borrowed and making coffee for yourself without offering anyone else. So, to be successful and popular at work you have to do a little more than just your job!

Other surveys have identified irritating workers to include: those who moan and grumble all the time, those who are obsequious (look up this word!) to the boss, those who tell tales and those who 'disappear' when there's an emergency or a lot of work to be done.

Hierarchical differences

All the above are common gripes about *colleagues*. In other words, people who work at the same level as yourself. But there will be people above and, eventually, below you. All these people have different expectations about you. How can you keep everyone happy and develop good working relationships with all the different people you work with?

- **Your superiors**. They are senior to you. *In addition to* complying with the responsibilities identified in your job description, they will expect you to be loyal, discreet, conscientious, reliable, to produce high-quality work, to use your initiative (by thinking ahead, not by having to be told everything), to remember what you have already been told, to tell them when you think there is a serious problem and to get on with other people.

- **Your subordinates**. These are people who are below you in any hierarchy (see Unit 1, page 99).

  When you have your own subordinates, treat them as you want your own boss to treat *you*. This means treating them all fairly, *listening* when they have a problem, not expecting them to do something you wouldn't do yourself (such as working late while you go home!), giving them clear instructions, being consistent and pleasant to work for.

Even if you are not directly responsible for someone else you will be dealing with other types of people – from canteen staff to cleaners. You need to respect them equally. If you are seen as 'stuck up', the cleaner might 'forget' to empty your waste bin and the canteen staff might 'accidentally' serve you lukewarm coffee. You are warned!

- **Coordinators**. These are people responsible for organising a particular task or project. In this case you may only relate to them over one particular matter. However, even if this is not very important to you, it will be to them. Treating their requests as important, keeping them informed, doing what you promised to do by the deadline and supporting them in their job are all important.

- **Section leaders**. They are responsible for a particular unit of a department. They may be senior to you but not *the* boss of the whole department. If you are part of this section then you should consider your section leader as your superior (see above). If they are the section leader of another area then you may relate to them in a similar way to coordinators (above). *Never* try to 'jump over' your section leader to tell tales to the departmental head, nor talk disparagingly about one section leader to another. They are likely to compare tales and you could find yourself extremely unpopular!

- **Team members**. If you are a member of a team then these are your immediate colleagues. If you get on well with your immediate colleagues then you will enjoy your working day much more than if you do not. Your responsibilities to the rest of the team are outlined on page 296.

Figure 4.11 Switch off your mobile when you go to meetings

A word of warning! Don't expect to be on close terms with everyone you meet at work. Much may depend upon the structure of the organisation and its size.

- In a hierarchical or pyramid organisation there is always some 'distance' between the managers and those below them. Even if they unwind on a night out with the staff, the following day it will be 'business as usual'.

- In a matrix organisation (see Unit 1.3, page 100) you may find you have to change teams or work with different people at different times. You may even have two bosses and their simultaneous requests to cope with!

- In a flat structure, it is likely to be more informal, and you may call the boss by his or her first name. However, you would be unwise to mistake informality for intimacy!

The best way forward is to find a mentor who will help you settle in when you first start a job. Some organisations appoint a mentor to new employees automatically (see page 285), but even if there is no formal system, you can unofficially ask a colleague you particularly like to guide you. A mentor is invaluable in helping you to get used to the 'customs' in the workplace and to give you an 'insider's guide' to the people you work with. Your mentor is also the person to turn to for guidance if you are worried or concerned about a particular aspect of the job – or the behaviour of a particular person you work with.

Your responsibilities to other people

To be effective at work, you need help and cooperation from other people, and they need it from you. If you purposefully help other people to be effective, you will normally find they are cooperative in return – and everyone benefits.

- **Meeting deadlines**. If work has to be done by a specific deadline then you *must* meet this. If unforeseen circumstances make this impossible then tell your boss well beforehand – so that alternative arrangements can be made in advance. Remember that the later you leave this, the more difficult it becomes.

- **Completing tasks to required standards**. It is no use meeting a deadline if the work is so sloppy it has to be redone. Take pride in your work and make sure anything with your name on it is of a high standard.

- **Exchanging information**. Communication is a key aspect of a job. No one is a mind reader and no one is psychic in the business world! Make sure people have the facts they need, in good time to take action. If you are unsure about something, ask for advice. At the start of your career you may find it difficult to decide whether information is important or not. Remember that it is always better to include something irrelevant than to omit something crucial.

- **Keeping promises**. A 'promise' is a serious undertaking. Never tell a colleague (or your boss) that you will definitely do something and then let them down.

- **Helping out**. If you get a reputation as someone who will 'roll up their sleeves' and help out when there is a crisis you will be valuable indeed. You will also find that when *you* have a problem, other people will be far more willing to help you.

- **Being positive**. Some people always find problems with an idea before they see the benefits. If your boss, or a colleague, suggests a new way of doing something then try to look enthusiastic! If you are genuinely doubtful then wait a little before suggesting there could be one or two drawbacks. But be certain these are *real* drawbacks rather than minor inconveniences which can soon be solved. If you are a problem solver, this is an added feather in your cap.

Team working

A key requirement of many jobs is the 'ability to work as a member of a team'. What does this mean? And would you qualify?

A team is a group of people working together to achieve the same goal (e.g. a football team or a cricket team). The goal of the team is more important than those of the individual members. You will often find teams operating in organisations with flatter structures, overseen by a **team leader**, who gives feedback on performance, encouragement to the members, clarifies any queries and monitors team performance. The captain of a football team is an example of a team leader. In many organisations, some teams will comprise a group of people who are at different levels in the organisation. The manager, or more senior member, may not always be the team leader – it would depend upon why the team had been formed and what its aims and objectives were.

Benefits of team working

- Ideally, a team comprises people with a mix of talents and abilities. (You wouldn't form a football team with 11 strikers or 11 goalkeepers!) Therefore each team has a **variety of expertise and abilities**.

- Within a team, each person can be allocated a job which maximises their particular strengths. They can concentrate on this and improve their abilities and skills. This is often known as **specialisation**.

- Within a team, certain people can be trained to do more than one job – so that the team can be changed to meet particular challenges or undertake certain tasks. Also, if one member is ill or absent, their work can then be covered by other people. This is called **flexible working**.

- The team support and help one another. They can share ideas, problems and achievements. Ideas can be 'bounced around' so that the final idea is improved by suggestions from different members of the team. If a 'problem shared is a problem halved' then team workers benefit by being able to discuss their difficulties with other team members. This encourages creativity and problem solving. An achievement can be celebrated by the whole team. In some organisations, bonuses are paid according to *team* performance, rather than *individual* performance.

Figure 4.12 The captain of the team is the leader

Benefits of being a team member

- Usually, team members are more **motivated** (see page 298) because they work with other people. Problems can be shared and work can be done more quickly. There is always someone to help if you are having difficulties.

- There is usually a friendlier atmosphere and people are keen to support and help each other. Team members may socialise together out of working hours and some members may become good friends.

As a team member . . .

Remember that team goals have priority over your own. In return you get the support of the members of the team. You have to prove you are loyal, supportive and cooperative – and willing to actively participate and communicate with the other team members. Learn to listen to other people and consider their suggestions. Don't over-react if you are criticised or sulk or take it personally. Equally, don't make hurtful remarks to someone else. Only criticise helpfully – by suggesting improvements tactfully. Contribute to discussions and be an active participant. Don't keep good ideas to yourself in case someone else gets the credit! Support other people when they are having problems. Always carry out your own commitments to the best of your ability. Finally, don't expect anyone to be perfect. Being a team member means having to accept other people's minor irritating traits. After all, you may have a few yourself!

ACTIVITY

1 Many colleges and schools include team-building activities in their induction programmes. This might include visiting a specialist centre for problem-solving activities. If your group has not participated in such an event ask your tutor if there is a chance of doing so.

If you have, ask your tutors' personal opinion (in an individual tutorial) about your own teamworking abilities. Be prepared to take action on any negative feedback you receive.

2 As a group:
   a decide upon the most important qualities of a team leader
   b suggest how a team leader could improve the situation if two or three members were often disagreeing with each other.

3 One activity that demands close teamworking is doing research together and preparing a presentation.

Dr Meredith Belbin, a management writer, said that an individual can never be perfect whereas a team can be. He meant that, given the right mix of abilities, a team can have more strengths than an individual person.

In teams of four, research and prepare a presentation on the benefits of teamwork for your tutor.
   a Include some of the work on team roles by Dr Meredith Belbin.
   b As a team, identify each member's strengths and the weak areas of the team as a whole. This means deciding if the strengths complement one another and whether the weaknesses mean there are skills that no member is particularly good at.
   c As a team, suggest how your weaknesses could be minimised, e.g. by people working together on difficult problems.
   d *In addition* to being graded on your presentation, ask your fellow students to grade you on your contribution as a member of the team.

Motivating individuals at work

Understanding motivation

People motivated to do their jobs are interested and enthusiastic about the work, want to do it well and work hard to succeed in what they do.

So, what factors motivate individuals at work? Studies have shown that the following have an effect:

- job satisfaction (feeling a genuine sense of achievement)

- financial rewards – wages/salary/bonuses (you work harder if you can earn more)

- non-financial rewards, such as social events or a staff restaurant

- benefits such as a pension or private health insurance

- working conditions, including health and safety

- hours of work

Figure 4.13 Working hard can bring you success

- promotion and responsibility

- praise and recognition.

It is easier to see how these link to motivation if you know how ideas about motivation have developed over the years.

Studies on motivation

Attitudes to work have changed. Early in the 20th century work was seen as a necessity and most people spent long hours doing hard, boring repetitive work to earn enough to buy the necessities to live. Most people were no more than 'human machines' and seen as only capable of doing routine, simple tasks.

As the century progressed, researchers such as Frederick Herzberg (see Unit 1, page 28), Abraham Maslow and Douglas McGregor studied the issue of work and people's attitudes to it. They discovered that people could be enthusiastic about work and described this as being motivated. Those who are motivated work hard to a high standard, and are eager to learn and improve themselves and their work. They are also willing to do extra duties at short notice.

The list above shows that there are many factors which can affect an individual's motivation.

There are factors which do not directly inspire people to be motivated, however they prevent them becoming disgruntled or unwilling to work hard. These are what Herzberg called **hygiene factors.**

Other factors have been called **social factors** by Maslow. These relate to getting on well with your colleagues. If you do not, then you are more likely to be demotivated, to do poor work or to take time off.

Herzberg and Maslow agreed that the type of work is the most important factor inspiring people to work really hard. These include:

- being praised for doing a good job

- enjoying the work that you do

- having responsibilities to make decisions and the satisfaction of seeing that something you have done has worked

- knowing that if you do well you could get a pay rise or promotion.

However, all people are different. What motivates you, therefore, may bore someone else – and vice versa. One person may be happy to do a dull, routine job if the pay is excellent. Another may prefer an interesting job with less money. Most people, however, realise that all jobs have some routine aspects and are prepared to put up with these so long as they find some aspects of the job challenging.

Douglas McGregor pointed out that the attitude of a manager is also a critical factor affecting an employee's performance. For example, you may work in a sports shop where you enjoy meeting customers and advising them. However, if your boss doesn't trust you and is too critical, you will find it hard to remain cheerful and enthusiastic doing your job. The days will seem long and you may look for another job.

Some managers do not trust staff to be motivated to work hard and do their jobs well. They believe you have to pressure them to do a good job and so push them hard. Many regard this approach as outdated. Today people want work to be interesting and fulfilling and are prepared to put the effort into tasks which are challenging.

ACTIVITY

1 Reread Frederick Herzberg's ideas on hygiene factors and motivators on page 28. To what

extent do you agree with him? Discuss your views with your tutor.

2 In a national survey in 1998, students ranked 'a friendly and helpful teacher' as the most important factor in helping to motivate them at college.

   a To what extent does your group agree or disagree with this statement?

   b How is this finding linked to the views of Douglas McGregor?

3 Look back at the list of factors affecting motivation on page 298. Rank them according to what is the most important to you, and compare this with your fellow students. How do you account for any differences?

Retaining employees

If you work in a human resources department, you will soon find that your manager is very concerned with statistics on absence and staff turnover. Absence figures show how many people have not turned up for work over a particular period. Staff turnover figures show how many people have left the organisation over a particular time period.

If you talk to your tutor, you are likely to find that he or she is also interested in the same thing! How many students attended each class, and how many were absent. And how many students have left the course since it began – and why.

The reasons for such keen interest are similar in both cases:

- Motivated employees have good attendance records. They are only absent for genuine reasons, such as illness. If a person is absent without good reason this is usually an indication that they are bored, unhappy or have other problems. Sooner or later they will leave altogether.

- Absenteeism also creates problems in that work is not being done and problems and delays are likely. It also puts greater pressure on other staff to cope.

- High staff turnover usually means there is a problem. Something is making people unhappy enough to want to leave. The manager will want to take action to prevent this – particularly as finding new staff can be expensive, both in terms of recruitment and training – and it is likely efficiency or output will be lower for a time.

Factors which can cause people to leave

Although these may vary between one individual and another, some common causes are often identified.

- The work is boring and monotonous – there is little or no job satisfaction for some employees.

- The conditions of employment or wage rates are better in other organisations in the area.

- The quality of the recruitment system is poor and unsuitable people are appointed to jobs.

- Insufficient training is given so people cannot cope with their jobs or the quality of training is poor so little is learned.

- There are no promotion prospects.

- People do not feel recognised or valued by their line manager(s).

- Employees feel isolated and there is little opportunity for social interaction between staff.

In the worst case, a combination of these factors means that the overall level of motivation is almost non-existent.

Investigating the problem

Organisations will collect statistics on staff turnover and monitor the situation regularly. If there is a problem it is important to investigate the type of staff who are leaving given that it is unlikely that staff turnover will be the same throughout the organisation.

Further study of the statistics may show the following:

1 Certain grades of staff (such as unskilled workers) leave more frequently than skilled staff or managers. Absenteeism may be higher, too. This may be because the work is poorly paid, less challenging and the type of workers who are hired may be less committed to permanent jobs or developing a career.

2 Certain departments, or sections, have higher staff turnover than others. This may be because a manager or team leader is poor at making appointments, is demotivating staff (by being overly critical or dictatorial) or because the type of work undertaken there is more tedious.

Action to take

The action to take will obviously depend upon the problem identified.

Three techniques, associated with **job design**, are used to try to make repetitive jobs more interesting:

1 **Job rotation** involves a group of people at the same level rotating or changing duties over a specific period. This allows people to learn new skills and makes the job less monotonous.

2 **Job enlargement** occurs when people are given additional duties to increase or enlarge the number of tasks they do. They may be trained to operate different types of machinery or different computer

packages. This is also sometimes known by the term **multi-skilling**.

3 **Job enrichment** is when people are given more responsibility for their own work and allowed to make a more active contribution. This is why **team working** is often so successful.

As an example, many modern motor manufacturers have abandoned the traditional assembly line, where workers undertook one small task routinely all day. Instead, teams are responsible for a specific number of tasks *and* for checking the quality of their own work. How they organise this is between them and their team leader. Motivation, job satisfaction, output and quality have all been increased by this method of working.

If the problem is more concerned with a particular section or department and a variety off different levels of staff are leaving regularly, then it may be necessary to find out if there is a problem with a particular manager or team leader – or even with the physical environment (such as an office which is over-crowded or poorly designed). One system used by many organisations is to hold **exit interviews** with staff when their views and opinions are sought.

Finally, if the problem is more widespread, the organisation will have to investigate its human resources policies and the ways in which these are perceived by managers and staff. This may include:

- reviewing the recruitment system

- retraining managers in recruitment and interview techniques (and checking no jobs are 'over-sold' at interview)

- providing better facilities for staff

- reviewing conditions of employment (such as working hours and holiday entitlements)

- reviewing pay rates

- reviewing fringe benefits and bonus payments

- reviewing the induction programme and how this is delivered

- checking that training and staff development opportunities exist for all staff

- checking that appraisal interviews are carried out sensitively and constructively

- ensuring all managers and team leaders understand the importance of motivation and how to motivate their staff.

ACTIVITY

1 The following are the staff turnover statistics for the last six months for groups of staff at Costlow supermarkets:

Floor managers	5%
Supervisors	5%
Check-out operators	25%
Office staff	20%
Shelf-fillers	60%
Warehouse staff	35%

   a Why do you think the leaving rate for shelf-fillers is so high?

   b What actions can Costlow take to improve this situation?

   c Why is it important Costlow takes action?

2 A sales supervisor in a call centre is a hard taskmaster. She routinely 'listens in' to conversations staff are having with customers and criticises them in front of everyone else if she doesn't like what she hears. She expects them to consistently reach their targets, per hour, on the number of calls they make. She is strict about lunch and break entitlements and is annoyed if staff take a day off, even if they are genuinely ill.

Sales are very high, so the organisation values her, but the human resources manager is concerned about the rate of staff turnover and the associated costs of having to recruit and train new staff. He is beginning to think it would be better if sales were lower and costs were lower too!

As a group, suggest:

a   what action the supervisor's own manager could take to improve the situation

b   what initiatives the human resources manager could introduce to decrease staff turnover in the call centre.

This unit concentrates on the different types of retail outlets that operate in the UK, their location and other differences between them. It focuses on the ways in which goods are sold, the environment of each different type of outlet and how health, safety and security are managed. It covers modern retail technology and the skills required to make a sale.

You may already have some experience in the retail sector through working in your holidays or in a part-time job. In this case you will be able to relate many of the topics covered to your existing knowledge. Even if retailing is new to you, you will have used retail outlets as a customer since you were very young. This unit will give you the ability to assess those outlets with a more professional eye and to identify important aspects of retailing you may never have considered before – as well as providing all the key facts you need to pass the external assessment linked to this unit.

5.1 The retail sector

There are six main types of retail outlet in the UK. The following points will help you to identify the key differences between each one.

Multiple retailers

A multiple retailer operates a number of stores, often on a nationwide basis. Each store is usually identical – so customers know what to expect. Some multiples such as Woolworths, Boots and Marks & Spencer sell a variety of goods. Others specialise, such as Dixons (electrical goods), Halfords (motor spares) and Next (clothing). A large multiple has more than 10 branches and a small multiple has fewer than ten.

Key features

- Same 'image' – so easily recognisable.

- Similar goods stocked (though large branches may have wider range).

- Goods bought centrally. Bulk purchases mean cheaper prices, so selling prices are competitive.

- All major decisions made at head office.

- National advertising possible because stores operate on large scale.

- May be found in town centres or in out-of-town locations.

- Large variety chain stores may have their own brand names on many items they sell, e.g. Winfield (Woolworths), St Michael (M & S) and Boots or British Home Stores own brands.

Department stores

Department stores were the first type of stores to offer 'one stop shopping', where customers could buy a variety of goods under one roof. A department store has different departments, each of which sells different types of goods. Each department operates independently and has its own staff. In many stores 'in-store merchandise concessions' are given to suppliers or manufacturers, e.g. Estée Lauder, Jaeger and Wedgewood. The aim of concessions is to offer a wider range of goods with no risk to the store itself, which charges for the rented space. Each concession

Figure 5.1 Merchandise concessions are a feature of department stores

is run as a 'shop within a shop' (see page 316). The location, number of staff and services offered by department stores means costs are relatively high so goods may be quite expensive. Examples include Harrods, Selfridges, John Lewis Partnership, House of Fraser, Debenhams and Beale's.

Key features

- Usually situated in a multi-storey building in a large town or city centre – though some now expanding to out-of-town shopping complexes.

- Allow customers to move freely and browse the range of goods on display without being pressured to buy.

- Quality goods (including designer ranges) offered in addition to budget priced goods. Some stores are renowned for quality goods (e.g. Harrods, Fortnum and Mason).

- Specialist staff to give advice on specific departmental products.

- Wide range of customer service facilities available which may include rest rooms, restaurants, coffee areas, car parking, telephones, export advice to tourists, own store cards.

Independent retail outlets

Many independent outlets are run by sole traders or are limited company family businesses. They may be situated in a town centre or serve a particular locality or neighbourhood. They are often known as **independent traders**. Some sell a limited range of items, e.g. a greengrocer, chemist or newsagent. Others are **general convenience stores** which sell a range of products, including groceries, wines and spirits and general household goods. Some are members of a voluntary **wholesale buying group**. This is where a group of retailers get their supplies from the same wholesaler to get the benefits of bulk buying, merchandising and advertising. Examples include Mace VG, Spar and Londis.

Key features

- Independently owned – even if a member of a voluntary group.

- Situated in town centres or local shopping areas.

- Individual shops which offer a personal service.

- Can be flexible about opening hours.

- May be specialist outlets or operate in a 'niche' market (see page 306).

- Pricing, discounts and other policies at owner's discretion.

- Operating costs can be kept down if family members employed or if shop is in low priced property area – or if owners live on the premises.

- Members of voluntary groups gain advantages of large-scale operations, e.g. bulk buying, so that costs are lower, regular deliveries, in-store advertising materials, national advertising campaigns.

Supermarkets and hypermarkets

Supermarkets are large stores, all on one level, which mainly sell groceries. Other goods may also be on sale, such as newspapers, sandwiches, flowers, clothing and some household and gift items.

There are three main differences between supermarkets and hypermarkets:

1   **The size of the selling area.** A supermarket has a selling area of between 25,000 sq ft and 50,000 sq ft (less than this and it is known as a mini-supermarket). The outlet is called a hypermarket if the selling space is over 50,000 sq ft.

2   **The range of goods sold.** Whereas both types of store will sell a wide variety of products (e.g. various brands and varieties of baked beans), a hypermarket will sell a wider range of goods. For instance, Asda's hypermarket chain, called Supercentres, sell computers and software, small electrical goods, branded sportswear, sports goods, fashion goods and housewares – as well as food.

3   **Their location.** Supermarkets may be out-of-town or in a town centre (such as Tesco Metro and Sainsbury Local stores) which offer a more limited range of goods. Hypermarkets are situated in out-of-town locations (see also page 308).

Both types of store sell goods at very competitive prices. The major supermarkets in Britain are those operated by Tesco, Sainsbury (which also runs Savacentre hypermarkets), Asda (owned by Wall-Mart), Morrisons, Safeway and Somerfield (see Figure 5.2). Netto and Aldi also operate supermarkets but sell goods more cheaply, concentrating on price rather than customer facilities, wide stock ranges or customer service.

Ranking	Name	Sales (£m)	Approx. no. of stores
1	Tesco	14,621	586
2	Sainsbury's	10,836	391
3	Asda	7,601	219
4	Safeway	6,979	486
5	New Somerfield*	6,000	1,460
6	Morrisons	2,533	1,000

*Includes Kwik-Save

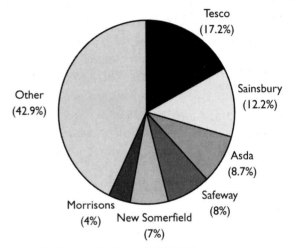

Sources: *Verdict Research, Verdict Analysis, Retail Intelligence*

Figure 5.2 The UK's main supermarkets, showing ranking and market share in 1998

Key features

- Large self-service stores which operate on one level.

- Large car parking areas at out-of-town locations, which often include a petrol station.

- Additional facilities in large stores which can include restaurant/cafeteria, cash machines, rest rooms, baby changing rooms etc.

- In-store facilities which can include an in-store bakery, fresh fish counter and delicatessen.

- Wide variety of goods on sale at competitive prices.

Specialist outlets

A specialist outlet sells only one type of product, such as spectacles, baby clothes, books or wine. The owner and staff have specialist knowledge and can give customers detailed information and advice. In some cases, small traders may decide to open an outlet as an extension of their own interest or hobbies, e.g. to sell fishing tackle, motorcycle spares, antiques, photographic or golf equipment or art and craft materials. However, do not be misled into thinking all specialist outlets are small scale – some may operate multiple outlets or quite large stores, especially for popular items such as sports equipment, computers, mobile phones, books or videos (think of Waterstones, PC World or Blockbuster Videos, for example).

The degree of specialisation depends upon the number of potential customers in an area. Therefore, especially in cities or areas which attract certain customers, you may find specialist outlets which operate in a **niche market**. For example, in Manchester the 'High and Mighty' shop specialises in selling clothes for tall men. Males who struggle to find suits or shoes large enough will be quite prepared to travel up to 30 or 40 miles to buy what they want. In some outlying areas you may find shops specialising in aquarium and pond supplies – because people interested in breeding fish will be prepared to travel for specialist advice and supplies. In some seaside areas you will find outlets selling equipment and clothing for yacht/boat owners or surfing enthusiasts. In the Lake District there are outlets specialising in equipment and clothing for climbers.

A likely future trend is for specialist suppliers to advertise their goods over the Internet and supply their goods by mail order. Books are already supplied by this method (by the American company Amazon.com and by Waterstones). This will mean that the physical location of specialist suppliers, particularly those operating in niche markets, will cease to be important. Whether you are interested in coin collecting, building models of helicopters or breeding pigeons, you will be able to obtain all the information and supplies you need through your computer!

Key features

- Specialist outlets sell only one type of product, e.g. ladies' fashions or toys. Those operating in a niche market are even more specialist, e.g. selling clothes for tall women or antique dolls.

- The owners (and staff) of small shops are often enthusiasts who can give specialist advice to their customers.

- Customers will travel many miles for the information and supplies they need.

- Locations which attract particular enthusiasts often have niche market shops, e.g. for surfers, skiers or climbers.

- Some specialist outlets operate on a large-scale, e.g. Toys 'Я' Us and Halfords.

The location of retail outlets

All outlets locate where they will attract customers. Where they locate affects what they sell and how much they sell. The location therefore depends upon the key type of customer for that particular shop or store. There are four main types of location to consider. Below, the main factors to consider are given under each.

Local shops

Local shops depend upon sales to people who live in the area and many also benefit from passing trade. In addition, you have already seen in the previous section that specialist outlets will locate in an area which attracts 'their' type of customer, such as sailing or climbing shops.

Local shops will stock and sell the type of goods it knows its customers want. This is why you will find Kosher and Halal butchers in Jewish and Muslim communities. In village areas you will find shops selling a wider variety of general goods than you may find in a town, simply because one village store may be serving all the needs of the local community. Although local shops cannot utilise the sophisticated customer research methods used by large stores (see page 313), they can keep a close check on popular lines and they often *know* their 'regulars'. This can help them to purchase items which their individual customers want and which fit their lifestyles and income levels.

All local shops benefit if their customers can park nearby, and if they are situated on a main road or in a corner location where they are visible from two directions. They are more likely to benefit from passing trade if they are located near a bus stop or tube station and if there are no other similar suppliers in the locality. Obvious examples include newsagents and fish and chip shops.

Within a local community you are likely to find a group of convenience shops clustered together. This means that customers can buy their groceries and greengroceries, visit the post office and the baker and call into their newsagent or off-licence all on one outing. Whereas these outlets are a boon for people without cars, many of them are struggling to survive because of the growth of supermarkets and out-of-town shopping complexes which sell a greater variety of goods more cheaply.

High street shops

Until the early 1990s there was a boom in out-of-town shopping centres (see below) but these damaged trade in town centres. Fears of 'ghost towns' prompted a change in government policy and local authorities now insist that companies must prove that there is no suitable site in, or near, the town centre before allowing an outlet to locate on the outskirts. This has resulted in a change of policy by large retailers. Tesco has developed its Metro stores, aimed at the people who are working who want fresh vegetables or ready meals. Sainsbury is expanding its Local stores and Asda is looking at 'half-sized' stores to be called Asda Fresh. These smaller supermarkets now only sell a more limited range of goods but open for shorter hours –to coincide with office hours – and do not have car parks attached. This is because many of their customers will be town centre workers who will visit them on foot and shoppers to the area are likely to use a municipal or shopping precinct car park.

However, for all traders who operate within a town centre, location is important. 'Core sites' such as the high street are very popular but side streets and back streets are not – because they don't get the passing trade. It is the main high street where you will find department stores, multiples and other major business outlets, such as building societies and banks. However, core sites are also more expensive (see Unit 2 page 182).

Shopping malls

A modern alternative to the traditional 'high street' is an undercover shopping precinct or shopping mall in the centre of a town, run by a specialist organisation. This has many benefits to shoppers and retailers.

- Shoppers are protected from traffic and bad weather.

- All major retail outlets are in the same place, under one roof, together with service outlets such as coffee and sandwich shops.

- The area is regularly cleaned and is decorated attractively to reflect seasonal variations, such as Christmas.

- The precinct or mall can be secured at night to prevent vandalism and security guards usually patrol unobtrusively during the day. CCTV cameras are also installed as a crime deterrent.

- There is usually a specialist goods delivery area beneath the centre where customers can also collect heavy or bulky purchases and large car parks either on the rooftop or adjacent to the mall.

The problem with such developments in towns and cities is that rents and rates may be high and outlets which are outside the precinct can find their business declines as fewer people walk around the traditional main shopping area. (See also Unit 2, page 171).

Out-of-town shopping centres

Huge shopping complexes have been built in several out-of-town sites in Britain, such as Cribbs Causeway (Bristol), Lakeside (Thorrock), MetroCentre (Gateshead), Merry Hill (Dudley), Trafford Centre (Manchester), Bluewater (Dartford), Braehead (Glasgow) and Meadowhall (Sheffield). These have the same type of attraction for customers as shopping malls – only on a larger scale. There is a wide range of facilities (shops, restaurants, cinemas, cash points), dozens of well-known outlets under one roof, they are near to main roads and/or motorways as well as train stations and provide large, secure parking areas.

Other out-of-town centres concentrate on a group of outlets situated in the same location, often adjacent to a by-pass or ring road. There are likely to be large multiple stores, such as Comet, Dixons, PC World, MFI, DFS and Carpetworld as well as DIY outlets such as B & Q. The reason for their popularity with shoppers is that it is easy to park, prices are competitive and the size of the outlets means a great variety of goods is

on sale. 'Drive-through' take-away outlets may be sited nearby so shoppers can even buy a snack on the way home!

Finally, hypermarkets have traditionally located out of town. All the Asda Supercentres will be located out of town, and Asda's chief, Allan Leighton, is currently considering the idea of a non-food hypermarket which would sell white goods (fridges, washing machines etc.), health and beauty products, clothing, music, videos and snacks. However, he will need planning restrictions on further out-of-town developments to ease first.

Other differences between retail outlets

Retail outlets differ in other ways, besides location. Although particular types of outlets may be similar, you will find individual differences between particular shops and stores. Below is a summary of some of the main areas where you need to compare different outlets. In each case, ask yourself *why* a particular outlet has chosen to operate in a certain way.

Opening hours

The Sunday Trading Act 1994 gave supermarkets and stores the freedom to open on Sundays. The trend spread to town centre shops and by 1999 more than half the shops in Britain were open on a Sunday. In 1997, 24-hour shopping arrived in Britain and by 1999, 63 branches of Tesco opened continuously from Monday morning until Saturday night. Other major superstores have followed. Local convenience stores also open long hours – as in the case of Spar which ran a promotion campaign '8 'til late'. These changes reflect the longer opening hours common in Europe and America and the changing working and shopping habits of their customers. Today, for instance, more women work and want shops to be open in the evening and all weekend. If one supermarket opens longer, then all the rest must do the same or lose business!

These hours contrast with town centre shops which usually open standard 9am to 5.30pm shopping times to reflect office hours when the town is busiest. Local shops may also close for half a day a week (often Saturday afternoon) as well as all day Sunday. It will depend upon the shopping habits of their customers.

Methods of payment

In many large outlets the range of payment methods you may expect to find includes:

- cash

- cheque

- debit card (e.g. Switch)

- credit card (e.g. Mastercard and Visa)

- store cards (e.g. Debenhams, Richards, Marks & Spencer)

- charge cards (e.g. American Express)

- credit facilities, e.g. paying in instalments or hire purchase facilities.

Legally, retailers must accept cash which is 'legal tender'. In England and Wales legal tender means Bank of England notes and coins. However, there is a limit on the number of coins below £1 which have to be accepted.

Cheques are normally accepted provided they are accompanied by a current cheque card. In this case payment up to the amount on the card is guaranteed – regardless of how much money the purchaser has in their account. Cheques are becoming less popular (see Unit 3, page 271) and debit cards more popular. These are 'swiped' and a special slip is issued in duplicate which the customer must sign.

The money is then transferred to the retailer through the banking system (see page 325).

Credit is an additional facility to customers – but is usually only available in outlets selling expensive goods or to encourage multiple purchases. Credit cards are the most popular method. Again the card is 'swiped' but the funds are not transferred from the purchaser's bank account. Instead, payment is made to the retailer by the credit card company and the customer receives a bill which can be paid immediately or over a few months. In this case interest is charged to the customer. The banks also charge the retailers for this service and fees average 1.6 per cent of the transaction cost – amounting to a massive £500 billion paid by retailers each year to banks. For this reason it is cheaper for large retailers to operate their own store card system and many offer incentives to shoppers to use these cards (e.g. 10 per cent discount during particular weeks or free alterations to store card holders). However, interest paid by customers on store cards is usually higher than on standard credit cards.

Figure 5.3 Debit cards are now one of the most common way of paying for goods

A charge card purchase is paid for in a similar way, except that charge card companies expect the purchaser to pay the account in full when it is received, unlike credit card companies.

Credit facilities may include **credit sales**, where the customer pays in instalments to spread out the cost, or **hire purchase**. The difference is a legal one. In a credit sale the goods belong to the customer immediately and if the payments are not made on time the retailer can sue the purchaser for the amount owing. Some clothing shops, furniture stores and electrical goods stores offer this facility. With a hire purchase agreement, ownership is only transferred when the final payment has been made, although there are legal protections for customers who have paid more than a third of the money but cannot keep up the payments. Expensive electronic goods and cars are examples of goods often sold on hire purchase. Hire purchase is usually available if the goods have a second-hand resale value and credit facilities if the goods have no resale value. You might be keen on buying a second-hand car but not so interested in a second-hand coat!

Because of the cost of sophisticated payment systems, such as credit cards, small retailers may only be prepared to accept cash – although some may take cheques from customers known to them. See page 325 for details of electronic payment systems.

Range of goods

You may hear retailers talking about the number of **lines** stocked or the number of lines in a sale. This term refers to the range of different goods which are stocked. This will be influenced by:

- the needs of the key customers
- the amount of storage space
- the capital available for stock
- the amount of display space.

As an example, take a general record/CD shop which stocks a wide variety of records, CDs, tapes and videos. A sample of all the stock must be on display, so that customers know what the shop is selling. If there are multiple copies of the same CD, one copy will be displayed and the remaining stock will be on shelves behind the counter. Decisions have to be made whether to purchase new releases or replenish stock which has been sold. Retailers cannot afford to buy every new release *and* replenish every item which has sold, otherwise they would be moving to larger premises every few years and have too much money tied up in stock. Buying decisions are based on the 'turn round' of an item, that is, how fast it is sold and converted back into cash. A CD gathering dust for two years wouldn't be replaced, whereas a popular one would.

Large supermarkets stocking over 25,000 lines need to make similar decisions. Unpopular lines will be discontinued so that new lines can be stocked – otherwise the store will run out of display space. Decisions are made on how many different brands to stock and in what quantities and in which sizes. Stocks will also vary during the year when extra space must be made for seasonal goods, such as barbecue fuel in summer and crackers at Christmas. Large stores take advantage of EDI (see page 324) to order goods on demand and obtain very speedy deliveries. This reduces the amount of 'back room' storage space required.

Own brands

Own brands are popular because they are seen as good value for money. Large retailers either produce their own brand goods or sub-contract their manufacture to standard producers. So the 'own brand' cornflakes you enjoy may be made by a cornflake producer who makes competing cornflakes!

Some retailers stock virtually all their own brands. Marks & Spencer is the best known. Outlets such as Boots and B & Q sell a mixture of own-brand goods and those produced by other suppliers. Local shops, of course, cannot sell 'own brand' labels, unless they belong to a voluntary group which offers these.

Role of staff

The number of staff and their roles varies from one retail outlet to another. A local store is likely to comprise the owner, his or her family and one or two assistants who may work part-time. Virtually all the major decisions will be made by the owner as to the layout of the store, what goods to buy, what prices to sell the goods, what times to open. The owner will also do much of the paperwork him/herself and pay all the bills.

A large supermarket or chain store, on the other hand, will have a professional manager who reports to a regional manager or director. Specialist staff will be employed within the store, including supervisors, customer service staff, checkout operators and shelf-fillers. Behind the scenes are warehouse staff, stock controllers and clerical staff – dealing with matters such as accounts payments, wages, personnel issues and written complaints. Larger supermarkets offer careers in merchandising, buying, finance, logistics (the movement of goods), store design, marketing and human resources. There will be a greater need for staff training in a very large store or hypermarket which sells a wide variety of goods or specialist products (such as Dixons). Large chain stores and department stores may employ buyers and display or merchandising specialists (see page 318). Careers in retailing usually focus on the type of job roles you can undertake in large organisations.

ACTIVITY

1   Divide into groups of four. Each group should investigate and report on
    a   local shops in one neighbourhood area
    b   the retail outlets in the town centre
    c   a local shopping precinct or shopping mall
    d   an out-of-town shopping area.

    In each case identify the extent to which your findings are similar to, or different from, the explanations on location and other differences between retail outlets on pages 306–311.

2   As a group, discuss how you would tactfully inform a customer that his or her debit card had not been accepted for payment – and what alternatives you would suggest. Bear in mind that this may not mean the card is stolen or the customer has no money – sometimes banks make mistakes!

3   Visit your student services or careers section and investigate careers in retailing. Alternatively, access one of the major supermarket chains on the Internet, e.g. www.tesco.co.uk, or www.asda.com or www.j-sainsbury.co.uk.

4   Ask your tutor if the owner of a small retail outlet and a manager of a larger outlet could visit your group to talk about his or her job and the number of staff employed. Prepare questions beforehand which will give you a better insight into how the role of staff varies between different retail outlets.

Customer incentives

Many surveys have been carried out to discover what customers want from particular outlets. Figure 5.4 shows comparative views from a recent survey and Figure 5.5 shows the main services offered by the large supermarket chains.

	1st choice (%)	2nd choice (%)
Ease of parking	20.5	7
Convenient location	20.5	12
Good value for money	12	9
Low prices	12	24
Good range of products	11	17
Quality 'own label' products	6	4
Clean and tidy store	5	6
High quality products	5	6
Good quality fresh products	5	7
Special 'in-store' promotions	1	3
Helpful staff	1	4
Other	1	1
Adapted from AC Nielsen Homescan Survey		

Figure 5.4 Preferred features in supermarkets

	Tesco	Sainsbury's	Safeway	Asda
Banking services	✔	✔	✔	
Cash machine	✔	✔	✔	✔
Credit card	✔	✔		
Petrol	✔	✔	✔	
Pharmacy	✔	✔	✔	✔
Post office		✔	✔	✔
Dry cleaning		✔	✔	✔
Loyalty card	✔	✔	✔	
Insurance	✔			

Figure 5.5 Services offered by supermarket chains

Retail outlets use a variety of incentives and sales promotion methods to increase sales (see Unit 1, page 78). Specific types of customer incentives used by retail outlets are described below.

Pricing strategies

In 1999 Asda dropped its customer loyalty card (one type of incentive) and replaced it with its Rollback campaign aimed at cutting prices on 4,000 products at a total cost of £200 million. It claimed that research showed customers preferred lower prices to promotional schemes. Cutting prices on selected goods is a pricing strategy used by all the major supermarkets – Tesco has its Value campaign and Morrisons has its Price Mission Plus campaign. This is a strategy which is often used for goods classed as 'price sensitive', i.e. where the customer wants to save money, or as 'loss leaders' to attract people into the store. Conversely, a small shop selling specialist items which are less price sensitive may deliberately sell at a high price to gain a reputation for being 'exclusive' and attract a particular type of customer.

Other common strategies include:

- using 'odd' pricing, e.g. £9.99 and not £10, to denote 'good value'

- having differential pricing (compare the price of Tesco Value goods, Tesco ordinary goods and Tesco Finest goods!)

- operating promotional zones, e.g. baskets of marked-down products to attract customers – often near the door

- holding sales and marking down prices to get rid of end-of-season goods

- offering a money-back guarantee if the goods are found to be on sale locally at a cheaper price within a certain period of time

- promoting a new product with a low introductory price or special offer (e.g. free trial size). The aim is to attract customers to buy a new line – or even attract new customers to a different type of product. The price will be raised once sales are established so that profits are increased.

Discounts

In most retail outlets the price of the goods is fixed. However, discounts are often available on expensive items, such as cars, computers and expensive electronic equipment, particularly for private individuals who pay in cash or by cheque (i.e. they do not require credit terms). In many outlets discounts will not be offered by the retailer but may be available if requested by the customer.

Discounts may be offered when a customer spends a large amount on buying several items. In some cases a retailer may offer to 'throw in' a few extra items for nothing (see also multi-packaging below), such as additional leads or earphones for a CD player, rather than give a discount.

Loyalty schemes

In 1999, Tesco announced it was extending its Clubcard scheme so that customers could obtain discounts on holidays and other items rather than using vouchers for free groceries. The aim of loyalty schemes is to reward regular shoppers – although there is some doubt as to whether this strategy is effective, given that the monetary benefit to the customer is relatively small.

One 'spin off' from loyalty schemes is the amount of data the companies have accumulated about their 'regular' shoppers and their buying habits – known as **precision retailing** or **market basket analysis.** From this they have created highly sophisticated databases which enable them to 'target market' particular customers. For instance, if you are a regular customer you may receive vouchers to give you money off items you frequently or occasionally purchase. This is no coincidence! The database knows exactly what you buy and how often! If you suddenly stop buying, a voucher could be sent to tempt you back (see also page 333).

Sale items

Many non-food retail outlets traditionally hold seasonal sales in January and July to clear out their stock ready for the new season. This also generates more business during times that are quiet, such as after Christmas and during the main holiday season.

Other reasons for goods to be offered at a sale price include:

* to get rid of surplus stock (when too many have been purchased in error)

* to dispose of damaged or shop-soiled items

* to promote one particular item for a limited period, e.g. 'limited special offer'

* to increase sales at other quiet times of the year

* as an incentive to regular customers (large department stores often hold special 'preview sales' evenings by invitation only)

* to sell off stock if the outlet is relocating or closing down.

All retailers have to comply with the Trade Descriptions Act 1987 in the sale of goods, in that the goods must be genuine sale goods. The previous price and the marked down price must both be clearly stated and the product should have been available to consumers at the previous price for at least 28 consecutive days in the previous six months in the shop where they are now on sale. If these conditions cannot be met then any differences must be clearly identified on the sale ticket (see Figure 5.6).

Multi-packaging

One of the most common examples of multi-packaging is a computer – which is often sold with a variety of free software, a mouse,

MID-SUMMER SALE

Sale price £15

Previous price £30

These goods were on sale
at the higher price from
1 – 21 May in this store.

Figure 5.6 A sale ticket

modem and other peripherals to make the whole package more attractive. Other examples include:

- 'buy two, get one free' offers

- free linked products, e.g. free stir fry sauce with any packet of stir fry vegetables, a free ballpoint pen with an A4 lined refill pad

- reduced price offers on linked goods, e.g. half price lipstick with every perfume sold

- multi-packs, e.g. three children's books wrapped together at a special discount price.

Free offers

In addition to the 'buy two, get one free' offers, other promotions may offer an item completely free of charge – provided certain conditions are met. This may involve the purchase of several items and the collection of receipts, vouchers or tokens which are then redeemed for a free item. However, many people stop collecting or forget to redeem what they have collected.

Credit terms

Credit is offered to encourage customers to make expensive purchases (see 310 for the difference between credit sales and hire purchase). Other incentives to take credit include the following.

- Free credit. This means that the customer will not pay any interest charges. This may be advertised as 0% APR. APR stands for the 'annual percentage rate' at which interest is charged. By law, this must be quoted on all credit agreements.

- A credit or payment 'holiday', i.e. 'buy today, pay nothing for 6 months'.

Delivery terms

Outlets which sell large, expensive items, such as furniture stores, normally offer a free delivery service. Stores which sell flat-packed or cheaper priced items, such as IKEA or MFI, usually charge delivery as extra.

Many retail outlets, such as Next, now offer a mail order 'Direct' service for a small delivery charge. Unsuitable goods can often be returned to a local branch. Supermarkets such as Tesco and Sainsbury's, which offer Internet shopping, charge for deliveries.

Customers who work full-time may wish to specify the date and time of delivery or give an alternative address, such as their workplace. Potential customers may be lost if the seller is inflexible about delivery.

After-sales service

After-sales service is important for expensive, durable items, such as cars and washing machines, where there may be a need for maintenance or spare parts. Even in the case of some less expensive products you would expect some help if they have a fault.

After-sales service is covered in Unit 1, page 87. Turn back to that page now and refresh your memory on this topic. (See also page 330.)

ACTIVITY

1 Examine the list of features preferred by customers in Figure 5.4. Note that this was for supermarkets. What features would you add if you were visiting:
   a   a large DIY store
   b   an electronics retailer
   c   a clothing store
   d   a department store?

2 As a group, draw up a checklist for assessing a retail outlet in terms of its features and facilities. Use your information from question 1 above to help you, together with the headings in the section above on customer incentives.

3 In groups of three or four, arrange through your tutor and the outlets concerned a visit to an outlet in each of the retail categories identified on pages 303–306. Assess and compare their facilities using your checklist.

4 Into which retail outlet category would you put each of the following stores? Give a reason for your decision and discuss your ideas with your tutor:
   a   Toys 'Я' Us
   b   Comet
   c   Oasis
   d   Debenhams
   e   B & Q
   f   W H Smith
   g   Waitrose
   h   VG.

5 Many large retailers offer an electronic shopping service – commonly known as **e-commerce**. Tesco launched a chain of cyberzones to provide Net access in its stores when it found that Internet shopping accounted for over 7 per cent of its turnover. Virgin operates www.virginunlimited.com to sell everything from cars and toasters to holidays.

In groups of two or three research at least one Internet shopping site and report back on the range of products you found, the 'user-friendliness' of the site and your opinions on whether this method of shopping will eventually replace the conventional one.

5.2 In-store environment

Every retailer has an image. This is expressed through the surroundings, the layout, the colour schemes, the general impression.

Toys 'Я' Us is young and lively – with a 'stack 'em high and sell it cheap' philosophy. Each store is run to a formula – identical in layout, stock and style. Staff are highly trained to follow set procedures in terms of displaying and selling goods. Debenhams or a high-class furniture store or clothing outlet have more orderly displays, carpeted areas, a quieter atmosphere, older staff. Staff are expected to use their initiative and selling skills to advise customers, particularly over the sale of

Figure 5.7 Toys 'Я' Us store layout

expensive or technical items, providing they do not go against company policy.

Before you start to analyse different outlets yourself, it is important to look at how a particular image is created by an outlet.

Store layout

If you have visited a Toys 'Я' Us store you will notice it is set out like a supermarket. You walk up and down long aisles. You don't do this in Debenhams. This is because these stores have a different type of layout. There are three basic store layouts (see Figure 5.8).

The grid layout

This layout virtually 'steers' customers around a store in a particular way. It is very economical in terms of space. Customers enter by a wall and continue to walk until they meet a vertical or horizontal unit at which point they can turn and move in another direction. You will find this type of layout in Toys 'Я' Us and other discount stores, in supermarkets, greeting card shops, large DIY stores, W H Smith's and Boots stores – and in the food section of Marks & Spencer.

The flow-through layout

This creates a more relaxed atmosphere and encourages customers to browse. You will find this layout used to sell clothes in Debenhams, Marks & Spencer, BHS, Oasis, Burton and Next. It is the main type of layout used by clothing stores, and goods are grouped together to allow customers to circulate between particular displays. There are usually cash points placed at strategic intervals among the displays.

The concessions layout

This is used in department stores which operate 'shops within shops' by offering concessions to particular manufacturers (see page 304). If you walk into the ground floor of a department store such as Debenhams you will usually find many different make-up counters – each operating as a concession. On the next floor you may find ladies' fashions organised in a similar way. Selfridges at Trafford Park made the deliberate decision to sell all ladies' fashions like this.

This layout may also be used to sub-divide the selling area into different product

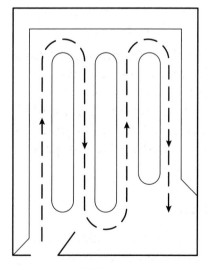
Grid layout

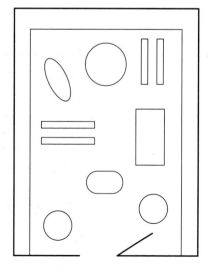
Flow-through layout

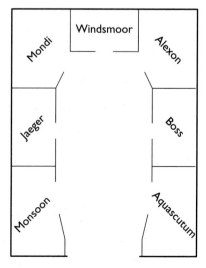
Concessions layout

Figure 5.8 Store layouts

groupings, perhaps for different types of customers. A large book store, for instance, could divide its selling space into fiction, non-fiction, special interest and children's books – and create a different atmosphere in each particular area.

Types of display

There are two basic rules about retail selling.

- The most valuable space in any outlet is 'selling' space. This is where goods are displayed. 'Sales per square foot' is an important measure of an outlet's success.

- Goods left in the stockroom don't sell – because customers don't know they are on sale. There is also little point in having a major display if very few of the items are in stock.

What products to display, where and how to display them are major decisions as they will have a direct impact on the quantity of goods sold. Displays are often called **visual merchandising** – as they are using the merchandise available to create a visual impact for shoppers (see also merchandising, page 318).

Displaying goods effectively is therefore a major method of promoting goods. In particular it makes items more desirable and encourages impulse buying. There are several types of display you will see in retail outlets, including:

- life-style displays
- coordinated displays
- theme displays
- speciality displays.

Life-style displays

Look at the pictures of students in any college prospectus and they look lively, happy, interested and surrounded by friendly people. The message is that you, too, will be happy if you study at this college; you will mix with great people and make lots of friends. This type of advertising is selling you a course of study, and a particular lifestyle.

Many commercial advertisers use this technique. Car manufacturers are renowned for it – advertisements targeted at young men show an attractive male driver and female companion, often in picturesque surroundings. Those targeting young women promote independence and a free spirit.

Retailers use the same technique. Products are linked to a lifestyle. The simplest way of doing this is to put the items in front of a large lifestyle graphic, e.g. beach wear in front of a picture of a cruise liner or mobile phones placed strategically around a graphic of young, busy people or executives on the move.

Coordinated displays

Look around any department store (or just in the windows) and you will find a number of coordinated displays. These consist of a number of 'linked' products, e.g. a television with lounge suite and integrated audio system, a bathroom display with towels, fittings, shower robes, toiletries, bed linen with coordinated wallpaper, lampshades and curtains. In each case the aim is to display products which would go together.

Retailers also use colour-coordination to assist product identification, when a group of products are related in some way. For instance, the Marks & Spencer 'Count on Us' low fat ready meals and Tesco Value products are all colour coordinated so that shoppers recognise them easily.

Theme displays

Goods can be linked by a particular theme. Some themes are seasonal. In February it may be the theme of Valentine's Day. In March, Mother's Day, in October Hallowe'en. A country might be a theme – a supermarket has a French week (cheese, wine, paté etc.) and then a Spanish week (wine, pasta, paella). Popular films are also used – *Titanic* and *Star Wars* were used in the late 1990s to group related products.

Speciality displays

A paint and paper shop may sell coordinated furnishings displayed against various wallpapers. A garden centre which specialises in lawnmowers and garden equipment may display these prominently.

These displays usually focus on a particular type of product the outlet wants to promote. The products may not be sold by many of its competitors. For example, a department store with a food hall may have window or in-store displays of fine food or wines.

Merchandising products and special displays

Imagine you have to display all the products in a new supermarket. You have an empty

area the size of two football pitches and a storeroom full of products. Where will you start?

This is the sort of problem faced by special display or merchandising teams employed by major chain stores and supermarkets. The aim of merchandising is to bring the products to the attention of shoppers – in the right quantity and in the right place at the right time. A **planogram** is usually devised for each store using a specialist software package, which takes account of the range of stock, the 'image' of the store, the size and weight of items, links between product groups and the profit margin on different types of goods. The aim is to maximise selling space and so maximise profits.

Special fittings will be installed so that goods can be displayed appropriately. The type of fittings will vary – from rails in a clothing store to wire baskets in a DIY outlet to browsers in a record shop and hooks for small packets of accessories. Most stores display goods on **gondolas** – free-standing units with shelves of different depths. These can be joined together to form a grid layout.

The number of items displayed horizontally is known as the number of **facings**. The most popular lines will be allocated the greatest number of facings, e.g. Coca-Cola 10, Pepsi-Cola 8, Virgin Cola 6. Manufacturers and visiting merchandisers (representing these organisations) will pressure stores to increase the number of facings for their product. Some offer a greater discount on purchases to stores which give them a large number of facings in a prime position.

Here are some 'tricks of the trade' used by retailers.

- Just below eye level is the optimum placement for popular lines.

- Items are blocked vertically on a shelf, with the most popular lines just below

Figure 5.9 Special window displays attract customers

eye level, those sold less frequently at the bottom and the slowest selling at the top.

- High demand items are placed at the back of the store so that customers are tempted past higher-price impulse lines, e.g. cosmetics and toiletries.

- The small top or bottom end of a long gondola will be used for 'special displays' – and goods here sell very quickly.

- Some everyday products will be placed near the door to start customers buying early.

- Confectionary, tobacconist and newspaper (CTN) areas are sited near the door so customers can call in just for these items. Sandwiches are often found in the same area.

- The aisle width between low profit, staple items will be narrower than between items with a higher profit margin. Narrow aisles tempt customers to move on quickly (e.g. past the baked beans) and wider aisles enable them to slow down (e.g. past wine or CDs).

- Large and heavy goods are placed near the exit – so customers don't fill their trolleys too quickly. So are frozen goods, so they don't defrost too quickly.

- Displays are placed in **hot spots**, i.e. busy areas, unless there is a deliberate strategy to tempt customers to a **cold spot** area which they normally ignore.

- Like products and related products are grouped together for convenience and to encourage 'add-on' buying, e.g. pasta and pasta sauce.

- Merchandise is moved around according to the seasons and to encourage impulse buying, e.g. barbecue fuel near the entrance in summer.

- Merchandise may be displayed differently to suit regional buying habits. So the planogram for a large multiple may differ for particular areas of the country.

- All goods on display must be clean and undamaged. Any goods being sold off must be put into a special display or in a bargain basket.

Once the goods have been set up by the display team this is maintained by store staff responsible for replenishing the stock regularly. Another name for this is **functional merchandising**. Stock is always **rotated** so that the oldest stock is sold first. Adjustments must be made for new lines and space allocated for these. In some cases this is created by selling off unprofitable lines (see page 313). Generally, products are moved around as little as possible in stores where customers see shopping as a chore, e.g. supermarkets, as they get irritated if they cannot find the products they want. Customers are less sensitive to changes in stores where shopping is seen as pleasurable, e.g. clothing outlets

Special displays

These can include:

- seasonal promotions, e.g. displays of sunglasses in summer on rotating stands

- manufacturers' displays, e.g. display stands for batteries or toothbrushes specially designed to hold every option (alternative) available

- point-of-sale displays, e.g. crisps or sweets near to checkouts

- impulse displays, e.g. special luggage locks displayed in a store selling suitcases

- operational displays, e.g. toys being demonstrated in a toy store

Figure 5.10 Mass displays attract the attention of shoppers

- mass displays of similar items, e.g. a display of books by a particular author in a bookshop.

Signposting

The aim of merchandising is to make goods easily available and easily found. This is achieved first by good displays and second by clear signposting. The type of signposting used will depend on the layout of the store and whether the store is self-service, assisted service (e.g. a multiple store) or whether personal sales staff are employed. Self-service stores need the most signposting, to help customers find what they want. General information about the location of items is on signs, and more detailed product information is given on tickets.

Signs

- Department stores have a 'directory' close to the entrance and by all lifts and escalators to show which goods are sold on which floor.

- Supermarkets, hypermarkets and mini-supermarkets have large signs hanging from the ceiling. These show the items sold at either side of each aisle.

- Smaller outlets have signs above particular displays. A record shop will label its browsers, as will a greetings card shop.

- Signs are also needed to identify customer facilities, e.g. changing rooms, customer service desk, coffee shop etc.

- Signs may also be used as a promotional aid. For instance, Tesco advertises its 'free computers for schools campaigns' with large promotional signs throughout the store.

Tickets

- Tickets are placed in front of goods giving key information. This may simply state the product or may give specific instructions, e.g. 'please check batch numbers are the same on all items'.

- Tickets may also **substitute** for goods. In many DIY stores, power tools are secured to the shelf and the customer takes a ticket giving the item code to the checkout instead of the item itself.

- Tickets should show the price of the item and a description, unless each item is priced individually.

- Tickets may also identify the number of facings for an item – although this is not known to the customer. This is often written in pencil so that it can be changed. Alternatively it may be identified on a bar code on the ticket or by the spacing between tickets.

Different kinds of checkout and counters

Positioning

Most outlets with a grid layout, such as supermarkets, have checkouts at the end of the grid so that customers automatically pass through the checkout at the end of their shopping. This maximises their opportunities to buy goods and is also a security measure. It is difficult to leave the store without going through a checkout! Most supermarkets have at least one 'rapid checkout' for baskets only – often situated near the CTN section.

An outlet with a flow-through layout will locate its cash points strategically at various points throughout the store. They are often sited so that customers have to walk past displays of merchandise to get to them, which encourages impulse buying.

An outlet with a concession layout will have cash points at each concession area – as each concession retains its own takings and pays the store holder rental for the site.

In both these cases the varied siting of cash points is convenient, as most shoppers in a large store who want to buy a specific item or two prefer to pay for it at a counter nearby. It also helps staff to keep track of items which are sold in their own department.

A small convenience store has two aims in mind when it positions its checkout – security and space. It will therefore usually site the counter near the door (to deter shoplifters), with valuable items (e.g. spirits and cigarettes) behind the counter. The counter is often placed near a wall and in a position giving the owner a good view of the shop as a whole – sometimes with the aid of close-circuit television.

Quantity

Except for the concession type, all outlets have to decide how many checkouts or cash points are needed – and how many should be operating at any particular time. The aim is to make sure there are enough cash points to minimise queuing – without wasting space or having staff doing nothing! There are sophisticated computer techniques to calculate the optimum number of cash points, and most stores have extra cash points or checkouts which only operate during busy periods.

Design

A store with a flow-through layout or which offers an assisted or personal service to customers will normally have counters. There must be enough counter space for folding and wrapping the items being sold. Below the counter there must be storage space for bags, carriers and other packaging materials. Counters must be wide enough to accommodate the number of staff employed at the cash point without being so wide as to take up too much valuable selling space. Special rails may be installed to encourage customers to queue at a particular side to maximise flow-through.

Checkouts in supermarkets and many self-service stores are usually self-contained areas with the operator comfortably seated. They are ergonomically designed to minimise unnecessary movement and to allow all the main operations to be within easy reach. This enables the checkout operator to process the items as quickly as possible and minimises bending and stretching. Most checkouts have a conveyor belt mechanism controlled by the operator to move the items along for processing. In a supermarket or DIY store the width between checkouts must be sufficient for the widest trolley to pass through. There must be space for customers to queue – so there has to be a space between the last display of goods and each cash point.

Security is important in all stores – not just in small convenience shops. For instance, plastic guards are often fitted on the cash drawer to prevent 'snatch and grab' crimes. Security is covered on page 338.

Customer amenities and customer comfort

The amenities that enhance the shopping experience depend on the type of outlet and whether the shopping trip is functional (e.g. a food store) or pleasurable (e.g. a clothing store). They depend on the key customer, his/her age range and the 'exclusivity' of the store.

Customer amenities include all the additional services customers may require, such as a creche, baby changing rooms, coffee shops, restaurants, toilet areas, cash machines, parking areas. There may also be an adjacent petrol station, assistance with packing and/or

Figure 5.11 Restaurants are a feature of many large outlets

carrying goods and rapid checkouts. There may be different trolleys to suit the needs of older people, families and people buying very large items. Car parks may be designed with extra wide spaces for family cars. Outlets without an adjacent car park may offer a 'collect by car' service.

In exclusive outlets there is less focus on speed. A more personal service is provided. There may be deep pile carpets and greater spaces between displays to encourage unhurried browsing. In clothes shops there may be spacious changing areas, seating, and partners may be offered coffee or tea while the shopper tries on a selection of outfits. There may be a concierge who will keep packages for collection later. There may be an alterations service – free to regular customers.

Heating, lighting and background music

Heating and lighting are key factors in outlets. If the outlet is too hot or too cold shoppers may cut short their visit. There should be appropriate heating in winter and air conditioning in summer.

Bright lighting is used in superstores so customers can clearly see the goods. Some areas may have different lighting for effect, e.g. pink for the in-store fresh meat area. Smaller outlets with big display windows can utilise natural light more effectively. This is very important in fabric and clothes shops for seeing colours in natural light. Lighting may be more subdued in specialist outlets and particular displays may be illuminated for effect. In a jeweller's shop, for instance, spotlights are used to intensify the brilliance of diamonds and other precious stones. In changing rooms, lighting is likely to be more subtle – and mirrors angled – to make the wearer look good. Coloured lights can be used effectively, especially in outlets whose key customers are young people. At Christmas, most outlets have coloured lights and appropriate music. Background music is used at other times to 'mask' unacceptable background noises, to avoid silence and to help shoppers relax. It is likely to be more muted in general outlets and livelier in 'young' outlets. Some stores play more upbeat music at weekends than during weekdays! Record stores will often play popular music or new releases to tempt customers to buy that particular music.

Many outlets try to appeal to all our senses. Smell is very important in some cases. The smell of freshly baked bread in a supermarket can attract shoppers to the bakery area to buy. The fragrance of perfume from the cosmetics area has the same effect. Touch is also part of the buying process – a customer who picks up an item is usually part way to making a purchase. Tasting sessions are held in many food stores to tempt customers to buy what is being sampled – cheese or pizza or wine.

Corporate image

Apart from what has already been discussed the image of an outlet is influenced by other factors.

- The type of building – compare a modern out-of-town supermarket structure with a small antique shop in an historic area of a town.

- The shop front – and the size of the windows. In markets and shopping precincts some outlets, such as greengrocers and cut-price stores, will have open fronts with displays on the pavement.

- The **fascia** (the board above the window). Many convenience stores use branded fascias – produced by a manufacturer or wholesaler to advertise particular products

Figure 5.12 The fascia helps convey the image

– because they are free. Look in your own town for examples of those provided by manufacturers such as Carlsberg or Cadbury's. Other outlets prefer to have their own fascia professionally designed. The design of the fascia (including the colour and lettering) helps to promote the image. Unless the outlet is well-known it is essential to give details of the trade carried out as well as the name of the store.

- The materials used inside the outlet, e.g. flooring can be wood, carpet, tiles or a mixture of these to signify different areas.

- The size of the interior and the degree of 'spaciousness'. The more cluttered an outlet the more 'down market' it will appear.

- The quality of the fixtures and fittings.

- The number of staff available to give personal assistance when required.

- The price of the goods on sale.

 ## ACTIVITY

I Visit sales outlets in your town and list the different types of display fittings you see. Try to find at least one example of:

a   wall shelving and wall hooks

b   gondolas at the end of a display

c   free-standing gondolas you can walk around

d   browsers

e   spinners which allow purchasers to rotate a display

f   glass-topped or glass-fronted display cases

g   chilled cabinets.

In each case identify the type of products which is displayed and compare your findings with other members of your group.

2   Divide into three groups. Group A is opening a cut-price clothes outlet for teenagers. Group B is opening a mid-range clothing outlet for men and women aged between 16 and 35. Group C is opening a top-priced outlet selling expensive yet trendy children's and baby clothes. In each case decide how you would design your outlet – both inside and outside. Be prepared to justify your decisions. Now present your ideas to your tutor and the rest of your group – and compare the results.

3   Visit a shopping complex, a large store or a shopping area near your home or college.

a   Critically assess the displays you see in shop windows and in-store. Select three displays you like and say why, in each case. Then select three displays which think are less effective and say why.

b   During your visit identify two examples of each type of store layout shown on page 316. Bear in mind that some outlets have a mixture of layouts in different areas. In such cases say why you think the layout changes and then check if other aspects change as well, such as the flooring or lighting.

5.3 Retail selling technology

Retail selling has been transformed over the last 10 to 15 years by new technology. This has speeded up transactions at cash tills and vastly increased the ability of retail outlets to assess stock requirements and replace stock quickly and easily. The following summarises the main developments.

Electronic point of sale (EPOS)

These systems enable:

*   information on the quantity of stock sold to be recorded electronically

*   stock sold to be matched against existing stock levels, for later analysis by store managers and executives

*   automatic stock re-order lists to be produced

*   prices to be stored automatically through a PLU (price look up) facility

*   till receipts to be printed containing product descriptions and price, as well as personalised or promotional messages.

A simple EPOS system may be used in a small outlet. Codes are stored in the cash register and these automatically identify the product and price when a sale is made. A more sophisticated system is operated by large superstores and linked to a bar code reader (see below). Fully itemised till receipts are issued. The insertion of any type of loyalty card will also update sales information against that particular customer – and will be used to inform the customer database (see pages 313 and 333).

Electronic data interchange (EDI)

EDI is a system for buying stock by computer. Orders are sent from the buyer to the seller by computer. Because orders are processed very quickly, EDI reduces the amount of stock that needs to be held and this reduces storage costs. Some buyers also produce their own invoices which they send to the supplier. Payment is also made by computer. Specific terminals are nominated as payment terminals and access is available only by means of a special 'smart card' and a personal security code. The payment computer communicates with the banks so that money is transferred immediately from the purchaser's bank to the supplier's bank. A computerised acknowledgement is also sent to the supplier's computer. Most large superstores use EDI. Tesco claims that 95 per cent of its orders and 60 per cent of its invoices are transmitted as EDI messages. This is linked to its EPOS system so that computerised terminals register the sales and this information is converted into orders sent to their suppliers via EDI.

Bar code readers

Bar code readers come in various forms. There are 'light pens', hand-held laser scanners and counter-sunk bar code readers. In each case the device reads the series of bars which identifies a particular product. Below each bar is a number. Most bar codes comprise 13 digits (see Figure 5.13) but some suppliers use fewer numbers – particularly if they produce all their own goods. Marks & Spencer uses a 7-digit code; smaller products are also often given an 8-digit code.

Figure 5.13 Understanding a bar code

Bar code readers can be linked to an EPOS system and the system programmed so that the bar code generates an item description and price. The advantages of this includes:

- rapid processing of goods at checkouts

- greater accuracy (fewer mistakes are made using readers than keying in digits)

- no requirement to price individual items on display

- price changes can be implemented quickly and easily.

The disadvantages are:

- damaged bar codes cannot be identified by a reader and have to be interpreted by the operator

- missing bar code labels cause hold-ups whilst the operator checks the price.

One of the latest developments is a type of magnetic tag. Each tagged item can be scanned, even if it is in a box of mixed goods. In warehouses this means that cartons don't have to be unpacked for goods to be scanned into a stock system. For retail sales it is likely to mean being able to pack your goods into a box which you then put through a scanner which automatically produces your bill. In five or ten years' time it may be goodbye to checkouts and goodbye to bar codes!

Electronic funds transfer systems (EFT)

EFT has revolutionised the way in which shoppers pay for the goods they have purchased. Under EFT systems the customer offers a debit card in payment – Barclays operate a Delta system and other banks operate the Switch system. The card is swiped through a terminal at the checkout or cash point and the amount owed is transferred electronically from the customer's bank account to the retailer's account. The customer has to sign a voucher to validate the transaction. Customers who hold a Switch card can also be offered a 'cashback' facility, currently up to £50. The customer may be asked to initial or sign the cashback entry on the till receipt, as an additional security measure.

Advantages include:

- less need for customers and retailers to carry large sums of cash

- money always available for 'impulse' purchases (providing the bank account is in credit)

- more rapid processing at the checkout than writing a cheque

- no danger of non-payment – if the customer has no funds in the account then the transaction will not be allowed.

ACTIVITY

1   Identify the benefits for customers who shop at a store which uses sophisticated retail selling technology. You should be able to list at least **ten** points.

2   Now repeat this exercise, but this time list the advantages from the viewpoint of the staff who work in the outlet.

Compare both your lists with those made out by your fellow-students.

5.4 Selling skills

Self-service has grown in popularity because it maximises space for selling, minimises staff costs in relation to total sales and therefore increases profitability. For the customer it is quick and easy.

However, for the selling of many goods sales people are essential. They may be needed simply to give information on the range of products available or on their features, as in the case of multiples. Personal selling skills are crucial however in outlets which specialise in highly technical products or expensive durable items. If you are buying a car, a computer or a fitted kitchen then you don't want to make a mistake. You need accurate technical advice as well as guidance on the product which most suits *your* particular needs. Some sales people are excellent. They know exactly when to help and when to leave you alone. They know what they are talking about. They can give you useful advice, helpful tips and assist you make the best decision. To do the job well needs certain skills and knowledge.

Pre-sales training

New staff are usually trained before they can deal with customers. In outlets selling very expensive or highly technical products this training is likely to be extensive. Carphone Warehouse staff, for instance, are trained intensively and must take an internal test before they can start selling to customers. Even stores selling more basic products often stay open late one day a week for 'staff training'. This is often an updating session on the latest products in stock and their features.

Pre-sales training is likely to consist of information on:

- product range, features and benefits of different items

- customer needs – and how to match products to customers

- customer policies – e.g. 'returns' policy, delivery charges, after-sales service

- selling skills.

Staff will also be taught the importance of appearance, tone of voice and body language. No-one wants assistance from a scruffy, loud-mouthed individual who approaches them with a yawn or a swagger!

Product range and product knowledge

Without good product or merchandise knowledge you cannot advise a customer about the best purchase to make. You will need to know:

- the goods which are normally kept in stock during the year

- which seasonal lines are stocked – and over what periods

- where particular goods are to be found in the store

- the price of individual items and the price ranges of particular types of products

- the variations that are available (e.g. colour, sizes, models, additional features, possible 'add-ons')

- the key selling features of each product

- the different uses of each product

- the delivery time for products currently out-of-stock

- how to advise on care and maintenance

- what after-sales service is available.

Identifying customer needs

A sales person's purpose is to help customers make decisions as to what meets *their needs*. What suits one person may not suit another. There are several key factors that have to be considered.

- **Price range/budget.** Most customers have a budget. It is no use recommending an ideal product the customer cannot afford.

- **Fashion/durability.** Young customers often want an item which is high fashion and are less interested in durability. Older customers may be less interested in fashion and more keen on reputation and reliability.

- **Performance/features**. High performance and additional features usually cost money. Sometimes a purchasing decision is a compromise between the ideal and what can be afforded.

- **Specific requirements**. A customer buying a table may need it to fit a certain space, a customer buying a carpet may need it to match an existing colour scheme or be hard-wearing because it will be placed in a frequently used area.

- **Personal circumstances.** A person living alone is unlikely to be interested in a large chest freezer, whereas someone with a large family may see this as a necessity!

Figure 5.14 The saleperson should explain how the product suits the needs of the customer

Matching products to customers

Sales people need to be able to identify the products that match a customer's requirements.

Some customers know nothing about the product they want and expect to be given all the information they need. This should be available in printed form so that 'just-looking' customers can take the information home. Those obviously not yet ready to buy should never be pressurised, as this may put them off buying from the outlet. Instead, sales staff should make sure they have everything they need to tempt them to return at a later date.

Other customers know exactly what they want. These are the easiest sales to make – providing the item is in stock. However, a good salesperson will make sure the customer has no misconceptions about the item – and that it can perform according to expectations. It may be the customer is not aware of other appropriate or better alternatives and these can be discussed, together with their comparative benefits.

Customers who are indecisive may be the most difficult. This is when the ability to assess customer needs and link the benefits of a product to those is invaluable. Sales staff should avoid confusing the customer by giving too many options at once and should take time to discover what the customer really wants.

Remember that it is only sales staff with good product knowledge and who take time to establish a customer's needs who can successfully match the right product to a particular person.

Selling the product

There are five steps to making a sale, each of them described below.

Step 1 – Opening the sale

Greet customers with a smile and a friendly greeting. 'May I help you?' is fairly standard – but often unsuccessful. It can frighten off people who are just looking. It's better to give customers time to look around and then approach them by commenting positively on the item (or items) they are looking at. Don't take a refusal for help personally. Reassure the customer, 'That's fine – but if you want to know anything please don't hesitate to ask me.' Keep one eye on the prospective buyer until you see them looking for assistance and then move forwards. You can usually tell this from their body language – instead of looking at the products the customer will be looking around for a sales person.

If you look friendly, personable and positive, then people will be more willing to approach you than if you 'crowd' them or appear too pushy.

Step 2 – Explaining benefits

Two golden rules. Never 'rubbish' a product (if it is rubbish, then why are you stocking it?) and never 'rubbish' a competitor (it's unprofessional). Instead *always* be positive. First, indicate the range of goods and find out which are within the customer's budget. A customer may clearly state how much they expect to pay – or you may have to 'sense' this from their reaction when you state various prices. Whatever you do, don't say 'How much can you afford?' The tactful version is, 'What price range were you thinking of?'

You can sometimes persuade a customer to spend more if there are clear benefits attached to a better version. However, it is important that you are ethical (look up this word!) and *never* deliberately mislead a customer into spending more for no good reason. Also, never make customers feel inferior because they can only afford a lower priced item.

Step 3 – Handling questions

This is where your product knowledge becomes invaluable! Answer honestly. If you don't know the answer to a question then say so – and then find out. If you are not sure about the technical features of a product then ask someone else to help the customer – and listen! If you do not sell an item that will meet the customer's needs then admit it – and advise the customer of an alternative source. Most customers will thank you for being honest with them – and remember you the next time they want something.

If you are selling a highly technical product then explain it in terms the customer will understand. Talking to a non-computer specialist and using jargon such as 'hard drive', 'cache memory' and 'bits per second' is meaningless.

Remember that a demonstration can be invaluable – you cannot describe 'quality of sound' for instance, but demonstrating the quality of a superb audio system might be enough to make the sale. If possible, let the customer handle the item – touching an item often helps convince a potential buyer of its quality.

Step 4 – Offering alternatives

If the customer hesitates, don't give up on the sale. Think carefully about other alternatives – and try to find out the reason for the hesitation. This is a clear barrier to the sale. Barriers may include price, size, colour, type of material, a bad experience with a similar item or an item from the same manufacturer, a bad report from a friend or poor timing (e.g. 'But we won't have room for it until the new extension is complete.')

A key phrase for most sales people is **overcoming objections**. This involves first finding out if the customer has any reservations which may prevent a sale. Some customers will voice their doubts outright, others will not. Good sales staff will know the main reasons why many customers hesitate – and will make sure they deal with these in certain ways, e.g. 'It's ideal as it's washable and doesn't need dry cleaning' or 'You can use it inside or outside as it's specially coated to be weatherproof.'

If the hesitation concerns the product or manufacturer then there may be other options to offer. You may be able to order a different model or show a range from other makers. A more senior member of staff may be able to make some useful suggestions if you run out of ideas or if you cannot think how to meet the customer's particular needs.

Don't offer dozens of alternatives, one after the other – this is confusing. 'Fine-tune' your suggestions to the customer's needs and discuss each option properly before moving on to the next. Remove rejected items so that the selling area stays free from clutter. If the customer still cannot decide but wants 'to think about it' then don't object. If you stay positive and helpful the customer may well return to buy the item later.

Step 5 – Closing the sale

This is the final stage of the process. Experienced staff move the discussion towards this point throughout the selling process and recognise when they reach it. One sign is when the customer asks questions about delivery, guarantees, after-sales service or credit facilities. The customer has moved on from assessing whether the product is suitable to other aspects of the purchase. They might ask if they can have a discount for cash. If the sale is for a large amount you should consult a supervisor, unless you know that the policy is to never give discounts.

If the customer is satisfied with the answers to the questions there is likely to be a

Figure 5.15 The sale has been made

decision. At this point the transaction details need to be concluded. This may mean wrapping the item and taking the money or arranging for delivery and credit facilities.

ACTIVITY

1 Select any product of your choice and gather information about it by visiting a variety of outlets and obtaining literature and asking questions yourself. Try to note the sales person's attitude and responses and identify which approaches you find helpful and which you do not.

2 Discuss with your tutor the following sales techniques and how they can be used.
   a 'Selling up' – where you identify the opportunity to sell a higher priced item.
   b 'Open questioning' – to find out information on customer needs if the customer is reticent.
   c Converting negative responses to positive selling points.

   d 'Substitution selling' – when the required item is not stocked or not currently in stock.
   e 'Related sales' – selling appropriately linked products after the first sale has been concluded.

3 Divide into pairs. One person should identify a product and then both write down as many possible objections to a sale as they can think of (without comparing at this stage). The second person now tries to sell the product and to overcome as many unspoken objections, or barriers, as possible. Score 'A' if the first person has no objections left at the end of the sale. Score 'B' if the first person has had to identify his/her own objections – but these have been overcome successfully. Score 'C' if there are still barriers which have not been overcome and the sale would therefore not be made. Then reverse roles.

4 Select any everyday item in your classroom (chair, table, whiteboard etc.) and spend five minutes listing the benefits. Then take turns at trying to 'sell it'.

5 Divide into pairs. One of you is the customer and the other the sales person (then you will reverse roles). Select one of the following products to buy/sell, research it properly (if you own one bring it to class to demonstrate) and follow all the stages above. Both your fellow student and your tutor should evaluate your performance.
   a An electric toothbrush
   b A digital answering machine
   c A mini disk player
   d A mobile phone
   e A pair of expensive trainers
   f A hairdryer
   g An electric shaver.

After-sales service

After-sales service was covered in detail in Unit 1, pages 87–88, under customer service.

The information below supplements this. So before you read it, check to make sure you remember the key points relating to after-sales service covered in Unit 1.

For this unit you also need to know:

- how to handle complaints
- how to handle exchanges of goods and refunds
- how to capture customer details to enhance future selling opportunities
- about warranties and guarantees.

Handling complaints

In many large stores complaints are handled by specially trained customer service staff. In smaller outlets the sales staff need to be able to deal with a customer making a complaint. In a large outlet a customer may complain to one of the sales staff.

Most retail outlets have a complaints procedure. This states how staff should deal with complaints. It is important that you know this and abide by it.

Figure 5.16 Be patient and listen to complaints

Complaints fall into two broad categories. There are complaints over minor issues which can usually be quickly resolved. Then there are complaints about major issues, some of which lead to customers taking legal action against the outlets involved.

Basic complaints

Typical examples are complaints about:

- location of goods (not being able to find a product)
- the price of an item (e.g. a price increase since last week)
- goods being out-of-stock or not available for some reason
- faulty goods or goods found to be damaged or with a part missing
- the attitude or behaviour of staff
- poor facilities (e.g. lack of trolleys or long queues at checkouts).

Information on how to handle this type of complaint is given below.

Serious complaints

These include:

- unsafe conditions that resulted in a customer having an accident
- a claim that food purchased contained a foreign object or caused illness
- a claim that an unsafe product caused injury
- serious allegations about a member of staff (e.g. swearing at a customer, drunkenness, fraud etc.).

Serious complaints must be reported to a senior member of staff immediately – if possible while the customer is still on the premises. If the customer has telephoned with a serious complaint then take full details of his/her name and address and telephone number. It is important that you remain non-committal, but explain that you are passing on the complaint to someone senior. Do not agree with the customer or in any way imply that your employer must be in the wrong. At this stage you do not know the facts, so you cannot form any judgements.

Handling standard complaints

There are golden rules for doing this.

- Listen carefully to the customer describing the problem. Make notes if necessary. If the customer is irate do *not* interrupt. Wait for the customer to 'run out of steam'.

- Apologise to the customer for the inconvenience he or she has been caused (this does not mean you are accepting responsibility).

- Either rectify the situation yourself (see below) or, if this is not possible, inform someone senior and reassure the customer that action will be taken.

- If there is a sensible explanation for the problem (e.g. you are genuinely short-staffed that day which is why there is a lack of trolleys) then explain the reason to the customer. But then inform your supervisor so that action can be taken.

- Record the complaint in the complaints log. Managers can use this information to monitor complaints in an effort to continually improve services and supplies and reduce further complaints.

Rectifying the situation

There is often two stages in this process. The first is satisfying the customer who is complaining. The second is preventing further complaints about the same thing.

This would apply in the following cases.

- Location of goods – first, direct the customer yourself or (better still) take the customer to where the goods are to be found. Then check your signposting to see if it can be improved.

- Out-of-stock/unavailable goods – these can be ordered if no other suitable products are stocked. Or you can check if the items are due to be delivered and inform the customer when they will be in stock or arrange to telephone the customer when they arrive. Another option is to direct the customer to an outlet which you know *does* stock the item. If you are constantly being asked for the same thing then your manager will also want to know so that the supplier can be contacted and the item regularly stocked from now on.

- Poor services – reassure the customer you will report the matter immediately – and do so.

- A minor complaint against other staff – stay neutral and take the details. Make sure your supervisor is aware of the complaint but do not report this verbally in front of other customers or staff.

- Faulty products – follow the procedures laid down in your company's returns policy (see below).

Handling exchanges of goods and refunds

All retail outlets have a refund policy (see Unit 1, page 87). If goods are broken or faulty then the retailer has a legal obligation to replace the item or, if the customer prefers, to give a refund. While some outlets may ask that customers produce a receipt this is not legally essential, provided that some other proof of purchase can be provided, e.g. a credit or debit card slip or a bank statement.

The situation is more complicated if the item sold is installed in the customer's home, as in the case of a television, washing machine or bathroom suite. In such cases the firm may send someone to visit the customer to assess the problem before discussing alternatives such as a repair or monetary compensation.

Some organisations have more liberal policies than others and will exchange any item if the purchaser changes his/her mind. This prevents complaints and usually generates sales as customers are more likely to buy something if they know it can be returned if it isn't appropriate. However, many retail stores, such as Marks & Spencer, which operate such a policy will only refund in cash if the customer paid in cash. If the goods were bought by credit card then a credit voucher is issued instead. This is to prevent people buying goods using a credit card and then immediately returning them to obtain cash as a refund!

The most difficult complaints are those made by buyers about an item some time after they purchased it. If the item is damaged this may arouse suspicion that the customer is responsible for it. The company's policy on such claims needs to be checked. In the case of expensive items you need to refer difficult problems to your supervisor. With cheaper goods, many outlets now replace the item as a matter of policy rather than risk losing a customer – and their own reputation.

Capturing customer details

As you already know (page 324), large stores operating a sophisticated EPOS system can capture customer details on each transaction that is made. The main reason for introducing loyalty cards was to gather information on customers so that they could be sent details of special offers and new developments. Those with store cards also receive such mailshots. Some stores also use video cameras linked to computers to monitor buyer behaviour. Savacentres and Boots use videos in large stores to measure the percentage of people who actually buy something. From the videos an outlet can check the length of queues, the number of people who pick up an item and put it back again, the items which sell and those which don't, those displays which attract customers and those which don't.

However, videos only provide general information on customers. They don't provide specific details – and many smaller retail outlets obviously don't operate national loyalty schemes. However, they may also keep a database of regular customers so that they can send them details of special offers, forthcoming sales, new lines etc. This means capturing the customer's name and address at least. If the store operates a delivery service then this information will be collected when the transaction is being completed. If the item is portable, then the customer must be

Figure 5.17 A camera can help to monitor the behaviour of customers

asked for the information. It is usual to do this after the transaction has been completed. The sales assistant explains the benefits to the customer (invitations to pre-sale previews etc.) and gives the customer the option of providing further details. This information is then recorded on computer so that the customer is included when mailshots about forthcoming promotions are sent.

Warranties and guarantees

A guarantee or a warranty is an agreement by the manufacturer of a product to repair or replace any parts which are defective, free of charge, within a specific period of time after purchase. No guarantee can overrule the customer's rights under consumer law. A guarantee only *adds* an additional benefit. A standard guarantee may include the following terms:

- the product will be repaired free of charge even if it is accidentally damaged

- the product will be repaired free of charge or replaced if it stops operating because of faulty materials or workmanship within 12 months from the date of purchase

- only the manufacturer's own service centres or agreed repairers may be used.

Some guarantees state that the customer must register their purchase to be valid. However, legally a customer can still claim under his or her statutory rights if a product malfunctions. If you are studying the option unit on consumer protection you will learn more about this.

An additional warranty period may be purchased to cover the item for longer periods. This may extend the time under which free parts will be fitted or under which no labour charges will be made. Most warranties have a list of limitations attached

which state the circumstances under which the customer would not be able to claim.

Many warranties have had a bad press. The Consumers' Association considers many of them to be over-priced and unnecessary and claims it is cheaper for purchasers to take the risk of paying for breakdowns on all household appliances except washing machines. However, warranties are often promoted by retailers who find them very profitable. Since the bad publicity, however, most outlets still make customers aware of the warranty options, but do not stress the benefits quite as keenly!

 **ACTIVITY**

1 As a group, discuss how the owners of a video, CD and computer games store could satisfy customers with genuine complaints yet protect themselves against customers copying the items and then trying to return them for a refund.

2 You work for a large toy store which also sells children's clothing for the under-tens. The manager wants to start a customer database so that regular customers can be sent promotional literature and information.
   a What details do you think should be captured from customers?
   b What methods would you suggest should be used to collect this information?

5.5 Health, safety and security

Retail outlets, like all other business organisations, must comply with health and safety legislation. This was described in detail in Unit 1, pages 35–41. Go back and refresh your memory about the main laws which govern health and safety – and the implications for organisations which do not comply with these laws. In particular, while you are reading this section, try to think how the laws may relate to the specific activities of retail outlets and their staff.

Health and safety

Identifying hazards

Hazards can relate to:

- the building itself or the layout of the store
- the delivery and storage of goods in the stockroom
- the fixtures and fittings in the store
- the way in which merchandise is displayed
- the equipment and appliances used
- cleanliness and 'good housekeeping'
- working practices.

Building and layout

Architects and designers are aware of the safety regulations they must consider when a store is built or refurbished. Standard requirements include clear and sufficient fire exits, safety glass in doors, handrails on steps and non-slip flooring. However, staff have to be vigilant in case hazards develop, such as a handrail working loose or a floor tile becoming dislodged. Such hazards should be identified and reported immediately.

Delivery and storage of goods

Workers in the stockroom should be fully aware of the Manual Handling Operations Regulations (see Unit 1 page 37) and use trolleys to move heavy loads. Items must be stacked safely and in compliance with specific labels (e.g. 'This Way Up', 'Fragile', 'Handle with Care'). Perishable goods are clearly marked and must be stored in appropriate conditions. Goods unloaded from refrigerated vehicles must be moved immediately to chilled or frozen food storage areas. Hazardous items (e.g. glass, kitchen knives or chemicals) must be stored safely.

Fixtures and fittings

Shelves must be stable and may have their front edges raised to prevent items falling forwards. The weight they can bear must be known to staff and never be exceeded. There should be no sharp edges on fixtures which could injure staff or customers. Plinths should not protrude so that people can trip over them. Staff must watch for general wear and tear that make fittings insecure and need repair. If a new member of staff stacks items unsafely, this needs to be rectified promptly.

Displays of merchandise

Displays should be constructed during quiet times so that customers are not at risk. They should be placed where they cannot be knocked against, and made secure so that items cannot fall off. Dangerous items should never form part of a display. Lighting should be installed safely, so that there is no risk of items overheating or catching fire. Displays of heavy items should be constructed so there is no chance of them toppling over and injuring someone – even if an item at the base is removed.

Equipment and appliances

Staff must be trained how to use potentially hazardous equipment (e.g. a bacon slicer) and must observe all the relevant safety precautions. Never use a broken or damaged machine and report the fault immediately. Equipment maintenance should be routinely carried out by specialists – this includes bakery equipment, refrigerators, heating and lighting. No member of staff should attempt to repair faults. There should be excellent control over pests such as flies and midges, e.g. through the installation of electrical devices which attract and kill them.

Cleanliness and 'good housekeeping'

General cleaning should be done after customers have left the premises, apart from accidents such as spillages and breakages, which should be cleaned up immediately. The area being cleaned should be cordoned off until the floor is dry and/or safe to walk on. Shelf cleaning and filling, and the cleaning of fridges and freezers should preferably take place during quiet periods. Large trolleys should not block the aisles. The whole area should be clean and tidy. Empty boxes should be removed immediately. Items on display must be clean. Bottles of liquid should be securely fastened.

For retail outlets dealing with food or catering, there are many legal regulations with which they must comply, such as the Food Safety Act 1990, the Food Safety (Temperature Control) Regulations 1995 and the Food Safety (General Food Hygiene) Regulations 1995. In

Figure 5.18 Spillages have to be cleaned up and the area made safe

addition staff who handle food must be trained how to do so – and often acquire special food handling qualifications – to reduce the dangers of contamination and food poisoning. Such staff will wear protective clothing and be trained how to guard against a wider range of hazards, such as hot pans, boiling water and sharp knives.

Working practices

General maintenance work should also take place when the store is closed. Any areas being repaired during opening hours should be cordoned off and merchandise re-sited. Stock repositioning should also take place 'out-of-hours' or at the quietest periods. Staff should receive regular training to maintain health and safety vigilance and be encouraged to report potential hazards.

Precautions to avoid hazards

Staff training, cordoning off areas which are hazardous, organising re-stocking during quiet periods are all *precautionary* actions. They seek to prevent or minimise the risk from potential hazards. Routine checking of fixtures and fittings and careful planning of displays are also precautionary actions. When senior staff walk around they should note potential hazards and arrange for action to be taken promptly. There may also be official safety inspections from time to time, although these are not substitutes for daily observations. Where possible hazards should be prevented. If this is not possible, then the potential risk should be minimised.

Actions to remove hazards

There should be a clear procedure for reporting hazards and action must be taken immediately. The type of action required will depend on the hazard. The key is to minimise delay. If a shelf is unsafe the goods must be removed immediately. If a glass bottle is broken then the area must be cordoned off straight away.

Emergency procedures

There are three main emergencies which staff may have to face:

- fire
- evacuation for some other reason (e.g. a bomb threat)
- accidents.

Fire

To comply with Health and Safety and Fire regulations, all retail outlets must have fire and smoke alarms fitted, an adequate number of easily accessible fire exists and provide staff training on how to respond if a fire breaks out.

This training should include regular fire drills. Staff should know the positions of the nearest emergency exits and how to instruct customers to evacuate the building. Certain members of staff should be appointed as fire marshalls. They are responsible for ensuring a rapid and calm evacuation from the building – often these will be supervisory staff specially trained to carry out this function. It is their responsibility to check no-one is left in service areas such as toilets and rest rooms.

Staff must know how to use the fire-fighting equipment which is installed, and the type of fires on which different types of equipment should be used. A small fire can be contained or extinguished quite quickly using the appropriate equipment, but staff should still raise the alarm if they have any doubts. This immediately alerts the fire brigade and ensures the building is promptly evacuated. In an emergency, it is important that each member of staff knows precisely what his/her responsibilities are – and follows these

exactly. This minimises the danger of a fire spreading and maximises the chance of an orderly and rapid evacuation taking place.

Other evacuations

Switchboard operators in large outlets should be trained in the procedure to follow if a bomb threat is received. The police must be immediately notified and the store evacuated. The public address system can be used to evacuate customers, without telling them why, so as not to cause panic. Staff should know what they have to do in an emergency evacuation and how to direct customers to the nearest emergency exits.

Accidents

All outlets have an accident book into which all accidents – whether staff or customer – must be recorded. There are also trained first-aiders in all large stores. Security staff are also often trained as first-aiders. It may be that copies of all accident report forms have to be sent to the company's legal department in case of future claims by a customer.

Figure 5.19 An injured person should be handled by a qualified first-aider

If a customer or a member of staff has an accident – or is taken ill – then a first-aider must be summoned. Someone who has slipped or fallen or has had a serious accident must not be moved. The outlet should have a standard procedure for calling assistance when required. In many large stores the first-aider will have a mobile telephone so that further assistance can be called for without leaving the patient.

Access and facilities for customers with disabilities

Most retail outlets do their best to accommodate the needs of disabled customers. These can include:

- ramps and automatic doors

- access for guide dogs

- clear signs showing where lifts are available (instead of escalators)

- disabled toilet facilities

- special trolleys which minimise bending and stooping

- assisted shopping for the disabled, the blind and visually impaired customers

- special shopping nights for the disabled.

However, staff also need to be trained to cope with disabled customers in an emergency when lifts must not be used. In this situation the member of staff in charge of a customer who is wheelchair bound must go to an appropriate point (e.g. the emergency stairwell) on an upper floor and identify their location to a fire marshall. The fire marshalls will communicate this information to the fire officers who will then arrange for the evacuation of the persons concerned.

Security issues

The theft of goods

Security is an important issue for all retail outlets. The Centre for Retail Research has reported that **shrinkage** rates (the retailing term for theft of goods) in Britain average 1.62 per cent and cost retailers 24 per cent of their profits. Total shrinkage in the UK retail industry was estimated at £1.4 billion by the British Retail Consortium – and retailers spent around £450 million on crime prevention measures.

Theft is committed by both customers and by staff – as you can see from the types of retail crime illustrated in Figure 5.20. Customers can obtain goods by shoplifting or through collusion with staff, mainly through refund fraud, false markdowns and 'sweethearting' (giving discounts or free goods to friends and families).

The Centre for Retail Research reports that the main methods used by store employees to steal include wearing or carrying merchandise out of the store, bogus refunds and stealing cash

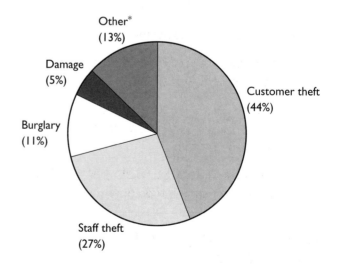

* Includes robbery and till snatches, frauds and other unexplained losses.

Source: Retail Crime Survey, British Retail Consortium

Figure 5.20 Types of retail crime in the UK, 1996–7

from the till. Studies show that new, part-time employees were more likely to steal, often being shown how to do so by a more experienced co-worker. They were likely to be caught within six months.

Stores try to minimise theft by preventing shoplifting, collusion and thefts by staff.

Shoplifting can be minimised by:

- employing store detectives
- excellent lighting throughout the store
- siting expensive merchandise at the back of the store
- 'tagging' goods so that an alarm sounds if the tag passes through a photo-electric curtain
- displaying expensive goods in locked cabinets
- 'chaining' expensive clothing such as leather coats to the rail
- installing convex mirrors in possible blind spots
- installing one-way mirrors between offices and sales floor areas
- installing CCTV cameras
- employing security guards to undertake constant surveillance
- having a specific changing room policy limiting and 'logging' the number of items per customer
- having clear warnings to shoplifters that they will be prosecuted for theft.

Theft of money can be minimised by:

- installing plastic shields above cash register drawers to prevent 'snatch and grab' crimes

- siting cash registers away from exit doors
- having a separate notes strongbox into which all notes are 'posted' immediately on receipt
- emptying tills regularly; staff who do this should work together as a team and wear protective helmets and goggles
- having an established procedure for providing additional change without the cashier having to leave the till
- locking tills when not in use.

Theft by staff can be minimised by:

- a clearly enforced procedure for genuine staff purchases and the storage of such items
- cloakroom areas for employee coats and bags – none of which must be allowed on the sales floor
- both systematic and random checks on cash registers against till roll records
- checkout operators 'logging on' with their staff code when they start to use a cash register – and 'logging off' when they hand over to another operator
- all refunds authorised by a supervisor
- all 'cashbacks' signed or initialled by the customer (see debit cards, page 326)
- only full, sealed cartons or boxes moved from the stock area to the sales floor
- a known policy that management have the right to search clothing or belongings if theft is suspected.

All retail outlets will have a special, secure office where the money is counted. Only authorised staff are allowed in this area. The money is usually transported to this area from cash registers in a special 'secure' trolley. Staff emptying the tills do not have access to the contents of the trolley. There will be a special strongroom or safe in which cash floats are stored. A large store will have the takings collected daily by a security firm. Smaller retail outlets should ensure that no money is left on the premises overnight and the till drawer should be left open – so that in the case of a break-in it is obvious that it is empty.

Security of premises

Virtually all retail outlets have security alarms to minimise break-ins. This is often essential before they can be insured against theft. However, not all thieves are deterred by security alarms. Ram-raiders, for instance, use cars or four-wheel drives to crash into the front of a shop or store, quickly steal what they can and drive away before the police arrive.

Measures retail outlets have introduced to minimise break-ins and damage include:

- security alarms and CCTVs which operate overnight

- illuminated shop fronts and car parks

- metal grilles over shop windows

- earth banks or 'moats' in front of stores

- concrete blocks, concrete flower rubs or metal bollards in front of windows

- security lights inside the shop itself

- secure 'dead' locks on all doors and windows

- separate entrances for staff and customers – with staff doors opened by a coded door lock

- anti-scaling devices such as spikes on roofs and external pipes

- locked gates and high metal fences at the back of the premises

- restricting key holders to the premises

- specific procedures for locking doors and windows at night

- checking all rooms carefully at the end of each day – especially toilet areas – to make sure no-one is concealed on the premises.

 **ACTIVITY**

1   If you work in a retail outlet part-time, summarise the health and safety precautions and the security procedures that are in operation at your workplace. Compare your report with those of your fellow-students who also work part-time.

2   Ask your tutor if he/she can arrange for the group to either visit a store in your area or be visited by a store manager to discuss both health and safety and security aspects.

3   In pairs, assess at least one retail outlet in your area for facilities for the disabled. Then compare your findings as a group and score each outlet to see which is best, and which is worst.

4   Your friend is starting a small retail business selling sports clothing near the town centre. He has asked for your suggestions on how he should maximise security. What advice will you give him?

Consumer protection

Many of us purchase goods and services that we later find to be defective or fail to match the promises of the salesperson or sales literature. What can customers do when this happens? What legal protection do they have? To whom can they turn for help? What remedies or compensation can be obtained, other than just a letter of apology?

This unit is concerned with all these issues. It examines the major aspects of consumer protection in Britain and why consumers need to have their rights protected by the law. It briefly looks at its development and the organisations which exist to help consumers today. Studying this unit will not only help you to gain your GNVQ Intermediate Business award but will also help you in your private life – and give you the confidence to take action if you are the victim of mis-selling.

This unit will be assessed through your portfolio work. Guidance on the assignment you must undertake will be given by your tutor.

6.1 Consumer protection and consumer rights

The first consumer protection law to be passed in Britain was the Sale of Goods Act 1893. Broadly, this stated that in any contract (agreement) between a buyer and seller the buyer had certain rights. However, it allowed the seller to deliberately add special terms to the contract to restrict the buyer's rights, which virtually destroyed the benefits of the Act. It wasn't until the Supply of Goods (Implied Terms) Act of 1973 was passed that sellers were prevented from taking away the most important rights of the buyers.

Subsequent Acts of Parliament improved the rights of buyers still further. Today anyone who purchases goods or services has considerable legal rights. Unfortunately many people do not know what their rights are, so do not know what action they can take if they have a problem with what they have purchased.

Before you can start exercising your rights, therefore, you need to know what they are! What you need is:

- a basic understanding of the law of contract
- a basic knowledge of the major consumer protection laws.

With this knowledge you will know how and when to take action.

The law of contract

A contract is a legal agreement between two or more people – e.g. a contract of employment between an employer and an employee. Here we are concerned with a **contract of sale.**

Formation of the contract

The law states that for a contract to be valid, five basic requirements must be met.

1 **Capacity.** Each party must be legally capable of making the contract. This means you must understand what you are doing. If a person suffers from a mental disorder or was drunk at the time of making the agreement then the contract

is likely to be invalid. There are also restrictions on the type of contracts people under 18 (minors) can make.

2 **Offer**. In most contracts the buyer must offer to buy an item from a seller. This must be a specific offer, either verbally or in writing, to buy a particular item at a stated price. It must be communicated directly to the seller. If you posted an order form to a mail order company, the offer isn't actually made until the company receives the document.

It may surprise you to learn that a retailer does not have to accept your offer – even if the goods are in the window and you offer the asking price. As long as the retailer isn't discriminating against you on the grounds of race or gender there is nothing you can do if you are refused the item.

An offer does not last indefinitely. If either party dies or if there is no acceptance within a reasonable time then the offer will lapse. The offer will also lapse if it is made subject to a particular condition which is not met. If you agreed to buy a set of glasses provided the shop assistant gift wrapped them for you, and you were told this service isn't available, then the offer will lapse. You can also **revoke** (i.e. withdraw) your offer at any time *before* it has been accepted.

3 **Acceptance**. If the offer is accepted, this must be communicated to the person making the offer. It may be:

- **by verbal or written statement** (e.g. a mail order firm sends you confirmation of your order)

- **by conduct** (e.g. a sales assistant wraps up the item, passes it to you and takes your money).

The acceptance must be **unqualified**. This means that it must exactly match

Figure 6.1 A contract being made

the offer. If you offered to buy a CD for £7.99 and the sales assistant tells you it is really £8.50 then this is a **counter offer**. It is then up to you whether you offer to buy it at the new price or refuse to make a further offer.

4 **Consideration.** In this case, the law of England and Wales differs from the law of Scotland. In England and Wales a contract must involve some kind of payment or other consideration. Generally, the law is not very interested in how much you paid. If you manage to buy a bargain, then that is your good luck. Only if the consideration seems very inappropriate (e.g. a computer for £5) might there be some concern that undue pressure has been placed by one party to the contract upon the other.

5 **Intention to create legal relations**. It is assumed that if you want to make a purchase you intend to create a legal relationship with the seller, i.e. you *want* to enter into the transaction. The courts will always presume this unless it can be proved otherwise.

Terms of the contract

The terms of the contract may be **express** or **implied**.

Express terms are specifically stated – either orally or in writing. For instance, you may agree to buy a computer provided it is delivered before a specific date because you need it to complete an assignment. If this is included as a condition in the contract then the seller has to comply. The correct phrase to use in this situation is 'time is of the essence'. It is sensible to have this in writing, then you have proof if there is a problem later.

Implied terms are those the courts are prepared to accept are the clear, but unexpressed, intentions of both parties to the contract. For instance, it is implied that you will pay a reasonable price for an item – you can't expect to receive it for nothing.

Terms can also be implied by Acts of Parliament, such as the Sale of Goods Act 1979 (as amended by the Sale and Supply of Goods Act 1994).

Terms are categorised in two ways and this distinction is important.

- **A condition** is a vital term. It is so important that the contract is invalid if these terms are not met. For instance, if you bought a computer you could reasonably expect it to contain a processor and some memory – so that it works. If this condition was not met you could reject the contract and claim damages.

- **A warranty** is a term of lesser importance. For instance, if your new computer had no modem fitted, even though this was part of the contract and you had ordered one, this would be classed as a warranty. In this case you could not reject the contract but could take action to claim damages so that you pay a lower price for the computer.

In Scotland no distinction is made between conditions and warranties although a similar distinction is made between 'material' and 'non-material' parts of the contract.

Exclusion clauses

The law is very suspicious of exclusion clauses. So much so that the **Unfair Contract Terms Act** 1977 prevents retailers from limiting or taking away a customer's legal rights under the Sale of Goods Acts (see page 345). The law is very strict on this matter. For instance, a retailer who tries to do this through a notice in the shop or statement in a contract or other document is guilty of a criminal offence.

Also, no notice or disclaimer can ever absolve an organisation from its liability to staff or customers if personal injury or death is caused through their negligence.

The only time that exclusion clauses are valid are when they are considered 'fair and reasonable'. If a jeweller loses your watch it had for repair, the shop would have to prove it took reasonable care of the goods and could not be held responsible for what occurred. If the loss or damage was through negligence

Figure 6.2 A contract is breached if the seller fails to take sufficient care in packing goods

on the part of an employee, then you would probably be entitled to compensation. Any exclusion clause which tried to limit the firm's financial liability would be carefully examined using the 'test of reasonableness'.

Guidelines are given in the 1977 Act as to what is considered a 'reasonable' exclusion clause. For instance, if you asked a carpenter to make you a special item to your own design, and he went to some trouble to obtain the wood and make it, it may be considered 'reasonable' for him to want additional protection against you later deciding you didn't want the item. He could do this by including a clause stating that you would still have to pay for the item.

Ending a contract

A contract is ended:

- **by performance** – you buy an article, pay for it and walk out of the shop with it

- **by agreement between both parties** – you return goods to a shop, the retailer accepts their return and refunds your money

- **by breach** – if one party to the contract does not carry out his or her part of the agreement.

Remember that if the breach relates to a condition (an important term) then the buyer may be able to choose whether to claim damages or end the contract altogether. If the breach relates to a warranty (a less important term) then the contract will still be valid but it may be possible to claim financial damages.

Privity of contract

Until 1999, in English law the only people who can take action if the contract is broken are the *parties* to the contract, i.e. the buyer and the seller. Therefore, if a benevolent uncle bought you a leather jacket which later proved to be faulty, *he* would have had to take

action against the retailer, not you. Since 11 May 2000, however, under the Contracts (Rights of Third Parties) Act 1999, it is not only the people who make a contract but also anyone who is intended to benefit from the transaction, who can claim. That includes you, if you were the recipient of a present.

 # ACTIVITY

1 You buy a bungee jumping experience for a friend's birthday. At what point would a legal contract exist.
   a When you saw the advertisement in the newspaper.
   b When you sent off the order form.
   c When you received the invoice.
   d When you made the payment.
   e When your friend made the jump?

2 When you receive confirmation you note the following terms in the contract. Which do you consider are reasonable and which are not?
   a Bungee jumps will not be held if there is a strong wind or other adverse weather conditions.
   b All bungee jumpers must be in good health and have no serious disabilities or heart conditions.
   c All bungee jumpers must be aged between 18 and 65 years of age.
   d If, for any reason, a person cancels and requests a refund, this must be done at least two months before the date the jump is scheduled.
   e All participants must weigh between 7 stones and 15 stones and must be at least 4' 6" tall.
   f The organisers will not be held responsible for any injuries no matter how they are caused.
   g The organisers reserve the right to refuse anyone to jump who is under the influence of drink or drugs.

3 When you arrive with your friend you are surprised to find that people are expected to pay extra to hire the safety harness. You and your friend refuse to pay and argue the company has breached the terms of its contract, especially as there was no mention of this in the advertisement or contract.

 a Are you right in making this statement?

 b If so, are the terms which have been breached a condition or a warranty? Give a reason for your answer.

 c Can you make a claim or will your friend have to do it on your behalf? Give a reason for your answer.

Consumer legislation

There are **five** Acts of Parliament you need to know. You do not need to know the details, but you must understand the rights they give buyers. These are summarised below. The first two are concerned with the sale and supply of goods and services. The second two are related to defective or dangerous goods – known as **product liability**. The final Act relates to buying goods on credit.

The Sale of Goods Act 1979 and 1995

One of the most important Acts today is the Sale of Goods Act 1979. Since it was passed this has been amended three times – by the Sale of Goods (Amendment) Act 1994, the Sale and Supply of Goods Act 1994 and the Sale of Goods (Amendment) Act 1995. This covers the fundamental requirements of purchasers, i.e. that goods must be:

- **as described** – this means that goods must conform to their description, e.g. waterproof must mean the item does not leak!

- **of satisfactory quality** – in relation to the price paid, the description, the age of the item

- **fit for the purpose for which they are intended** – goods must carry out the purpose they are made for, e.g. a pen must make a clear legible mark.

Another requirement is that:

- the goods must be fit for any specific purpose which the buyer has made clear to the seller at the time of the sale (e.g. if you specified your pen must write at any angle)

If the goods are not of satisfactory quality the courts would take into consideration various factors, such as whether the goods were free from minor defects, satisfactory in appearance and finish, safe, durable and as described (whether by the seller, on the packaging or on any labels). The buyer of unsatisfactory goods is entitled to a refund within a reasonable time after purchase from the seller (not the manufacturer). The buyer does not have to accept a credit note. A buyer who agrees to a free repair does not lose the right to a refund if the repair is unsatisfactory. If goods go wrong after a period of use then, instead of obtaining a refund, the buyer can claim compensation which may be the repair, replacement or a price reduction on the original item. Do note, however, that this does not mean you can make a claim for an item you bought several years ago and which has stopped working through general wear and tear!

Both second-hand goods and sale goods are covered by this Act. In relation to second-hand items the buyer's right to compensation will depend on the age of the item, how much was paid and how the article was described. If the sale price of an item has been reduced because of a specific fault which is pointed out to the buyer (e.g. shop-soiled) then the buyer cannot later complain about that particular fault, but can complain if something else goes wrong. However, if any fault is so obvious it can be clearly seen when the goods are examined you cannot complain later about this particular fault.

The Supply of Goods and Services Act 1982

Service standards are covered by this Act, as in buying the services of a plumber to repair central heating or a garage to service a car. Buyers are protected against shoddy workmanship, delays and exorbitant charges. The Act states that all services should be carried out:

- for a reasonable charge

- within a reasonable time

- with reasonable care and skill

- using satisfactory materials.

The government is currently proposing tighter legislation to prevent 'cowboy' builders operating. These are unqualified builders who mislead people into paying for unnecessary repairs. The legislation is needed because the

people 'duped' often have no records to prove what happened, or the 'cowboy' builder has no permanent address and has vanished from sight.

The Consumer Protection Act 1987

This Act relates to price and safety. Under the Act it is an offence:

- to mislead consumers as to the price of goods, services, accommodation or facilities (e.g. by missing out the VAT when quoting the price)

- to mislead consumers over sale prices and claim exaggerated price reductions

- to supply goods which are not reasonably safe.

Note the words 'it is an offence'. These are important when you come to the section on civil and criminal law on page 350.

The Consumer Protection Act (CPA) is enforced by Trading Standards officers. It is also an offence not to cooperate with Trading Standards officers during any investigation.

The Trade Descriptions Act 1968

This Act is designed to prevent the false or misleading description of goods, e.g.:

- selling goods which are wrongly described by the manufacturer

- implied descriptions, e.g. a picture on a box which gives a false impression

- other aspects of the goods, including quantity, size, composition, method of manufacture etc.

Usually the spoken word of the seller overrides the written description of the goods as the buyer can rely on the expertise of the salesperson. However, this is obviously harder to prove if there is a dispute.

Figure 6.3 There is legal protection against poor work

The Consumer Credit Act 1974

This requires all businesses which offer credit to have a specific licence – otherwise they will be committing an offence. Most retailers will have a licence which enables them to offer all forms of credit to a customer up to a value of £15,000. Those retailers (e.g. garages) who arrange for customers to obtain credit through a separate finance company need a different licence.

The Act provides for:

- customers who sign a credit agreement in their own home to be allowed a 'cooling off' period of five days. During this period the customer can change his/her mind and **cancel** the agreement without any penalties (see below).

- customers to demand (within 28 days) that retailers provide details of the name and address of any credit reference agencies which have been used to ascertain their credit worthiness. It is an offence for a retailer not to do this.

- the credit reference agency to provide full details to the customer if the request is made in writing, and a small administration fee is paid. Any incorrect information must be corrected if further information is provided by the customer.

- advertisements offering credit must include the total charge for credit and the APR (annual percentage rate of charge). The Act also restricts the way in which advertisements are worded and the prominence of financial information relating to charges.

- sellers must provide written details of credit terms if requested by the customer (or his/her representative) in writing or orally, either in person or on the telephone, unless such a quotation has already been provided.

You should know the difference between cancelling an agreement, withdrawing from an agreement and terminating an agreement.

Cancelling an agreement

The customer is allowed to cancel a signed credit agreement if:

- action is taken quickly – within the five-day 'cooling off' period

- the agreement was signed after talking to the lender or supplier in person (not on the telephone)

- the agreement was not signed on the lender's or seller's premises

- the amount is between £50 and £25,000 and the borrower has offered his/her property as security for the loan.

At the point the agreement is signed the customer should be given a copy which sets out the cancellation rights. A further copy should also be sent by post to the customer.

Withdrawing from an agreement

A customer can withdraw from any agreement before it has been signed by both parties. If the customer has already signed, it is important to notify the lender immediately – by phone, fax or email – before the lender also signs.

If an amount is borrowed and a person's home is offered as security, then there is a seven-day consideration period during which the borrower can study an advance copy of the agreement. During this time it is possible to withdraw from the arrangement.

The effects of withdrawing are identical to cancelling an agreement.

Terminating an agreement

This means paying off an outstanding debt to end the agreement earlier than was originally agreed. Customers who are in a position to pay off outstanding amounts in one lump sum should do so, as they save on further interest payments. Some agreements allow for a rebate for some of the charges which would have been made during the remainder of the loan period – others do not. Anyone wanting to terminate an agreement must find out, first, what the settlement figure would be. After this amount has been paid, the agreement ends or is terminated.

Anyone wishing to buy goods on credit should read the terms of the agreement carefully before signing. This avoids nasty shocks later – such as finding out there is an *additional* charge for early settlement.

ACTIVITY

1 Under which part of the Sale of Goods Act would you have cause to complain if you bought the following? Bear in mind you may be able to claim under more than one heading.

  a A purse or wallet labelled 'real leather' which turns out to be plastic.

  b A hairdryer which overheats and catches fire the first time you use it.

  c A video tape which has such a poor picture it is unwatchable.

  d An all-weather tent from a camping shop for £200 which lets in water.

  e A computer printer which jams after two weeks of use.

  f A mobile telephone advertised for £60 which costs you £70.50 because they didn't tell you about the VAT.

2 a Do you think it would have made any difference if the tent in 1(d) had cost £20 and was advertised as a 'children's play tent'?

  b If the salesperson had described the tent you bought as being suitable for your needs – and showed you a picture on the box of the tent in a snowy field – what Act could you quote to support any claim you made?

3 Under which other Act could both the supplier or the manufacturer of the hairdryer and the mobile telephone company be prosecuted by the Trading Standards Office?

4 Divide into groups of three. Then – either from your own experiences or using your imagination – think of **three** further problems you could experience under each part of the Sale of Goods Act or the Sale of Goods and Services Act. Then compare your ideas as a group.

5 An elderly lady near you is distressed because she was visited by a double glazing salesperson and signed an agreement to have new windows. The cost is £5,000 but interest payments alone would add on another £3,000 – which is far more than she can afford.

  What would you advise her to do and why?

6.2 Solving consumer problems

Consumers with a problem need to know what to do. The main stages include:

• knowing which sources give help and advice

• understanding how to make a complaint

• realising how the court system operates – and how they can take legal action

• understanding how to make a claim

• knowing the likely outcomes of such claims.

Each of these stages is described in more detail below.

Sources of help and advice

There are dozens of sources of help and advice today. These are covered on pages 353–358. Most have web pages – and you will find it much more interesting finding out about them using the Internet. In your own area, there is likely to be a Citizens Advice Bureau and a Trading Standards office. Both provide free advice to consumers. There is also a wealth of information you can get from national bodies.

Making a complaint

The Office of Fair Trading is a national organisation concerned with consumer protection. They give guidance on making a complaint to anyone who telephones their consumer information line on 0345 22 44 99. The following is a summary of the action to take.

1   Complain to the supplier of the goods or service as soon as possible. Always give the supplier the opportunity to put the matter right *first*. Bear in mind that if you leave your complaint for too long you may lose some of your legal rights.

2   Make sure you take any receipt or proof of purchase with you. Don't part with this – in case you need it later.

3   If the supplier is some distance away, or if you get no satisfaction after calling in person, then you will need to put your complaint in writing. It's a good idea to ring the organisation and to get the name of their customer services manager so you can send the letter to that specific person.

4   Keep your letter short and to the point. In the first paragraph state when and where you bought the goods or service. In the second, state what has gone wrong clearly and unemotionally. If you have already visited the firm without any success, say when and where you called, the name of the person to whom you spoke and the outcome. In the last paragraph state what you want done and set a realistic deadline.

5   Keep copies of all correspondence. If the company telephones you, make a note of what they said and the date.

6   At this stage the problem is usually solved. Remember that you don't have to accept the first offer you receive, if you feel it is a poor one.

7   If you are getting nowhere then get expert advice. This could include expert opinion on the problem (e.g. by asking another trader to put their views in writing), by contacting your local trading standards department or another source of help and advice (see pages 353–358).

OFFICE OF FAIR TRADING

Figure 6.4 The Office of Fair Trading logo.

ACTIVITY

1   You bought a Stirling exercise bike by mail order from Huttons Direct, 14 Weybridge Road, London N1 4PE, for £95. After two months it became very difficult to use, no matter what setting it was on. Now – one month later – the pedals have jammed and it will not work at all.

   a   Decide what action you would like Huttons to take.

b Write a letter of complaint to their customer services manager, Miss Jennifer Checkland.

2 You receive a response from Huttons arguing that you must have misused the bike and offering you £20 in vouchers against their sportswear.
a Would you accept their offer?
b If not, what would you do and why?

Taking legal action

The vast majority of consumer problems and complaints are settled without too much difficulty by the parties involved. However, if a consumer cannot settle the problem out of court then he or she may consider taking legal action. Before taking this action, however, it is important to get advice and help from a specialist. In the case of the exercise bike, for instance, you should contact your local Trading Standards office, which may suggest you contact the Mail Order Traders' Association in Liverpool to check if Huttons is a member. If so, the association may help you with your case. Equally, if you had seen the bike advertised in a newspaper or magazine, you could contact one of the mail order protection schemes which operate to help consumers to resolve such problems.

If all else fails you may decide to take legal action. Most solicitors offer free legal clinics (often on a Saturday morning) or complainants can ask their local Citizens Advice Bureau for help. It is useful to know from the outset how the legal system operates in Britain. Bear in mind that the court system is different in Scotland. Both are covered below.

Criminal and civil actions

There are two types of court systems in Britain:

- those concerned with **criminal** matters

- those concerned with **civil** matters.

What is the difference and how does this relate to consumer protection?

1 **Criminal law**. A criminal is an individual who has committed an action against the interests of society. Such actions are defined in **statute law**, which will list these as 'offences', i.e. 'it is an offence to . . . .' A criminal action is normally brought by a representative of the state (e.g. the police or a Trading Standards officer or an environmental health officer). It may (rarely) be brought as a private prosecution by the aggrieved party.

The case is either tried in a magistrates' court or before a judge and jury in a crown court (or in a sheriff court in Scotland).

The remedy can be imprisonment or a fine (i.e. a punishment for wrongdoing).

2 **Civil law**. This is concerned with relationships between individuals. Note that the term 'individuals' can also mean companies. In this case one individual brings a civil action against the other. To bring this action there must be two factors:

- there must be loss or damage

- there must be a legal obligation owed to the party bringing the action.

The action will normally be started in a county court (or sheriff court in Scotland) by the aggrieved party – known as the **claimant**. This person starts court proceedings against the individual accused of causing the loss of damage – known as the **defendant**. The small claims procedure (see below) is a speedy and easy way of bringing action for claims for small amounts (in 1999, up to £5,000 in England and Wales, £1,000 in Northern Ireland and £750 in Scotland).

The remedy is usually damages (i.e. monetary payments) to either refund the money or pay compensation to a successful claimant. The aim is to reimburse the aggrieved party.

In some cases an action may be taken against a trader in *both* courts. If I bought a defective product which caused me personal injury then I may sue the manufacturer in the civil court. Trading Standards may also prosecute the manufacturer in the criminal court for breaching product safety laws.

The small claims procedure

The small claims procedure was introduced to help private individuals to bring a claim cheaply and easily. There is no need to use a solicitor. The process is started by completing a summons form with the relevant names and addresses and giving a brief outline of the case. There is a small fee, but this is repaid if the claimant wins the case. Anyone who needs help filling in the forms can go to their nearest Citizens Advice Bureau for help.

The court 'serves' the summons on the defendant and then informs the claimant of the next stage. If the defendant decides to go to a solicitor then this will be at his or her own cost – unless the claimant is bringing a frivolous action. The steps involved are shown in more detail in Figure 6.5.

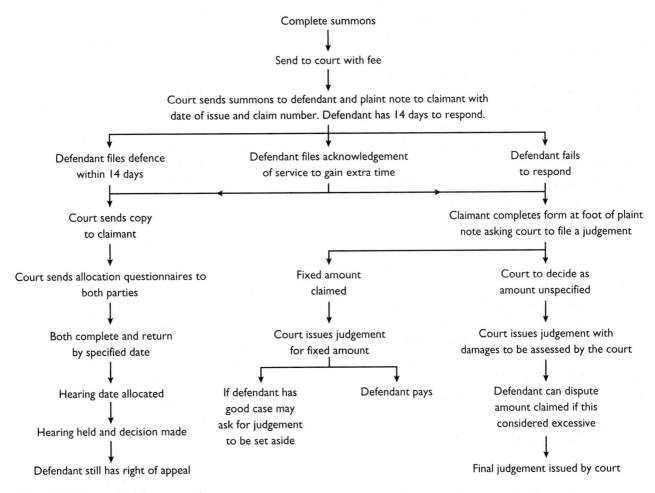

Figure 6.5 The small claims procedure

ACTIVITY

1   Look back at the Consumer Protection Act 1987 on page 346 and note the actions which are listed as an offence.

2   Three traders are prosecuted by Trading Standards officers in the criminal court.
    a   The first has misled customers by quoting prices without VAT despite a previous warning.
    b   The second has retained a notice saying 'NO REFUNDS ALLOWED' despite a previous warning.
    c   The third was unqualified to carry out a repair to a gas boiler which blew up and killed the occupant of the house.

    Identify the Act under which each trader would be prosecuted and then discuss, as a group, the type of 'remedy' you think would be appropriate in each case.

3   Nominate one member of the group to contact your local county court to obtain a copy of the leaflet which explains the small claims procedure. Discuss how this operates with your tutor. Look also at Figure 6.5 and check that you understand what you would have to do to pursue a valid claim to a successful conclusion.

4   You leave a valuable ring at a jeweller's for repair.
    a   The ring is stolen from the shop when the assistant leaves it on the counter while she is attending to the next customer. What action should you take and why?
    b   Would it have made any difference if:
        i   the ring had been stolen overnight despite the premises having an alarm.
        ii   the shop had a notice which said 'All goods left at the owner's risk'

        iii the shop had made you sign a contract which said that their liability for any loss was limited to £15?

    Discuss your ideas as a group and with your tutor.

6.3 Citizens' and customer charters

Many organisations are reputable and, indeed, go beyond their rights under law by offering a range of additional services to customers. An example is the 'no quibble exchange or refund' policy that some retail shops have if you change your mind about something you have bought.

Often the organisation will advertise their charter, or customer service standards. This tells customers what their rights are, how problems will be dealt with and how to bring any complaints. The **citizens' charter** was introduced by the government in 1991 to focus on consumer rights in areas such as health, education, transport, welfare, tax, customs procedures etc. Today there are over 200 national charters and dozens of local charters which relate to regional services, such as your local authority, benefit office or hospital. Organisations which consistently prove they can offer a high standard of service to the public are awarded the **Chartermark**.

Figure 6.6 The Chartermark sign of excellence

Customer charters are issued mainly by private organisations (e.g. retail stores, manufacturers, service suppliers) – although you may find your local council calling their charter a 'customer charter' – just to confuse you! However, the fundamental idea is the same. The **purpose** of charters is to:

- publish standards of service

- continuously improve customer service standards

- provide full information on customer rights

- ensure all customers are treated equally and fairly

- ensure all customers know how to complain.

ACTIVITY

1 Divide this task of collecting as many of the following charters as you can among members of your group.
   a Obtain a copy of your college charter.
   b Visit your local post office and ask for a copy of their charter.
   c Visit your nearest Inland Revenue office and ask for the taxpayers' charter.
   d Contact your nearest HM Customs & Excise office and obtain a copy of the travellers' charter.
   e Visit your local hospital or GP and ask for a copy of the patients' charter.
   f Visit your local authority and ask for a copy of their charter.
   g Surf the Net and print out examples of at least five charters (try to make sure some of these are from private organisations in the UK). You can do this by accessing a main search engine (e.g. www.yahoo.com or www.altavista.com) and typing in

'customer charter'. If you put quotes around the two words then you will be searching for the phrase, not the individual words, and will be more successful.
   Then as a group, study the charters you have obtained and identify aspects which are common to them all.

2 Divide into four groups. Study the charters and write down all the particular points you identify under the following headings. Then compare your answers.
   a The rights they give to customers.
   b The additional protection they offer to customers (in addition to their legal rights).
   c The remedies which are identified for dissatisfied customers.

6.4 Sources of help and advice

There are many organisations to help consumers who have problems. Details are on pages 353–358.

The functions of consumer organisations

Consumer organisations may carry out one function or several, e.g.:

- **advisory** – those that give advice to consumers, e.g. the Citizens Advice Bureau

- **regulatory** – those ensuring that organisations operate according to specific regulations, e.g. the rail regulator which oversees train operating companies such as Virgin.

- **promotional** – those involved in promoting and advertising consumer rights, such as the Office of Fair Trading

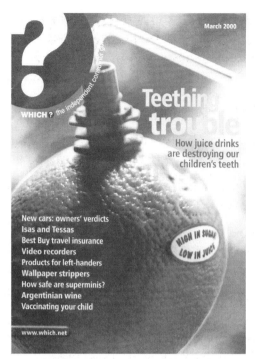

Figure 6.7 The Consumers' Association publishes its own magazine

- **investigatory** – those that investigate reports of breaches of regulations, e.g. the Trading Standards officers

- **lobbying** – those pressing the government for changes in the law to further protect consumers, e.g. the Consumers' Association

- **information** – those involved in providing information to manufacturers, retailers and consumers, e.g. the Office of Fair Trading, the Department for Trade and Industry, Trading Standards

- **representation** – those that represent consumer interests on committees or in consumer groups, e.g. the National Consumer Council or the Consumers' Association, or represent consumers in court, e.g. Citizens Advice Bureau advisers.

Consumer organisations

The main organisations and their key functions are listed below. You should note that they all have web sites – the address of which is given after each heading. To undertake the activity which then follows you will ideally need access to the Internet.

The Office of Fair Trading (OFT)

The role of the OFT is to:

- identify trading practices which are against consumer interests

- put these right, wherever possible

- regulate the provision of consumer credit

- investigate and remedy activities by industry and commerce which are against the interests of consumers (such as fixing prices or limiting the supply of an item).

The OFT also produces a quarterly consumer magazine called *Fair Trading,* which your tutor can obtain free of charge (check your library first, to see if it is stocked). The address is 15-25 Bream's Building, London EC4A 1PR, enquiry line: 0345 22 44 99, web page www.oft.gov.uk.

Citizens Advice Bureau (CAB)

There are nearly 800 Citizens Advice Bureaux in Britain. They give independent advice on a range of problems – not just those relating to consumers. They also advise people who are in debt, have problems with benefits or housing, legal concerns or other difficulties connected with issues such as employment or immigration.

They will help clients complete forms or write letters to organisations and even represent them in court.

Each CAB is an independent charity and many of the advisers and other people who work there do so on a voluntary basis.

You can find your local CAB in the telephone book. On the Internet you can access the

Figure 6.8 A Citizens Advice Bureau gives advice on a range of problems

National Association of Citizens Advice Bureaux (NACAB) on www.nacab.org.uk and use this site to search for your local CAB website. Online information and advice is available on www.adviceguide.org.uk.

If you live in Scotland then the Scottish Association of Citizens Advice Bureaux (known as Citizens Advice Scotland) covers this area and the 54 CAB which operate across Scotland. Their web site is www.cas.org.uk.

National Consumer Council (NCC)

This independent body was established in 1975. Its aims are to:

- promote action which improves and safeguards consumer interests

- represent consumers when major decisions are being made which will affect them

- ensure that the interests of all consumers are taken into account.

The NCC publishes several research papers and reports each year. It is best accessed through the Internet on www.ncc.org.uk.

Trading Standards

The Trading Standards offices throughout the country are there to:

- provide free help and advice to consumers and traders

- give help on using the small claims procedure against traders who are providing unsatisfactory goods or services

- investigate complaints made by consumers, e.g. in relation to misleading prices or descriptions of goods or services or inaccurate weights and measures

- enforce legislation in their own area. To do this they make test purchases, they also have the power to enter premises to inspect and seize goods and documents to make sure that traders are operating within the law. They can also seize dangerous goods and prevent them from being sold.

You can find the address and telephone of your nearest Trading Standards office in your local phone book or Yellow Pages. There are various web sites. Trading Standards Central is the web site for the Institute of Trading Standards Administration (ITSA). The web address is www.tradingstandards.gov.uk. This site gives you the opportunity to view or order useful leaflets. You may also find it interesting to access the safety warning pages – identifying products which manufacturers are recalling because of problems. It also includes useful teaching resources relating to consumer protection and provides links to a wide range of other consumer sites (e.g. BBC Watchdog On-Line, European Young Consumer Competition, plus regulators and ombudsmen). There is also a link to TSnet – another Trading Standards site run by a Trading Standards officer (www.xodesign.co.uk/tsnet/).

You may also find your own local area has a web site, such as Oxfordshire Trading Standards on www.oxon-tss.org.uk. From this site you can link to your own local site. You will see from the legislation pages just how many Acts exist to protect consumers!

Ombudsmen

The ombudsman scheme operates in many service areas, each of which has its own ombudsman. The job is to impartially investigate unresolved complaints and problems. There is no charge for the service. Ombudsmen are a last resort, rather than a first resort and customers are expected to try to resolve the problem with the supplier first. If there is no satisfaction, then the case can be referred to the ombudsman.

Ombudsmen operate in the following areas. Note that where there is no mention of a web site this is because there wasn't one at the time of writing.

- The Health Service Ombudsman investigates complaints about the National Health Service (www.ombudsman.org.uk).

- The Parliamentary Ombudsman investigates complaints relating to government departments. Complainants must be referred by their MP. (www.ombudsman.org.uk).

- The Local Government Ombudsmen investigate complaints against major local authorities (but not small town or district councils) (www.open.gov.uk/lgo/).

- The Legal Services Ombudsman is concerned with complaints about solicitors, barristers and other members of the legal profession in England and Wales

(tel: 0161 236 9532). There is a separate Scottish Legal Services Ombudsman (www.scot- legal.ombud.org.uk).

- The Northern Ireland Ombudsman investigates complaints relating to government services and health services in Northern Ireland (www.ombudsman.nics.gov.uk/).

- The Insurance Ombudsman Bureau is concerned with complaints about insurers – this may relate to the small print of insurance documents, inefficient service, disputes over claims (www.theiob.org.uk).

- The Banking Ombudsman scheme covers individual complaints about any bank in the UK (www.obo.org.uk).

- The Building Societies Ombudsman investigates complaints about UK building societies – in relation to mortgages, savings accounts or other services (tel: 0171: 931 0044).

- The Independent Housing Ombudsman investigates complaints about landlords. (tel: 0345 125973). There is a separate Housing Association Ombudsman for Scotland (tel: 0131 220 0599).

- The Estate Agents Ombudsman investigates complaints from private individuals – whether buyers or sellers – against estate agents, surveyors, valuers or auctioneers (www.oea.co.uk/).

- The Funeral Ombudsman investigates complaints against member funeral directors (tel: 0171 430 1012).

- Three ombudsmen currently deal with investments and pensions – the Investment Ombudsman, the Pension Ombudsman and the Personal Investment Authority Ombudsman Bureau – but all financial services will be covered by one ombudsman from autumn 2000 to simplify the system. This will cover banking and insurance as well as investments (see Financial Services Authority below).

Details of all ombudsman schemes in the UK and other complaint-handling bodies (e.g. the Police Complaints Authority and the Broadcasting Standards Commission) can be found on the government website – www.open.gov.uk.

Oftel

Office of Telecommunications

Figure 6.9 The Oftel logo

Regulators

Regulators are commonly known as 'watchdogs'. They oversee a particular industry. The aim is to obtain quality, choice and value for money for consumers. Although many regulators are government departments they operate independently, so that they can take an impartial view.

The government appointed regulators to oversee all the utility companies (i.e. water, gas and electricity) when these were privatised. They include:

- Oftel – the Office of Telecommunications – regulator for the UK telecommunications industry (www.oftel.gov.uk).

- Ofwat – the Office of Water Services – regulator for the water industry (www.ofwat.gov.uk).

- Ofgem – this is the new name for the regulator of the Office of Gas and Electricity Regulation. The web sites are currently still accessed through the 'old' names for gas and electricity, i.e. Ofgas and Offer (www.open.gov.uk/offer or www.ofgas.gov.uk).

In addition, there are regulators for other industries, e.g.:

- The Office of the Rail Regulator (Ofrail) is the government department responsible for all the train operating companies in the UK (www.rail-reg.gov.uk/).

- The Office of the National Lottery (Oflot) is the government department which overseas the regulation of the National Lottery (information telephone line: 0845 7129956).

- The financial services industry has several bodies to protect investors. The most powerful organisation is the Financial Services Authority (FSA) – a 'super-regulator' which overseas the whole financial services industry. The FSA has four objectives:

  ○ to promote confidence in financial markets

  ○ to protect consumers

  ○ to increase public awareness of the financial system

  ○ to reduce financial crime.

It has been given the power to operate as the regulatory body to oversee:

  ○ managers who hold money on behalf of other people (e.g. pension fund managers)

  ○ stockbrokers and market traders

○ independent financial advisers who advise or act for private investors.

You can find out more from its web site at www.sib.co.uk/.

Other consumer organisations

There are many consumer organisations in Britain. Some of these focus on a wide-range of issues concerning consumers, others are related to a particular industry. A selection of both types is given below.

- The Consumers' Association is an independent body which tests and examines goods and services and provides information to consumers. It is probably best known for its *Which* magazine (www.which.net/ – note that this is a subscription site and only a limited amount of information is available to non-subscribers).

- The Advertising Standards Authority (ASA) oversees press advertising and investigates complaints by consumers about the content of advertisements. It publishes case reports of complaints it has investigated and the action taken (www.asa.org.uk).

- Trade associations are bodies associated with specific trades (e.g. the Association of British Travel Agents). A list is normally included in all local telephone directories and community directories.

- The Office of the Data Protection Commissionaire administers the Data Protection Act. Consumers can complain about personal information held about them on computer (www.dataprotection.gov.uk/).

- The Welsh and Scottish consumer councils represent and safeguard consumer interests in those countries, as does the General Consumer Council for Northern Ireland. (www.wales.consumer.org.uk or www.scotconsumer.org.uk or alexandra.nics.gov.uk/gcc/).

- The National Federation of Consumers Groups is run by volunteers with the aim of promoting and coordinating consumer action, representing the views of members and campaigning to promote awareness of consumer issues and bring about change. They publish a magazine, *Consumer News*, which can also be read on the Internet (www.nfcg.org.uk).

You can access other consumer organisations through Net links attached to Trading Standards Central or the Office of Fair Trading. Other sites you may find useful if you are researching are:

- www.lawrights.co.uk – which gives free legal information on consumer issues in England and Wales

- www.consumers.gov.uk – the consumer gateway site of the Department of Trade and Industry which again includes links to other useful consumer organisations

- www.bbc.co.uk/watchdog – which gives information related to the BBC's Watchdog consumer programme

- www.consumerworld.org – which gives information to consumers on a wide range of current issues.

ACTIVITY

I   Find out if your tutor can arrange for a local Trading Standards officer and/or a Citizens Advice Bureau representative to talk to your group about their work in relation to consumer protection.

2 In pairs or groups of three, select one of the following organisations to research, so that your group as a whole is investigating each organisation listed. Supplement the information above with your own findings. Prepare a 10-minute talk for the rest of the group about the work of the organisation you have been allocated, using visual aids if possible. Supplement your talk with a one-page A4 information sheet for your audience on the main function and purpose of the organisation.

Note that if you use the Internet as a research tool to prepare your presentation, you should be able to use this task to supplement your key skills portfolio for IT and communications.

a Office of Fair Trading
b Consumers' Association
c National Consumer Council.
  If you live in Scotland, Wales or Northern Ireland, then the Scottish or Welsh Consumer Council or the General Consumer Council for Northern Ireland
d National Association of Citizens Advice Bureau or Citizens Advice Scotland
e Trading Standards
f Ombudsman scheme and details of at least one ombudsman service
g Regulators and details of the operations of at least one regulator
h Advertising Standards Authority
i National Federation of Consumer Groups
j If you live in Scotland, Wales or Northern Ireland, then the Scottish or Welsh Consumer Council or the General Consumer Council for Northern Ireland.

This option unit gives you the basis for studying administration. It concentrates on helping you to understand what is meant by administration systems as well as giving you an insight into the role of administrators in relation to handling information and organising meetings – two major parts of most administrative jobs.

This helps provide you with a firm basis for progressing to study Administrative Operations at Advanced level or to undertake an NVQ Administration qualification – which you are likely to do if you leave your Intermediate course and immediately start work or transfer to a training scheme.

This unit will be assessed through your portfolio work and your tutor will give you information about what you will need to provide.

7.1 Administrative systems

You first started to learn about administration in Unit 1, when you looked at the administrative function, its purpose and the activities which are carried out there. Turn back now to pages 53–57 and refresh your memory. In particular, note the difference between **centralised** and **decentralised** administrative functions. Check with your tutor that you clearly understand this difference.

Understanding systems

A system is defined as a pre-planned process or a set of activities which has been designed to achieve a specific result.

Take a simple example. A bank cash machine is a type of system. You enter your card and your PIN number. The process starts when you tap specific keys to request a mini-statement, an account balance or cash. The result is the statement or cash you receive.

Many 'systems' are mechanical or electronic. A camera is a system for taking photographs. You put in the film, take the picture and then take your film to be developed (another process!). The end result is the pictures you receive.

If you take photographs you will know that the quality can be variable. This may be because the film or the camera is faulty, you

Figure 7.1 Drawing money from a bank cash machine

made a mistake (by pointing the lens at the sky, for instance) or the person who developed the film made an error.

Many systems are variable because machines or equipment can develop a fault and also because *human beings* are involved – and human beings can make mistakes. So, even the most sophisticated system in the world is never perfect!

ACTIVITY

A road traffic system is very complex. Road users must follow rules to help reduce the number of accidents. However, problems still occur.

As a group:

a Look at the definition of a system above. What 'result' do you think road planners and traffic system developers hope to achieve?

b What 'equipment' or other non-human problems can spoil this result?

c Give five examples of human errors that can have an effect.

d How is the traffic system *controlled* in this country – i.e. what and who regulates it to stop people 'breaking the rules'?

e What document contains the rules of the system for new users?

Adding controls

Your modern, expensive camera adjusts the settings automatically. This is one type of control to reduce human error. If you are a driver you will be aware that you have to follow the Highway Code and that the police can prosecute you if you break the law.

The following are all features of systems.

a There are guidelines, instructions or even rules which everyone must follow.

b These state, in sequence, the procedures people have to follow.

c There are controls to try to stop people doing things differently and spoiling the end result.

d Every user of the system is trained to do the same thing.

The aim is to have a successful outcome every time.

ACTIVITY

1 a Where or how would you find out how to:
   i use a bank cash machine
   ii set a new video recorder
   iii drive a car
   so that you could obtain a 'successful outcome'?

b As a group, list as many consequences as you can of 'doing your own thing'.

2 Think back to when you enrolled at college. This is another type of system.
   a What guidelines were you given?
   b What procedures did you have to follow?
   c What would have been the result if you had ignored these?
   d Why do you think it is sensible for everyone who enrols to have to follow the same procedures?

Applying systems to administration

All businesses are crucially dependent on their administrative systems for their success. Three administrative systems you will study in this unit are for:

- filing papers
- receipt and distribution of mail
- despatch of mail.

Administrative systems can also be applied to many other jobs, such as the system of dealing with visitors at reception, the system for controlling photocopying or for sending faxes or emails. Having a *system* to follow means that jobs can be done successfully most of the time. This means that anyone who has to do the job for the first time has to do it in a certain way. This may vary from one organisation to another, but only slightly. So, if you move from one organisation to another to do the same job you will know what to do.

In very large organisations, where many activities are **centralised**, every department follows the same system. In a small organisation, different departments may do much of their own work, and the systems may vary slightly between one area of the organisation and another.

A system may become out of date and need to be reviewed. In some cases the system may not 'work' because it is too complicated and staff do not understand what to do. You can measure the effectiveness of a system by checking the outcome. If the work is done properly, staff understand what to do and the 'customers' are satisfied, then the system is successful. If there are problems, these need to be identified and changes made to the system to make it work.

ACTIVITY

A medium-sized business decides to operate a new system for all the photocopying. Currently anyone can do their own photocopying, but the machine keeps breaking down – the engineer says this is through misuse. The manager decides that in future only one person, Julie, can do the photocopying and the work must be put in her 'in' tray each day. After a week several complaints are received that there are too many delays and

urgent documents take too long to copy. In other cases Julie has misunderstood the instructions (which she claims were unclear) and the work has had to be redone, wasting paper and time. On Friday Julie was off sick so no copying was done. On her return she told the manager she was looking for a new job because photocopying all day was boring and she got the blame when things went wrong. Obviously the new system is not working!

As a group discuss with your tutor:

a why the 'old' system was changed
b the problems with the 'new' system
c how the system could be changed to make it effective.

7.2 Collecting and storing information

Information is often described as the 'life blood' of an organisation. Why? Because an organisation needs a constant flow of information to survive. You know the importance of information from your own experience. Take a simple example. You plan

Figure 7.2 Up-to-date information is essential to doing business on the Stock Exchange

to meet your friends tonight several miles away but start watching a video before you go out. You are so engrossed in the video that you haven't looked out of the window or, of course, seen the weather forecast on TV. So you have no idea that it has been snowing outside. You are also unaware that your mobile phone is dead because you forgot to renew the batteries. You get ready to go out and only when you open the front door do you realise you have a problem. The problem has occurred because you had no way of receiving the latest information – that the weather had changed dramatically.

Now just think of the hundreds of people in an organisation who are making dozens of decisions every day based on the latest information they have. Imagine all the mistakes and problems that can occur if information is delayed, inaccurate, unavailable or lost!

All administrative staff play a key role in:

- **collecting information** (whether it arrives in the mail, electronically, by telephone or is passed on by word of mouth)

- **processing information** (i.e. inputting it, merging it with other information, sorting it, reorganising it, reproducing it or updating current records)

- **storing information** (in filing systems and on computer)

- **distributing information** (i.e. passing on messages, forwarding electronic mail to the right people, giving out mail).

The storage and retrieval of information

It is useless 'storing' something if you cannot find it when you want it! The test of a good storage system is that:

- you can find things quickly

- the items stored are kept in good condition.

Staff in a CD store or video shop need to find what customers want within a few seconds – so their storage systems must be excellent. In offices, information is stored and retrieved in manual filing systems and on computer systems. Again staff must be able to find anything within a minute or so.

 **ACTIVITY**

Test yourself! How quickly can you find each of the following documents – and what condition are they in?

a   Your birth certificate
b   Your last bank statement
c   Notes your tutor gave you last week
d   Your GCSE results slip (or certificate)
e   A receipt for something you bought a few days ago.

Manual filing systems

Manual filing systems are used for paper documents – often known as 'hard copies'. Paper documents can include business letters, memos, reports, purchasing documents (quotations and orders), financial documents (invoices, statements, banking documents), leaflets, brochures, booklets, catalogues and legal contracts.

There are often different methods for storing these items – you can punch holes in a piece of paper for filing in a folder, for instance, but you couldn't do this with a thick catalogue! Also, some items need to be kept for a long time for legal reasons, whereas others only need to be kept for a few days or weeks. So the type of documents or files to be kept determines the storage system and the methods of storage. Examples include:

- documents fastened together in a brown manilla file folder

- documents kept together in an envelope wallet

- A4 lever arch files (for punched documents)

- A4 box files (for catalogues and other booklets)

- A3 files – often used for computer print-outs.

Storage systems

There are usually a variety of filing cabinets in offices. These include:

- **vertical cabinets** with a number of large drawers (usually four). These are fitted with special 'suspension' pockets into which document folders are placed. Tabs attached to these pockets make it easy to identify the files.

- **horizontal cabinets** with several large, shallow drawers. They are ideal for storing large documents, such as architects' drawings.

- **lateral cabinets** are like large, open cupboards with a sliding door or blind which can be pulled down when the cupboard is not in use. The cabinet contains suspended pockets in rows into which file folders are slotted. Multipurpose cabinets have a combination of lateral and vertical files and may include shelves and storage space for box files, ring binders and other items.

Filing cabinets can usually be locked and are fire and impact resistant. They also have safety features (e.g. only one drawer of a vertical cabinet can be opened at once so that the cabinet doesn't tilt towards the user).

Methods of classification

If you had a pile of documents, how would you sort or order them so that it would be easy to find whatever you wanted? This, of course, depends on the type of document. You may keep your pay slips or bank statements in date order and if you were filing invoices from suppliers you would probably have a separate file for each supplier. You would then have to decide the order in which to organise the files. You may decide to do this alphabetically – or according to the supplier number.

In business, files are usually stored using an **alphabetical** or a **numerical** system, e.g.:

- **Alphabetical by name.** In this case papers are filed under the **surname** of the person or the **name of the organisation**. This is the most commonly used system for storing customer or personnel files. If you want to see how this system works, look in the phone book.

- **Alphabetical by subject.** Here the method is to group the material according to the **topic**. This is frequently used for filing information on products and services and for filing paperwork relating to an executive's areas of responsibility. Yellow Pages is a good example of classifying information alphabetically by subject.

Figure 7.3 Different filing cabinets

- **Alphabetical by geographical area**. In this system the **place** or **location** is the key. The method is often used to organise information into sales territories, especially by mail order companies or by companies importing or exporting goods.

- **Numerical by sequence**. This is grouping documents by **number**. It could be a customer number, employee number or supplier number. An index is created so that users can find the number quickly if they need to. In a sequential system, each new file is simply given the next number.

- **Alpha-numerical**. This combines both alphabetical and numerical filing. It is simply a method of sub-dividing numerical files using the letters of the alphabet. Instead of each new file being

given a new number, files are divided in 26 groups, A-Z, and each of these groups has its own numbers, e.g. A1, A2, A3, B1, B2, B3 etc.

- **Chronological**. Here the **date** is used, as for filing birth certificates, examination certificates, travel documents.

There are advantages and disadvantages to each of these methods and these are summarised in Figure 7.4. A key factor in choosing a system is how much **cross-referencing** will be required. This is needed when a document is placed in two (or more) files. The original is usually placed in the most obvious file and a photocopy, or cross-reference note, placed in other file(s). Cross-referencing is usually more likely to be needed in an alphabetical method than the numerical one.

Classification method	Advantages	Disadvantages
Alphabetical by names	Easy to use A miscellaneous file for each letter can be created for 'one-off' papers	Popular letters become congested Difficult to expand Names can be confused
Alphabetical by subject	Easy to add new topics Easy to sub-divide main topics Sensible grouping for writing summaries and reports on a topic	Can be overlaps between subjects resulting in duplication, much cross-referencing or confusion May be several files on a particular topic
Alphabetical by geographical area	No need to know complex foreign names Simple and easy if location is known	Expansion can be difficult Similar place names can be confused, e.g. Boston, Lincolnshire, and Boston, USA
Numerical by sequence	Capable of infinite expansion Each file has a unique number The number can be used as a reference number in correspondence	An index is essential for files to be found Transposition of figures can cause problems Miscellaneous documents are difficult to store
Alpha-numerical	Easy to expand under each letter Numbers can be used as a reference number	Can be confusing unless system understood Index essential to find files
Chronological	Useful when date most significant item Easy to use and understand	Too specialised for general use More information required to find specific items (e.g. name of traveller as well as date of travel to identify correct tickets)

Figure 7.4 Advantages and disadvantages of methods of storing information

Operating a manual storage system

Everyone who uses a filing system must know exactly how to use it. Otherwise files could get lost, documents might be misfiled, papers damaged. This is why filing is a type of administrative *system*. There are clear rules and procedures that must be followed for the system to work.

Rules and procedures

These must include instructions on:

- the general rules of filing
- how to cross-reference documents
- how to control the lending of files and how to trace these if they are overdue
- how long to retain documents and files
- how to deal with confidential documents
- what to do if a problem occurs and the person to whom this should be reported.

ACTIVITY

1 The general rules of filing are outlined in Figure 7.5. Check that you understand all the terms and examples used. Then check your own file folder to see how well you punch documents!

2 Refer to your local Yellow Pages and find three examples of cross-referenced entries.

3 a As a group, discuss how you would control the lending and return of files for which you are responsible.

   b How would you amend these ideas to cope with confidential files and documents?

4 Why do you think it is important that some documents must be retained? Refer back to page 363 if you are stuck. Now give three reasons why you think it is important to remove old files (or old documents) at regular intervals.

5 As a group, discuss what you think should be done if the following problems occur:
   a a senior member of staff borrows files but doesn't return them
   b an important document that arrived yesterday cannot be found
   c your colleague never does her share of the filing, leaving you to do it all.

6 a Obtain an office equipment catalogue and identify the different types of storage

DO	● File daily – to avoid a backlog and documents getting 'lost' in the filing tray. ● Pre-sort documents *first*. Use a concertina file to pre-sort into alphabetical order quickly and easily. ● Remove paper clips as these 'hook' other papers – staple related documents together. ● Repair torn or damaged documents or photocopy them. ● Punch documents *squarely* by aligning them with the guide rule on the punch or align them using the centre arrow so the holes are always in the same place. ● Learn the rules for alphabetical filing – the phone book is a useful guide.
DON'T	● Guess where to file something – ask first. ● Squeeze papers into a full folder – split into two and write 'to' and 'from' dates on each. ● Pull out folders by the tabs – they tear. ● Remove individual documents from a file – take the complete file and follow the official procedures for 'borrowing' a file. ● Start a new file for every new name. 'One-off' documents are usually put in a miscellaneous file. ● Overload a filing cabinet with too many folders.

Figure 7.5 Rules for filing

systems described on page 364. See how many other storage systems you can find which are *not* listed above.

b You already know that controls in a system are not infallible! Vertical cabinets have been built not to tilt – but what sort of carelessness can create safety hazards? Discuss your ideas as a group.

7 How would you check how successful a filing system is? Discuss your ideas as a group.

Computer-based filing systems

If you use a word processing package or a database then you are using a type of computerised filing. The other main method is electronic document management systems (EDMS). In this system documents are scanned into a computer and stored via a special computer program onto optical disks. Each of these systems is briefly described below.

- When you produce a document on a word processor you give it a title and can store it in its own 'file folder'. In this way you can store documents methodically on

Figure 7.6 File folder containing documents

a hard disk. Your disk directory will show all the folders and you can access each of them to find out the contents, using a program such as Windows Explorer.

- A database is for storing details of customers, suppliers or personnel. It is a computerised index card system. The

	Advantages	Disadvantages
Manual filing systems	Allow access by multiple users Files can be removed for reference and used elsewhere Notes can be attached to documents to give additional information Relatively cheap to install/maintain Confidential files can be kept in special locked cabinets	Take up floor space Need systematic sorting to remove 'dead' files Papers can be misfiled Papers may be damaged Files can be lost or misplaced Filing often considered a 'chore' Backlog of unfiled documents creates a problem
Computerised filing systems	Space-saving – about 13,000 A4 documents can be stored on one optical disk Scanning is quick and easy Access by different people possible from PCs Indexing and cross-referencing done automatically Back-up files created automatically – can be kept off premises for security	Inappropriate for some documents, e.g. legal contracts Expensive Computer failure means no files available Staff training required Hard copies still taken for reference or to work on – so still some paper to store

Figure 7.7 Advantages and disadvantages of manual and electronic filing systems

advantage is that the 'cards' can be sorted under different (and multiple) headings quickly and easily to find particular groups, e.g. all the customers in a certain district and/or in a particular age group.

- EDMS is filing of the future. Here incoming and copies of outgoing documents are scanned into the system and stored on special optical disks. The documents are indexed, which makes it easy to retrieve them using appropriate search criteria.

The advantages and disadvantages of paper-based versus computerised filing systems are summarised in Figure 7.7.

ACTIVITY

Bill Andrews owns his own computer firm. His administrator is ill and the staff forget to give him the following documents before he leaves by car for a two-day conference. Instead they simply put them in his in-tray after he has left.

1 A letter from a very large company asking Bill's company to design their new web site. They want him to give a presentation to them on Monday in London. He must confirm immediately whether he will be attending or not.

2 A telephone message from his insurance company that his car insurance is overdue.

3 A report from the financial manager, attaching a spreadsheet showing the company's latest cash flow position, which Bill wanted to study while he was away, as he thinks there are some problems.

   a What could be the result in each case? Discuss your ideas as a group.

   b If you were Bill, what action would you have taken if you had known about these documents and in what way would the outcomes have been different?

7.3 Using information

Information is used for three main purposes:

- **To make decisions**. Decisions are always better if you have up-to-date, accurate and complete information. If you are missing a critical piece of information, you are likely to make the wrong decision. In Bill's case, not responding to the presentation invitation could mean losing valuable new business.

- **To satisfy legal requirements**. In some cases information has to be handled (or documents must be signed) promptly, in other cases information must be retained for a specific time period. Tax and VAT returns, for instance, must be returned by a specific date or the business owner is fined. Different types of documents must be kept safe for a specific number of years, by law, e.g. accounts for 6 years and accident reports for 30 years. In Bill's case, he could have been driving to the conference in an uninsured car – which is illegal.

- **To monitor business activity**. Most organisations have computerised accounts systems or produce spreadsheets or reports which show the level of sales activity and the amount of money being received. If this information shows a fall in sales or any other type of problem then action must be taken promptly. If you have studied Unit 3 on Business Finance you will realise how important financial information is to an organisation – particularly information about the cashflow. Bill will need to take action if there are cashflow problems or the bank may 'bounce' cheques if there is insufficient money in the account to cover them.

For all these reasons it is important that information is processed and distributed quickly so that it is available when it is needed. Otherwise the results could be very serious indeed – and a firm may even go out of business.

7.4 Methods of processing and communicating information

Information is processed when it is changed or converted in some way. It may be improved or may be prepared for a particular use, e.g.:

- scribbled jottings from a telephone call are written out into a legible and clear message

- notes made during a meeting are summarised into action points and sent to those who were present (see page 381)

- notes made during researching are written up into a report or summary

- information on a customer's account is obtained before a reminder letter for payment is sent

- sales figures are input into a spreadsheet and analysed for sales trends. An accompanying graph may be prepared.

- customer names and addresses in a database are merged with a promotional letter being sent as a mail shot.

In many cases information stored in manual filing systems and computer-based systems is being accessed and processed to help create new communications. In some cases entirely new information is being processed. In other cases new and old information is being linked together.

Information can be received or communicated in one of three ways:

- orally – when you talk to someone face-to-face or on the telephone or when you attend a meeting (see page 374)

- in writing, such as memos, letters and reports

- electronically, e.g. emails, faxes and video conferencing.

Different methods, different recipients

In Section 1.4, pages 110–114, you learned about the differences between written and oral communications, and the advantages and disadvantages of each method were summarised in Figure 1.78 and the variety of methods available was summarised in Figure 1.79. You also learned that the method to use depends on various factors.

- The reason for communicating.

- The person who will receive the information – particularly whether the communication will be internal (staying within the organisation) or external (sent outside the organisation).

- Whether it is urgent or non-urgent.

- How complex the message is.

- Whether or not feedback is required.

Reread pages 110–114 again to refresh your memory, before learning more about electronic methods below.

Electronic methods of communicating

During the 21st century, electronic methods of communicating are likely to become more and more popular. It saves time, money and effort to attach a file electronically to an email than to print it out and send it by post – providing you know what you are doing.

The following are the key facts you need to know about the main methods of communicating electronically.

Email

As a student you may have your own email site at college for sending emails to fellow students or communicating over the Internet. Electronic mail is a simple and easy method of transmitting messages internally and externally. The benefits are that:

- any other document produced on computer can be attached to the email and transmitted at the same time

- complex information can be sent – and because the details are written down there is little risk of misunderstanding, which could happen if you were communicating by telephone

- emails can be prepared and sent at the sender's convenience – any hour of the day or night – and the recipients can read incoming messages and respond when it suits them

- emails can be sent simultaneously to a group of people, e.g. all the people who normally attend a particular meeting

- a copy of an email can be printed out for the file or for further discussion

- all email systems are protected by a password and a user ID so that only the named user can access the mail.

Fax

Fax machines are versatile, useful and cheap. Most offices have them, for transmitting documents over any distance quickly and easily. Automated fax machines can undertake many operations independently. Frequently used numbers can be stored in the machine's memory, which has a search facility for speedy retrieval, so that faxes can be sent automatically during cheap-rate and off-peak times. The machine can be programmed to preface each message with a specially printed

Figure 7.8 A fax machine

cover sheet giving the name of the organisation and sender, and to print a previously stored signature at a specific point.

The main benefit is that the document does not need retyping. Also more people have access to fax machines than to email. You can send a fax on headed paper so that the document looks more official than an email message. Faxes also have the advantage of being able to transmit graphics, maps and photographs.

Video conferencing

Video conferencing is simply a method of holding a meeting when the participants are in different locations. It can be done simply over the Internet, between two people who have video conferencing software and a tiny camera on top of their computers! Instead of just typing messages they can see and hear each other as well. This is known as **desktop conferencing**. If more people are involved, special equipment can be hired for group conferences or the participants can go to their nearest video-conferencing studio. There is one in all the major cities in the UK and most places abroad. Video conferencing is normally a cost-effective option if the participants would otherwise have to travel long distances to attend – as it saves both time and expenditure on travel.

ACTIVITY

1   Faxes and email systems are used for rapid transmission. How often then do you think users should:

   • check their electronic mailbox for new messages

   • check fax machines for incoming messages?

2   Fax messages can be signed whereas email messages cannot. Identify three occasions when this may mean that a fax is more appropriate than email.

3   Many colleges have a room where video conferencing can be demonstrated – even if just between two computers. Try to find out if this is available in your college. Alternatively, find out about NetMeetings by accessing the Microsoft site on www.microsoft.com. You can then go to the products or catalogue page and search for NetMeeting to find out the latest information. Print out any details you find useful.

Internal and external mailing systems

Another method of obtaining and sending information is through mail systems. Each morning millions of documents are delivered to business premises all over Britain by the Royal Mail. Faxes and emails arrive throughout the day and couriers may deliver urgent packages. Internal mail is sent from one department to another within the organisation.

Figure 7.9 Mailing systems

Every organisation also sends faxes and emails and arranges for urgent items to be collected by courier. Standard items of mail are processed and despatched daily through the Royal Mail system.

To work in any business you need to understand how the standard items of incoming and outgoing mail are processed, and how both external and internal post systems operate. You also need to know when to use more rapid transmission systems, such as fax, email and courier services.

Internal mail

The aim is always to:

   • distribute mail as quickly as possible each morning

   • make sure no mail is damaged, lost or wrongly delivered.

A centralised mailroom operates in most organisations where mail is delivered by Royal Mail – often at a specific, pre-arranged time each day. In a small firm, one particular person may be responsible for opening all the incoming mail. This involves the following tasks.

1 Pre-sorting the mail into:

- urgent items (for immediate delivery or collection)

- personal or private and confidential items – which are not opened unless special instructions have been given

- guaranteed delivery mail, such as registered and recorded delivery items which are signed for on receipt and usually recorded in a special book

- monetary items, such as cheques, which may be listed separately

- routine mail – first class items are usually opened before second class

- circulars, such as brochures and advertising literature. Many organisations have a 'circulation slip'

which is placed on these (see Figure 7.10) to reduce photocopying.

Any wrongly delivered mail is usually reposted unopened with an appropriate note on the envelope, e.g. 'not known at this address'.

Parcels are usually not opened in the mailroom but delivered to the department it is addressed to, where the contents will be checked.

2 Checking the mail to ensure all enclosures are included and clipping these to the main document.

3 Date-stamping all documents unless they are financial or legal documents, such as cheques or legal contracts.

4 Sorting the mail into departments and placing it in baskets for distribution or collection. The order for placing documents is:

- urgent on top

- private and confidential or personal letters

- first class items

- second class items

- circulars and magazines.

5 Checking all envelopes to make sure they are empty before being discarded. Some organisations retain all envelopes for 24 hours to make sure no important enclosure has been overlooked.

CIRCULATION SLIP

Name	Date received	Date passed on

Please return to ....

Figure 7.10 Circulation slip

 ACTIVITY

1 Use an office equipment catalogue to decide the furniture and equipment you would require if you were responsible for processing the incoming mail in a medium-sized organisation. Discuss your suggestions with your tutor.

2 The Home Office and the police provide information to businesses on dealing with suspicious items in the post. You can obtain government information on this over the Internet by downloading files using Acrobat. If you cannot do this, select two members of the group to visit the local police station to ask the crime prevention officer for a leaflet. You can also search the Net for information on suspicious packages (use a search engine such as Altavista or Yahoo). Much of this is American – but the information is just as valuable.

3 You accidentally open an envelope marked 'strictly personal' and addressed to your boss. It contains a letter from a debt collection agency regarding non-payment of a large bill. Discuss as a group what action you should take.

External mail

In offices or departments items are prepared for the external post throughout the day.

- Letters are typed, signed and placed in envelopes.

- Larger envelopes are prepared for more bulky items.

- Weighty items or items that could be damaged are packed into jiffy bags.

- Parcels are packed and wrapped securely.

Many organisations use window envelopes for most of the routine post, to save retyping the name and address. The most usual size of envelope is known as 'DL' – A4 sheets can be folded three times to fit inside.

Once the mail has been taken or sent to the mailroom the staff:

- sort the mail into:
  - special items (e.g. registered and recorded delivery items)
  - foreign mail
  - routine mail (separated into first and second class)
  - parcels

- weigh the items on special postage scales to calculate the correct postage rate

- complete any forms required for special items

- frank or stamp the mail.

The mail is then collected by the Royal Mail at a pre-arranged time or taken to the nearest post office. Franked items are delivered in a special bag – they are *not* posted in the normal way.

Internal mail systems

External post costs money, so most organisations operate a system of internal post between departments and between branches. Costs are kept down by:

- special re-usable envelopes for internal mail items

- bulk envelopes holding a number of items to be sent to branch offices

- an internal delivery system – which may include packages and envelopes being moved from one branch to another by internal personnel.

A special type of internal/external system is used by some small businesses, such as solicitors and estate agents, who contact one another frequently. Each is given a DX number and their mail is collected locally, sorted and delivered for a specified charge.

Courier services

Couriers and private delivery services are now commonly used for urgent packages and parcels. The price varies depending on the journey to be made. A private parcel delivery service may charge a similar rate to

Figure 7.11 A special delivery by courier

Parcelforce for standard items but a special delivery by motorbike courier will be much more expensive. Given that many documents are now transmitted instantly by computer or fax, couriers are usually only used when *original* documents, disks or CD-Roms have to be transported. Examples are a legal document which needs an immediate signature or an advertising proof which needs urgent approval.

ACTIVITY

I   Divide into groups of two or three and research the Royal Mail postal services on the Internet by contacting either http://www.royalmail.co.uk or http://www.parcelforce.co.uk.

Each group should select one of the following topics to research:

- choosing and using envelopes and addressing these

- packing and wrapping parcels securely

- identifying items which must not be posted

- special delivery and how this operates

- guaranteed delivery services

- electronic mailings and electronic services

- sending small mailings abroad

- different methods of paying for postage

- standard services within the UK

- calculating postal charges

- parcel services within the UK (Parcelforce)

- parcel services overseas (Parcelforce).

2   Find out as much as you can about franking machines and how these operate by referring to equipment guides published by the major manufacturers or to an office equipment catalogue (check in your college library). Try to arrange to see one in operation.

3   Identify the additional equipment which may be needed in a large organisation to process outgoing mail.

7.5 The purpose and administration of business meetings

One eminent psychologist, Dr David Lewis, estimated that people can spend up to two years of their working lives in meetings. Other studies have shown managers spend up to 65 per cent of their working week at meetings. Why are meetings held at all – and why so many?

Meetings are held for several purposes. Their main one is face-to-face communication between people who need to:

- give out or exchange information

- obtain the views and opinions of others

- decide on action to be taken

- solve problems

- generate ideas and suggestions

- coordinate activities to be undertaken by different people

- report on an event or activity

- discuss issues of mutual concern

- broaden involvement in a project

- obtain assistance

- organise special events or occasions.

Only when a meeting has a particular purpose – or aim – is it likely to be effective. The meeting must also be **well organised**. This means that:

- the time, date and venue must be fixed in advance

- the time and date should be convenient for those whose attendance is vital

- the venue must be large enough for everyone and in a convenient location to minimise travel time and cost

- those attending must know what they need to do to prepare for the meeting

- one person must be nominated to chair (run) the meeting and another to take notes

- paperwork must be prepared in advance and either circulated to members beforehand or handed out on the day

- the chairperson must be capable of running the meeting properly – so that everyone is encouraged to contribute, and

no-one is allowed to distract or 'take-over' the meeting

- minutes, or action notes, which summarise what was discussed and the action people promised to take, must be circulated afterwards.

Two major roles are **chairperson** and **minutes secretary**. A good chairperson can make the difference between an efficient, well-run meeting and a chaotic free-for-all. The minutes secretary is usually responsible for the administrative arrangements before, during and after the meeting. The role of each person is shown in Figure 7.12. You may like to note that the term 'minutes secretary' is rarely used by small, private organisations – but there is still someone who has to do these duties!

 **ACTIVITY**

1 Read through the tasks listed in Figure 7.12 and then decide the skills required for a person to be:
   a a good chairperson
   b an effective minutes secretary.

2 Assume you are a member of the health and safety committee at your workplace. As a member what do you think your role and responsibilities are? Discuss your ideas with your tutor.

Making arrangements

The success of a meeting will depend on how well the arrangements are organised. However, meetings also cost money, so you must be able to arrange a meeting which is cost-effective in achieving its aims. Meetings must be safe, so you must also consider the health and safety aspects. The key issues are summarised below.

Chairperson	Minutes secretary
Knowing the rules and regulations relating to the meeting	Check availability of main participants
Start the meeting on time	Book and check venue
Introduce new members	Order refreshments
Follow the agenda (see page 379)	Send out notices or invitations
Explain the background to topics being discussed	Prepare paperwork required
Encourage relevant discussion	Book equipment required
Ensure members 'address the chair' and do not converse amongst themselves	Nominate person to take messages while meeting is in progress
Check each person has the opportunity to contribute	Welcome arrivals
Decide when to end discussion on a topic and summarise the points made	Arrange paper, pencils, pens
	Pass out papers and information
Arbitrate when there is disagreement over an issue (if there is deadlock the chair has the casting vote)	Give apologies for those not able to attend
	Take notes of meeting
Check everyone is clear on the action agreed	Tidy room and remove surplus papers
Close the meeting properly	Type up notes or minutes
Check and sign the minutes	Check these with chairperson
	Circulate any other papers
	File spare papers
	Enter date of next meeting in chairperson's diary

Figure 7.12 Roles and tasks of chairperson and minutes secretary

Cost implications

All business meetings have a budget. The aim is to keep costs to an acceptable level within this budget.

The costs include:

- time travelling to and from the meeting and attending it
- travel
- accommodation – for those who need to stay overnight
- hiring the venue
- refreshments or meals
- photocopying and postage
- other paper and stationery required.

Internal meetings are usually held in special meetings rooms in the office building. If it involves people travelling from different parts of the country, the meeting may be held in a central location. Hotels, universities, business centres and chambers of commerce have facilities for this. To save on time and the cost of travel, some organisations use video conferencing (see page 370)

Arranging accommodation

The major considerations include:

- the convenience of the venue
- the suitability of the room
- the facilities
- the cost.

The meeting room must be large enough to seat everyone comfortably and there must be facilities for taking notes. Traffic noise must be muted, any video or projection screen must be easy to see and the room must be warm, well-lit, clean and tidy. There should be side tables if refreshments are to be served. The windows should have blinds to close out light if audio/visual equipment is to be used.

For external venues, such as hotels, other factors should be considered, e.g.:

- ease of access – the venue may be near a main road or miles away in the countryside
- car parking space
- availability of sleeping accommodation
- friendly and professional staff
- appropriate facilities and good food
- a good safety record (see below).

Usually most meetings have people sitting around a large boardroom style table or a u-shaped table. You will need to specify the kind of seating arrangement you want.

Health and safety aspects

Most external meetings start with a rundown of 'housekeeping arrangements' for participants. These include information about what to do in the case of fire (e.g. fire alarm, nearest fire exit, nearest assembly point). In a large building there should be smoke alarms, heat detectors and a sprinkler system, as well as fire-fighting equipment such as extinguishers and hoses. In hotels every bedroom must clearly display a fire notice showing the quickest escape route. The fire certificate, which is a legal requirement, lists the equipment installed, shows a plan of the building, gives details of the fire precautions taken, how the alarm is raised and other relevant information.

'Housekeeping arrangements' should also include information on the location of the nearest toilets, cloakrooms and first-aid facilities. A good organiser will be prepared for any health emergencies. If the meeting is internal, normal procedures should be followed, such as immediately contacting a first-aider. At an external venue emergencies are usually dealt with by reception or by security. These include health emergencies and emergencies such as power failure or a bomb warning.

The facilities themselves should, of course, be safe. This includes the building itself and the way in which routine operations are carried out. Cleaning or maintenance work, for instance, should not be a risk to visitors. All electrical equipment must be checked – many external venues do not allow untested or unchecked electrical equipment to be used on their premises. Safety signs should identify any hazards or risks to visitors or employees.

Finally, there must be safe access and egress (exits) for individuals. Usually this involves having a separate area for loading and unloading, speed limits on drives or car parks and crossing points or barriers where pedestrians must cross a vehicle route. Inside the building 'traffic routes' must be kept clear and floors must be appropriately covered and not be uneven or slippery. There must be handrails on stairs, landings and galleries and glass doors should be clearly marked. Doors that open both ways and ordinary doors on main traffic routes should have a transparent panel for seeing through.

All organisations in the UK are bound by the Health and Safety at Work Act 1974 (see Unit 1, page 36) and the Management of Health and Safety at Work Regulations 1992 applies as much to hotels or business centres as it does to shops and factories. Anyone who uses or visits the premises – including employees, outside contractors, members of the public and visitors – must be able to do so safely.

Organising refreshments

For internal meetings most organisations have a system for ordering light refreshments or sandwiches from the catering department. Tea or coffee is often available on arrival – particularly for those who have travelled some distance. If it is going to be a long meeting then fresh water or a variety of non-alcoholic cold drinks may be available throughout the day.

If the meeting is held at lunchtime it is usual for sandwiches or a buffet to be provided. Sticky or messy food should be avoided – and don't forget the plates and serviettes!

If a meeting is to last all day, the participants may break to have lunch at an external venue. In a small firm there may be no catering department and only the facilities to provide tea, coffee and biscuits in-house. In this case, a lunchtime meeting may involve buying in sandwiches from the local sandwich shop.

Sending letters of invitation

A letter of invitation is sent to those outside the organisation who are attending the meeting.

Figure 7.13 Meetings often need catering

To those within the organisation, it is usual to send a notice of meeting and agenda in one document – either through the internal post or by email if the meeting is informal.

The invitation and information about the meeting should be sent in good time to allow people to make arrangements to attend. Key participants may be contacted by telephone first, to ensure the proposed date is suitable for them. It is pointless calling a meeting that no-one can attend! The organiser should keep a list of those who cannot attend and 'send their apologies'. This list is read out at the meeting.

Providing documentation

Some types of documentation must be sent to participants before the meeting. This includes the agenda for the meeting (see page 380), any papers people need to read beforehand – and a map if the meeting is to be held at an unfamiliar location. Other papers are **tabled**. This means they are produced at the meeting itself. It is sensible to have spare copies of all documents which have been sent out in advance in case anyone forgets to bring their copies.

Meetings documents

The minutes secretary, or administrator, not only has to carry out the duties listed in Figure 7.12, he or she also needs to know how to prepare all the documentation required – and when to produce them.

Letters of invitation or notice of meeting

These **must** state:

* the name and address of the organisation, if people outside the organisation are being invited

HIGHTOWN COLLEGE
Cheyne Walk
HIGHTOWN
HG3 9NP

Tel: 01892-303809

Fax: 01892-399889

Principal: Janine Stott B.Litt, MA (Oxon)

25 January 2000

Mr M Grimmer
Chief Paramedic
St Catherine's Hospital
Riverside Road
HIGHTOWN
HG2 9PD

Dear Mr Grimmer

PLANNING MEETING – PUBLIC SERVICES COURSE PROVISION

I would like to invite you to attend our planning meeting for next year's Public Services course which will be held in Room F224 in the main building of this college on Monday, 23 February, at 1530 hours.

As you are aware, we are always keen to link our course provision to current trends and last year you were kind enough to help us by suggesting events and activities for students linked to your own specialist area. As we now want to finalise our plans for next year we would again value your assistance and advice.

We should be grateful if you could confirm as soon as possible if you will be able to attend. We will then send you the agenda for the meeting and arrange for a car parking space for you and a visitor's badge to be available at reception.

Yours sincerely

Louise Kemple
Course Leader

Figure 7.14 Personalised letter of invitation

- the date, day and time of the meeting

- the place (room and location address, if different from the company address) where the meeting will be held

- the type of meeting, if appropriate

- the date of the notice or invitation.

Any special issues to be discussed, may also be described.

Imagine your college runs a public services course and is planning provision for next year. Teaching staff and experts are invited to give their views. An example of the letter of invitation is shown in Figure 7.14. This would be personalised for each individual invited.

ACTIVITY

1   Study the letter in Figure 7.14 carefully and then identify:
    a   whether all the key requirements are included
    b   what reason has been given for holding the meeting
    c   how the writer has tried to make the participant feel his contribution would be useful
    d   what other information has been included for the benefit of the reader.

2   The health and safety committee of Hightown College is interested in improving access for the disabled. At the last meeting it was agreed that the best person to contact for expert advice is Mr John Ashton, the Disablement Officer, who is based at Hightown Council, 14 Riverside Walk, Hightown, HG3 4MP. The chairperson, Carolyn Strachan, has already telephoned him and he has agreed to attend your next meeting which will be held two weeks on Thursday, at 1430 hours in room J20.

    Write a formal letter of invitation to Mr Ashton for her to sign.

The agenda

An agenda for a meeting provides information about the business to be discussed. It also lists the 'order of business'. Routine meetings usually start and end with specific items of business. These are items 1, 2, 3, 6 and 7 in the list that follows.

1   **Apologies for absence.** This is the first item. The minutes secretary reads out the list of those who cannot attend and the reason why. Their names are recorded and appear on the minutes separately (see below).

2 **Minutes of the previous meeting.** The minutes of the previous meeting are circulated (unless they have been sent out previously) and checked for accuracy. The phrase often used is 'taken as read'. This means they do not have to be read out aloud. If an inaccuracy is noted then the previous minutes are never altered. Instead the correction is noted in the current minutes.

3 **Matters arising.** This covers comments and queries relating to actions taken since the last meeting. Discussion should not take place on any items which are specifically listed on the current agenda.

4 **Correspondence.** This is only included if a communication has been received which is of interest to the meeting as a whole.

5 **Specific items(s).** These comprise the main business of the meeting. However, the meeting should avoid trying to cover too many items, as discussion will be rushed. List the most important items first, in case some people have to leave before the meeting ends.

6 **Any other business.** Commonly shortened to AOB, this item is for minor, general items of discussion that are not included on the agenda or have arisen since the agenda was issued. Important items may be mentioned, but only for inclusion as an item on the next agenda.

7 **Date and time of next meeting.** This item can be moved forward if anyone has to leave early.

For internal participants the notice and agenda is often combined into one document to save stationery, postage and time! The combined notice and agenda for the health and safety meeting to which Mr Ashton has been invited is shown in Figure 7.15. At a meeting with an 'outsider' present other

---

NOTICE AND AGENDA

Hightown College
Cheyne Walk
HIGHTOWN
HG3 9NP

15 January 2000

HEALTH AND SAFETY COMMITTEE

The next meeting will be held in the boardroom at 1500 hours on Wednesday, 6 February 2000.

AGENDA

1 Apologies for absence
2 Minutes of the previous meeting
3 Matters arising
4 Correspondence
5 Improving access for the disabled – Ian Ashton, Disablement Officer, visiting for this item
6 Report on recent fire drills (KP)
7 Accident statistics for previous year (please refer to report already circulated)
8 Any other business
9 Date and time of next meeting

Secretary

Figure 7.15 Notice and agenda of meeting

items may not be discussed, in case they are confidential. This is sometimes called a 'one-line agenda'. One other way is to invite the visitor to attend only the discussion of the particular item they will be talking about. We will assume this in the case of Mr Ashton.

Finally, it is useful if the agenda includes the names of the people who will 'lead' particular items and if it also refers to documents or information which have been circulated and which members need to read. If participants have comprehensive information they cannot complain they didn't know what was expected of them!

Minutes

The term 'minutes' is the formal word used for a report or summary stating what took place at a meeting. Minutes are *always* written in the third person and the past tense. A set of minutes usually includes the following information.

- The name of the organisation.

- The type of meeting, the place, date and time.

- The names of those present. The chairperson is usually listed first and the minutes secretary last, with other participants in alphabetical order. Anyone else invited for a specific reason (such as Mr Ashton) is identified as being 'in attendance' (see Figure 7.16).

- A numbered list of the items discussed, which should match the agenda. Under each heading is a brief record of what has been discussed and decided.

- An action column showing the initials of those who have promised to undertake particular tasks and report back at the next meeting.

- Space for the chairperson to sign and date the minutes once they have been agreed as correct.

ACTIVITY

An example of the minutes from the health and safety committee meeting is given in Figure 7.16. Look through these carefully and note, in particular, the style and language used to describe what took place.

MINUTES

HIGHTOWN COLLEGE – HEALTH AND SAFETY COMMITTEE

Minutes of the meeting held in the boardroom at 1500 hours on Wednesday, 6 February 2000

Present
Carolyn Strachan (Chair)
Ian Ashton (in attendance for item 5)
Ian Bentley
Ashraf Hussain
Kate Parker
Bill Stevens
Maria Gomex (Secretary)

ACTION

1. **Apologies for absence**
Apologies were received from Keith Watson who is in hospital.

2. **Minutes of previous meeting**
The minutes of the previous meeting were taken as read, agreed as a true and correct record and signed by the chair.

3. **Matters arising**
Ian Bentley commented that the new overalls had been received and distributed to all laboratory staff.

4. **Correspondence**
The secretary read a letter from a visitor who had complained about the surface on the car park which was pot-holed and uneven. She had sprained her ankle, although not badly, but felt action should be taken to improve the surface. It was agreed this should be an agenda item at the next meeting.

5. **Improving access for the disabled**
Ian Ashton, Hightown Disablement Officer, visited for this item. He had inspected the college campus and produced several recommendations including ramps to two buildings and an automated wheelchair lift for short stairways. It was agreed Bill Stevens, estates manager, should obtain costs on these suggestions before the next meeting.   **BS**

6. **Report on recent fire drills**
Kate Parker produced a summary of the findings. Timings were good but in one building the emergency doors had jammed. Bill Stevens agreed to investigate and report back at the next meeting.   **BS**

7. **Accident statistics for previous year**
These had been circulated previously. Carolyn Strachan reported a noticeable improvement from the year before. No serious accidents had been reported over the period.

8. **Any other business**
Ashraf Hussain said that recent staff changes had meant a fall in the number of qualified first-aiders. It was agreed that Kate Parker should contact all staff to see who was interested in volunteering for training.   **KP**

9. **Date and time of next meeting**
It was agreed the next meeting should be held at 1500 hours on Wednesday, 8th May 2000.

Signed .... (Chairperson) ....((Date)

Figure 7.16 Minutes of health and safety committee meeting

Action points and other papers

You will find variations in the paperwork at different meetings and in different organisations. Here are some examples.

- At formal meetings there is an official notice sent out, then an agenda. If there is to be a vote then voting papers have to be prepared and proxy forms sent so that those who cannot attend can nominate someone else to vote on their behalf.

- At some meetings the chairperson may request a special 'Chair's agenda' which leaves space alongside each agenda item for the chairperson to make notes.

- The type and style of minutes can vary. Minutes of narration are more detailed than minutes of action – which simply list the conclusion and action agreed. In some organisations a separate list of action points may be summarised and circulated for some meetings, rather than official minutes.

An administrator may have to check that action has been taken on the particular action points agreed at the meeting by the people concerned. This may involve telephoning people to give them a tactful reminder of the date they promised to submit a report or find out some information. You will soon find out who is very efficient, who is relatively good and who always needs reminding in plenty of time. Which group would your tutor place you in?

ACTIVITY

Plan your own meeting to discuss a day out for your group. Ask your tutor whether this has to be an educational trip linked to your course or whether it can be an 'end of term' fun day out!

a Decide on the date, time and location for your meeting.

b Discuss with your tutor if you can afford refreshments and, if so, book these.

c Select a chairperson and a minutes secretary.

d Decide on the topics for discussion (where to go, cost, date etc.) and prepare a notice and agenda. Bear in mind that as this is your first meeting you will not have to include 'minutes of previous meeting' or 'matters arising'.

e Include your tutor as an 'external' visitor and write him/her a letter of invitation.

f Prepare and circulate the remaining documentation.

g Hold the meeting – ask your tutor to assess how well each person contributes as a member of the group and supports the chairperson.

h Prepare and check the minutes and action points. You may find it useful if each person

writes up their own version and then you compare the results!

i Two weeks' later, check whether anyone has failed to complete the action they were supposed to carry out.

j Plan and hold a follow up meeting, if required.

7.6 Administrative systems and the law

At the start of this unit you learned about systems and how they can be controlled. You looked at the road traffic system and you should already know that there are laws to control the way it operates, the behaviour of drivers and pedestrians and the road-worthiness of vehicles.

Similarly, certain administration systems are controlled by the law. The two main areas of law you need to understand are:

• data protection legislation – and its effect on the storage and use of certain records

• health and safety legislation – and its relevance to administrators.

Finally, it is useful to have a broad overview of the law of copyright – given that many administrators are asked to photocopy a variety of documents.

Data protection legislation

Data protection is concerned with protecting the collection, storage, processing and distribution of personal information which relates to living individuals. The first Data Protection Act regulated the use of information processed on computer. This was introduced because there was considerable public concern about the type of information which was held about individuals on computers, such as whether this was correct, whether personal and sensitive details were held against people's wishes and whether the information could be given or sold to someone else without the person's consent. The Act gave people rights about the information which could be held about them, who could hold it and how it could be used.

In March 2000, the Data Protection Act 1998 was introduced to replace the original Act. This extended several of the requirements and, in particular, covered data held in manual filing systems as well, provided these are in 'structured' files. Basically, this means there is a set of information about a person, such as an employee or customer.

Organisations have until 23 October 2001 to check that all their new data and files comply with the Act. However, manual data held in filing systems prior to 24 October 1998 will not be completely covered by the Act until October 2007. This extension period is to give **data controllers**, i.e. businesses and organisations which hold personal data, time to check which files must comply with the law and take the required action.

If an organisation fails to comply or contravenes the Act, then the Data Protection Commissioner has the power to issue an **enforcement notice** or an **information notice** against that data controller. An enforcement notice instructs the data controller what action it must take (or what activities it must cease). An information notice is a request for details. The Commissioner also has the power to apply for a warrant to enter and search premises if there is evidence of contravention. Failure to comply with a notice or to obstruct a search are criminal offences.

Figure 7.17 gives more details of the Act and the information it covers.

ACTIVITY

Study the Act with your tutor and then answer the following questions:

1 Three of the following five types of data are included within the Act. Which are they?
   a Personnel record held on computer.
   b Customer records held in an alphabetical filing system.
   c A data base of friends and contacts you keep on your home computer.
   d Manual files on individuals held by a credit reference agency.
   e Police records on individuals.

2 Three of the following are an offence under the Act. Can you identify them?
   a An employer sells its personnel database of an insurance company so that it can sell its products to them by direct mail.
   b Your employer provides information about your income to the tax office without your consent.
   c You write to your bank asking for details of the information they hold on you but they say this is confidential.
   d Your college asks you if you will voluntarily identify your ethnic origin when you complete your enrolement form.
   e Your father, who owns a small business, refuses give notification saying the Act doesn't apply to businesses with fewer than 20 employees.

Health and safety and administration

In Section 1.2 you learned about the Health and Safety at Work Act (pages 35–42). Many people consider that accidents only happen in factories or dangerous environments, such as

The Data Protection Act 1998 required all organisations and businesses which process personal data on individuals (a **data subject**) to give notification that they should be included in a register of **data controllers**, unless they have already registered under the 1984 Act. They must state

- their name and address and the name of their representative, if any
- a description of the personal data being processed and the types of data subject which it covers (e.g. customers, employees, students etc.).
- a description about why the data is being processed
- a description about any recipients to whom it may be disclosed
- a description of any countries outside the EU to which it may be sent.

The term 'data' which is covered by the Act relates to

- information recorded or processed by computer
- information which is part of a relevant filing system or forms part of an accessible record, e.g. health records, social services records etc.

All data controllers must comply with the eight principles of the Act in relation to the handling of personal data.

- Data must be obtained and processed fairly and lawfully. Normally this means the individual has given his/her consent. Explicit consent is required for 'sensitive' data relating to religious or political beliefs; racial origin; trade union membership; physical or mental health or sexual life; criminal convictions.
- Personal data must be held only for one or more specified and lawful purposes and should not be processed for another reason.
- The data should be adequate, relevant and not excessive.
- Personal data must be accurate and kept up-to-date.
- Personal data must be kept no longer than is necessary.
- It must be processed in accordance with the rights of data subjects (see below).
- It must be stored to prevent unauthorised or unlawful access, loss, destruction or damage.
- It must not be transferred outside the EU unless the country to which it is being sent also protects the rights of data subjects.

The rights of individuals (data subjects) include:

- the right to access data held about them
- the right to prevent processing which would cause damage or distress
- the right to prevent processing for direct marketing purposes
- rights in relation to automated decision-taking (e.g. evaluating job performance or credit-worthiness on the basis of personal information)
- the right to take action to correct, block, erase or destroy inaccurate data
- the right to compensation if damage is suffered through contravention of the Act.

Exemptions

The Act allows for certain exemptions, although in many cases specific conditions are attached. Broadly, the categories of exempt data include that held for

- purposes of national security
- crime detection and taxation purposes
- health, education and social work
- research, history and statistics
- domestic use only.

Figure 7.17 The Data Protection Act 1998

on oil rigs or at sea. It is true that these are more hazardous places to work. It is untrue that the law only applies to these areas or that accidents never happen in offices!

The specific legislation which you need to know in more detail if you are involved in administration includes many of the regulations listed on page 37. In particular:

- the Display Screen Equipment Regulations 1992

- the Provision and Use of Work Equipment Regulations 1998

- the Manual Handling Operations Regulations 1992.

The Display Screen Equipment (DSE) Regulations 1992

These regulations introduce minimum standards for the use of VDUs and the design of workstations. If you use a VDU, you are protected in that your employer must

- analyse and assess display screen workstations to assess and reduce risk

- ensure that all workstations meet minimum requirements in relation to the display screen equipment itself, any related furniture, the working environment and software used

- ensure operators receive regular breaks or changes in activity – it is illegal for VDU users to work continuously at a computer all day

- arrange an eye examination, on request, for those who use a VDU for more than one hour a day, and provide special spectacles if the test shows that these are required

- provide users with adequate health and safety training relating to their equipment.

The Regulations also require the following.

- **Display screens** must have well-defined characters of adequate size, a stable image, easily adjustable brightness and contrast, be able to tilt and swivel easily, and there must be no reflective glare.

- **Keyboards** must be tiltable and separate from the screen with enough space in front to provide a 'rest' space. The surface should be matt and the keyboard should be easy to use with clearly contrasted symbols on the keys.

- **Work surfaces** must be sufficiently large and must have a low reflective finish. The arrangement of the equipment must be flexible so it can be adjusted to suit the needs of the user.

- **Work chairs** must be stable and allow the user easy movement and a comfortable position. The seat height must be adjustable and the seat back tiltable to give good back support. Foot rests must be provided on request.

- The **working environment** must provide satisfactory lighting but with the minimum of glare. Windows should have blinds and/or workstations should be positioned to avoid reflections. Noise and heat levels should be such that they do not cause distraction or discomfort. Radiation levels must be negligible and humidity must be controlled and maintained at a satisfactory level.

- **Software and systems** must be suitable for the task, user friendly and appropriate to the level of knowledge of the user.

Many of the Regulations have been the result of concerns expressed about repetitive strain injury (RSI) – an injury caused by continually making awkward or repetitive movements and, in particular, tensoynovitis, which is the inflammation of the tendon sheaths in the hand, wrist and arms.

There have also been concerns about the stress levels of VDU workers, particularly those who are required to input a high number of characters per day. Staring at a screen for long periods without a break can cause headaches and migraine attacks and there have been concerns it can also trigger epileptic fits (although it cannot cause epilepsy where the condition does not already exist). The Regulations also specifically state that, in the light of scientific evidence, pregnant women need not stop working with computers. They do, however, recommend that female VDU operators who are pregnant or planning a family should be able to discuss any concerns they may have with an appropriate specialist.

The Provision and Use of Work Equipment Regulations 1992

These Regulations relate to the maintenance and upkeep of equipment in the workplace. They relate to its

- positioning
- usage
- maintenance.

First, large items of electrical equipment need positioning where they will not be continually knocked or banged and to be installed in accordance with the manufacturer's requirements. They should only be moved by someone who knows what they are doing. A large photocopier, for instance, needs checking to ensure it is on a level surface and that there is sufficient air flow around it. There must also be room for the operator to work safely.

Staff must be trained how to use equipment properly. A simple machine, such as a fax, can be used by referring to the handbook. A more complex operation, such as rectifying a paper jam in a photocopier, should only be undertaken by someone who has had special training. Basic instructions can be included on notices near the equipment itself, such as reminding staff using a photocopier to close the lid during its operation and not to look at the bright light.

Electrical equipment needs checking regularly to ensure wires are not left hanging or trailing, that no wires or plugs are damaged and that there are sufficient sockets so that adaptors are not used. Many types of office furniture now incorporate **wire management** where the wires are positioned in special channels under the desk tops.

Equipment maintenance should be carried out regularly. However, the Regulations recognise that the type of checks and maintenance will vary depending upon the complexity of the equipment, its usage and the degree of risk. A check can therefore range from a basic inspection of a hand-held device, such as a stapler, to a more rigorous inspection programme for complex machinery and equipment.

The Manual Handling Operations Regulations 1992

Anyone who has ever moved a large amount of paper will tell you how heavy it is! Yet moving stationery items and even small items of equipment around a building is often necessary. Under these Regulations the provision of trolleys (and even trucks) to lift and move heavy loads is essential. In addition, staff must know how to lift items safely. This includes:

- disconnecting electrical equipment before trying to move it
- never attempting to lift a load which is too heavy

• lifting lighter loads by bending the knees first. This means the weight is taken by the legs and not the back.

A final word!

In most offices the key to safety is not just abiding by the law but by being tidy, concentrating and using the right tools for the job.

• **Tidiness** (better known as **good housekeeping**) means you will not be hit by files falling off a shelf, you will not slip on spilt liquid, you will not cut your hand on a pair of scissors which was hidden under the papers piled on your desk.

• **Concentrating** means you will not staple your finger instead of the page, you will not fall over the bottom drawer of the filing cabinet you forgot to close earlier.

• **Using the rights tools for the job** means you will make the effort to find the safety stool and not risk life and limb by standing on a swivel chair to open a window, you will not risk losing a nail (or tooth) by trying to remove a staple without a staple remover!

 **ACTIVITY**

I Which of the following products do you consider would
  a provide additional protection for VDU users under the DSE regulations
  b simply be useful to have around?
     i special computer cleaning products including screen wipes and keyboard sprays
     ii wrist rests to reduce discomfort and fatigue
     iii ergonomic keyboards which reduce the dangers of RSI
     iv 'stretch and exercise' computer software for keyboard users to relax shoulders, neck, hands and back
     v fully adjustable seating with back and height adjustments, a swivel seat and castors as well as footrests.

Discuss your ideas with your tutor.

2 A few years ago, a job centre worker in north London received a severe electric shock at her computer terminal. Although she later recovered, investigations revealed that her desk, which contained metal, was not earthed. When the cabling from her computer frayed the metal frame of the desk became live. The cost of rectifying the problem and making sure it could never occur again was £6 million.
  a Under which Regulations could the worker's employer have been prosecuted?
  b What precautions are taken at your college to check computer equipment?
  c What precautions do *you* take to check any computer equipment you have at home?
  d List four ways in which laser printers could become hazardous for staff. Discuss your ideas with your tutor.

3 Photocopiers are one of the easiest items of equipment to use, provided you know what you are doing. However, there is a law which limits what you can photocopy – the Copyright, Designs and Patents Act 1988.

Visit your college library and research this Act. Your librarians will be well aware of it! Find out
  a what you can copy as a student, legally
  b what your tutor can copy for the class, legally
  c whether you could hire a video and show it to your class, and charge them for admission
  d what I would have to do, as an author, if I wanted to reproduce an article from a newspaper in this book.

KEYS TO UNIT 3

The keys to this unit relate to the practical examples and the activities in section 3.3 relating to business documents. Group activities and section reviews are revision exercises and will be checked by your tutor.

Section 3.1

Practical example – 1

1   £27,000

2   £2,250 + £1,300 + £400 + £600 = £4,550

3   £22,450

4   Tax = £4,013.50; money left = £18,436.50

5   £18,436.50 – £1,200 = £17,236.50/12 = £1,436.38

6 a Could lose business, work fewer days/weeks, gross income could fall overall even though rate is higher.
   b Should check rates other plasterers charge through his builder friends, making sure he stays competitive but charges current rate.

Practical example – 2

1   8,600

2   8,600/5 = £1,720

3 a £2,580
   b £2,150

4 a 75p and maximise revenue at £2,580
   b Aim to sell 3,440 copies

5   £250

6   £2,580 + £250 = £2,830

7   3,440 × 0.40 = £1,376

8   Profit = £1,454

9   May not sell as many as predicted – students may share a copy or pass it on, may not sell all advertising space, difficult to produce exact number to sell. All unsold copies add to costs not to profit. If very successful someone else may try to compete. If first few issues not good value sales may decline. Preparation/distribution may cost more time/commitment than people are prepared to give – shared profit of £1,454 between 3 = £484.66 for three months work!

Practical example – 3

1

Rent advance	£1,000
Business rates	£200
Redecoration	£500
Fixtures and fittings	£2,500
Furniture	£2,000
Insurance	£450
Stock	£850
Sundry items	£750
Telephone	£150
Advertising	£500
Total	**£8,900**

2   £100

3 a Clients paying to have their hair done.
   b Selling products to clients.

4   Find out what competitors charge. Work out number of clients she could manage each week and estimate earnings per week. Check if this will cover costs of running the business and give her enough to live on after paying tax and National Insurance.

5   Items: equipment (portable hairdryers etc); mobile phone; supplies of consumable products (shampoo, colourant etc.); towels/overalls/gloves; liability insurance; van or car – could be secondhand; vehicle insurance and road tax.

6   Jacqui is more likely to make the most profit as she will be able to manage some clients simultaneously. Unless Sara deals with a family, she will only be able to deal with one client at once. Using time productively is usually one good way of increasing revenue!

Practical example – 4

1   £5,040

2   £4,125

3   £9,165

4   1,665

5   £4,995

6   £4,170

7   £450

8   £3,720

Practical example – 5

Sales revenue		(£)
September	340 single T-shirts	2,040
	84 packs of 3	1,260
October	210 single T-shirts	1,260
	62 packs of 3	930
November	320 single T-shirts	1,920
	92 packs of 3	1,380
	180 single packs of socks	360
	68 packs of 3 socks	340
December	420 single T-shirts	2,520
	230 packs of 3	3,450
	275 single packs of socks	550
	184 packs of 3 socks	920
	Total	**16,930**

Cost of sales

Single T-shirts   1,290
Packed T-shirts   468 packs × 3 = 1,404

Total T-shirts sold = 2,694 @ £3 = £8,082

Single socks   455
Packed socks   756

Total socks sold = 1,211 @ £1 = £1,211

Total cost of sales = £9,293

Gross profit = sales revenue – cost of sales = £16,930 – £9,293 = £7,637

Expenses – market stall for 2 days a week for 16 weeks at £25 = £800

Net profit = £6,837

Section 3.2

Case study – test 1

1   Missing item is royalty payment to Jack – £200 for the year.

   Total start-up costs = £2,500

2   Fixed costs: rent, insurance, advertising, stationery, accountant, telephone, salary, gas, electricity, miscellaneous supplies and expenses, contingency fund for emergencies.

   Variable costs: raw materials, packaging and distribution costs.

3   **a**   £1,300 per month
   b   £2,000 per month
   c   £3,300 per month

4   Fixed costs do not vary with output. Variable costs depend upon the number of items produced. The more items produced, the higher the variable costs.

5   Fixed costs and variable costs – see page 217.

Case study – test 2

1   £7.50

2   £2.50

3   $\dfrac{1300}{(7.50 - 2.50)} = \dfrac{1300}{5} = 260$ characters

Case study – test 3

   a   360
   b   340
   c   474
   d   Increasing the fixed (or variable) costs raises the break-even point because costs have increased. Lowering fixed or variable costs lowers the break-even point. This is why businesses try to keep their costs as low as possible.

   The selling price also affects the break-even point. If the selling price is raised, then fewer need to be sold to break even. However, in this case Max has lowered his selling price so he will need to have to sell more characters to meet his costs.

Practical example – 7

Questions 1 – 4

Profit/Loss Forecast – Nixa Hire Cars

	April	May	June	July	Aug	Sept
Sales	2,200	4,160	6,750	10,175	10,175	6,000
Cost of sales	400	640	900	1,100	1,100	800
Gross profit	1,800	3,520	5,850	9,075	9,075	5,200
Expenses	3,400	3,800	4,700	6,400	6,800	4,200
Net profit/loss	–1,600	–280	1,150	2,675	2,275	1,000

5   April and May.

6   Sales are not at break-even level so revenue does not cover total costs.

7   June–September.

8 £5,220.

9 Nixa is more likely to make a loss out of season because trade will be slower.

10 **a** Main sales revenue would be received between October and January with sales peaking in November/December.

b Peak sales would be in summer and would be even higher in hot weather. However, ice cream is purchased all year round from supermarkets so firms will aim to cover costs during the winter but make maximum profits in the summer.

c Busiest time for bookings will be in January and February. December and March also quite busy. Late booking offers are used to tempt people to buy late holidays to sustain revenue during other months.

11 **a** £760
b £4,500.

Case study – test 4

Profit/Loss Forecast – Max's characters

	Aug	Sept	Oct	Nov	Dec	Jan
Sales revenue	0	1,800	4,800	6,000	5,400	2,400
Cost of sales	2,000	2,000	2,000	2,000	500	500
Gross profit	(2,000)	(200)	2,800	4,000	4,900	1,900
Expenses	1,300	1,800	1,800	1,800	1,600	1,300
Net profit/loss	(3,300)	(2,000)	1,000	2,200	3,300	600

Profit/loss over period = profit of £1,800

Practical example – 8 – Activity 4

1 **Nixa Hire Cars – monthly balance**

Monthly summary	April	May	June	July	Aug	Sept
Opening bank balance	6,500	4,620	5,450	9,610	15,945	22,230
Plus total receipts	62,200	5,160	8,750	12,675	12,675	9,000
Minus total payments	64,080	4,330	4,590	6,340	6,390	4,990
Closing bank balance (D)	4,620	5,450	9,610	15,945	22,230	26,240

2

	(£)
Opening balance	6,500
Plus total receipts	110,460
Minus total payments	90,720
Closing balance	26,240

3 Move surplus funds to interest-bearing account. This will add to her reserves which will help her if she wants to expand the business further.

4 **a** She could tell from looking at her cashflow – and seeing how quickly her bank account would recover from the initial purchase of the cars.

b An overdraft is a temporary arrangement for the bank account holder to spend more money than is in the account. A loan is taken over a fixed period, by arrangement with the bank, and interest is charged. Usually monthly payments are made.

Case study – test 5 – stage 3

1 and **2 Max's characters cashflow forecast**

	Aug	Sept	Oct	Nov	Dec	Jan
INFLOWS/RECEIPTS						
Cash sales	0	360	960	1,200	1,080	480
Credit sales	0	0	1,440	3,840	4,800	4,320
Loans received	0	0	0	0	0	0
Grants received	0	0	0	0	0	0
Owner's capital	1,500	0	0	0	0	0
Sub-total – all inflows (A)	1,500	360	2,400	5,040	5,880	4,800
OUTFLOWS/PAYMENTS						
Variable costs (purchases, stock etc.)	0	2,000	2,000	2,000	2,000	500
Wages/salaries	900	900	900	900	900	900
Capital items	920	0	0	0	0	0
Rent and rates	1,260	0	0	420	420	420
Light/heat/power	80	80	80	80	80	80
Loan repayments	0	0	0	0	0	0
Stationery and printing	100	100	100	100	100	100
Telephone	50	50	50	50	50	50
Insurance	20	20	20	20	20	20
Advertising/promotions	100	100	100	100	100	100
Licence fee	200	0	0	0	0	0
Miscellaneous expenses	90	90	90	90	90	90
Sub-total – all outflows (B)	3,720	3,340	3,340	3,760	3,760	2,260
Net cashflow (C)	(2,220)	(2,980)	(940)	1,280	2,120	2,540
MONTHLY SUMMARY						
Opening bank balance	50	(2,170)	(5,170)	(6,090)	(4,810)	(2,690)
Plus total receipts	1,500	360	2,400	5,040	5,880	4,800
Minus total payments	3,720	3,340	3,340	3,760	3,760	2,260
Closing bank balance (D)	(2,170)	(5,170)	(6,090)	(4,820)	(2,690)	(150)

3   **Quick check key**

	(£)
Opening balance	50
Add total receipts	19,980
Deduct total payments	20,180
Closing balance	(150)

4   He could aim to borrow £6,000 to prevent problems being overdrawn (apart from £90 in October).

Activity 5

1   Sue has estimated Max's revenues from February to April to increase the overall inflow of money at a time when the inflows/outflows will be more balanced. She has included his start-up capital which immediately improves the situation at the outset, as Max was very under-capitalised. She has reduced costs where she thinks this is practical, e.g. advertising after the initial promotional period. She has included the loan repayment but allowed for a possible 'repayment holiday' of six months.

The overall effect is an improvement in Max's cashflow and in his resulting bank balances.

2   His sales peak around December. After his initial period his sales steadily improve and then there is a slight downturn.

3   If Max thinks he may be overdrawn he must notify the bank. Otherwise he will have to pay high bank charges if he has an unauthorised overdraft. The bank could also choose to 'bounce' (reject) any cheques he writes – which will make suppliers very wary of him.

4   Total receipts in a month will fall if debtors do not pay promptly and yet the business still has to make payments. If costs rise, then the surplus between receipts and payments is reduced. If the two occur simultaneously, a positive cashflow can easily become negative.

5   A cashflow forecast is the only forecast which provides information on the predicted flow of receipts into the business and payments out of the business. Identifying the trends assists business owners to make informed decisions to prevent problems occurring.

6   Discuss with your tutor.

Section 3.3

Activity 6

1   Check with your tutor.

2   £846.10

3   Business Supplies should contact DigiTech and advise them of the delay. It should offer DigiTech a new delivery date or the opportunity to change the order to items that will be available for the date required. The customer should not be left to think the goods will arrive when they will not. If the customer needs items urgently, then they must have the opportunity to obtain them elsewhere, if necessary.

4   To prevent goods being ordered without permission.

5   a   200 reams of paper would have been delivered to DigiTech.

   b   Legally, the supplier does not have to take these back. However, it is unlikely Business Supplies would want to upset DigiTech in case they lost future business. If Joel rang, apologised and explained his mistake, provided the goods had not been used or opened, Business Supplies would probably collect them and issue a credit note for the returned items.

6   a   Details of order to be checked by your tutor.
   b   £134.28

7   a   Address is incorrect – Brampton instead of Brompton. Inclusion of postcode meant order arrived safely, but address details should be carefully checked.

Unit price for Cyberbugs should be £70 not £84.

Order was sent unsigned.

   b   Action to take depends on the type of error. Often a quick telephone call will clarify errors of quantity, reference code, description and price. An unsigned order should not be accepted. Confirmation of amended/authorised order should be requested by fax, so details are in writing in case there are any queries later.

Activity 7

1   Delivery notes are sent with the package and list the contents. They enable the customer to check the items delivered are correct and match the order.

2   False. This would delay delivery people – especially if packages were large or contained many items. If the package appears to be undamaged on receipt then the delivery note should be signed. If the package is damaged then this should be noted on the form.

3   On computerised systems which update stock levels with every transaction low stocks are identified quickly and new stocks can be ordered (or produced) before the stock runs out.

4   Paper records can be filed under the unique customer account number. Keying in the number on a computer system automatically provides details of the customer and a record of previous transactions.

5   For ease of reference and so that the recipient can check which order the delivery note relates to.

Activity 8

1 A goods received note is made out to list the contents of a package which has been delivered. It notes any shortages or damage to goods. It confirms to accounts staff the exact items which should be paid for.

2 A GRN is an internal document. A copy is sent from the checker to the accounts department.

3 In case there is a query about a comment on a GRN, or if damage or a shortage is identified later, after the package is delivered to the purchaser.

4 Because several staff may have identical initials.

5 b It depends whether the firm still wants the extra cartridge or not. Contact Swift Office Supplies. Either arrange for the missing cartridge to be delivered or ask for a credit note to adjust the discrepancy.

Activity 9

1 An invoice is a request for payment that lists the items which have been purchased with the price of each and the total amount due.

2 a Inaccuracy means the wrong amount will be charged. Whilst this can be rectified with either a credit note (for an over-charge) or a supplementary invoice (for an under-charge) it gives a poor impression to the customer. It also creates additional work for staff, correcting the error. If an under-charge was not noticed, then the business will not be paid for goods it has sent.
   b It is likely the customer will stop dealing with the firm altogether. First, it may suspect whether the errors are always accidental! Second, the 'nuisance value' of having to notify the supplier and check the adjustments have been made will be too great if this is a regular occurrence. It is easier to find an alternative supplier! Therefore a firm which regularly makes mistakes is likely to find itself losing customers.

3 If an over-charge is made then the supplier sends a credit note to the customer (see page 263).

4 The calculations are correct. However, you know that only 2 laser cartridges were delivered whereas 3 are listed on the invoice. If you had arranged for another to be delivered – and this had arrived and been checked in on a GRN – then the invoice could be passed for payment. If a credit note was due you should attach a note to the invoice saying that a cartridge was missing and referring the accounts staff to the GRN you made out.

5 Check your invoice with your tutor. The total amount due should be £2,757.13.

6 £142.

Activity 10

1 A credit note is sent when a customer is owed money for some reason. It confirms the amount which will be deducted from the customer's account with the supplier.

2 a Check the credit note was made out to the correct customer and that the name, address and reference number are accurate.
   b Check the date was included, plus any returns reference supplied by the customer.
   c Ensure the invoice number was quoted and that the credit note was numbered correctly.
   d Check the quantity, description and unit price matched that on the invoice for the goods which are to be credited.
   e Check the calculations.
   f Ensure that discount and VAT rates are identical on the credit note and the invoice.

3 Check your credit note with your tutor. The amount to be refunded is £370.12.

4 Petra will have checked that all the items agreed have been returned and that they are all in perfect condition.

5 £146.14.

6 The supplier should be contacted and the mistake pointed out, so that it can be rectified without delay.

Activity 11

1 To list/confirm the month's transactions on the account and to remind the customer of the total amount due.

2 A running balance is the balance after each transaction. The total balance is the amount showing at the end of the month.

3 Notify the supplier immediately and have available details of the invoice number, date paid, cheque number and date the money was transferred out of the account.

4 Beacon could be told that they will exceed their credit limit with the new order and the order could be refused. However, if Beacon are an excellent customer, with whom there have been no previous problems, it is likely their credit limit could be revised or a temporary increase allowed.

5 Your tutor needs to check your statements, particularly that you have listed everything in the correct (date) order and used the correct columns. In addition, your running balance must be correct throughout. The total balance for Hemple's should be £3,974.63 and the total balance for Kids 'n' Toys is £7,313.50.

Activity 12

1   It makes it easier for the customer to pay – and for DigiTech staff to link the payment to the correct account when the payment is received.

2   Cheque number, amount being paid, date of payment, account reference.

3   Because an amount listed on the statement is being disputed but the company is paying the rest – both as a gesture of good faith and so that it will stay within its credit limit in case it wants to place another order.

4   Inform your supervisor. The sender will have to be notified promptly. It is likely the amount has been transposed on the cheque in error. The firm may wish to cancel that cheque and send another, so it should not be banked at this stage.

5   So that the accounts staff receiving the cheque will know why it has been sent.

Activity 13

1   a   the payee
    b   the drawer.

2   a   it has been incorrectly written
    b   the drawer has insufficient funds in the account

c   the drawer has instructed the bank to 'stop' payment of the cheque, for some reason.

3   The cheque number, the account number, the bank sort code.

4   Date of payment, name of payee, reason for payment, amount paid.

5   The cheque number and payment appears on the bank statement.

6   When a business cheque is signed by a representative of that organisation.

Activity 14

1   They provide evidence for a cash transaction.

2   It is quicker than producing receipts by hand. The cash register will also keep a running total of all the money taken and an automatic copy of every receipt.

3   Receipts vary, but you would expect to find the name of the firm, date of transaction, amounts paid, total paid. Some large retailers issue itemised receipts, where each item is described. If VAT is added, this should also be shown.

4   As a security measure – in case an unscrupulous employee tried to sell the goods to commercial organisations.

Blank documents for photocopying

DigiTech Characters Ltd
Unit 5
Brompton Industrial Park
BROMPTON
Newshire
BR4 9DK

Tel: 01232 788488
Fax: 01232 601090
Website: www.DTcharacters.co.uk

VAT reg. no. 830/38473/99

Email: orders@DTcharacters.co.uk

PURCHASE ORDER

To:

Supplier no.:

Official order no.:

Date:

Please supply:

Quantity	Description	Item code	Unit price

Delivery: ....

Signed: .... Designation: ....

Suppliers should note that orders are only valid if signed by a designated executive of the organisation.

DigiTech Characters Ltd
Unit 5
Brompton Industrial Park
BROMPTON
Newshire
BR4 9DK

Tel: 01232 788488
Fax: 01232 601090
Website: www.DTcharacters.co.uk

VAT reg. no. 830/38473/99

Email: orders@DTcharacters.co.uk

D E L I V E R Y   N O T E

To:

Delivery address (if different):

Date:

Your order no.	Customer account no.	Despatch date	Invoice no.	Delivery method

Item code	Quantity	Description

Thank you for your order. Please retain this delivery note for your records.

Received in good condition (or comment here)

....

Signed ....   Date ....

Please print name ....

White copy: customer   **Pink copy:** carrier   **Yellow copy:** DigiTech

GOODS RECEIVED NOTE

D C **DigiTech Characters Ltd**

Supplier:

GRN no.:

GRN date:

Delivery note no.:

Supplier a/c no.:

Delivery note date:

Carrier:

Checker:

Order no.	Quantity ordered	Quantity delivered	Description	Tick box or enter details if goods damaged or discrepancy identified

White copy: Purchases file
Pink copy: Accounts

DigiTech Characters Ltd
Unit 5
Brompton Industrial Park
BROMPTON
Newshire
BR4 9DK

Tel: 01232 788488
Fax: 01232 601090
Website: www.DTcharacters.co.uk

VAT reg. no. 830/38473/99

Email: orders@DTcharacters.co.uk

INVOICE

To:

Your order no.	Customer account no.	Despatch date	Invoice no.

Item code	Quantity	Description	Unit	Unit price	Gross value	Discount value	Net value
				TOTAL			
						VAT 17.5%	
						TOTAL DUE	

Terms: net 28 days
Carriage paid
E & OE

White copy: customer
Pink copy: sales
Yellow copy: accounts

DigiTech Characters Ltd
Unit 5
Brompton Industrial Park
BROMPTON
Newshire   BR4 9DK

Tel: 01232 788488

Fax: 01232 601090

Website: www.DTcharacters.co.uk

VAT reg. no. 830/38473/99

Email: orders@DTcharacters.co.uk

CREDIT NOTE

To:

Your returns ref.	Customer account no.	Date/tax point	Invoice no.	Credit note no.

Item code	Quantity	Description	Unit	Unit price	Gross value	Discount value	Net value
			TOTAL				
				VAT 17.5%			
				REFUNDED CHARGE			

Reason for return:

White copy: customer
Pink copy: sales
Yellow copy: accounts

DigiTech Characters Ltd
Unit 5
Brompton Industrial Park
BROMPTON
Newshire   BR4 9DK

Tel: 01232 788488   VAT reg. no. 830/38473/99
Fax: 01232 601090
Website: www.DTcharacters.co.uk   Email: orders@DTcharacters.co.uk

STATEMENT OF ACCOUNT

To: Customer a/c no.:

                                       Credit limit:

                                       Date:

Date	Details	Debit (£)	Credit (£)	Balance (£)

AMOUNT NOW DUE:

REMITTANCE ADVICE

From: Customer a/c no.:

                                       Date of statement:

AMOUNT ENCLOSED: ....   CHEQUE NO.: ....

Your ref.: ....   Date of payment: ....

All cheques should be made payable to DigiTech Characters Ltd

DigiTech Characters Ltd

Unit 5
Brompton Industrial Park
BROMPTON
Newshire   BR4 9DK
Tel: 01232 788488   Fax: 01232 601090

REMITTANCE ADVICE

To: Supplier a/c no.:

                                           Statement ref.:

                                           Date of statement:

AMOUNT ENCLOSED: .... CHEQUE NO.: ....

YOUR REF.: .... DATE OF PAYMENT: ....

Date _____

● Newshire Bank plc
Main Street
Brompton BM1 3PH

61–01–48

Date _____

Pay _____

A/C PAYEE ONLY

£ [   ]

For and on behalf of
DIGITECH CHARACTERS LTD

£ _____

| Cheque No. | Branch Sort Code | Account No. | Transaction Code |

000877

⑈000877⑈ 60⑈0148⑆ 4731⑈605⑈02

_____

Authorised Signatory

DigiTech Characters Ltd

Unit 5
Brompton Industrial Park
BROMPTON
Newshire   BR4 9DK
Tel: 01232 788488   Fax: 01232 601090

VAT reg. no. 830/38473/99

CASH SALE RECEIPT

Name:

Address:

Receipt no.:

Date:

Received by:

Quantity	Description	Price	Total

Sub-total:

VAT at 17.5%:

Total paid:

Index